DATE DUE

[JUL 1 6 2002	
JUL 1 4 2003	
3-17-04 IL:24 3564	
10/29/08:IL, 4585702	

GAYLORD   #3523PI   Printed in USA

Supervisory Leadership

Focus on Instruction

Don M. Beach

*Tarleton State University
of the Texas A&M
University System*

Judy Reinhartz

University of Texas at Arlington

Allyn and Bacon

Boston ■ London ■ Toronto ■ Sydney ■ Tokyo ■ Singapore

This book is dedicated to teachers—who are the foundation and cornerstone of instruction—and to two special teachers—our spouses, Linda and Dennis, who provided the love, encouragement, and support that made this book possible.

Editor in Chief, Education: *Paul A. Smith*
Series Editor: *Arnis E. Burvikovs*
Editorial Assistant: *Karin Huang*
Marketing Manager: *Brad Parkins*
Editorial–Production Service: *Chestnut Hill Enterprises*
Composition and Prepress Buyer: *Linda Cox*
Manufacturing Buyer: *Suzanne Lareau*
Cover Administrator: *Jenny Hart*
Electronic Composition: *Omegatype Typography*

Copyright © 2000 by Allyn & Bacon
A Pearson Education Company
160 Gould Street
Needham Heights, Massachusetts 02494

Internet: www.abacon.com

A previous edition was published in 1989 by HarperCollins under the title *Supervision: Focus on Instruction.*

Between the time Website information is gathered and then published, it is not unusual for some sites to have closed. Also, the transcription of URLs can result in unintended typographical errors. The publisher would appreciate notification where these occur so that they may be corrected in subsequent editions.

Library of Congress Cataloging-in-Publication Data

Beach, Don M.
    Supervisory leadership : focus on instruction / Don M. Beach, Judy Reinhartz.
        p. cm.
    Includes bibliographical references and index.
    ISBN 0-205-30601-2 (alk. paper)
    1. School supervision—United States.   2. Educational leadership—United States.   I. Reinhartz, Judy.   II. Title.
    LB2806.4.B433   2000
    371.2′03—dc21   99-26285
                                                                           CIP

Photo Credits: Will Faller: pp. 3, 102, 157, 185, 209, 232; Miles Brothers, National Archives: p. 25; Will Hart: pp. 46, 71, 127, 263, 296.

Printed in the United States of America

10   9   8   7   6   5   4   3   2   1   04   03   02   01   00   99

CONTENTS

Preface   ix

About the Authors   xi

PART ONE   Setting the Stage for Supervisory Practice   1

1 Supervision as a Field of Study   3

Organizing Principles   5

Views of Supervision   7

Assumptions Related to Supervision   9

A Theoretical Framework for Supervision   12

Roles of the Supervisor   16

Setting the Stage and Getting Started   18
    A View from the Field   18

Summary   19

Your Turn   20

References   22

2 The Changing Contexts for Viewing Supervision   25

Early Beginnings—The Colonial Period (1600–1865)   29

Expansion and Growth—The State and National Period (1865–1910)   30

Science Applied to Learning and Organizations—The Scientific
and Organizational Period (1910–1920)   31

Becoming a Profession—The Professionalization and Bureaucratic
Period (1920–1935)   33

Changing the Way Schools Are Viewed—The Progressive and
Cooperative Period (1935–1955)   33

Rewriting Curriculum—The Curriculum Development and
Change-Oriented Period (1955–1970)   35

Dealing with Differences—The Clinical and Accountable Period (1970–1980)   36

The Reform Influence of Business—The Entrepreneurial and Reform Period (1980–1995)   37

What's Next?—Supervision and the Future   40

Summary   41

Your Turn   42

References   43

3 Schools as Organizations: The Workplace for Teachers and Supervisors   46

Characteristics and Perceptions of Organizations   48
  A View from the Field   51

Historical Views of Organizations: Their Descriptions and Purposes   51
  Organizational Structure and Bureaucracy   52
  Organizational Functions and Relationships   54
  A View from the Field   58
  Behavioral Organizational Processes   58
  Organizational Influence   59

Organizational Culture   60

Principles of Effective Organizations   62

An Organizational View of Effective Schools   63

Summary   66

Your Turn   67

References   68

4 Supervisors as Leaders   71

Leadership: Views and Definitions   73

Leaders and Managers   75

Essential Leadership Qualities   76

Theoretical Models of Leadership   80

Supervisory Leadership Styles   87

Leadership Principles   88

Power and Authority: Their Use in School Organizations   90
A View from the Field   93

Summary   96

Your Turn   97

References   98

5   Communicating Effectively: A Critical Component for Supervisors   102

Definitions and Characteristics of Communication   104

Supervisor Responses That Promote Effective Communication   109

Responses That Create Barriers to Communication   112

Communicating in Descriptive, Nonjudgmental Language   114

Other Forms of Communication   115

Communication Principles   118

Summary   120

Your Turn   121

References   122

PART TWO   Models and Mechanics of Supervision   125

6   Supervision Processes: A Framework for Action   127

Clinical Supervision   129
Five-Step Cycle   130
Guidelines for Use of Clinical Supervision   132
The Instructional Supervision Training Program   134

Developmental Supervision   137

The Clinical and Developmental Models Working Together   139

Collegial and Collaborative Supervision   141
Peer Coaching   141
Cognitive Coaching   142
Mentoring   144

Self-Assessment Supervision   145

Summary   149

Your Turn   151

References   153

7   Classroom Observation: Collecting Information about Teaching
and Learning   157

Preparing to Observe in Classrooms   159

General Guidelines for Classroom Observation   160

Procedures for Collecting Data   162

Data Analysis   171

Interacting and Conversing with Teachers   174

Summary   178

Your Turn   179

References   181

PART THREE   The Instructional Dimension
of Supervision   183

8   Curriculum Development: The Role of the Supervisor   185

Definitions and Views of Curriculum   187

The Role of Philosophy in Developing Curriculum   188

A Curriculum Development Model   192

Curriculum Designs   197

Operationalizing the Curriculum Development Process   199

Resources for Curriculum Development   202
A View from the Field   203

Summary   204

Your Turn   205

References   207

9 Teaching: A Complex Process   209

   Definitions and Views of Teaching   211

   Concerns Related to Classroom Teaching   212

   Effective Teaching Behaviors: Process–Product Focus   215

   Beyond Process–Product: New Views of Effective Teaching   221

   Teaching: The Role of the Supervisor   223

   Summary   225

   Your Turn   226

   References   227

10 Assessing the Complexity of Teaching: Characteristics and Components   232

   Performance Assessment and Views of Teaching   235

   Characteristics of Performance Assessment Systems   240

   Components of Assessment Systems   242
      Classroom Observation   242
      Portfolios   244
      Case-Based Methods   246

   Formative and Summative Assessment Phases   249
      Formative Assessment   250
      Summative Assessment   251

   Summary   253

   Your Turn   255

   References   256

PART FOUR   Reflection, Growth, and Change   261

11 Professional Growth and Development: Staff Development Opportunities for Teachers   263

   Definitions and Views of Staff Development   265

   Reasons Why Teachers Participate in Staff Development   267

Teachers as Learners: Developmental Characteristics   270

Successful Staff Development Programs: What Research Says   277
A View from the Field   278

Professional Growth: Using Models from Other Organizations   282

Self-Assessment for Supervisors: Linkages
to Professional Growth   285

Summary   288

Your Turn   289

References   291

12 Making Decisions and Facilitating Instructional Change   296

The Decision-Making Process   298
Steps in Decision Making   299

Principles to Guide Decision Making   301

The Change Process   303

Resistance to Change   304

Stages in the Planned Change Model   307

Change and School Culture   309
Facilitating Change   311

Principles of Change   312

Summary   313

Your Turn   314

References   315

Author Index   318

Subject Index   323

PREFACE

Supervisory Leadership: Focus on Instruction is designed to provide school personnel, who serve in a variety of supervisory positions, with the necessary concepts, principles, and skills needed to be successful. This book is meant to be comprehensive, realistic, and well researched. In recent practice, a supervisor's position has increasingly shifted from a deficit or helping model to a collegial, cooperative, and mentoring role. Current practice is emphasized in this book, and students are urged to reflect upon and apply the information presented in each chapter. The central theme of this book is the development of supervisors who interact with teachers, students, parents, and community members in ways that create a school culture that focuses on learning.

Two questions that guide our thinking are: (1) What supervisory processes promote teacher professional growth and development, which results in quality instruction? (2) What knowledge and skills do supervisors need in order to coach and mentor teachers who are at various stages of professional development? Clearly, in responding to these questions, we view the teacher as the single most important instructional entity in the teaching–learning process. Likewise, we view supervisors as leaders and the supervision process as critical to promoting continuous growth and development, which results in school improvement.

This book has evolved from our combined experience of over 50 years in various educational settings: elementary and secondary classrooms; preservice teacher training; staff development programs at the national, state, district, and classroom levels; and graduate education. We have solicited input from practicing educational leaders, classroom teachers, and our graduate students. This book has been a collaborative effort in which we have tried to "speak with one voice," and we feel that the result is a unique blend of our two perspectives.

The book provides an overview of supervision and school leadership as well as a historical context for the supervision process. We have also included both a theoretical foundation for supervisory practices within school organizations and principles and skills that contribute to effective collaboration with teachers. Further, we have cited and analyzed the theoretical and research studies related to the field of supervision, schools as organizations, school improvement, leadership and supervisory behavior, communication, curriculum development, and teaching effectiveness.

The book is divided into four major parts. Part One, Setting the Stage for Supervisory Practice, provides an introduction to supervision as a field of study and the school as a learning organization, with an examination of the change in the supervisor as a leader. These chapters establish a theoretical framework for supervisors to employ as they develop a personal sense of supervisory leadership and build their individual professional supervision repertoire.

The chapters in Part Two, Models and Mechanics of Supervision, represent the pragmatic aspects of the supervisory process. Whereas Part One includes the knowledge and understanding of supervision, which is primarily theoretical in nature, Part Two is more practical and stresses the application of appropriate supervisory behaviors and attendant skills within the context and implementation of the supervision process. The clinical, developmental, collegial, and self-assessment models of supervision reinforce the notion that a variety of options exist from which supervisors may select, as they work collaboratively with teachers.

The third Part is The Instructional Dimension of Supervision. The emphasis in these chapters is both on instructional planning and implementation and on the role of the supervisor in facilitating quality teaching and learning. For us, Part Three describes the process by which schools become learning organizations through planning (curriculum development), the delivery of instruction (teaching), and the assessment of teaching (continuous growth and development).

Finally, Part Four, Reflection, Growth, and Change, focuses on fostering reflection to assist educators as they become more collaborative in participating in school improvement efforts, supporting teacher professional development, and making decisions that promote instructional change. Part Four establishes the context in which supervisors use the concepts, principles, and skills they have learned to create a culture in which teachers and students are successful.

"A View from the Field" segments represent the reflections of practicing supervisors as they implement the presented concepts. The "Your Turn" section at the end of each chapter provides opportunities for the readers to interact with, reflect upon, and apply the concepts, principles, and skills presented in the book. The tasks in these sections ask the readers to consider the information presented in the chapter and then to apply it to real-world situations or to their own work. The application step is essential for supervisors to become reflective practitioners.

This book has been a labor of love as we have incorporated most, if not all, of the suggestions offered by reviewers and professors. We are particularly indebted to the following reviewers for their insightful comments and suggestions: Constance Goode, Northern Illinois University; Thomas H. Metos, Arizona State University; and Judith A. Ponticell, Texas Tech University.

As the title suggests, we have presented a theoretical and programmatic framework for supervisors to employ as they become leaders and as they continue to grow and develop in their understanding of teaching and learning. As a result, we hope that this book represents a significant contribution to a better understanding of the complexities of supervisory leadership.

ABOUT THE AUTHORS

Don M. Beach is currently professor of education at Tarleton State University, Texas A&M University System. He received his Ph.D. in Curriculum and Educational Leadership from George Peabody College of Vanderbilt University. His master's in secondary education and administration is from Texas Tech University. He has taught at both the elementary and secondary levels in the schools of Texas and Tennessee and served in numerous supervisory positions in education. He is an active writer, researcher, and teacher and has served a variety of leadership roles in numerous professional organizations, including the Association of Teacher Educators, the Association for Supervision and Curriculum Development, and the Council of Professors of Instructional Supervision. He continues to conduct workshops at the state and national levels and publish in professional journals. Don is the author of numerous textbooks and monographs concerning supervision and elementary and secondary curricula.

Judy Reinhartz is currently professor of education in the School of Education at The University of Texas at Arlington. She received her doctorate from the University of New Mexico in the area of science education and instructional supervision. Her master's degree was conferred by Seton Hall University. In her more than 30 years of experience in education, Dr. Reinhartz has served in various teaching assignments and supervisory leadership positions at all levels of education in New Jersey, Virginia, New Mexico, and Texas. In 1985, she was the recipient of the Amoco Foundation's Outstanding Teaching Award at The University of Texas at Arlington. Dr. Reinhartz is actively involved in professional organizations, including Phi Delta Kappa, the Association of Teacher Educators, and the Association for Supervision and Curriculum Development. With her varied educational experiences, Judy has published extensively and has frequently served as a consultant to a number of school districts on topics such as effective teaching, supervisory leadership, and instructional assessment.

Setting the Stage for Supervisory Practice

Chapter 1: Supervision as a Field of Study

Chapter 2: The Changing Contexts for Viewing Supervision

Chapter 3: The Workplace for Teachers and Supervisors

Chapter 4: Supervisors as Leaders

Chapter 5: Communicating Effectively: A Critical Component for Supervision

Part One sets the stage by providing various contexts for supervisory practice. Supervisors must have an understanding of (1) their roles and the nature of the supervision process to effectively work within the organizational structure of schools, (2) the historical forces that shape supervisory practice, (3) the nature of being a leader, and (4) the importance of communication. Chapter 1, Supervision as a Field of Study, begins by presenting various views of the supervision process, different definitions and approaches, and assumptions related to supervision. A theoretical framework that links theory to practice is described, and the roles of the supervisor are discussed. Chapter 2, The Changing Contexts for Viewing Supervision, provides descriptions of the changing historical contexts in which supervision occurs. Each historical period identifies the political and social forces that have implications for educational supervision. Chapter 3 describes schools as organizations and the workplace of supervisors and teachers. The structure and function of organizations as well as the processes that occur in organizations are discussed. Organizational culture and characteristics of effective organizations and schools are also among the topics.

As the title suggests, Chapter 4 defines supervisors as leaders and identifies the salient qualities of leadership they need to be effective. In addition, the chapter distinguishes between leaders and managers and presents theoretical models of leadership. As supervisors serve as leaders in schools, they utilize various styles and types of power. Promoting effective communication is the focus of Chapter 5. Effectiveness is described in terms of responses that facilitate or inhibit communication and that occur in descriptive and nonjudgmental language.

1 Supervision as a Field of Study

OBJECTIVES

The objectives of this chapter are:

- Discuss the purpose of supervision and the complexity of the roles and functions supervisors fulfill.
- Identify the organizing principles and discuss the various views and definitions of supervision.
- Identify and describe the theoretical perspectives of supervision.
- Explain the various assumptions related to supervision.
- Discuss the roles associated with the supervision process.

Examining principles, concepts, and skills generated from research is the first step in the journey to understanding supervision as a field of study. Elements from research that provide the backdrop for supervisory practice include organizational theory, effective instruction, leadership theory, teacher development, and communication theory. In addition to these elements from research, three general or theoretical perspectives provide lenses for viewing the supervision process and include an organizational, people, and instructional focus. An understanding of these research elements and theoretical perspectives can assist supervisors as they become skilled in working with teachers, parents, and community members. Supervision as a field of study provides a knowledge base, which is "passed hand to hand among those who are willing to dare similar voyages of their own" (Wheatley, 1992, p. xi), and helps supervisors better understand the complexities of their roles and responsibilities.

The primary purpose of supervision, as presented in this text, is to support and sustain **all** teachers in their goal of career-long growth and development, which ultimately results in quality instruction. Such growth and development rely on a system that is built on trust and is supportive of teachers' efforts to be more effective in their classrooms. As Tracy and McNaughton (1993) note, "Teachers …often desire supervision at all stages of their career" (p. 3). Calebrese and Zepeda (1997) view supervision as "linking the facilitation of human growth to that of achieving organizational goals" (p. xiii). Other texts may view supervision as being conducted primarily by central office personnel. We view supervision as a general function of instructional leadership that occurs throughout the educational community, which is essential to the effective operation of schools and, ultimately, student learning. As Sheppard (1996) notes in his review of research, "In the broad view, instructional leadership entails all leadership activities that affect student learning" (p. 326). Supervisory positions may include but are not limited to: peer coaches, lead teachers, team leaders or department heads, specialists–consultants, facilitators, curriculum directors, principals, assistant superintendents, and/or superintendents. For us, supervision focuses on the interactive nature of teaching and learning and involves numerous people in different roles and contexts, at multiple levels of the school organization. It has its focus on teaching–learning and teacher development.

Firth (1987) speaks of the complexity of roles and functions of supervisors when he notes that superintendents and principals have their administrative roles defined by law or clarified in state school codes, but others who also function as supervisors do not. Such individuals "may have different responsibilities but the same title, or identical responsibilities but different titles" (p. 2). In examining the typical administrative structure of schools (Chapter 3), the superintendent generally supervises the work of building principals and the central office staff as well as oversees instruction for the entire school district. Accordingly, central office staff also serve as supervisors as they work with teachers and administrators within the school district. At the campus level, the principal supervises the instructional program in that school; on each campus, there may be other personnel, such as team leaders, department heads, or lead teachers, who also assume supervisory roles as they coach and mentor teachers. It is these roles and responsibilities within the organization that define supervisors, not simply a title. Bolman and Deal (1995) caution that "leadership lies in the hearts of leaders," and as they work with colleagues, they must remember to remain in touch "with a most precious human gift [the] spirit" (p. 6).

In this chapter, we will present an overview of supervision, describe the organizing principles that guide supervisory practice and compare various views of supervision. In addition, we will discuss some of the basic assumptions related to the field of supervision and provide a theoretical framework for the supervision process. The chapter describes various supervisory roles within the school organization and sets the stage for supervisors by presenting a scenario that puts this field of study in a context.

Organizing Principles

Knowledge about the history of the supervisory process; the various models of supervision; the specific principles, concepts, skills, and procedures; and the elements from research form the organizing principles for supervision as a field of study. The four interrelated principles that guide professional practice are:

1. "Historical roots" of supervisory practice—The knowledge and ways of thinking that have been accumulated and, as Wheatley (1992) notes, handed down regarding past and current professional behavior along with views of supervision.

2. Models of supervision—[Clinical (Goldhammer, Anderson, and Krajewski, 1993), developmental (Glickman, Gordon, and Ross-Gordon, 1998), collegial and collaborative (Costa and Garmston, 1994; Showers and Joyce, 1996), and mentoring (Reiman and Thies-Sprinthall, 1998)]—The knowledge of various ways of working with teachers to foster professional growth and development that promote quality teaching and learning, as well as self-assessment (Reinhartz and Beach, 1993).

3. Specific techniques and procedures—The skills supervisors use as they converse with teachers, observe in classrooms, collect and analyze data, and discuss possibilities for action (Good and Brophy, 1997).

4. Research elements—The knowledge of effective organizations, schools, instruction, leadership, communication, teacher development, decision making, and change that validate and support supervisory behavior.

The historical issues associated with supervision will be addressed in detail in Chapter 2. Various periods covering the last 300 years will be discussed, along with the implications of the social, political, and historical dimensions of the development of supervision. The second organizing principle, models of supervision, will be discussed in Chapter 6. Specifically, the clinical, developmental, collegial and collaborative, mentoring, and self-assessment models will be described. Specific conferencing, data-gathering, and analysis skills are presented later in Chapter 7. The elements of the research derived from schools as organizations, supervisors as leaders, communication, effective teaching, and teacher development are also discussed in separate chapters. When the elements from these chapters are integrated, they provide a composite portrait of supervision.

Figure 1.1 presents the conceptual organization of the book and serves to illustrate the cumulative nature of supervision as a field of study. To demonstrate how these principles and elements fit together, we have organized the book into four major parts. Part One includes Chapters 1 to 5 and sets the stage by providing a knowledge base in the areas of (1) assumptions, roles, and theoretical framework; (2) views and historical contexts; (3) organizations and effective schools; (4) leadership behavior; and (5) communication. Part Two includes descriptions of supervision processes, and data collection procedures. Part Three provides an

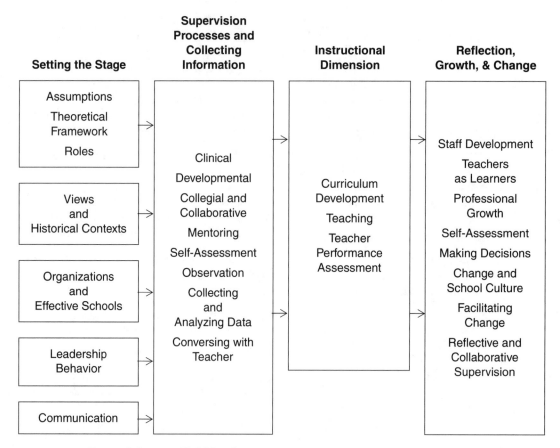

FIGURE 1.1   **Supervision as a Field Study**

analysis of the instructional dimension of supervision which includes curriculum development, teaching, and teacher performance assessment. Part Four addresses the issues of reflection, growth, change, professional inquiry, decision making, reflection, and collaboration.

Effective supervisors need to be visionary as they confront outmoded and noncollaborative procedures found in school settings. Likewise, the field of supervision is in transition and redefinition (Sergiovanni and Starratt, 1998); it needs a renewed pioneering spirit, creative energies, and proactive leadership strategies, which will serve to shape the dynamic nature of supervision for the next millennium (Smith and Thompson, 1997). Glanz and Neville (1997) advocate continued use of supervision by having it "be dynamic, integrated, and evolving" (p. 29). According to these authors, supervisors have more important responsibilities than ever before because they address the changes that need to occur. Supervisors are being called upon to initiate and facilitate the change process as they execute their varied responsibilities (Daresh and Playko, 1995). If the field of supervision is to remain vital, so too must the supervisors (Smith and Thompson, 1997). To see change as being a positive process, supervisors are challenged "to reshape [their] fundamental world view" (Wheatley, 1992, p. xi).

Views of Supervision

No single unifying definition of supervision appears in the literature. In fact, a great many terms are often used interchangeably (i.e., peer supervision, cognitive coaching, instructional leadership, instructional supervision, supervisory leadership). As Daresh and Playko (1995) note, "Educational supervision is a field in search of a definition [since] no real consensus has ever been reached concerning what supervision should be" (p. 7). Krajewski (1997) also observes that educators have failed "to arrive at an agreeable, workable, comprehensible, nonthreatening definition...and none [of these definitions] have gained an overall acceptance and understanding by a majority" (p. 34). The great number of definitions for supervision is largely due to the various historical, political, social, and economic forces at work in any given time period (Chapter 2) or developed and touted by various proponents or gurus (Krajewski, 1997). The definitions tend to change over time in response to the priorities present in the social milieu of schools and have often been seen by teachers as veiled attempts at evaluation. White and Daniel (1996) have noted that definitions and theoretical orientations presented in the literature tend to be evaluation-based or clinically based.

One of the earliest definitions of supervision comes from the Latin root that means to "oversee" or "have oversight of." Dictionary definitions expand on this early meaning and indicate that to supervise translates into directing or managing the work of others. In the early 1930s when supervisory roles and responsibilities were emerging, the leaders in the National Education Association (1931) defined supervision as leading efforts to improve teaching, observing in classrooms, and conferencing with teachers. By the late 1950s, supervision was viewed as an activity that helped teachers do their job better and improve the learning situation of children (Wiles, 1956). During the 1960s, supervision was seen as a change process (Harris and Bessent, 1969). Over the last two decades, various authors have defined and grouped supervision in the following ways, according to three perspectives that are described in the theoretical framework section of this chapter.

Instructional

■ A multidimensional interpersonal process that involves curriculum development, learning environments, grouping of students, teacher utilization, and professional development (Pfeiffer and Dunlap, 1982)

■ A way of offering specialized help to improve instruction (Oliva, 1993; Oliva and Pawlas, 1997)

■ The function that brings together the components of instructional effectiveness into schoolwide efforts (Glickman, 1985, 1990; Glickman, Gordon, and Ross-Gordon, 1998)

Organizational

■ A management function within the school production system (Alfonso, Firth, and Neville, 1981)

■ A leadership function involving administration, curriculum, and teaching (Wiles and Bondi, 1980, 1986)

■ For Alfonso (1997),

> Supervision…contributes to effectiveness [and] to goal attainment…by gaining commitment to…mutually shared objectives; by assisting people in making their work efficient, effective, and personally rewarding; by building communication networks…; and by helping to create an organization that values human beings. (p. 13)

People

■ A way of modifying teacher behavior (Wiles and Lovell, 1975)

■ A means of facilitating professional growth by providing teachers with feedback about their classroom interactions (Glatthorn, 1984, 1990)

■ Activities that improve and stimulate professional growth (Goldhammer, Anderson, and Krajewski, 1993)

■ A matter of human relations and the development of human resources (Doll, 1983; Sergiovanni and Starratt, 1993)

■ A moral quality that involves both promoting teacher development and nurturing and articulating a vision of what a learning community should be (Sergiovanni and Starratt, 1998)

We define the term *supervision* as a *complex process that involves working with teachers and other educators in a collegial, collaborative relationship to enhance the quality of teaching and learning within schools and that promotes the career-long development of teachers.* We have deliberately avoided using the word "help" in our definition because this word often connotes a deficit model and implies that teachers lack something and need supervisors to help them "fix" some aspect of instruction. Supervision liberates, improves, and seeks to make needed changes throughout the educational community; as Bolman and Deal (1995) note, "Leading with soul" requires that supervisors breathe spirit and passion into their lives and organizations (p. 12).

Supervision is contextual, and the interactions with teachers depend on the degree of experience of both teachers and supervisors. We believe all educators have personal and professional aspirations that have not yet been achieved. Ideally, supervisors serve as a bridge that supports and sustains efforts, leading to achieving these personal and professional objectives.

Our view of supervision is not one in which teachers are "lacking" or deficient, and supervisors have what it takes to "fix" the deficiency. As stated in the assumptions, we believe that ultimately the only people who can change are the people themselves. Supervision is a reciprocal process in which both supervisors and teachers grow through their various interactions. For us, the supervisor is not some "super" person who is all-knowing and can handle all issues and concerns. As a catalyst, a guide, a supporter, or an encourager, the supervisor together with teachers moves along a growth continuum, which is infinite.

Supervisors are educators who have been formally or informally designated as resources for teachers; as resources, teachers have someone to talk with regarding various ideas, issues, or concerns. Supervisors, in most educational organizations, are empowered and in turn empower others as they access information, link people and materials, and facilitate change in such a way that teachers are successful in their efforts. Supervisors can play such a role for beginning as well as for veteran teachers because to teach is to learn.

The use of various terms, such as mentor, coach, or supervisor, tends to complicate our understanding of the process rather than clarify it because each term carries with it value-laden meanings. For example, for some, it is difficult to conceive of a supervisor both as a resource and a source of authority or as a friend and an evaluator. Granted, this type of thinking may be somewhat contradictory to one's belief system. So, instead of providing clarity, many times the terms expressed in the literature add to the ambiguity and uncertainty of the context of supervision. As you read this book and consider the context in which supervision occurs, we hope you will be able to sort out these issues.

Assumptions Related to Supervision

As supervisors, teachers, and other educators interact, their behavior is based on several assumptions that guide the process and serve to establish a mind-set or frame of reference for those engaged in the improvement of instruction. These assumptions are based on a view that is characterized by an open, nonthreatening, trusting, and empowering relationship between the teacher and supervisor, which leads to two-way growth for both. Secondly, such a view addresses instructional issues by using various data obtained from dialogues, class visits, observations, and reflections. To clarify this view of supervision as lifelong learning, six assumptions (Goldhammer, Anderson and Krajewski, 1993; Beach and Reinhartz, 1989; Boyan and Copeland, 1978) are central to this perspective.

1. *Teachers can resolve instructional situations by modifying their behavior.* When teachers encounter instructional challenges, the initial question to ask is: "What actions or behaviors can I exhibit that will bring about positive actions from my students so that they learn?"

It should be noted, however, that many factors other than those related to teacher behaviors impact student learning; teachers are not in control of social, legal, and budgetary factors that influence schools and the teaching–learning process. Some examples of the problems that are beyond the direct control of teachers, which they feel interfere with students' ability to learn, are listed in the Metropolitan Life Survey of American Teachers (*Teacher Education Reports,* 1992).

When teachers focus solely on student behavior, they miss opportunities for enhancing their interaction with students. As teachers and supervisors work together to identify those factors that are beyond their control, they then focus on those over which they have control. In this interaction, they begin to identify instructional behaviors that increase student achievement.

2. *The recognition of a need to modify behavior comes from within rather than being imposed by others.* By engaging in professional dialogue, it prompts teachers to examine their belief system and causes them to think about making changes. This level of recognition and awareness, coupled with feedback from the supervisor, serves to initiate a change process that starts with the teacher.

3. *Through informal discussions, classroom visits, and systematic observations, instructional behaviors can be identified and examined.* There are a variety of ways in

Issues cited in the Metropolitan Life Survey of the American Teacher (*Teacher Education Reports,* 1992) include:

- Poverty, 41 percent
- Parents' drug and alcohol problems, 32 percent
- Physical or psychological abuse, 22 percent
- Poor nutrition, 21 percent
- Students' own alcohol problems, 13 percent
- Violence in the schools, 11 percent
- Students' own drug problems, 9 percent
- Poor health, 7 percent

which supervisors can gather information about classroom practices. Informally, this can be accomplished by having conversations with the teacher and by spending time in classrooms. A more formal approach can be achieved by using specific observation techniques and instruments. It is at this stage that the models and mechanics of supervision (Chapters 6 and 7) can prove helpful.

4. *By coaching, facilitating discussions, and spending time in classrooms, supervisors can provide another perspective.* Such insight can be useful as the supervisor and teacher "relive" a teaching–learning episode. At this point, the supervisor can serve as a coach and mentor for the teacher in the quest for greater instructional effectiveness. Even when the process is supportive and rapport is established, ghosts from past experiences, such as "old resentments and suspicions," need to be overcome (Goldhammer, 1964/1992, p. 5).

5. *When the information generated is acknowledged as accurate, teachers assume the major role in identifying where changes are needed.* For instructional change to be lasting, teachers should reexamine their beliefs, perceptions, and assumptions about teaching, learning, and their students. Ultimately, the job of the supervisor is directed toward fostering career-long professional development; for this process to be successful, it takes effort from the teachers themselves. This assumption is predicated on the belief that teachers, when supported and encouraged, have the desire, willingness, and competence to make changes in their behaviors and procedures.

6. *The level of productivity for both the teacher and supervisor is enhanced when the relationship and interactions are collegial in nature and based on trust, cooperation, mutual respect, and reliance upon each other.* Such a partnership leads to the development of a shared vision of quality education for all children. The supervision process is productive when the teacher and supervisor work together to create a culture of continuous growth. Together, supervisors and teachers become partners in developing a cooperative plan of action.

These six assumptions form the framework for a philosophical base from which to operate. In a sense, these assumptions provide benchmarks for explaining and understanding the theoretical and practical dimensions of supervision. As noted earlier, teachers are at different professional stages with varying instructional abilities, professional experiences, and developmental levels. The range of teacher abilities, taken together, can be viewed as a continuum of professional development with the most capable teachers at one end and the less capable teachers at the opposite end. This variety of teaching abilities and potential requires that supervisors modify their approach so that they can meet the needs of teachers who are at different stages of professional development. To accommodate such diversity in the range of teacher behaviors, supervisors can select from several models and use a variety of strategies. A more complete and detailed discussion of data collection procedures, teacher developmental stages, and supervision models is presented in Chapters 6, 7, and 11.

A Theoretical Framework for Supervision

Examining the beliefs that guide supervisory practice is the first step toward an understanding of the theoretical foundation of supervision. Such an understanding is important because supervisors use a theoretical base for making decisions and taking action. The linkage between theory and practice, however, is not always clear. In the following section, we will seek to provide a response to the question, How does theory guide practice?

A theory involves the generalization and application of the most advanced and valid knowledge to specific situations (Ornstein and Hunkins, 1988). A theory may also be viewed as a way of interpreting information or providing an explanation for a set of facts (Helms and Turner, 1986). For Reinhartz and Beach (1988), a theory is needed to help explain and validate practices that supervisors employ. Getzels (1960) has further explained the importance of a theory by saying that supervisors "think and work from within some conceptual framework, some theoretical bias [or] some intellectual stance" (p. 38). Theory, then, aids our understanding of supervision. As Sergiovanni and Starratt (1998) point out, "The question for most supervisors…is not whether they are being theoretical or not but what are the theories (implicit hunches and operating principles)…[which] provide the basis for professional decisions and practice" (p. 6).

To determine the implicit hunches and operating principles that guide supervisory practice, Reinhartz and Beach (1988) reviewed 10 supervision books published during the decade of the 1980s to identify the components presented by the various authors that support a theoretical perspective of supervision. This initial work has been replicated by Pajak (1990), Anderson (1993), and White and Daniel (1996). In the original Reinhartz and Beach (1988) study, the definitions of supervision, the use of supporting fields and related research, and the overall or general approaches to supervision were used to identify the authors' general perspective or theoretical orientation.

By first examining the screen of related fields and supporting research, the most frequently mentioned elements in the texts were:

- Organizational theory, climate, and culture
- Effective instruction and schools
- Leadership theory and behavior
- Teacher development and staff development
- Communication theory and communication skills

As seen in the earlier section on definitions, taken together these components form the beginnings of a theory of supervision, and three general perspectives or points of view emerge. One perspective focuses on school organizational structure and behavior in schools. Another perspective is primarily concerned with people (teachers) and their professional development. The third perspective is instructional, which focuses on the teaching–learning process.

The *organizational perspective* emphasizes goals and objectives as the driving force in schools. In such a view, leadership, along with school culture and climate, is central to successfully accomplishing the objectives. Supervision is described as "management of people and resources," "goal accomplishment or task orientation," and "organizational effectiveness." The way to improve the organization is to improve the structure or establish new goals and objectives.

A *people perspective* focuses on the continued professional growth and development of teachers through staff development activities. This perspective goes beyond just activities and suggests that schools exist to meet basic human needs; it requires a supervisory approach that is sensitive to the needs of teachers and views teachers as "precious resources." Such terms as "professional development" and "staff development" are often linked to this perspective. In order to improve the supervisory process in this perspective, the interpersonal "fit" (the relationships between and among teachers and supervisors) must exist.

An *instructional perspective* is more specialized because it stresses the unique aspects of the teaching–learning process. Supervisors who have this perspective are frequently concerned with the school curriculum and the implementation of the curriculum in individual classrooms. Such phrases as "delivery of instruction," "curriculum development and alignment," "teacher effectiveness," and "improving classroom instruction" are used when describing the supervision process. This perspective often puts the supervisor in a clinician role, using a diagnostic and prescriptive approach to observe classroom instruction and provide feedback to the teacher.

Based on these three theoretical perspectives of supervision, Reinhartz and Beach (1988) suggest that supervision is indeed a diversified field of study and concur with Pfeiffer and Dunlap (1982), who note that there does not seem to be one single theory of supervision that is adhered to or accepted by all. If a theory can be seen as a way of interpreting information, a supervisory paradigm seems helpful in understanding the roots of supervisory practices and values. The three perspectives and the related fields or supporting research, coupled with definitions and approaches, provide several different theoretical underpinnings.

What appears to happen is that supervisors interpret information using the related fields or supporting research to produce a theoretical base, which guides their practices. Selected supervision textbooks reveal, through their definitions, the various theoretical perspectives. A summary of the definitions and approaches of supervision is presented in Figure 1.2.

As seen in Figure 1.2, the three theoretical perspectives (organization, people, and instruction) become the lenses through which supervisors "see" or interpret information relative to supervision. When the perspectives are coupled with the supporting research elements (organizational theory, effective instruction, leadership theory, teacher development, and communication), a clearer view or theory of supervision emerges. Each supervisor selects one or more of the perspectives to give meaning and direction to practice.

A theory of supervision is dependent upon a combination of factors, which includes at least one general perspective or viewpoint. However, a theory of supervision—a view of reality—is dependent upon the unique selection of factors made by each supervisor and the research base they draw on (Chinn and Brewer,

FIGURE 1.2   Selected Supervision Textbooks: Definitions and Approaches

Authors	Definitions of Supervision	Related Fields of Study (Research)	Approaches to Supervision
Alfonso, Firth, and Neville (1981)	Integration of processes and procedures to enhance effectiveness of the organization; supervision viewed within an organizational production system, (school is a production system); form of management	Organization, leadership, communication, decision making, and change theories	Improvement of organizational efficiency and effectiveness through behavioral and systemic supervision (ISB)
Lovell and Wiles (1983)	Improvement of student learning by maintaining, changing, and improving the design and actualization of learning opportunities	Communication, motivation, change, leadership, organization, group development, teaching, and learning	A behavior management system that focuses on improved instruction as an outcome of supervision
Goldhammer, Anderson, and Krajewski (1993)	Use of data from observation in face-to-face interactions with teachers to improve performance opportunities	Clinical methods, observation and analysis skills, and business and medical leadership skills	A process that seeks to provide teachers with the development of qualities, skills, and practices to be effective
Kosmoski (1997)	Leadership process that seeks to improve instruction to promote successful student achievement	Organizational development, human development, leadership styles, effective teaching and school research, curriculum design, and development, and staff development	Improvement of student success by applying principles of of effective instruction and leadership principles
Oliva and Pawlas (1997)	Service to teachers through specialized assistance	Historical contexts, instructional and curriculum development, staff development, and assessment procedures	Provision of services to help teachers in improving their instructional effectiveness

Calebrese and Zepeda (1997)	Process of linking human growth and potential to achieving organizational goals	Organizational development, leadership and vision, data gathering, decision making, change, and team building	Application of effective organizational principles in a moral and responsible way to accomplish school goals and outcomes
Sergiovanni and Starratt (1998)	Process of helping teachers as a community of learners gain a vision of educational possibilities through reflective insight	Human relations and human resources, school improvement and restructuring, learning communities, and moral action	Transformation or redefinition of the school into a community of learners—people with a common set of professional and moral concepts that guide behavior
Glickman, Gordon, and Ross-Gordon (1998)	Assistance given to teachers based on their developmental levels	Interpersonal and technical assistance skills, teacher and adult development, effective schools, organizational goals, professional development, and curriculum development	Both a process and a function that provide assistance to teachers for the improvement of instruction and attainment of school goals

1993; Kennedy, 1997). Although the theory base is often complex, knowing about theory leads supervisors to a greater understanding of what they do and why.

Roles of the Supervisor

Supervisors have different titles and positions but perform many similar roles. Titles, such as coordinator, facilitator, assistant principal, principal, or superintendent, are specific to their individual jobs or positions as designated by the organizational structure of the school district. Supervisory roles refer to broader general behaviors. In this context, an individual may have the title of assistant superintendent of instruction but have many roles that are similar to others with different titles. For example, an assistant superintendent must be a leader, planner, and communicator, but so does a building principal. The roles are partly dependent upon the expectations and job descriptions developed by each school system and adapted to meet the needs of the campus or context. Supervisors, regardless of title, are typically called upon to perform the following roles, and the performance of one role is often related to others.

Leader.   In order to be successful, a supervisor must be a leader and, as such, be able to get others to work toward a shared vision through team learning (McAdams, 1997). For instance, the supervisor must be able to work with teachers to accomplish the instructional goals of the school or modify instructional plans to provide equity and excellence in learning opportunities for all students. In addition, persuading teachers to adopt new curricular programs or instructional models is often a part of the supervisor's role. Being a leader is "akin to the 'diagnostician' role of organizational developers and human resource professionals" in that it involves "broad change efforts that combine a variety of performance improvement interventions" (Carr, 1995, p. 61). Being effective in leading others is therefore a role that the supervisor should welcome.

Planner/Organizer.   Within the operation of schools, planning is one of the most important roles for the supervisor and, according to Kosmoski (1997), "is required at all levels" (p. 75). Planning involves the ability to anticipate what should be done and how it should be accomplished. Whether the supervisor is engaged in macro-planning, by organizing a school staff development, or micro-planning, by focusing on a specific staff development session, prior thought is essential to the success of the endeavor (Reinhartz and Beach, 1997). Short- and long-range planning are prerequisites for supervisors and involve setting goals and prioritizing. Whether the duties of the supervisor involve class scheduling or obtaining the necessary curricular materials (including textbooks), the ability to link people and resources with a time frame is essential to school operations.

Facilitator.   As supervisors, their primary objective is the professional growth of teachers as they expand their teaching repertoire. It is imperative that supervisors function as facilitators and be supportive as they function in a variety of settings with teachers who have different needs and levels of professional competence. "Rearranging and restructuring of teacher thinking...is facilitated by the supervisor during conferences, and contacts by encouraging the teacher to imagine, describe, and prepare" (McGreal, 1997, p. 94). In the role of facilitator, for example, the supervisor provides direct assistance to teachers, by coaching, and gives indirect assistance, by securing needed resources/materials, funding, promoting collegial relations, observing, and listening to teachers as they reflect on their concerns and elaborate on their strengths.

Appraiser/Assessor.   This role may be one of the most controversial because there is disagreement as to whether anyone other than the building principal should evaluate or appraise teachers. Waite (1997) asserts that evaluation or appraisals pay "homage to the organization, the bureaucracy, and not the teacher" (p. 57). Other individuals, such as consultants or coordinators, who are asked to become part of the teacher evaluation process may compromise the trust relationship they have developed with teachers. Although supervisory personnel have historically been associated with staff development, there is an increasing trend to involve others besides principals in teacher appraisal. The ability of the supervisor to appraise teaching within the formative evaluation parameters, along with coaching and assisting the teacher, is an important part of the improvement of instruction.

Motivator/Encourager.   One of the most important roles performed by a supervisor is to motivate others "to become productive members of the organization" (Kosmoski, 1997, p. 44). Motivation enhances a person's desire to do something and is enhanced by encouragement, which is the process that builds a "person's self-esteem, self-confidence, and feelings of worth" (Dinkmeyer and Eckstein, 1996, p. 16). Supervisors can help teachers develop a positive attitude by using strategies that will foster an intrinsic desire to grow in their instructional performance. Being able to motivate is vital to the supervisor's ability to foster and sustain change and improvement.

Communicator.   Supervisors must be good communicators, and their ability to effectively work with others depends on their ability to listen and respond. As Daresh and Playko (1995) describe the process, "Communication takes place daily on many different levels and within various subsystems [and]...clarifies an organization's goals, procedures, and rules...bringing to light the unique identity of the organization—what it stands for" (p. 163). It is imperative that supervisors be able to communicate ideas and information to all segments of the educational community, and to the public as well.

Decision Maker.   Supervisors have to be able to make split-second decisions affecting individual students, teachers, staff members, or the entire school—which type of gifted program to implement, whether to support the use of uniforms for all students, etc. These decisions "fall within the three domains [of] instructional, curriculum, and staff development" (Oliva and Pawlas, 1997, p. 453). The supervisory process requires continuous decision making and involves working with teachers, parents, students, and other administrators to determine what is best for all involved. The ability to make a difference in the quality of instruction in a classroom may depend on the supervisor's ability to make sound decisions based on data.

Change Agent.   Supervisors, because of their position within the school structure, also serve as change agents. They are officially designated or empowered by the school organization to bring about change, primarily in instruction, but also with regard to the school itself. McAdams (1997) notes: "In reality, organizations change only when the people in them are willing and able to do so" (p. 141). Supervisors work within the school system to bring about changes in programs and procedures that will positively impact classroom instruction.

Coach/Mentor.   Although the role of mentor has appeared in the literature before, the role of coach is an emerging role for the supervisor. Costa and Garmston (1994) suggest that "skillful…coaches apply specific strategies to enhance another person's perceptions, decisions, and intellectual functions" (p. 2). For Makibbin and Sprague (1997), coaching involves acting as a resource to improve instructional practices. As supervisors coach teachers, they provide valuable resources, feedback, and support.

With a variety of titles and job descriptions, some supervisory roles become more important than others, depending on the particular situations or context. Regardless of the specific title, one can see from these roles that a supervisory position carries with it a great deal of responsibility.

Setting the Stage and Getting Started

In the earlier parts of this chapter, we focused on the academic aspects of supervision by providing views, roles, guiding principles, and a theoretical framework. Thus far, this discussion has been without practical linkages to the real world of schools. Supervision, however, occurs in schools with real people and issues. The larger context of supervision is the school district, but where supervision can and should make a difference is at the person-to-person level with teachers. As teachers and supervisors work together to address issues, such as curriculum alignment, standards-based curriculum, and student assessment, they must establish a working relationship and a vision that result in increased student achievement.

A View from the Field

Let's examine the following scenario. It is October, and Trish has been in her present position as the assistant principal at Morningside Elementary School for several weeks. As she entered the workroom one Monday morning, several teachers were standing at their mailboxes discussing the many issues that made demands on their time. That very morning several teachers were notified that they were expected to attend an orientation meeting for the technology grant their school had been awarded. The orientation meeting would be from 6 P.M. to 9 P.M. in a location 35 miles from their school. These teachers had to make arrangements for after-school care for their own children. In addition, they had to be thinking about ways to meet the needs of all students and work toward raising achievement test scores.

Trish remembers what it was like to be a classroom teacher; she smiles as she realizes that the demands on her time related to her professional life have not decreased but, in many ways, have increased. Her role as their supervisor was to listen and be aware of their needs and concerns, then to problem-solve and brainstorm with them regarding their immediate dilemma today. Trish suggests they ask for volunteers to attend the meeting, making sure that all grade levels are covered. Having these teachers as resources in the building, they can then instruct others during the next scheduled campus meeting.

Welcome to the field of supervision. The possibilities for handling these and other issues are limited only by Trish's understanding of the supervision process. Factors Trish has to consider, as she becomes more comfortable and effective in her role as assistant principal, include giving attention to relevant educational issues and concerns at her school; offering a systematic approach to examining problems; and generating alternative options to address the teachers' concerns. Drawing upon her past experiences as a classroom teacher and team leader as well as using her knowledge of theoretical perspectives and views of supervision, Trish is now ready to initiate a supervisory plan that is compatible with the mission of the school and the vision of the school culture.

Her response to the teachers may be immediate—a snapshot of supervision—yet the response is based on her understanding of the nuances of supervision. How she establishes her supervisory style becomes very personal.

Viewing supervision as a field of study, with multiple roles and no single unifying definition, makes the selection of a plan of action difficult in different contexts. Despite frequent ambiguity voiced by those in the profession, the field of supervision has made progress in refining practice based on a deeper understanding of the educational issues that challenge supervisors. Trish has an enhanced understanding of the supervision process when she has the ability to conceptualize a response to the teachers that is relevant to them and their situation.

Summary

Understanding supervision as a field of study is important as supervisors work with various individuals and groups and promote the career-long development of teachers. The organizing principles and views of supervision were presented and discussed as the heart of the field of supervision. To better understand the evolution of supervision, our conceptual organization of the book, along with a section on views, was included.

Any individual, regardless of his or her title, who functions in a supervisory position in the school system is an instructional supervisor. For example, superintendents, principals, consultants, and directors are just a few of the titles used that also have supervisory roles as part of their job responsibilities. Those functioning in a supervisory capacity must be people-oriented as well as task-oriented to be effective in developing a vision for improving instruction.

Six assumptions that establish a framework for the supervisory process were presented. Within this text, supervision is viewed as a process of working with teachers and other educators in a collegial, collaborative way to improve classroom instruction and student learning and to foster professional growth and development. Each assumption focused on a key area (teacher behavior, teacher concerns, reflection and self-discovery, and role of the supervisor), which will help supervisors when they work with teachers.

The supervision process is complex and requires formulating, implementing, and evaluating goals and objectives; developing, implementing, and evaluating curriculum; supervising and appraising personnel and providing for staff development; developing and managing resources for the teaching–learning process; and evaluating materials, programs, and classroom instruction. Specific roles discussed included leader, planner/organizer, facilitator, appraiser/assessor, motivator/encourager, communicator, decision maker, change agent, and coach/mentor. Supervisors perform these roles as they help teachers improve their instructional behaviors.

The last section of this chapter created a context for implementing supervision by describing a school episode. To be effective, supervisors must be able to serve as the leaders, supporters, and colleagues of faculty, parents, and other community members.

As discussed in the next chapter, the events of the late 1990s may place supervisors in leadership roles that they have not experienced in several decades. The supervisor will become the glue for these new school-based endeavors. In the final analysis, the supervisors will be held accountable for specific programs because they will be doing the leading, rather than just following mandates issued from external sources. Anyone desiring to become a supervisor should be aware of the rewards as well as the challenges of the position.

YOUR TURN

1.1. As someone who has been supervised, what comes to mind when you hear or see the word supervision? Write five words that you associate with the supervision process. What do you remember when you had an issue regarding your teaching schedule or teaching assignment? Review the major sections of the chapter, and add five additional words that might be used to describe the supervision process. In what ways are the lists the same? In what ways do they differ? Why do you think they are the same and/or different? Over the next several weeks, continue to add to your lists; consider developing a concept map for supervision, using the terms in these lists.

1.2. Using your experiences as a teacher and your understanding of the supervision process, develop a list of suggestions that, as supervisor, you might follow as you work with new teachers who will be part of your team.

1.3. Select a supervisory position (such as curriculum director, assistant principal, principal, elementary/secondary consultant, team/department leader) and interview or "shadow" the person holding that role.

Describe a typical day in this position, based on your interview and/or experience, discussing the roles and responsibilities as outlined in Chapter 1.

Develop a Venn diagram. The left circle would represent school issues that teachers experience, the right circle would be the person you selected to shadow, and the area where these circles overlap would be how they would interact.

1.4. As an elementary or secondary consultant in your district, you have been given the assignment of investigating standards-based education. Your responsibility is to find out about the key principles, assumptions, and current approaches used to define outcomes and apply this approach to daily practices in the classroom.

Once you are familiar with the standards-based movement, you are asked to present your findings to teachers, parents, and building administrators at a meeting.

What would be included in your strategic plan to communicate the essential components of the standards-based curriculum and assessment? What discipline area will you select to demonstrate standards-based curriculum development, alignment, lesson/unit development, and assessment? What questions would you anticipate from the audience?

How will you deal with the questions, What's in it for me? What would your recommendations be for phasing in standards-based education in your school?

1.5. In this current atmosphere of school restructuring, supervisors (you) may be asked to assume a variety of responsibilities. As you prepare for these new and varied responsibilities and as you continue to read this text, reflect on the strengths and shortcomings that you bring to this position. What are these, and how will they work to your advantage and/or disadvantage? Record the responses to this question.

To facilitate this reflection process, keep a journal, setting aside several pages for the heading "Skills, Talents, and Qualities That I Bring to the Supervisory Position" and a few pages for the heading "Talents and Qualities That Interfere With My Supervisory Position."

Over a period of time (a month or longer), add to your journal; at the end of the semester, reflect on and analyze your qualifications for assuming a leadership position as a supervisor.

Decide what role, if any, you will play in the changes that occur on your campus.

REFERENCES

Alfonso, R. J. (1997). Should supervision be abolished? No. In *Educational supervision: Perspectives, issues, and controversies.* J. Glanz & R. E. Neville (eds). pp. 13–19. Norwood, MA: Christopher Gordon Publishers.

Alfonso, R. J., Firth, G. R., & Neville, R. F. (1981). *Instructional supervision: A behavior system.* (2nd ed.). Boston: Allyn & Bacon.

Anderson, R. H. (1993). Clinical supervision: Its history and current context. In *Clinical supervision: Coaching for higher performance,* pp. 5–18. R. H. Anderson and K. J. Snyder (eds.). Lancaster, PA: Technomics.

Beach, D. M., & Reinhartz, J. (1989). *Supervision: Focus on instruction.* New York: Harper & Row.

Bolman, L. G., & Deal, T. E. (1995). *Leading with soul.* San Francisco: Jossey-Bass Publishers.

Boyan, N. J., & Copeland, W. D. (1978). *Instructional supervision training program.* Columbus OH: Charles E. Merrill.

Calebrese, R. L., & Zepeda, S. J. (1997). *The reflective supervisor: A practical guide for educators.* Larchmont, NY: Eye on Education.

Carr, A. A. (1995). Performance technologist preparation: The role of leadership theory. *Performance Improvement Quarterly, 8,* 59–74.

Chinn, C. A., & Brewer, W. K. (1993). The role of anomalous data in knowledge acquisition: A theoretical framework and implications for science instruction. *Review of Educational Research, 63,* 1–49.

Costa, A., & Garmston, R. (1994). *Cognitive coaching: A foundation for renaissance schools.* Norwood, MA: Christopher-Gordon Publishers.

Daresh, J. C., & Playko, M. A. (1995). *Supervision as a proactive process.* (2nd ed.). Prospect Heights, IL: Waveland Press.

Dinkmeyer, D., & Eckstein, D. (1996). *Leadership by encouragement.* Delray Beach, FL: St. Lucie Press.

Doll, R. C. (1983). *Supervision for staff development: Ideas and applications.* Boston: Allyn & Bacon.

Firth, G. (1987 March). Recognition by professional organizations: A better way to clear up role confusion. *Update.* Alexandria, VA: Association for Supervision and Curriculum Development.

Getzels, J. W. (1960). Theory and practice in educational administration: An old question revisited. In *Administrative theory as a guide to action.* R. F. Campbell and J. M. Lepham (eds.). Chicago: University of Chicago Press.

Glanz, J., & Neville, R. (1997). *Educational supervision: Perspectives, issues, and controversies.* Norwood, MA: Christopher-Gordon Publishers.

Glatthorn, A. A. (1984). *Differentiated supervision.* Alexandria, VA: Association for Supervision and Curriculum Development.

Glatthorn, A. A. (1990). *Supervisory leadership: Introduction to instructional supervision.* Glenview, IL: Scott, Foresman and Company.

Glickman, C. D. (1985). *Supervision of instruction: Developmental approach.* Boston: Allyn & Bacon.

Glickman, C. D. (1990). *Supervision of instruction: Developmental approach.* (2nd ed.). Boston: Allyn & Bacon.

Glickman, C. D., Gordon, S. P., & Ross-Gordon, J. M. (1998). *Supervision for instruction: A developmental approach.* (4th ed.). Boston: Allyn & Bacon.

Goldhammer, R. (1964/1992). Observations on observation and observations on observations on observation. In *The Robert Goldhammer papers: Early writings of a distinguished educator.* Stephenville, TX: Council of Professors of Instructional Supervision.

Goldhammer, R., Anderson, R. H., & Krajewski, R. J. (1993). *Clinical supervision: Special methods for the supervision of teachers.* (3rd ed.). Fort Worth: Harcourt Brace Jovanovich.

Good, T. L., & Brophy, J. E. (1997). *Looking in classrooms.* (5th ed.). New York: Addison-Wesley.

Harris, B., & Bessent, W. (1969). *Inservice education: A guide to better practice.* Englewood Cliffs, NJ: Prentice-Hall.

Helms, D. B., & Turner, J. S. (1986). *Exploring child behavior.* Monterey, CA: Brooks/Cole Publishing Co.

Kennedy, M. M. (1997). The connection between research and practice. *Educational Researcher, 26,* 4–12.

Kosmoski, G. J. (1997). *Supervision.* Mequon, WI: Stylex Publishing, Co., Inc.

Krajewski, R. J. (1997). Can we put back the s in ASCD? No. In *Educational supervision: Perspectives, issues, and controversies,* pp. 32–42. J. Glanz and R. F. Neville (eds.). Norwood, MA: Christopher-Gordon Publishers.

Lovell, J. T., & Wiles, K. (1983). *Supervision for better schools* (5th ed). Englewood Cliffs, NJ: Prentice-Hall.

Makibbin, S. S., & Sprague, M. M. (1997 February). The instructional coach: A new role in instructional improvement. *NASSP Bulletin, 81,* 94–100.

McAdams, R. P. (1997 October). A systems approach to school reform. *Phi Delta Kappan, 79,* 138–142.

McGreal, T. (1997). Can a supervisor be a coach? In *Educational supervision: Perspectives, issues, and controversies.* J. Glanz and R. F. Neville (eds.). Norwood, MA: Christopher-Gordon Publishers.

National Education Association. (1931). The fourth yearbook of the department of supervisors and directors of instruction of the National Education Association. *Evaluation of supervision.* New York: Teachers College Press.

Oliva, P. F. (1993). *Supervision for today's schools.* (4th ed.). New York: Longman.

Oliva, P. F., & Pawlas, G. E. (1997). *Supervision for today's schools.* (5th ed). New York: Longman.

Ornstein, A., & Hunkins, F. P. (1988). *Curriculum: Foundations, principles and issues.* Englewood Cliffs, NJ: Prentice Hall.

Pajak, E. (1990 April). Identification of dimensions of supervisory practice in education: Reviewing the literature. Paper presented at the annual meeting of the American Educational Research Association, Boston. ERIC Document Reproduction Service No. ED 320 285.

Pfeiffer, I. L., & Dunlap, J. B. (1982). *Supervision of teachers: A guide to improving instruction.* Phoenix: Oryx Press.

Reiman, A. J., & Thies-Sprinthall, L. (1998). *Mentoring and supervision for teacher development.* New York: Longman.

Reinhartz, J., & Beach, D. M. (1988). The search for a theory of supervision. *Pedamorphosis, 4,* 4–8.

Reinhartz, J., & Beach, D. M. (1993 Fall/Winter). A self-assessment model for supervisors: Increasing supervisor effectiveness. *Record in Educational Administration and Supervision, 14,* 35–40.

Reinhartz, J., & Beach, D. M. (1997). *Teaching and learning in the elementary school: Focus on curriculum.* Upper Saddle River, NJ: Merrill Publishers.

Sergiovanni, T. J., & Starratt, R. J. (1993). *Supervision: A redefinition.* (5th ed.). New York: McGraw-Hill.

Sergiovanni, T. J., & Starratt, R. J. (1998). *Supervision: A redefinition.* (6th ed.). New York: McGraw-Hill.

Sheppard, B. (1996 September). Exploring the transformational nature of instructional leadership. *The Alberta Journal of Educational Research, XLII,* 325–344.

Showers, B., & Joyce, B. (1996 March). The evaluation of peer coaching. *Educational Leadership, 53,* 12–16.

Smith, J. M., & Thompson, B. S. (1997). Can we put back the S in ASCD? Yes. In *Educational supervision: Perspectives, issues, and controversies.* J. Glanz and R. Neville (eds.). Norwood, MA: Christopher-Gordon Publishers.

Teacher Education Reports. (1992 September 22). Latest Met Life survey finds teachers unprepared to meet student problems, *14,* 3–7.

Tracy, S. J., & McNaughton, R. H. (1993). *Assisting and assessing educational personnel.* Boston, MA: Allyn & Bacon.

Waite, D. (1997). Do teachers benefit from supervision? No. In *Educational supervision: Perspectives, issues, and controversies.* J. Glanz and R. F. Neville (eds.). Norwood, MA: Christopher-Gordon Publishers.

Wheatley, M. J. (1992). *Leadership and the new science.* San Francisco: Berrett-Koehler Publishers.

White, B. L., & Daniel, L. G. (1996). Views of instructional supervision: What do the textbooks say? Paper presented at the Mid-South Educational Research Association Meeting, Tuscaloosa, AL, November 6–8.

Wiles, K. (1956). *Supervision for better schools*. Englewood Cliffs, NJ: Prentice-Hall.

Wiles, J., & Bondi, J. (1980). *Supervision: A guide to practice*. Columbus, Ohio: Charles E. Merrill.

Wiles, J., & Bondi, J. (1986). *Supervision: A guide to practice*. (2nd ed.). Columbus, OH: Charles E. Merrill.

Wiles, K., & Lovell, J. (1975). *Supervision for better schools*. (4th ed.). Englewood Cliffs, NJ: Prentice-Hall.

2 The Changing Contexts for Viewing Supervision

OBJECTIVES

The objectives of this chapter are:

- Discuss the impact of social, political, economic, and historical events on supervisory practice.
- Identify the periods of supervision and discuss the implications from each period on supervision today.
- Identify and discuss possible future trends in supervision.

As indicated in Chapter 1, an understanding of the historical roots of supervisory practice helps to set the stage for the supervision process. An awareness that supervision is a process that occurs within the context of time and place is essential to functioning as a supervisor in schools today because practices and procedures are often the result of changes that occur over time in society and in schools. Supervision practices are the result of the history of American public education as it has grown and evolved. In describing this evolutionary process, Tanner and Tanner (1987) note that public education and supervision as a field of study are so tightly linked that supervisors need to recognize the importance of past practices on their current roles as supervisors. Programs and procedures relating to supervision in schools are in response to changes that have taken place in the social and educational milieu, and these behaviors and practices should be viewed in relation to not only the present situation but earlier events and conditions as well.

As social institutions, schools are not immune to shifts that take place within society; in fact, schools have historically reflected the values and attitudes of each generation. In the late nineteenth and early twentieth centuries (between 1890 and 1910), schools were called upon to educate the waves of immigrants that came to this country. Schools continue to educate the immigrants who arrive each year. As schools experience the social, political, and technological developments of the time, they are frequently called upon to be instruments for social change. The dynamic nature of the American culture has been fueled by international as well as domestic developments. For example, the launching of *Sputnik I*; the Cold War; the desegregation of schools; nuclear weapons and technology; the breakup of the Soviet Union; tax rollbacks at the local, state, and national levels; increased global economic competition; and changes in the family structure have all impacted education in various ways. Because of these and other developments that have taken place in society, the missions of schools have continued to change, and supervisory practices must be continually modified to meet the needs of a given time and place.

Depending upon the current social, economic, and/or political conditions, new educational priorities are established; these priorities range from decisions made at the local level by school boards to actions taken at the national level by task forces, legislators, and/or the Supreme Court. The school context in which supervision takes place is therefore dynamic, and with new educational priorities, practices related to supervision are modified as well.

Numerous reports, published during the decade of the 1980s, chronicled the less than satisfactory conditions of public education: *A Nation at Risk*, 1983; *Crossroads in American Education*, 1989; *Everybody Counts*, 1989; *Science for All Americans*, 1990; *Learning to Read in Our Nation's Schools*, 1990; and *Learning to Write in Our Nation's Schools*, 1990. As a result of these and other reports, the period of 1980–1995 may become known as the era of school reform. American education has been continuously confronted with conflicting demands for reform and counterreform. Schools have come to view these attacks from every conceivable and inconceivable source as part of the educational process that creates changes in supervisory practice.

As we move into the twenty-first century, issues that may impact teachers and supervisors include: curriculum development that centers on thematic, integrated planning or makes connections across the curriculum (Frazee and Rudnitski, 1995; Fredericks, Meinbach, and Rothlein, 1993); the effective use of technology in the teaching–learning process (Bradsher, 1995; Buckley, 1995; Etchison, 1995); authentic assessment of students (Newman and Wehlage, 1993; Stiggins, 1994; Valencia and Place, 1994; Wiggins, 1993); teachers as reflective practitioners engaged in action research (Eby and Kujawa, 1997; Henderson, 1992); and the development of career-long educators through professional growth activities (Guskey and Huberman, 1995). As these changes are implemented in the schools, new roles and responsibilities will be assumed by the supervisor. For some, their supervisory positions require them to continue to document teaching effectiveness, while others will be more directly involved with teachers by working side by side in action research projects, planning thematic integrated units, or keeping reflective journals.

More recently, Showers and Joyce (1996) have suggested that supervisors may be involved with peer coaching teams, which allow teachers to continuously study their teaching in a collaborative way. Schools have also begun to endorse standards-based curriculum and site-based management plans in order to give each school campus greater autonomy in developing plans and evaluation procedures that will improve student performance. Some schools (such as those in Johnson City, New York; Littleton, Colorado; and Phoenix, Arizona), have implemented comprehensive plans to improve instruction and foster greater student achievement (Glasser, 1990).

As change continues to occur in education, the supervision process takes on additional characteristics. Supervisors have become instructional leaders, working with campus teams composed of teachers, parents, and administrators to develop school mission statements and develop campus goals and objectives. To accommodate the current as well as future changes in education, additional adjustments will continue to be made in the roles and responsibilities of supervisors. In the midst of change, when there are shifts in educational priorities, the focus of supervision becomes one of purpose setting; during times of rapid change, one especially significant function is to interpret and give meaning to the perceived chaos. With social changes come changes in supervisory practices to meet the goals and objectives of each social context and historical time period.

There are a variety of timetables that can be used to identify major periods in educational practice, but each is an arbitrary framework. We have identified periods that, for us, represent a time of unique educational practices or social events. The timetable presented shows the evolution of supervisory practice over time and how programs and procedures in supervision are influenced by the social context of the various historical periods. To establish an historical perspective, Figure 2.1 provides a timeline that traces the development of supervision practices through different decades and identifies the time period and theme, the role of the supervisor at that time, and the resulting supervisory focus.

The dates given in the figure are not absolute indicators but serve as benchmarks in charting the changes both in society and in supervisory practice. Each of

FIGURE 2.1 Charting the Changes in Supervisory Practice

Time Period/Theme	Supervisory Roles	Supervisory Focus
1600–1865 (The Colonial Period) Early Beginnings	Authoritarian and autocratic committees	Inspecting to maintain conformity to lay standards
1865–1910 (The State and National Period) Expansion and Growth	State and local administrators and managers of schools, students, and curriculum	Overseeing of state and local curriculum and instruction
1910–1920 (The Scientific and Organizational Period) Science Applied to Learning and Organizations	Efficiency experts and scientific managers	Implementing standardization and regimentation of curriculum and instruction
1920–1935 (The Professionalization and Bureaucratic Period) Becoming a Profession	Career managers and educational specialists (bureaucrats)	Monitoring progress of teachers and students toward educational goals
1935–1955 (The Progressive and Cooperative Period) Changing the Way Schools Are Viewed	Facilitators and counselors	Providing direct assistance to teachers in improving instruction
1955–1970 (The Curriculum Development and Change-Oriented Period) Rewriting Curriculum	Curriculum specialists and writers	Assisting teachers in developing curriculum and implementing instructional change
1970–1980 (The Clinical and Accountable Period) Dealing with Differences	Clinicians and analytical observers	Helping individual teachers be more effective and accountable by analyzing the teaching–learning process
1980–1995 (The Entrepreneurial and Reform Period) The Reform Influence of Business	Instructional leaders and managers	Coaching teachers in the fine points of effective instruction while reconfiguring the school organization
Supervision and the Future What's Next?	Multitalented and collaborative partners	Creating schools as learning organizations through professional development

the periods referred to in the timeline is described in greater detail in the sections that follow.

Early Beginnings—The Colonial Period (1600–1865)

This earliest period in our development as a nation was marked by the establishment of schools in the local communities and planted the seed for the concept of local control of education. Typically, in this early period, each school was under the control of a lay committee that had general oversight of the schools. Supervision was conducted by the lay committee and took the form of inspection, which was designed to ensure adherence to community standards and expectations. Throughout the colonies, selectmen served as supervisors as they visited schools and made reports (Tanner and Tanner, 1987). This lay committee, which often included ministers, screened and selected teachers and established standards for employment; these members also visited schools to inspect the buildings and verify teacher and pupil performance (Burton and Brueckner, 1955).

During this colonial period, the *Massachusetts Law of 1647*, frequently referred to as the Old Deluder Satan Act, was one of the first laws passed that was in support of compulsory education. The Dame school, common during this period, "was a necessity of the times.... Miss Betty making the figures on the sand[y] floor with her rod,...[had] her pupils with their square pieces of birch bark and bits of charcoal, copying the sums she gave them" (Small, 1914, pp. 162–164).

During the 1700s, the one-room school was common in rural areas as settlers moved inland toward the Mississippi River and beyond. Conrad (1996) provides a description of the one-room school by suggesting that it was stark in appearance, with "tall windows at either side of a simple, rectangular structure.... Inside, most had a teacher's desk on a platform at the back of the room, slate blackboards, maps of the United States, a picture of George Washington, and a hand-held school-bell" (p. 11).

Wood (1987) provides insight into the life of pioneer teachers during this colonial period when one-room schools were often isolated places. A glimpse into this past comes from the diary of Miss Lucy Eliza Richards, who describes her first day of class in a one-room schoolhouse. By the time the day was over,

> I [had] rushed from one to other, giving each an assignment, and trying to return to check the work by the time it was completed. Most of them tried. Only [one] refused...I do not want to be the fourth teacher "run-off" from White Star. (p. 17)

During the early 1800s, the *common school* became the blueprint for the organization of schools across the country. The common school was designed to create a stable society, a sense of nationalism, and an education that was practical and had market value. As Spring (1986) notes, "School reformers placed their hope for a better tomorrow on the growth of the common school. The rhetoric...was full of promises to end poverty, save democracy, solve social problems, end crime, increase prosperity, and provide for equality of opportunity" (p. 336).

Characteristics of supervision during this early period included: (1) the authority of lay committees over the educational process; (2) the autocratic rule of committees in supervising teachers and pupils; and (3) inspection to ensure strict adherence to the rules and standards set by the lay committees. Initially the emphasis was on local control; however, by the 1860s (toward the end of the colonial period), local school districts had grown, and state school educational agencies began to take greater responsibility for education.

Supervisors during the colonial period were lay members of the community, not educators; they typically monitored and verified compliance with local rules and procedures. They were enforcers of local codes and customs and often carried out their responsibilities in an autocratic, authoritarian way. For example, in many communities, teachers were not to marry, and if they did, they would automatically lose their teaching positions. Even with laypeople serving as supervisors, the issues related to teaching and learning were similar to today's issues—the need for dedicated teachers who have their students' welfare at heart, along with social policies related to ending poverty, providing equity, and preparing students for a democracy.

Expansion and Growth—The State and National Period (1865–1910)

With the end of the Civil War and the question of the unity of the nation settled, the period of 1865–1910 was characterized by westward expansion and the continued growth of cities and states. The growth of cities, spurred by industrialization, produced a marked increase in school enrollments (Pierce, 1935); as a result, a new school format was developed. The graded school used chronological age as a basis for assignment to grade level, and the curriculum was organized and presented in a sequential manner, which was compatible with grade-level assignments. The qualities of the graded school in the late 1800s are described by Reisner (1935) as follows:

> There was...more material included in the graded course of instruction,...[but] the quality of teaching and instruction was improved hardly at all.... The business of school being what it was, any movement, any conversation, any communication, were out of order. The spirit of control was military and repressive, not constructive and cooperative. (pp. 427–428)

As schools grew, the question of who would control the schools also became an issue. The district system of organization, which began as the common school movement in Massachusetts, "led to the creation of a school board that was responsible for all of the schools in a local area" (Reinhartz and Beach, 1992, p. 27). Local control within the common school districts had originally evolved to meet the needs of a sparse and rural population. The district system, however, became popular with growing cities because it minimized the power and control of the state and allowed communities that wanted schools to organize districts, levy taxes, build schools, and hire teachers (Tanner and Tanner, 1987).

When local districts failed to raise sufficient revenues to support schools and maintain standards, problems emerged concerning the quality of education. States then engaged in a series of maneuvers that were related to the goals of the common school movement. One of the major aims of this movement was to establish some form of state control over local schools (Alfonso, Firth, and Neville, 1981). States began to institute statewide systems of education and took more responsibility for the supervision of education by passing laws that gave general oversight for the operation of the schools to the state or a central educational agency.

The growth of cities and the increasing diversified student populations in schools produced another change. The day-to-day management of schools was turned over to an educator, and this position became what today we call the *principal* (Pierce, 1935). A variety of titles, such as *headmaster* and *head teacher*, were originally used to designate supervisory roles and responsibilities within a school; the specific period when all duties were first centralized around one individual called a principal cannot be precisely determined. When the title of principal did appear during this period, the five supervisory duties, as identified by Spain, Drummond, and Goodlad (1956), consisted of the following:

1. Maintaining discipline in the school
2. Establishing rules and regulations for the performance of students and teachers
3. Administering the physical plant (opening school, closing school, maintaining the building)
4. Classifying pupils according to grade level or assignment
5. Scheduling and regulating classes

With the establishment of the principalship during this period, supervision generally became the responsibility of a single individual, who fulfilled one or more of the five supervisory duties listed; these duties have continued to spiral through the years to the present. The roles of the supervisor became more complex in order to meet the requirements of the graded school campus. However, the authoritarian inspections, characteristic of the earlier colonial period, were often continued by those individuals in their new supervisory positions. During this period, teachers looked to the principal rather than lay committees for guidance and direction in meeting their responsibilities.

Science Applied to Learning and Organizations— The Scientific and Organizational Period (1910–1920)

As advances in learning theory and psychology were made during the decade of 1910–1920, educational practice began to incorporate these principles within the teaching–learning process. The work of William James and others in applying the principles of scientific inquiry to the field of psychology produced results that were pertinent to teaching and learning in schools. Schools used information gained from research in the business community regarding time and motion studies (efficiency experts) and applied this to daily classroom routines. School operations and procedures were also influenced by the scientific management principles developed and implemented in business and industry. With the growth of graded schools (with multiple grades and at least one teacher per grade), the school structure was the educational equivalent of specialization and the division of labor. Organization of the educational process led to the adoption of scientific management for schools, and the influence of standardization within this management model impacted the supervisory process.

This preoccupation with efficiency and regimentation led to standardized classes and schedules. Teachers at each grade level were expected to be doing roughly the same activities at the same time each day. At the high school level, the Carnegie unit, which has become the unit of course credit for secondary schools, was developed during this time period, and instruction was standardized based primarily on hours spent in the classroom.

The regimentation and standardization of procedures were viewed as helpful in dealing with large numbers of students and were readily adopted as schools were called upon to educate children who had recently come to the United States from different backgrounds. The emphasis on regimentation can also be seen in this time period in the concept of the "melting pot." As immigrant children were "standardized" by the schools, they were to lose their ethnic identities and become "Americans." In 1909, Israel Zangwill dramatized this popular concept of standardizing the American culture when the hero in his play, *The Melting Pot,* says:

> America is God's Crucible, the great Melting Pot where all the races of Europe are melting and reforming! Here you stand...in your 50 groups, with your 50 languages and histories and...hatreds and rivalries. But you won't be long like that... into the crucible with you all! God is Making the American. (p. 37)

Although large numbers of immigrants came to the United States during this time period, it was also a

> time of national transition as growth and westward expansion further enlarged the pluralistic nature of the society.... The successive immigrant populations from Asia and Mexico, along with the relocation of native peoples and the abolition of slavery created a more diversified society. (Reinhartz and Beach, 1997, p. 11)

Supervision during this period was characterized by a preoccupation with standardization and regimentation of educational programs and procedures. The focus of educational supervision was helping teachers become more efficient in the use of classroom time by routinizing various instructional activities and standardizing the curriculum. This mechanistic view of teaching defined the supervisors' role as efficiency monitors who checked to see that teachers were using time effectively and ensuring that the lessons were basically the same for all.

Becoming a Profession—The Professionalization and Bureaucratic Period (1920–1935)

During the period of 1920–1935, the educational bureaucracy resulting from scientific management became well established. As a result of the earlier concern for efficiency, development of the school organization led to divisions of labor and technical specialization. The trend to include specialized subjects in the school curriculum also brought forth supervisory specialists (Alfonso, Firth, and Neville, 1981). This transfer of supervisory responsibility and the development of multiple levels of supervisory professionals expanded the earlier mode of enforcement and inspection. As Bolin (1986) notes, it marked a significant change "in thinking about instructional supervision because it represent[ed] an official turning over of supervision of classroom teachers to middle management personnel" (p. 27).

The result was an increase in the development of middle management positions and a bureaucratic structure. A school organization that had its infancy in this period typically included the school board, superintendent, principal(s), other specialists, and teachers. This organizational structure is discussed in detail in Chapter 3. State departments also developed hierarchies with many different staff levels, which increased the size and scope of the state educational bureaucracy.

Monitoring the progress of both students and teachers was the primary function of supervisors. The practice of regularly visiting teachers' classrooms to "check up" on teachers with regard to instructional and procedural matters led to the use of the term "snoopervision" because of the mechanical procedures and evaluative nature of the supervision (Wiles and Bondi, 1986). An anonymous poem published in 1929 illustrates how a "snoopervisor" functioned:

> With keenly peering eyes and snooping nose,
> From room to room the Snoopervisor goes.
> He notes each slip, each fault with lofty frown,
> And on his rating card he writes it down;
> His duty done, when he has brought to light,
> The things the teachers do that are not right… (Anonymous, 1929)

The teachers felt, and frequently feared, that they were constantly being watched by those holding supervisory positions in the educational system.

Changing the Way Schools Are Viewed— The Progressive and Cooperative Period (1935–1955)

A significant change in the perception of supervision occurred during the 1935–1955 time period. The attitudes of authoritarian inspection and enforcement of rules, often associated with the previous era, gave way to a new attitude, which was one of providing help or assistance to teachers. Supervisors began to assume roles that were helpful and facilitative, and teachers began to view supervision as guidance rather than inspection (Lucio and McNeil, 1969). The 1946 Association for Supervision and Curriculum Development (ASCD) yearbook, *Leadership Through Supervision,* described the supervisor as an educational leader who possessed such virtues as a love of children, a belief in people, a vision, and the ability to be a friend. Supervision became a process for helping teachers improve their performance through classroom observation and cooperative problem solving.

As a result of Mayo's emphasis on human relations in the corporate setting, a similar focus on human relations behavior emerged as a major theme in education during the 1940s and early 1950s. The human relations approach to supervision viewed teaching and learning as processes rather than products. Within this framework, the primary responsibility of the supervisor was to provide assistance to teachers in improving classroom instruction; less emphasis was placed on monitoring, judging, and/or evaluating teachers.

The progressive education movement led by John Dewey (1902, 1906) also had significant impact on supervisory practice during this period by further emphasizing the need to provide assistance to teachers. Progressive educators saw teaching and learning as a complex process that involved the interaction of people—teachers and students—within the humane classroom environment of child-centered schools. The primary purpose of schools was to prepare students to be citizens of a democracy. As Pajak (1993) describes the movement, "Dewey's notion of cautiously reasoned cooperative problem solving, rather than rules generated by science, became a major guiding principle of supervisory leadership" (p. 164). Alfonso, Firth, and Neville (1981) further indicate that schools struggled to promote the innovative, creative, and humanizing potential described by early progressives and were led by Dewey (1906), who "had an abiding faith in the child's creative spirit and potential for good…[and] warned teachers and others not to diminish this natural curiosity and creativity" (p. 28). Educational terms and concepts associated with Dewey that evolved from the progressive education movement include child-centered curriculum, inquiry teaching and learning, thematic planning and teaching, critical reflection and analysis, and the role of experience in constructing knowledge (Dewey, 1902).

With this more caring approach, the supervision process changed from snooping, monitoring, and enforcing to meeting the needs of teachers as they met the diverse needs of their students. Teachers regularly met with supervisors to discuss ways to meet the needs of students and improve instruction. Pajak (1993) describes the instructional supervisor of this period as a democratic leader whose methodology was problem-centered and collaborative. For Barr, Burton, and Brueckner (1947), the change from autocratic heritage and inspection practices is reflected in the renaming of the position from supervisor to consultant or advisor. Perhaps Franseth (1955) best captures the spirit of this period by suggesting that supervision is a process whereby supervisors work with teachers in an open, supportive environment to solve problems related to teaching and learning.

Rewriting Curriculum—The Curriculum Development and Change-Oriented Period (1955–1970)

As public education entered the post–World War II era, two historical events of this period had a major impact on the operation of schools. The first was the 1954 decision of the Supreme Court in *Brown v. Board of Education*, which began the process of desegregating the schools. The second, and the one with the most immediate impact, was the launching of Sputnik I by the Soviet Union in 1957, which started the space race and resulted in a major reform of the public school curriculum. Primarily as a response to these two historical events, the role of the federal government in educational programs increased significantly, as seen in such programs as the Head Start legislation for preschoolers.

The 1954 Supreme Court decision in *Brown v. Board of Education* helped to shape some educational programs during the 1960s. As a result of this decision, "separate but equal" segregation policies were repudiated and replaced by a Court mandate to integrate schools. As each community sought relief through the courts to integrate the schools, the range of student ability and the diversity of backgrounds increased significantly. Coleman et al. (1966) found that by placing disadvantaged, underachieving students with achieving students, the underachievers benefited without significantly impacting the learning of others. Within this context of a wide range of student ability, the thrust of supervision was to help teachers assess and maximize the learning potential of each student. To accommodate this wide range of student abilities, many textbook publishers developed curriculum materials with an individualized format, and schools embraced other individualization strategies such as learning centers and learning activity pockets (LAPs). To meet the disparate needs of students, schools established a variety of special programs to help socially and economically disadvantaged students succeed.

With the launching of the Soviet satellite, American education changed almost overnight as the United States began its race into space, with particular emphasis on the goal to put a man on the moon. Suddenly, the American educational system was perceived as inferior to the Soviet system and was criticized for a lack of rigor and an insufficient emphasis on mathematics, science, and foreign languages. There was a clamor to turn away from the human relations view of teaching and learning and return to the traditional study of subjects in the curriculum, including an increased emphasis on science and mathematics courses. University programs funded by the National Science Foundation brought teachers to campus in the summers to attend special science and mathematics institutes.

As new educational programs were developed and implemented, supervisors became curriculum specialists and writers, spending much of their time redefining and strengthening the content of each subject area in a massive overhaul of the public school curriculum. In what has become known as the "alphabet soup" curriculum reform, each content area was carefully scrutinized by many of the most knowledgeable people in the field. Bruner (1960) convened leading experts from a variety of academic fields at the Woods Hole Oceanographic Institute to discuss the teaching of content in the curriculum and later wrote about his findings in his book, *The Process of Education*, which outlines his concept of the spiral curriculum. This emphasis on content led to the development of new curriculum guides for nearly all subjects. In addition, new curricular programs—such as the Biological Sciences Curriculum Study (BSCS), English 2000, Greater Cleveland Math Program (GCMP), Man: A Course of Study (MACOS), Elementary School Science (ESS), and Science: A Process Approach (SAPA)—were developed for elementary and secondary students. Few if any content areas were exempt from the scrutiny, and many new textbooks and educational programs were developed to help students catch up in science, mathematics, and other areas.

During this period, supervisors were called upon to assist teachers in developing and modifying curriculum, which often included writing curriculum materials or preparing learning packets for individualized instruction. New curriculum guides were written, and many individualized programs were developed at the local district and campus levels. Writing at the time, Cunningham (1963) saw the role of the supervisor as a change agent. Pajak (1993) described the supervisor as an organizational change agent who sought to bring about social change through curriculum implementation. According to Bolin (1986), instructional supervisors were "looking at the curriculum as the focal point of school improvement and seeing the teacher as instrumental to curriculum implementation" (p. 27). Educational supervisors during this period were engaged in analyzing and modifying the curriculum, collecting and organizing instructional materials, and aiding teachers in the transition to new materials and programs that met the needs and abilities of students in their classrooms.

Dealing with Differences—The Clinical and Accountable Period (1970–1980)

Supervision during the decade of the 1970s was patterned along the lines of a medical or clinical model. Emphasis was placed on the diagnosis and treatment of instructional problems, using data obtained from teacher conferences and classroom observations. Using research from human behavior and guided by a desire to help individual teachers be more accountable, supervisors adopted a clinical model for use in the schools.

The intent of the clinical model was to diagnose classroom problems and/or identify areas for improvement, then prescribe appropriate courses of action to correct the situation. This clinical approach to supervision incorporated the ingredient of "objective" classroom observation to aid in the analysis or diagnosis of teacher–student interaction. The purpose of the model was to help teachers "see" what needed to be done by holding up a mirror on the classroom, using data collected from observations. The clinical model was designed to promote awareness of teaching behaviors and classroom interactions that impact student learning; then, working with supervisors cooperatively, a course of action was identified. The clinical perspective was also helpful as supervisors worked with teachers to address the implementation of Public Law 92–142 and the education of handicapped students as well as meet the needs of students whose first language was not English.

The accountability dimension of the period was not only evident in the analysis of the teaching–learning process but in the public funding of education as well. In what has become known as the taxpayer revolt, spurred by Proposition 13 in California, schools became fiscally accountable. Educators were informed by local and state entities that financial support would be limited and schools would have to be more cost-effective. Supervisors also began to calculate the per-pupil instructional cost, analyze the results of various instructional programs, and provide data for making decisions about the cost-effectiveness of each. Schools had to become more accountable for the tax dollars they spent in relation to the results they achieved, and supervisors worked in concert with business managers to contain educational/instructional program costs.

The Reform Influence of Business—
The Entrepreneurial and Reform Period
(1980–1995)

The concern for more cost-effective measures, which also produced increased achievement, and the influence of business on educational practices intensified during the decade of the 1980s and is evident in many ways today, as we move toward the twenty-first century. School–business partnerships have increased, and business leaders have been involved in numerous local and state task forces and committees that deal with issues regarding American public education. Perhaps as many as 30 different reports were issued during this period. A representative sample of these reports was cited earlier in the chapter.

In addition to dealing with calls for reform, schools have had to learn to do more with less as many communities reduced budgets or experienced reduced funding as a result of tax rollbacks. During this period, supervisors were often called upon to secure additional resources for districts through grant writing or business partnerships. Many of the funding concerns that emerged are still present and have prompted a reduction in central office and other supervisory positions as schools have sought to become "lean and mean."

In recent years, there has been a managerial tone to the operation of schools; the ideas of the entrepreneur, one willing to take risks, have been applied at the school campus level as well as the district level. Consistent with business practices, supervisors serve in a variety of managerial positions, and they have learned to speak a management language as they have become part of the management team. Pajak (1993) has described these educational supervisors as corporate visionaries.

The influence of the business literature has also been seen in the preparation and practices of effective educational supervisors. Blanchard and Johnson (1982) describe effective managers as those who care about people, help individuals set and obtain goals, give them praise, and train winners. Likewise, the influence of the research of Peters and Waterman (1982) and their eight characteristics of excellent companies has often been applied to the operation of schools. Although some characteristics seem to fit the instructional setting better than others, each characteristic has the potential to promote excellence in education (Reinhartz and Beach, 1984).

The eight characteristics originally identified by Peters and Waterman (1982) and described by Reinhartz and Beach (1984) are as follows:

1. *A bias for action*—Emphasis is on planning for action and putting ideas into practice, rather than spending an inordinate amount of time analyzing issues and consequences; school structure should be fluid and flexible, giving value to an idea and acting upon it.

2. *Close to the customer*—Supervisors and educational leaders should be good listeners and seek input from their clients; rather than being insensitive to students, parents, and community members, educators/supervisors listen more and seek input from those people directly affected by the educational enterprise.

3. *Autonomy and entrepreneurship*—Successful organizations value and encourage creativity and risk taking in order to maintain a competitive edge; supervisors are problem solvers and creative thinkers who encourage and reward teachers for the same skills that contribute to quality education.

4. *Productivity through people*—Members of excellent organizations feel they are partners in the day-to- day activities and believe they are crucial to the success of the organization; morale in schools is greatly enhanced by programs and procedures that emphasize the value and worth of people and involve everyone in ways that communicate that they truly make a difference.

5. *Hands-on, value-driven*—Excellent organizations have values that they live by, and these values are in a form that can be easily communicated to their members as well as to others; schools, at both the district and campus levels, must clearly articulate mission statements, goals, and objectives.

6. *Stick to the knitting*—Successful organizations emphasize those things they do best, such as manufacturing a product or providing a service; faculty and staff of schools need to recognize and accept that they cannot be all things to all people, and to be more effective, each school should identify its specific strengths, develop a campus improvement plan, and provide resources for those areas that help achieve the stated goals.

7. *Simple form, lean staff*—Successful organizations have structures that are basically simple and are guided by clearly stated goals; simple form and lean staff translate into an organizational structure that limits the number of central office or middle management personnel in large districts and concentrates on the delivery of instruction at the campus level.

8. *Simultaneous loose-tight properties*—This last characteristic is a synthesis of the previous seven because organizations that exhibit this trait give local units control in making decisions, yet there is a central monitoring process to ensure that the mission and goals drive the operations and actions; applied to schools, site-based management and collegial groups provide greater autonomy to faculty and staff at the building level in making decisions.

Supervisors during the decade of the 1980s sought to improve teaching and learning, using these general traits, as they worked with teachers and staff within their districts. Effective schools, as well as organizations, have begun to realize that they are dependent upon people, and "if schools are to [continue to] improve the quality of instruction, it will be at the local building level (loose-tight properties) with the teacher at the heart of the improvement process (productivity through people)" (Reinhartz and Beach, 1984, p. 29).

As schools enter the last decade of the twentieth century, the corporate model has given direction to improvement efforts as supervisors assume greater responsibility for promoting excellence. The influence of business and industry on supervisory practice can be seen in the writings of authors who call for a complete change in supervisory practice and a reverse in the supervisor's role from inspecting, policing, and inhibiting to helping, coaching, facilitating, building, and improving people (Costa and Garmston, 1993; Olson, 1986; Showers and Joyce, 1996). It should be noted, however, that schools deliver a service and are not driven solely by the concern for the "bottom line" or profit. Certainly schools should be cost-effective and not wasteful, but their primary concern is the education of the children entrusted to them.

Covey (1989) has suggested that most organizations focus on production (results) at the expense of production capability (those who work to produce the results). If organizations are to be effective in the next decade, they must achieve a balance between production and production capability. There are organizations that talk about the customer but completely forget the employee. To bring balance to the process of production (P) versus production capability (PC), "always treat your employees exactly as you want them to treat your best customers. You can buy a person's hand, but you can't buy his [or her] heart.... You can buy his [or her] back, but you can't buy his [or her] brain" (Covey, 1989, p. 58). The heart is the site of enthusiasm and loyalty. The brain is involved with creativity, ingenuity, and resourcefulness. Covey continues by saying that supervisors should work with employees as if they were volunteers because that's just what they are: They volunteer their hearts and minds.

It is too soon to tell how long the business influence and managerial emphasis will continue. There are indications that supervisors will become even more involved with teachers in the improvement of instruction. As Glickman, Gordon, and Ross-Gordon (1998) note, "Supervisors who hold formal leadership roles will have to redefine their responsibilities—from controllers of teachers' instruction to involvers of teachers in decisions about school instruction" (p. 29). Such involvement may involve not only the use of classroom observations to record teacher–pupil behaviors but the use of peer coaching, mentoring, and reflection.

What's Next?—Supervision and the Future

This chapter has traced the development of the supervision process as conditions and priorities have changed within the American culture. Historical, political, and social forces have produced changes in the way we view schools as well as the teaching and learning that occur in schools. Individuals who serve in supervisory positions must be cognizant of the ever-changing conditions that produce alterations in the supervision process. As supervisors move into the uncharted future, Poole (1994) suggests that "the roles of the supervisor and teacher are also changing. The supervisor is no longer…the expert, passing along judgments and advice to teacher technicians. Instead the teacher is…an equal who contributes valuable expertise and experience to the supervisory process" (p. 287).

Predicting the future course of supervision in the new century may prove difficult at best. In the coming decades, supervisors will most likely need to be multitalented individuals who can: work with teachers in adjusting to rapidly changing conditions; coach teachers to be more reflective; promote instructional excellence; and (based on an awareness of the growing diversity in schools) work in collaborative ways with teachers to foster continued professional growth. For Pajak (1993), supervisors of the late 1990s and early twenty-first century will most likely work in a decentralized, team-focused learning organization and will need to be able to model and promote effective instruction. Supervisors will also be called upon to encourage teachers to participate in decisions that impact the quality of instruction, not only in their classrooms but on their school campuses and in the whole district.

Successful organizations of the next century will be places of learning, capable of adapting to rapidly changing conditions. Supervisory leaders will be expected to accurately assess instructional programs and classroom instruction, and to make the adjustments required to meet changing circumstances. The challenge confronting supervisors, which will need to be addressed, is recognizing that schools have been primarily teaching organizations, not learning organizations. Koestenbaum (1991) says that "leaders think differently," and they will be called on to "construct…the leadership mind: an inner space, unified with room enough for conflict, paradox, and contradiction, committed to greatness in vision, realism, ethics, and courage" (p. 31). The purpose of most schools is to transmit information rather than generate or create it. Those schools that are effective at teaching may not be good at learning; rather than getting schools to teach better, the future will require that they learn better (Pajak, 1993).

Senge (1990) describes the role of the supervisor in such a learning organization as someone who helps people reorganize their thinking so they can look below the surface and determine the underlying causes. If current trends continue, supervisors will also be called upon to create a climate for learning. This creation of learning spaces will require restructuring schools in ways that nurture learning for all students and emphasize the capabilities of teachers to see new possibilities.

Supervisors must also be cognizant of the diversity represented in public schools. Teachers and student populations are changing, and demographic studies are predicting an even greater change in the twenty-first century. Ryan and Cooper (1993) have described the future of minority populations by saying, "By the year 2000, over one-third of all school-age children, and by 2020, nearly half, will fall into this category" (p. 350). Meeting the challenge of an increasingly pluralistic society will require that supervisors recognize that social and cultural forces of society impact the educative process. As Ravitch (1993) notes, "the future of education will be shaped...by changes in demography, technology, and the family" (p. 43). Schools of the future will have children who reflect the pluralistic nature of society, which requires that supervisors and teachers plan and implement instruction that is learner-centered (Reinhartz and Beach, 1997).

Finally, Fullan (1998) has suggested that supervisors will need to develop a new mind-set, breaking the bonds of dependency created by overload and "packaged solutions" and thinking outside the box. He offers the following four principles for supervisors, which may prove helpful in informing and guiding their actions:

1. Respect those you want to silence.
2. Move toward the danger in forming new alliances.
3. Manage emotionally as well as rationally.
4. Fight for lost causes. (p. 8)

With baby boomer supervisors looking toward retirement, there will be more educators moving into the field of supervision. The advice for supervisors who want to be effective comes from Fullan (1998), who says that "there are not clear solutions"; nevertheless, you need to be prepared to look for answers close at hand and reach out (p. 10).

Summary

As indicated in Chapter 1, knowledge of past trends in supervision provides a foundation for current practices and procedures. This chapter identified major historical periods that have influenced supervisory practice. Each period had a unique set of circumstances—a political, social, and/or economic milieu—that impacted the way we view teaching and learning as well as supervision.

The grouping of the periods by date is somewhat arbitrary, but there is general consensus about the major periods within the historical framework. The nine major historical periods identified in this chapter included the following:

1. Early Beginnings—The Colonial Period (1600–1865)
2. Expansion and Growth—The State and National Period (1865–1910)
3. Science Applied to Learning and Organizations—The Scientific and Organizational Period (1910–1920)
4. Becoming a Profession—The Professionalization and Bureaucratic Period (1920– 1935)
5. Changing the Way Schools Are Viewed—The Progressive and Cooperative Period (1935–1955)
6. Rewriting Curriculum—The Curriculum Development and Change-Oriented Period (1955–1970)
7. Dealing with Differences—The Clinical and Accountable Period (1970–1980)
8. The Reform Influence of Business—The Entrepreneurial and Reform Period (1980–1995)
9. What's Next?—Supervision and the Future

Each period identified events that have shaped the supervision practices and procedures based on the particular political, social, and economic characteristics of the time. The school does not exist apart from society, and the conditions existing at the time serve to guide and shape teaching and learning as well as the supervisory process. Clearly, the trend for supervisors during the decades of the 1980s and 1990s has been to be more directly involved with the improvement of instruction and increased academic achievement in collaboration with teachers. Lessons from the past and current trends suggest that supervisors will need to be multitalented individuals who have a repertoire of skills as they work with teachers at different professional levels within the increasing diversity of the individual classrooms and schools; they need to think outside the box and seek new solutions to issues confronting all educators in the twenty-first century.

YOUR TURN

2.1. You have been asked to speak to a group of principals, consultants, and other supervisory personnel who are attending a three-day workshop on "Being an Effective Supervisor." You have been given the topic "Our Historical Roots: The Connection for Being an Effective Supervisor." At first you think, "Oh, no. How dull! What does history have to do with being an effective supervisor?" As you prepare your presentation, consider using an interactive, cooperative learning approach. You may decide to look at various periods and examine the effects that supervisory practices have had on present instruction. Outline your thoughts as you prepare for your session.

2.2. The members of your local school board have expressed frustration and confusion about all the educational reports and reforms. They have asked the staff to write a position paper that addresses two issues:

a. What are the changes in society that will impact programming for teachers and students (for instance, latchkey kids, values, violence in schools, and an older society)?

b. Devise a five-year plan that supervisors and teachers can use in adjusting to the current political, social, and economic realities. Identify trends in the areas of funding or budget development (proposed school bonds), instructional facilities, curriculum materials, instructional technology, and educational personnel.

2.3. Based on the following quotation, how would you respond, and what specific suggestions would you have for supervisory personnel?

"What the writers of excellence in industry are calling for is a 180-degree change in direction in supervising people—one that changes the role of the supervisor from that of inspecting, policing, and inhibiting to one that helps, coaches, facilitates, builds, and improves people. Should we in education do anything less?" (Olson, 1986, p. 61)

2.4. Your school district is looking for an additional instructional supervisor in the central office. Your district is located in the heart of a large metropolitan area that has an active teachers' union/organization, collective bargaining, a diverse ethnic enrollment (57 percent), and growing illiteracy and dropout rates. Write down a job description for this person (1) based on the current social and educational circumstances and (2) in light of what his or her duties will be beyond the year 2000 for this school district.

2.5. You are a firm believer that educational practices and procedures occur in cycles. Based on this belief, identify recurring trends from various time periods that are currently impacting supervision.

2.6. Your superintendent has chosen "A Learning Organization" as the theme for this year's staff development. As a supervisor in the school district, describe some activities and programs that should be included to meet this year's theme. You may find P. M. Senge's book, *The Fifth Discipline: The Art and Practice of the Learning Organization,* helpful.

REFERENCES

Alfonso, R. J., Firth, G. R., & Neville, R. F. (1981). *Instructional supervision: A behavior system.* (2nd. ed.). Boston: Allyn & Bacon.

Anonymous. (1929). The snoopervisor, the whoopervisor, and the supervisor. *Playground and Recreation, 23,* 558.

Applebee, A. N., et al. (1990). *Learning to write in our nation's schools.* Princeton, NJ: Educational Testing Service.

Applebee, A. N., Langer, J. A., & Mullis, I. V. S. (1989). *Crossroads in American education.* Princeton, NJ: Educational Testing Service.

Association for Supervision and Curriculum Development. (1946). *Leadership through supervision.* Washington, DC: ASCD.

Barr, A. S., Burton, W. H., & Brueckner, L. J. (1947). *Supervision: Democratic leadership for the improvement of learning.* (2nd ed.). New York: Appleton-Century.

Blanchard, K., & Johnson, S. (1982). *The one minute manager.* New York: William Morrow.

Bolin, F. (1986 December). Perspectives on the definition of supervision. *Wingspan, 3,* 22–29.

Bradsher, M. (1995 October). Networking with kids around the world. *Educational Leadership, 53,* 42.

Bruner, J. (1960). *The process of education.* Cambridge, MA: Harvard University Press.

Buckley, R. B. (1995). What happens when funding is not an issue? *Educational Leadership, 53,* 64–66.

Burton, W. H., & Brueckner, L. J. (1955). *Supervision.* (3rd ed.). New York: Appleton-Century-Crofts.

Coleman, J. S., Campbell, E. Q., Hobson, C. J., McPartland, J., Mood, A. M., Weinfield, F. D., & York, R. L. (1966). *Equality of educational opportunity.* U.S. Department of Health, Education, and Welfare. Washington, DC: U.S. Government Printing Office.

Conrad, M. (1996 Spring). The fourth "R"—Schoolhouse R'cheology. *Mirage, 13,* 9–11.

Costa, A. L., & Garmston, R. J. (1994). *Cognitive coaching: A foundation for renaissance schools.* Norwood, MA: Christopher-Gordon Publishers.

Covey, S. R. (1989). The *7 habits of highly effective people.* New York: Simon & Schuster.

Cunningham, L. L. (1963). Effecting change through leadership. *Educational Leadership, 21,* 75–79.

Dewey, J. (1902). *The child and the curriculum.* Chicago: University of Chicago Press.

Dewey, J. (1906). *Democracy and education.* New York: Macmillan.

Eby, J. W., & Kujawa, E. (1997). *Reflective planning, teaching, and evaluation: K-12.* (2nd ed.). Upper Saddle River, NJ: Merrill Publishers.

Etchison, C. (1995). Tales from a technology teacher. *Science and Children, 32,* 19–21.

Franseth, J. (1955). *Supervision in rural schools.* U.S. Department of Health, Education, and Welfare. Washington, DC: U.S. Government Printing Office.

Frazee, B., & Rudnitski, R. A. (1995). *Integrating teaching methods.* Albany, NY: Delmar Publishers.

Fredericks, A. D., Meinbach, A. M., & Rothlein, L. (1993). *Thematic units: An integrated approach to teaching science and social studies.* New York: HarperCollins Publishers.

Fullan, M. (1998 April). Leadership for the 21st century: Breaking the bonds of dependency. *Educational Leadership, 55,* 6–10.

Glasser, W. (1990). *The quality schools.* New York: HarperCollins Publishers.

Glickman, C. D., Gordon, S. P., & Ross-Gordon, J. M. (1998). *Supervision of instruction.* (4th ed.). Boston: Allyn & Bacon.

Guskey, T. R., & Huberman, M. (eds.). (1995). *Professional development in education.* New York: Teachers College Press.

Henderson, J. C. (1992). *Reflective teaching: Becoming an inquiring educator.* Upper Saddle River, NJ: Merrill Publishers.

Koestenbaum, P. (1991). *Leadership: The inner side of greatness.* San Francisco: Jossey-Bass Publishers.

Langer, J. A., Applebee, A. N., Mullis, I. V. S., & Foertsch, M. A. (1990). *Learning to read in our nation's schools.* Princeton, NJ: Educational Testing Service.

Lucio, W. H., & McNeil, J. D. (1969). *Supervision: A synthesis of thought and action.* New York: McGraw-Hill.

National Commission on Excellence in Education. (1983). *A nation at risk: The imperative for educational reform.* U.S. Department of Education. Washington, DC: U.S. Government Printing Office.

National Research Council. (1989). *Everybody counts: A report card to the nation on the future of mathematics education.* Washington, DC: National Academy Press.

Newman, F. M., & Wehlage, G. (1993). Five standards of authentic instruction. *Educational Leadership, 50,* 8–12.

Olson, L. C. (1986 December). In search of excellence in supervision. *Wingspan, 3,* 58–61.

Pajak, E. (1993). Change and continuity in supervision and leadership. In *Challenges and achievement of American education.* G. Cawelti (ed.). Reston, VA: Association for Supervision and Curriculum Development.

Peters, T. J., & Waterman, R. H. (1982). *In search of excellence: Lessons from America's best-run companies*. New York: Harper & Row.

Pierce, P. R. (1935). *The origin and development of the public school principalship*. Chicago: University of Chicago Press.

Poole, W. L. (1994 Spring). Removing the "super" from supervision. *Journal of Curriculum and Supervision, 9,* 284–309.

Ravitch, D. (1993 September 11). When school comes to you. World topics and current affairs. *Economists, 328,* 43–49.

Reinhartz, J., & Beach, D. M. (1984). In search of educational excellence: Will the corporate model work? *Teacher Education and Practice, 1,* 51–54.

Reinhartz, J., & Beach, D. M. (1992). *Secondary education: Focus on curriculum*. New York: HarperCollins Publishers.

Reinhartz, J., & Beach, D. M. (1997). *Teaching and learning in the elementary school: Focus on curriculum*. Upper Saddle River, NJ: Merrill Publishers.

Reisner, E. H. (1935). *The evolution of the common school*. Upper Saddle River, NJ: Merrill Publishers.

Rutherford, J. F., & Ahlgren, A. (1990). *Science for all Americans*. New York: Oxford University Press.

Ryan, K., & Cooper, J. M. (1993). *Those who can, teach*. (6th ed.). Boston: Houghton Mifflin.

Senge, P. M. (1990). *The fifth discipline: The art and practice of the learning organization*. New York: Doubleday.

Showers, B., & Joyce, B. (1996 March). The evolution of peer coaching. *Educational Leadership, 53,* 12–16.

Small, W. H. (1914). *Early New England schools*. Boston: Ginn and Company.

Spain, C., Drummond, H. D., & Goodlad, J. (1956). *Educational leadership and the elementary school principal*. New York: Holt, Rinehart.

Spring, J. (1986). *The American school*. New York: Longman.

Stiggins, R. J. (1994). *Student-centered classroom assessment*. Upper Saddle River, NJ: Merrill Publishers.

Tanner, D., & Tanner, L. (1987). *Supervision in education: Problems and practices*. New York: Macmillan.

Valencia, S., & Place, N. (1994). Portfolio: A process for enhancing teaching and learning. *The Reading Teacher, 47,* 666–671.

Wiggins, G. (1993). Assessment: Authenticity, context, and validity. *Phi Delta Kappan, 75,* 200–214.

Wiles, J., & Bondi, J. (1986). *Supervision: A guide to practice*. (2nd ed.). Columbus, OH: Charles E. Merrill.

Wood, J. R. (1987). *The train to Estelline*. New York: Bantam Doubleday Dell Publishing Group.

Zangwill, I. (1909). *The melting pot*. New York: Macmillan.

3 Schools as Organizations

The Workplace for Teachers and Supervisors

OBJECTIVES

The objectives of this chapter are:

- Describe the characteristics and perceptions of organizations.
- Discuss the historical development of organizations.
- Define organizations' culture and explain the importance of culture building within organizations.
- Identify and apply principles of effective organizations to school settings.
- Describe the characteristics of effective schools as organizations.

This chapter is about people and how they work together in groups to achieve specific goals and objectives within organizations. Because virtually every individual has had some experience in working in a group to achieve a goal, the concept of an organization is not foreign; it is a part of daily existence. Civic clubs, corporations, governmental entities, and special-interest groups are just some examples of organizations that individuals may belong to or interact with in their communities. Schools, as organizations, are also the workplaces for teachers and supervisors.

Schools, like other organizations or workplaces, do not exist independently of the society, or of other organizations in the society in which they operate, but rather are products of that society (Stacey, 1996). As a result, they are dynamic, ever-changing entities and considered to be open systems that transform resources (input) into some result or product (output) (Katz and Kahn, 1978). For example, students come to school with varying talents; at the end of 12 years, they are expected to become productive citizens. The factors that shape that process are the result of not only schools but also many other components of society. Etzioni (1964) has commented on how organizations, such as schools, are part of our total existence:

> Our society is an organizational society. We are born in organizations, and most of us spend much of our lives working for organizations. We spend much of our leisure time paying, playing, and praying in organizations. Most of us will die in an organization, and when the time comes for burial, the largest organization of all—the state—must grant official permission. (p. 1)

Therefore, the workplace of the school is shaped by both the sociocultural system and the school's desired outcomes. As institutions of society, schools can be viewed as multifaceted organizations that are both similar to and different from other workplaces in form and function. It is not surprising, then, that the organizational structure of schools mirrors the complexities of other organizations as they seek to accomplish their goals by getting "other organizations and people to interact with them" (Stacey, 1996, p. 23).

Organizations may be thought of in general terms as the vehicles for accomplishing goals or performing a function within the context of a human social system (Hershey and Blanchard, 1993). However, if an organization's policies and supervisory practices are not carefully monitored, the organization may be restrictive to its members rather than provide an operational structure. In such a situation, the organizational environment becomes demeaning for its members rather than supportive of them. In any organization, tension is created as the result of a constant struggle to accomplish tasks, perform a service, or produce a product without alienating or subjugating the people involved in the process.

Unfortunately, some organizations forget that people are the core of productivity; such organizations apply rules and procedures in order to achieve maximum results, but ultimately these regulations can inhibit, restrict, and negatively impact the members of the organization rather than encourage, support, and affirm them. At their worst, such organizations become oppressive places in which the focus is solely on the task; the emphasis is on production, and there is a general disregard for the needs of people. Schools, as organizations that provide a service rather than produce a product, must constantly seek to affirm and enhance people. At the same time, educators must guard against developing too many restrictive rules and procedures that may contribute to a stifling environment. Supervisors walk a tightrope as they supervise within the school organization in their efforts to achieve results and at the same time obtain a commitment from the educational staff to work toward improved campus goals and objectives.

Schools have a variety of designs and configurations, depending upon their size, history, nature, and functions. Since the supervisor works within the context of the school organization, it is helpful to analyze various organizational structures, behaviors, and functions and then apply this knowledge specifically to schools. For supervisors, the school organization is the professional work environment in which decisions are made and leadership is exercised. When supervisors have a better understanding of the variables of the workplace and the features that help to shape and define the work, they can be more effective in their positions as they involve teachers and other staff members in accomplishing the school's educational goals.

In describing the organizational environment of schools, Sergiovanni and colleagues (1992) note:

> Perhaps the most critical difference between the school and most other organizations is the human intensity that characterizes its work. Schools are human organizations in the sense that their products are human and their processes require the socializing of humans.... [and they] are labor intensive. (p. 167)

As labor-intensive organizations, schools rely heavily on people with skills to get the work done, which is primarily the task of educating students. It is important, then, for supervisors to identify aspects of school operations that will improve and strengthen the results desired for the school. Critical to this process is the ability to work within the organization to link the behavior of members to the goals and structure of the school system. When there is a mismatch between a supervisor's ability to work with people and the purposes and goals of the school organization, the effectiveness of the organization ultimately suffers.

To be effective, it is necessary for instructional supervisors to study organizational theory, structure, and behavior and to analyze schools as organizations with attendant bureaucratic operations. This chapter provides supervisors with a description of characteristics of organizations, an historical overview of organizations (organizational theory), a discussion of organizational culture, a profile of an effective school, and principles of effective organizations.

Characteristics and Perceptions of Organizations

Organizations have great variety: Some are large, and some are small; they have complex or simple structures; and they exist for different reasons. Yet with all their diversity, there are some common characteristics that most, if not all, organizations share. In a generally accepted analysis of organizations, Gross (1964) says that organizations may be regarded as a group or cooperative system that has the following five characteristics:

1.   An accepted pattern of purposes—Members recognize the primary need or reason for the organization to exist.

2.   A sense of identification or belonging—All members, regardless of their position, have an identity with their work and see themselves as an integral part of the organization.

3.   Continuity of interaction—Members of the organization interact with each other with a degree of regularity and continuity; there are established patterns or channels of communication.

4.   Differentiation of function—Members of the organization perform different and/or specialized roles.

5.   Conscious integration of organizational goals—Members of the organization work together with deliberate efforts to achieve organizational goals.

Applying these five characteristics to schools suggests that, as organizations, schools have a *raison d'etre*—a reason to exist—which is the education of students in the community. Furthermore, schools have a special identification as faculty, staff, and students work together to build school spirit. There are formal and informal interaction patterns among members of the school organization in faculty meetings, newsletters, and other joint activities. The various positions and responsibilities as identified on a school organization chart reflect different roles and functions for members of the organization. Finally, there is a conscious integration of goals as each school develops a mission statement with objectives, based on a collective vision that addresses student learning.

Kowalski and Reitzug (1993) view organizations as links between structures (e.g., departments, grade levels) and/or groups (e.g., teachers, staff). Others see human organizations as complex and adaptive networks of people who interact with each other to perform the tasks to carry out their aims or purposes (Charan, 1992; Nohria and Eccles, 1992; Stacey, 1996). They are "structured social system[s] consisting of groups and individuals working together...in social units...to attain a common goal" (Greenberg and Baron, 1997). And Drucker (1997) defines organizations as how different work is accomplished in the marketplace. He adds, an organization is social, involving people, and it bespeaks values.

Schools are integrated systems of structures and groups, with each group comprised of individuals (Berrien, 1976). Within the organization called school, individuals and groups work together in various structures to accomplish educational goals. Parsons (1965) has provided a definition of an organization that can also be applied to the school workplace:

> An organization is a system which, as the attainment of its goals "produces" an identifiable something which can be utilized in some way by another system;...[For] an educational organization, it [the product] may be a certain type of "trained capacity" on the part of the students. (p. 63)

Other insights into understanding organizations have been provided in the following descriptions and definitions:

1. Social units that seek the attainment of specific goals (Pfeiffer and Dunlap, 1982)

2. Contrived designs or arrangements that serve a specific function or meet a need while transmitting values and accomplishing goals (Alfonso, Firth, and Neville, 1981)

3. Social units that are constructed and reconstructed to seek specific goals and that have (a) a division of power, labor, and communication; (b) one or more centers of power that direct the organization toward goals; and (c) substitution and recombination of personnel through removal, transfer, or promotion (Etzioni, 1964)

4. A system of cooperation (Barnard, 1938)

5. A grouping of personnel to accomplish established purposes through allocation of functions and responsibilities (Gaus, 1936)

Although these definitions differ in various ways, some common themes emerge, which portray organizations as groups of individuals (1) working together within a structure or system; (2) seeking the attainment of goals or objectives; (3) having differentiated roles, functions, and responsibilities; and (4) sharing a set of beliefs or principles. If we take all these themes into account, a comprehensive definition emerges. For us, an *organization consists of individuals who are united by a set of values or principles and who work together within a structure that promotes shared decision making in order to accomplish specific goals and objectives.*

The concept of an organization as the workplace, however, is more than just a physical setting (Johnson, 1990); it includes other variables that help to characterize or define an organization. These variables are physical, economic, organizational, cultural, psychological, political, and sociological (Johnson, 1990). Within each of the seven variables there are unique features that help to establish the parameters of a workplace.

The first, physical features, relates to the size and architectural design of the building. Economic features involve salaries and benefits as well as rewards and incentives. Within the organizational variable, features that would be of interest or concern to teachers and supervisors would be the distribution of authority, assignment and schedule, type and kind of supervision, specialization of work, and interdependence that exists among the community, educators, and schools. Cultural features include traditions, values, and beliefs that support the vision. Psychological variables comprise such items as dedication or level of commitment of the members, levels of stress, and opportunities to grow and learn. Political features involve the kind of governance and decision-making processes employed. Finally, sociological variables include the characteristics of the students, parents, community, teachers, and supervisors.

A View from the Field

The following example shows how these variables operate at Newton Middle School Academy. The academy is a new school of 800 students, with a traditional as well as flexible curriculum that benefits the students in a variety of ways. There are two active teacher organizations on the campus, and one group is closely aligned with a union. The salaries are above state average but are still low compared to the national average.

Teachers are marginally involved in governance issues and site-based decision making. As a new school, the faculty and students have few traditions and are establishing a reputation and a new culture to best live up to its mission as an academy within the public school for middle school students across the district. The faculty had to apply and interview for positions in the new school and therefore have a high level of commitment and dedication. For them, teaching is a passion, and they view working with supervisors and colleagues as a collaborative process. Parental involvement has been a high priority as students represent many different ethnic and income levels. Parents take an active role in all aspects of the school program—especially Saturday School, which provides enrichment and tutorial opportunities. Because the school is new, it has taken on a mission to house special programs that encourage the implementation of various pedagogical ideas. There is a greater distribution of power among supervisors, teachers, and community members. The school has attempted to support teachers in curriculum and program development by providing two periods for professional activities—one directed toward instructional and noninstructional tasks, and the other to meet with a cadre of students to discuss issues and concerns. This scenario serves to illustrate how all seven variables contribute to the creation of an organizational workplace called Newton Middle School Academy.

Historical Views of Organizations: Their Descriptions and Purposes

Views of organizations have changed over time based on the events, situations, and emphasis during a particular era. Thus, a better understanding of organizations as workplaces comes from an examination of the structure, function, and characteristic behaviors associated with each view. Four major organizational views can be identified:

1. Structure and bureaucracy—scientific management
2. Functions and relationships—human relations and human resources
3. Processes—behavioral approach
4. Influence—power and persuasion

These four views are discussed in detail to provide an understanding regarding the framework that undergirds schools as organizations and helps to explain how they function. The four views can be used as a focus for analysis of contemporary organizational theory as it applies to the school setting.

Organizational Structure and Bureaucracy

Scientific management, or the classical theory of organizations as it is sometimes referred to (developed by Taylor, 1911, 1947), emphasizes the structure and bureaucracy of an organization as a way to create better, more efficient workplaces. As an organizational theory, scientific management contains two fundamental issues: "*motivation*, the explanation of why a person participates in an organization, and *organization*, specifically, techniques for dividing up specialized tasks and the various levels of authority" (Owens, 1970, p. 46).

Taylor's view of motivation was primarily economic. He believed that people work for an organization because they need money to meet basic physiological needs. Therefore, pay periods should be short to maximize reinforcement of work. The structure of an organization emphasizes the division of labor, where jobs are organized into small-scale tasks, and each employee functions in a highly specialized area requiring a specific skill. In such a structure, strong central control and close supervision are essential to keep activities and functions coordinated. The characteristics of organizations using the classical theory include specialization, control, hierarchy, and division of labor. Such views of organizations comprise what is commonly called the *formal organization*, where people fit into the organization on its terms (Owens, 1995).

Taylor's work (1911, 1947) prompted schools to adopt an organizational structure that emphasized specialized skills and functional organizational lines of responsibility. Because the teaching dimensions of public schools lack hourly wages or production schedules, the structured aspects (rather than the motivational dimensions) of classical theory are more apparent in school operations, even today. When such terms as lines of authority, organization charts with centralized control, specialized skills, functions and responsibilities, and channels of communication are used, schools are described in classical theory terms. In schools, an early response to the concern of organizational behavior and structure can be seen in a focus on the functional lines of responsibility, such as staff line charts. In addition, there may be an emphasis on the operation of the organization, with little regard for human factors. It is not that people do not matter, but the focus is on organizing the workplace in a way that gets the job done.

As schools follow a pattern set by corporations, structure and control become the primary mechanisms for bringing about instructional changes within the school. Corporations first followed the principles of scientific management advocated by Taylor (1911), and later the principles of bureaucracy proposed by Weber (1947). The typical model for school organizations was the bureaucratic structure, which included, among other things: (1) a division of labor with a hierarchical structure that adopted written policy manuals and their regulations; (2) impersonal interactions between and among personnel; (3) long-standing careers within the system; and (4) an operation characterized by efficiency, stability, and orderliness (Pfeiffer and Dunlap, 1982). Fayol (1949) also developed a set of principles that emphasized scientific management and bureaucracy. He established a pyramidal, hierarchical structure and incorporated such concepts as specialization, subordination, centralization, and remuneration as part of the operation of the workplace.

An examination of the structure of American schools, as seen in their organizational charts, reveals an affinity for the formal bureaucratic organization and reflects a pattern characteristic of many business corporations. While there are differences in the roles supervisors and managers play within the business setting, their supervisory functions can be viewed as somewhat parallel to those held by supervisory personnel within the school organization. Figure 3.1 provides an example of the parallel nature of the organizational structures of schools (on the left) and corporations (on the right).

The formal administrative arrangement of the organization is usually expressed as an organizational chart that, as Schultz and Schultz (1998) note, "may be the most famous symbol of the bureaucratic approach" (p. 277). The line chart shows the relationships between and among administrative and supervisory per-

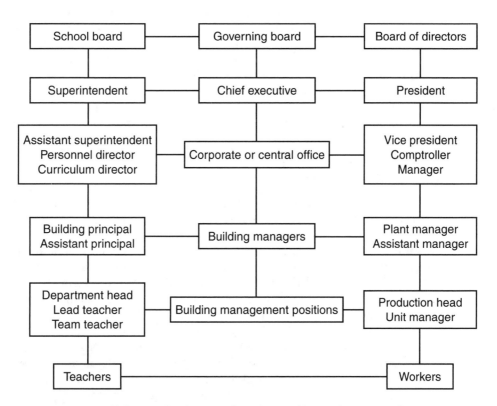

FIGURE 3.1 Parallel Organization in Education and in Business or Industry

sonnel and other members of the organization. Organization line charts identify those individuals who function either directly in the chain of authority (usually a solid line) or indirectly in an advisory capacity (usually a dotted line). Most line charts of school district staff identify direct administrative authority along with other advisory, auxiliary, and technical staff members, who may have input in the operation of the school organization but who lack any direct authority.

Today, most school districts and state educational agencies have some form of bureaucratic organizational structure that shows the direct lines of authority as well as indirect advisory relationships. Schultz and Schultz (1998) caution that "Although organization charts look nice and give [supervisors] the feeling that their employees are in their proper places and that the organization is running smoothly, these neat lines and boxes on paper do not always reflect daily operation on the job" (p. 278). Perhaps the school organizational structure will slowly begin to change and incorporate new ideas related to corporate structure, function, and behavior. Townsend (1984), in his book *Further Up the Organization,* raised some legitimate concerns about this organizational view when he suggested ways to prevent management from stifling people and strangling production. According to Townsend, it is time to change organizational structure and behavior so that people can work together when given an opportunity, and he advocates that organizations begin by asking for ideas, trying them out, rewarding employees as groups, and even singling out individuals in front of their peers and saying, "Thanks!" and by "treating everybody from top to bottom as respected adults rather than children or criminals" (p. x). Harper (1992) found that the greatest challenge facing CEOs and supervisors was the need for more employee involvement and participation in making decisions related to the quality of work life. Using such a high-involvement organizational approach in schools could create an organizational climate that results in improved teacher morale and greater student achievement.

Organizational Functions and Relationships

The second view of organizations that emerged in the 1930s in response to the classical theory (or scientific management) emphasized the human relations aspects of the workplace and the human resources model. Managers and organizational leaders recognized that scientific management was not adequate to explain the complex interactions that occur within organizations. As Sergiovanni and colleagues (1992) have observed in a bureaucratic system, "such issues…as individual personality and human needs,…conditions [such] as job satisfaction, motivation, and morale, and such values as liberty and empowerment seem clearly secondary" (p. 42).

While the scientific management view emphasizes structure and bureaucracy (formal organization), the human relations model is more concerned with human factors (motivation and morale) and interpersonal relationships (communication). In the organizational functions and relationships view, the construction and reconstruction of social interactions, unity, and systems are designed to improve work processes and outcomes by fostering decision making, improving communication, and facilitating the allocation of resources. Iannacconne (1964) described the complex interactions within the organization in terms of the struggle that exists between the formal legal power and authority of the organization itself and the informal extralegal power and influence of groups.

The recognition of the social dynamics of the organization was supported in the work of a management research team headed by Elton Mayo and Fritz Roethlisberger at the Western Electric Company in Cicero, Illinois. Their work is considered to be the beginnings of the human relations movement in organizations and is the result of "the impact of the Hawthorne studies, which focused attention on workers instead of on production" (Schultz and Schultz, 1998, p. 205). Owens (1970) attributes the following basic concepts of the human relations view to Mayo (1945) and his associates (Roethlisberger and Dickson, 1939): (1) A highly specialized division of labor is not necessarily the best way to maximize organizational efficiency; (2) employees respond to the hierarchy, rules, and reward system of an organization not as individuals but as members of a group; (3) the production results of employees are determined more by their social capacities than by their physical capacities; (4) money may serve as a motivational factor for working in an organization, especially in the beginning, but employees seek other, perhaps more important intangible rewards; and (5) worker motivation and job satisfaction are related to improved production. Other investigators (Blanchard and Johnson, 1982; Levering, 1988; Peters and Waterman, 1982) have contributed to the discussion concerning the importance of the human factor in the degree of organizational effectiveness.

Lewin (1951), in his *group dynamics* or *field theory*, describes how relationships in organizations are based on the following elements: (1) the needs, values, and desires of the individuals; (2) the characteristics of the group; (3) and the psychological environment or cultural norms of the organization. These determinants, when taken together, create a field of forces based on relationships, which in turn influence how people behave in the workplace. Figure 3.2 represents the overlap of these determinants to create a force field within the workplace: the greater the overlap, the stronger the field and its impact on behavior. If there is to be a meaningful change in behavior, then both the group norms and the cultural norms must respond to and address the needs, values, and desires of individuals. This human relations view suggests that it is important for supervisors to recognize the powerful influence of both school culture and norms of teachers as they seek to impact the force field of the school. If teachers are to make changes in their instructional behaviors and their classrooms, they must be supported not only by supervisors but by colleagues and the total school culture.

Argyris (1957) was particularly concerned about the *dissonance,* or lack of congruence, between the needs of individuals and the demands of the formal organization. A dissonance can cause frustration, conflict, and failure. As individuals function in the formal organization, their needs are often ignored or neglected.

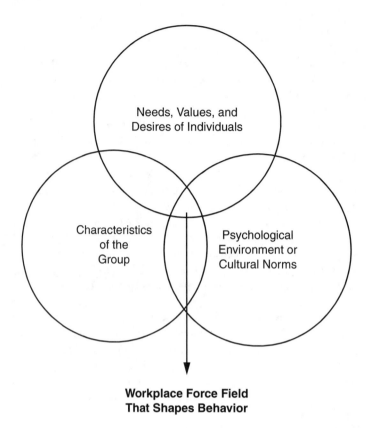

**Workplace Force Field
That Shapes Behavior**

FIGURE 3.2   Determinants of Workplace Force Field

They sometimes experience competition, rivalry, and insubordinate hostility; they focus on parts rather than the whole. Therefore, supervisors must remain sensitive to the needs of individual teachers in order to minimize dissonance in schools. By knowing the needs of their faculty and staff, supervisors can attend to the characteristics of the organization (e.g., schedule of classes, types of observations) as a way to reduce frustration and alienation.

Rogers (1958) carries the idea of support further by suggesting that counseling programs be established to provide helping relationships. Owens (1970) says that "within the helping relationship framework, efforts to produce more effective behavior should be developmental and not coercive and supervisors should accentuate the intrinsic satisfaction that teachers can get from being involved" (p. 87).

The human relations framework recognizes that teachers' feelings, needs, and motivations are important factors that contribute to more productive relationships within a school and with other faculty and students. Many organizations have created self-managing work groups, which involve members in monitoring all aspects of their work and empower them to perform their tasks (Manz, Keating, and Donnellon, 1990). Gould and Letven (1987) and Glatthorn (1987) have also emphasized a cooperative, interactive approach. For example, in the Wisconsin Regional Staff Development Center, educators from all grade levels and disciplines come together to learn with and from one another. It is in this collaborative approach that "members help each other maintain the spirit of inquiry crucial to the healthy intellectual life of all faculty members" (Gould and Letven, 1987, p. 51). In commenting further on this helping relationship framework, Glatthorn (1987) notes that "when districts provide supporting conditions, teachers can work together...using a variety of collaborative methods, for their professional growth" (p. 31).

Herzberg's (1966) *job enrichment* or *motivation-hygiene* theory suggests that there are two views or sides to human nature. One side deals with fundamental needs such as safety, nourishment, and other basic drives. The other side of human nature has a "compelling urge" to be successful, to reach full potential through continuous psychological growth. This view recognizes that some organizational (job-related) factors can lead to job satisfaction while other conditions can lead to job dissatisfaction. Factors that can affect job dissatisfaction are called "hygiene factors," which include salary, work conditions, and job security; elements that can contribute to job satisfaction are called "motivational factors" and include recognition, responsibility, and opportunities for growth (Herzberg, 1966).

The job enrichment or motivation-hygiene theory suggests to supervisors that teachers whose greatest needs are met by salary, job security, and orderly work environment tend to get little satisfaction from their work per se. These teachers also show little interest in job performance and are often chronic complainers when at work. On the other hand, teachers who receive a great deal of personal satisfaction from and are motivated by their instructional activities and other professional accomplishments tend to be less affected by hygiene factors and respond to opportunities for professional growth and responsibility.

The principles that guide the human relations approach have caused supervisors to adopt a more democratic or collaborative approach when working with teachers. Sergiovanni and colleagues (1992) suggest that the ideal school is one where teachers are highly motivated and committed to obtaining school objectives and, in so doing, derive intrinsic satisfaction. Teachers, then, are linked together in highly effective work groups, and these work groups "are characterized by commitment to common school objectives, by group loyalty, and by mutual support" (p. 138). Smylie (1995) further advocates that teachers be given opportunities to work together in team-building activities that have common goals, responsibilities, and items for action.

In such a school, supervisors must be able to foster rapport with teachers. Rapport is built on trust, which creates "a harmonious relationship with and between people" (Goldhammer, Anderson, and Krajewski, 1993, p. 66). In the human relations view, supervisors are aware of anxious feelings teachers may have and support them in enhancing their personal and professional self.

A View from the Field

In the following example, the importance of cultivating harmonious relationships among teachers is emphasized. At an elementary school, there had been a high incidence of personal tragedies, including family illnesses and death of loved ones (a husband and mother of two teachers). The members of the hospitality committee responsible for doing acts of kindness, such as sending cards and flowers, as well as acknowledging these events were inconsistent, which caused hard feelings. In a memo, the members of the committee apologized for any hurt feelings, and they established some general guidelines for the future. In this particular situation, the supervisor recognized how important it was to attend to personal feelings of faculty and staff. Supervisors have often found it difficult to deal with the realities of the hierarchical structure, which emphasizes power and central control, while at the same time trying to maintain an open, responsive style in building trust and rapport. In this example, personal and professional lives of teachers are essential to consider when fostering a supportive school culture.

Behavioral Organizational Processes

The third view of organizations uses a behavioral approach and regards the processes within the organization as a complex system with both a formal and an informal structure. This perspective examines the ways organizations operate and the instructional effectiveness that results as supervisors study the interactions that occur in the social units or systems of the school. The behavioral approach to organizational processes is also helpful in analyzing the factors that have an impact on individual behavior within schools. Getzels and Guba (1957) suggest that there are two dimensions related to organizational behavior: One is personal and the other is institutional. The formal structure has identifiable organizational positions, roles, and job descriptions. People who occupy the roles "behave" according to established guidelines or expectations and are rewarded or reinforced for such behavior. People act in a prescribed fashion, based on their role in the organization, and the performance in the role remains constant even though there are changes in personnel.

But the behavioral view of organizations also acknowledges an informal structure. People who occupy roles in the formal structure interact with each other face-to-face as they communicate, plan, make decisions, and examine procedures. Because some degree of the human dimension is inherent in any social interaction, individuals seek social interactions and friendships within the organization. Informal groups may be based on such characteristics as age, gender, personal interests, marital status, and/or work orientation. The evidence from research suggests that an informal structure is necessary to the proper functioning of an organization and that, within an informal structure, primary groups have great power (Owens, 1970).

An extension of the behavioral view of organizational processes is a technique known as management by objectives (MBO). Drucker (1954) is generally credited with this approach, which focuses organizational behavior on the specification of organizational goals, the development of an action plan, and the evaluation of results. MBO programs have been credited as being effective in improving performance in a number of organizations (Kondrasuk, 1981; Midas and Devine, 1991).

Within a school context, the behavioral approach to organizational processes suggests that an individual has the role of teacher, based on employment status and job description, and also functions as a person who works with others. Such association with others is based on similar characteristics or common work experiences. To illustrate this informal organizational principle, Owens (1970) says:

> Teachers of the same grade level or in the same department, or those whose workplaces are close together tend to belong to the same primary groups...it is almost impossible to think of a school organization today that does not...develop primary group affiliations that will reward [members] with...social and psychological satisfactions. (p. 50)

Such a model suggests that supervisors must recognize that their behavior and that of teachers are influenced not only by the expectations of the school and the needs and characteristics of the staff (Campbell et al., 1985) but by the rewards and reinforcers. One of the greatest potential uses of the behavioral process approach is the opportunity for organizational development. Using this perspective, supervisors work with teachers and staff to develop a campus improvement plan based on key organizational goals (such as developing specific strategies and programs to meet the needs of at-risk youth). Supervisors then apply behavioral principles by rewarding and reinforcing both individuals and groups in a planned and sustained effort as the desired outcomes are attained.

Organizational Influence

The fourth view focuses on the use of influence or the power of persuasion in the operation of the organization and seeks to answer the question, Who are the truly powerful and influential people in the organization? The sources and distribution of power and influence are critical to understanding this view. Blase (1991) has suggested that this view acknowledges "the use of formal and informal power by individuals and groups to achieve their goals...[and] political actions result from perceived differences between individuals and groups, coupled with the motivation to use power to influence and/or protect" (p. 11). Drory and Romm (1990) describe organizational politics as actions that are not officially approved by an organization but are taken to influence others. This view often places one's own interests above the interests of others—even the organization's—in order to move ahead (Greenberg and Baron, 1997). Using this organizational perspective, the supervisor is put in a political arena where operational decisions and procedures are most often derived from political maneuvers or actions of powerful or influential individuals.

An examination of the effects of influence in organizations also looks at the behaviors associated with power, authority, and persuasion. These behaviors have their origins in the social and behavioral sciences. Wiles and Bondi (1986) note that "the study of influence is comprised of at least four subareas: studies of change, of leadership, of decision making, and of the role of politics" (p. 36). These subareas are important factors in the study of power and influence, and three of them—change, leadership, and decision making—will be discussed in detail in later chapters. Like other organizations, schools constantly seek leadership, make decisions, implement changes, and initiate strategies for dealing with the pressures exerted by the politics of the environment.

The major views of schools as workplaces include organizational structure and bureaucracy, functions and relationships, processes, and influence; they add to our present understanding of organizational structure, function, and behavior. These four different views concerning the operations within organizations help supervisors recognize the importance of the school as an organization. Knowledge of how organizations are structured and operate presents instructional supervisors with a basis for the critical understanding of their professional work environment, and how schools carry out long-term and short-term tasks. As Wiles and Bondi (1986) state: "Once the supervisor knows the [organizational] environment and understands how it works, he or she must then compare that purpose with his or her own conception of what schools should be doing" (p. 26). Supervisors can then use this common ground of agreement as they work with teachers to develop strategies to improve instruction.

Just as there are many different school districts or systems, there are many ways to organize education to meet the goals of the schools; this information is essential for supervisors. They can increase their effectiveness by becoming aware of the major views of organizational structures and the different factors that operate in each. For instance, the behavior of a supervisor in a school district that operates within the general guidelines of scientific management would be quite different from that of a colleague whose school district adhered to the organizational influence model. Knowing the difference between the two organizational models and what factors influence the structure, functions, and behaviors of individuals within each view can determine the effectiveness of supervisors as they, along with teachers, seek to enhance the teaching–learning process.

Organizational Culture

As one of the variables that helps define and shape the school organization (see Figure 3.1), the influence of school organizational culture on the teaching–learning process has become central to understanding the operation of effective schools. Jewell (1998) defines organizational culture as "the collective meaning of an organization's social environment,…[the] widely shared values and assumptions that create particular behavior patterns in an organization" (p. 445). Culture is a term used by anthropologists to describe the various patterns of life in different groups; normally, it involves (among other things) the values, attitudes, beliefs, rituals, and customs of the people in the group or organization (Owens, 1995). Deal and Peterson (1990) note:

Culture is a historically rooted, socially transmitted set of…patterns of thinking and ways of acting that give meaning to…experience, that…dictate how experience is seen, assessed, and acted on…[while helping] us perceive and understand the complex forces that work in…human groups and organizations. (p. 8)

Other scholars in the field have viewed organizational culture somewhat differently; their definitions include:

- The way things are done (Bower, 1966)
- The shared beliefs and values that hold the group together (Deal and Kennedy, 1982)
- A product (the accumulated wisdom of the organization) and a process (the continuing system of sharing and learning the old ways) (Bolman and Deal, 1991)
- The body of solutions to problems taught to new members as a way of perceiving, feeling, and thinking about problems (Schein, 1991)
- The strategic body of learned behaviors that provides meaning for group members (Cunningham and Cresso, 1993)
- A set of beliefs, customs, practices, and ways of thinking that [people] share…[by] being and working together (Stacey, 1993)

The study of culture is central to the study of organizations. Social psychologists and social scientists also describe behavior patterns within organizations as culture. Kanter (1986), in discussing organizational culture, suggests that synergy is achieved and "the 'whole' contributes something above and beyond the value of the parts" (p. 91), when organizations focus on their mission, clarify and reinforce their value and belief systems, emphasize cooperation, and eliminate extraneous activities. Chatman and Jehn (1994) have identified seven elements that help to shape the culture of an organization. These seven elements include: (1) innovation or the way members are creative and develop new ideas; (2) stability or the establishment of rules and procedures that create a predictable workplace; (3) people orientation or the way in which interactions between and among individuals are fair, supportive, and respectful of rights; (4) results orientation or the focus on achieving desired results; (5) easygoingness or the creation of a relaxed work tempo or atmosphere; (6) attention to detail or the concern for precision and getting things right; and (7) collaborative orientation or an emphasis on working in groups or teams.

Ott (1989) has identified various ways that organizational culture is transmitted. Symbols are material objects, such as school buildings, that connote meanings. Stories are also used to transmit organizational culture as members recount important events or incidents that helped to define the organization's history (Neuhauser, 1993). Jargon is the special language that helps members define their identities in the organization. Especially significant for schools are the ceremonies or special events that reinforce the values of the organization. Ceremonies help members to celebrate their successes and sustain their behavior. Finally, mission statements or statements of principle codify the beliefs of the organization and, when posted, serve as reminders of what the organization values.

The work of Purkey and Smith (1981/1982) suggests that the organizational effectiveness of a school "is distinguished by its culture: a structure, process and climate of values and norms that channel staff and students in the direction of successful teaching and learning" (p. 68). In addition, Saphier and King (1985) suggest that effective schools have an organizational culture that articulates expectations for students and faculty; stresses excellence and academic effort; views all students as capable of achieving; and creates a safe, orderly, and respectful environment.

As teachers and supervisors learn the symbolism of the school organization, they become encultured through direct and extraceptive learning (Cunningham and Cresso, 1993). For us, *school culture is powerful because it serves as the memory of the past and helps to shape and mold the collective vision for the future of what teaching and learning should be. It ultimately guides decisions that help define the school.* Sergiovanni (1991) has noted that all schools have an organizational culture: Some are strong and functional while others are weak and dysfunctional. Effective schools have strong and functional cultures supported by a vision of excellence. Visions are generated by educational leaders who, in concert with teachers, establish values and traditions for the school setting. Such values and traditions help complement those articulated by the total school community.

Principles of Effective Organizations

Characteristics of effective organizations are summarized in the following principles, based on research gathered from a variety of organizational settings (Alfonso, Firth, and Neville, 1981; Deal and Peterson, 1990; Lovell and Wiles, 1983). These 10 principles can be used to guide supervisors as they work in school organizations:

1. In order for schools, as organizations, to be successful and function effectively within the community, their purposes must be consistent with the values and culture of the community they serve and its members—students, parents, and community residents.

2. An effective educational organization treats individuals with dignity and respect by maintaining an open, responsive, cooperative posture and treats educators as professionals.

3. An effective educational organization encourages individual members to take risks and to develop and capitalize on their creativity and potential, which in turn enhances the organization's effectiveness.

4. To be successful, an educational organization must have the necessary resources and talent, and the members of the organization must have a knowledge of organizational structure, an understanding of each member's role within the structure, and an understanding of the operational procedures that guide the organization.

5. Educational organizations are dynamic places, and changes occur within them to meet changing societal conditions and circumstances.

6. The morale of an educational organization will be enhanced when there is continuous interaction among members of the group, and when the members understand, perceive as important, and share a common set of values, goals (mission), and objectives.

7. An effective educational organization has members who act in ways that reflect shared values and clearly defined goals, and who periodically examine their behavior in relation to the organization's mission and goals.

8. Effective school organizations assist members by directly supporting, enhancing, and rewarding teacher instructional behavior that results in increased student achievement.

9. An effective educational organization has an organizational structure that allows for both formal and informal responsibilities and interaction.

10. Effective educational organizations establish procedures and strategies for regular or frequent analysis of the overall effectiveness of the organization, and they assess the degree of submission and alienation among members and constituents.

These principles are an integral part of creating schools that are more effective as organizations and workplaces for teachers and supervisors. Figure 3.3 further elaborates on the parallel characteristics of effective schools and effective organizations.

An Organizational View of Effective Schools

While many of the descriptions provided in earlier parts of this chapter have centered on characteristics and views of organizations in general, this section examines the specific organizational characteristics associated with effective schools. Within the last three decades, studies have been conducted to identify characteristics of effective schools or those that produce greater student achievement. Zigarelli (1996) notes that this quest has produced a myriad of studies that can help to inform supervisors and other educators.

This research is qualitative in nature and is generally expressed in case studies that examine the organizational characteristics and work behaviors found in effective or high-performing schools (Wohlstetter and Smyer, 1994). Assumptions that have given definition to these research studies include these five beliefs: (1) Effectiveness is based on the measurement of student success in learning (knowledge, skills, and attitudes); (2) student learning is the central purpose/focus of teaching; (3) the attitudes and behaviors of teachers and staff are key components of

FIGURE 3.3   **Parallels Between Effective Schools and Effective Organizations**

Effective Schools	Effective Organizations
Coherent ethos with agreed-upon ways of doing things; agreement on instructional goals	Strong culture with shared ways and values; a consensus on "how we do things around here"
Importance of principal as leader	Importance of leader as hero or heroine who embodies core values, or who anoints other heroic figures
Strong beliefs about teaching and learning	Widely shared beliefs about the organization's mission
Teachers as role models; students with positions of responsibility	Employees as situational heroes or heroines who represent core values
Ceremonies, traditions, and rituals centered on events such as arrival in the morning, the first day of school, and graduation	Ceremonies, traditions, and rituals centered on events such as greeting employees in the morning, opening a new plant, and the retirement of a senior executive
Orderly atmosphere without rigidity, accountability without oppression	Balance between innovation and tradition, autonomy and authority
Teachers involved in technical decision making	Employee participation in decisions about their own work

Source: Deal, T. E., & Peterson, K. D. (1990). *The principal's role in shaping school culture.* U.S. Department of Education. Washington, DC: U.S. Government Printing Office.

effective schools; (4) schools accept the responsibility of the academic performance of students and reinforce the belief that all students are capable of learning; and (5) schools as organizations must be examined holistically, rather than dissecting and isolating parts—tinkering with the parts does not work (Owens, 1995). These assumptions provide a framework for examining the various studies and data presented in the following section.

In the 1970s and 1980s, Edmonds (1979, 1982) identified five factors that characterize effective schools. These factors include: (1) high teacher expectations for students; (2) frequent monitoring and measuring of student achievement; (3) school goals that emphasize academic instruction; (4) a school environment that is safe, orderly, and supportive of teaching and learning; and (5) instructional leadership provided by the principal. These factors are evident in mission statements, the general atmosphere of the school, and the slogans found written on the walls of halls and classrooms.

In the 1980s, Purkey and Smith (1981/1982, 1985) identified four process variables and nine organizational characteristics that result in effective schools.

The four process variables include: (1) establishing a sense of belonging or community in the school; (2) creating an environment conducive to learning; (3) utilizing collaborative planning; and (4) developing consensus on goals with high expectations regarding student performance. Schools do not function in a vacuum, and the process variables point out the importance of having a school organization that involves its faculty, staff, and community members in making decisions regarding goals, expectations, and ultimately the total educational program for all learners. Effective schools are not top-down schools; they are places where collaboration is occurring at all levels—starting with the individual classrooms, continuing at the campus level, and coming together at the district level.

The nine structural or organizational characteristics of effective schools identified by Purkey and Smith (1981/1982, 1985) help to provide the specifics for understanding why these schools are so successful. These characteristics include: (1) campus-based management and decision making; (2) schoolwide emphasis on and recognition of success; (3) more time devoted to instruction during the school day; (4) campuswide staff development based on teacher needs; (5) curriculum alignment, organization, and articulation; (6) strong instructional leadership provided by principals or other teachers and administrators; (7) parental support and involvement in school; (8) stability in staffing; and (9) support provided at the district level. These characteristics provide specific terminology, which can be used to describe effective school organizations. Working to develop a K–12 educational program through the alignment of the curriculum for example, means educators at all levels talk to each other. Supervisors play a critical role in establishing the environment for this dialogue to take place and ensuring that the communication between elementary and secondary teachers becomes an ongoing process.

Hill, Foster, and Gendler (1990) also have added mission and organizational strength to the list of characteristics. By mission, they mean providing students with experiences that emphasize outcomes or results. Organizational strength refers to the ability of the schools to initiate action in order to accomplish their mission. Bryk, Lee, and Smith (1993) have found that the communal nature of schools impacts school effectiveness. Schools that are smaller and have a caring faculty and staff create positive faculty and student interactions and provide common learning experiences for students that are described as communal in nature and that produce greater learning results. In fact, Bryk, Lee, and Smith (1993) argue that large, bureaucratic, and comprehensive schools are impersonal and therefore less effective.

More recently, Zigarelli (1996) reviewed not only the earlier studies of Edmonds and Purkey and Smith but also the studies of Block (1983), Downer (1991), and Coyle and Witcher (1992) to identify variables or constructs of effective schools that are most often cited. Zigarelli (1996) found six variables that were consistent in the research. These six factors include: (1) employment of quality teachers, (2) teacher participation and satisfaction, (3) principal leadership and involvement, (4) a culture of academic achievement, (5) support and cooperation from the school district administration, and (6) high parental involvement. The results of Zigarelli's analysis of these six variables show that student, parent, and school controls "strongly affect student achievement" (p. 106).

Wohlstetter and Smyer (1994) examined four different organizational models that have been shown to produce high-performing schools. These models advocate restructuring as a way to improve student academic achievement. The first model, Effective Schools, seeks to implement the characteristics identified by Edmonds and others, cited above. The School Development Program uses school-based decision making as a way to foster student achievement (Comer, 1980, 1988). The decisions made by a school-based community serve to improve student behavior and academic performance. The Accelerated Schools model advocated by Levin (1987) is designed to enhance the academic performance of disadvantaged, at-risk students. Students participate in a challenging curriculum based on the existing strengths of students and teachers. The Essential Schools model also targets at-risk and poor-performing students. Sizer (1992) advocates that Essential Schools provide an intellectual focus, simple achievement goals, universal goals, personalization, active student learning, student exhibitions, attitudes of trust and decency, a generalist staff, and financial support to serve as the guiding principles for such schools.

As leaders in the school organization, supervisors can use these characteristics and models to work with others to inform practices by affirming values, shaping the school's tradition, using language that reinforces qualities of effectiveness, and overseeing the change process. Supervisors are potters, poets, actors, and facilitators who affirm values and traditions in the way they dress and behave, and in the language they use. They have tremendous influence in shaping a school's vision and mission, but they are also impacted both by stories they are told about the heroes and heroines and by participation in school ceremonies. Most importantly, it is a give-and-take; as supervisors oversee transitions in the life of a school, they too have been changed through the process of collaboration as they become deeply involved in the professional growth of teachers and the teaching–learning process of the school organization.

Supervisors should look at schools in terms of possibilities, not what is actually there, and work toward creating a vision of what can be. The Norfolk, Virginia, schools have been cited as premier effective schools because the educational programs have been developed within the context of a shared vision and a set of mission goals and objectives for school improvement (Cunningham and Cresso, 1993). The role of the supervisor is central to developing such a comprehensive commitment to school effectiveness.

Summary

Organizations are fundamental components of society. They are a part of our total existence, and schools are no exception. Schools share many common characteristics with other organizations. Chapter 3 focused on the four major historical views of organizations. The four views of organizational development include: (1) organizational structure and bureaucracy, (2) organizational functions and relationships, (3) organizational processes, and (4) organizational influence. Knowledge of these views is important as supervisors work with teachers because it provides supervisors with a frame of reference to guide their behavior as they work within the context of the organization called *school*. Since organizations are composed of people, knowledge of the organizational setting can also guide supervisors as they work with teachers.

The chapter described the aspects of organizational culture and its role in shaping behavior, as well as the vision and mission of the workplace. The school culture is powerful because it is the memories of the past and the blueprint for the future. It is the invisible glue that holds the organization together. The chapter also presented 10 principles that synthesize research about effective organizations and provided a comparison of the characteristics of effective schools and organizations.

The chapter ended with a discussion of the characteristics of effective schools. These characteristics are presented as an overview that provides a context for supervisors. The chapter emphasized those components that help to explain how and why effective schools operate the way they do. By gaining information about organizations in general, and about schools as organizations more specifically, supervisors will have greater insight into the school environment or workplace.

YOUR TURN

3.1. Organizations share many common characteristics. Cite three traits all schools share regardless of type, size, purpose, student population, and/or tax base. Make an appointment to meet with your principal and ask him or her questions regarding the school as an organization and its impact on the teachers and students.

3.2. Some administrators in the central office are making all the decisions while others appear to function only as advisors. You have been asked to develop a line staff chart that reflects shared decision making relative to the reorganization of the central office and the way it interfaces with individual schools within the district. Your responsibility is to construct the chart in such a way as to clearly communicate lines of authority, duties, roles, and decision-making responsibilities.

3.3. According to the tenets described in organizational theory, schools function as organizations. As a supervisor, what environmental factors will you encounter that may hinder and/or help you as you work with teachers to develop and improve their instructional skills?

3.4. In what ways would the role of a supervisor in a large urban or suburban school district differ from that role in a small, rural district? (Refer to your response to item 2.2 in the Your Turn in Chapter 2 for help.)

3.5. In discussing organizations, Etzioni (1964) says:

Most organizations most of the time cannot rely on most of their participants to carry out their assigned tasks voluntarily, to have internalized their obligations. The participants need to be supervised, the supervisors themselves need supervision, and so on all the way to the top of the organization. In this sense, the organizational structure is one of control, and the hierarchy of control is the most central element of the organizational structure (p. 12).

Do you agree with this statement? Why or why not? What specific examples can you cite from school organizations to support your answer?

REFERENCES

Alfonso, R. J., Firth, G. R., & Neville, R. F. (1981). *Instructional supervision: A behavior system.* (2nd ed.). Boston: Allyn & Bacon.

Argyris, C. (1957). The individual and the organization: Some problems of mutual adjustment. *Administrative Science Quarterly, 2,* 1–4.

Barnard, C. I. (1938). *The function of the executive.* Cambridge, Mass.: Harvard University Press.

Berrien, F. K. (1976). A general systems approach to organizations. In *Handbook of industrial and organizational psychology.* Dunnette, M. (ed.). Chicago: Rand McNally.

Blanchard, K., & Johnson, S. (1982). *The one minute manager.* New York: William Morrow.

Blase, J. (ed.). (1991). *The politics of life in schools: Power, conflict, and cooperation.* Newbury Park, CA: Sage Publications.

Block, A. W. (1983). *Effective schools: A summary of research.* Arlington, VA: Educational Research Service.

Bolman, L. G., & Deal, T. (1991). *Reframing organizations.* San Francisco: Jossey-Bass Publishers.

Bower, M. (1966). *Will to manage.* New York: McGraw-Hill.

Bryk, A. S., Lee, V. E., & Smith, J. B. (1993). *Catholic schools and the common good.* Cambridge, MA: Harvard University Press.

Campbell, R. F., Cunningham, L. L., Nystrand, R. O., & Usdan, M. D. (1985). *The organization and control of American schools.* (5th ed.). Columbus, OH: Charles E. Merrill.

Charan, R. (1992 September/October). How networks reshape organizations for results. *Harvard Business Review, 12,* 479–494.

Chatman, J. A., & Jehn, K. A. (1994). Assessing the relationship between industry characteristics and organizational culture: How different can you be? *Academy of Management Journal, 37,* 522–533.

Comer, J. (1980). *School power.* New York: Free Press.

Comer, J. (1988). Child development and education. *Journal of Negro Education, 58,* 125–139.

Coyle, S., & Witcher, A. (1992). Transforming the idea into action. Policies and practices to enhance school effectiveness. *Urban Education, 26,* 390–400.

Cunningham, W. E., & Cresso, D. W. (1993). *Cultural leadership: The culture of excellence in education.* Boston: Allyn & Bacon.

Deal, T. E., & Kennedy, A. (1982). *Corporate cultures.* Reading, MA: Addison-Wesley.

Deal, T. E., & Peterson, K. D. (1990). *The principal's role in shaping school culture.* U.S. Department of Education. Washington, DC: U.S. Government Printing Office.

Downer, D. F. (1991). Review of research on effective schools. *McGill Journal of Education, 26,* 323–331.

Drory, A., & Romm, T. (1990). The definition of organizational politics: A review. *Human Relations, 43,* 1133–1154.

Drucker, P. (1954). *The practice of management.* New York: Harper & Row.

Drucker, P. (1997). Introduction: Toward the new organization. In *The organization of the future.* F. Hesselbein, M. Goldsmith, & R. Beckhard (eds.). San Francisco: Jossey-Bass.

Edmonds, R. (1979). Some schools work and more can. *Social Policy, 9,* 28–32.

Edmonds, R. (1982). Programs of school improvement: An overview. *Educational Leadership, 40,* 4–11.

Etzioni, A. (1964). *Modern organizations.* Englewood Cliffs, NJ: Prentice-Hall.

Fayol, H. (1949). *Administration industrielle et generale*. Trans. Constance Storrs. In *General and industrial management*. London: Sir Isaac Pitman and Sons.

Gaus, J. M. (1936). A theory of organization in public administration. In *The frontiers of public administration*. J. M. Gaus, L. D. White, & M. E. Demock (eds.). Chicago: University of Chicago Press.

Getzels, J. W., & Guba, E. G. (1957). Social behavior and the administrative process. *School Review, 65*, 423–441.

Glatthorn, A. A. (1987 November). Cooperative professional development: Peer-centered options for teacher growth. *Educational Leadership, 45*, 31–35.

Goldhammer, R., Anderson, R. H., & Krajewski, R. J. (1993). *Clinical supervision: Special methods for the supervision of teachers*. New York: Holt, Rinehart & Winston.

Gould, S., & Letven, E. (1987 November). A center for interactive professional development. *Educational Leadership, 45*, 49–52.

Greenberg, J., & Baron, R. A. (1997). *Behavior in organizations*. (6th ed.). Upper Saddle River, NJ: Prentice-Hall.

Gross, B. M. (1964). *The managing of organizations*. New York: Free Press of Glencoe.

Harper, S. C. (1992). The challenges facing CEOs: Past, present, and future. *Academy of Management Executive, 6*, 7–25.

Hershey, P., & Blanchard, K. H. (1993). *Management of organizational behavior*. Englewood Cliffs, NJ: Prentice-Hall.

Herzberg, F. (1966). *Work and the nature of man*. Cleveland: World.

Hill, P. T., Foster, G. E., & Gendler, T. (1990). *High schools with character*. Santa Monica, CA: RAND Corporation.

Iannacconne, L. (1964). An approach to the informal organization of the school. *Behavioral science and educational administration*. 63rd yearbook of the National Society for the Study of Education. D. Griffith (ed.). Chicago: University of Chicago Press.

Jewell, L. N. (1998). *Contemporary industrial/organizational psychology*. (3rd ed.). Pacific Grove, CA: Brooks/Cole Publishing Co.

Johnson, S. M. (1990). *Teachers at work: Achieving success in our schools*. New York: Basic Books, a division of HarperCollins Publishing.

Kanter, R. M. (1986). *When giants learn to dance*. New York: Touchstone Books, Simon & Schuster.

Katz, D., & Kahn, R. (1978). *The social psychology of organizations*. New York: Wiley.

Kondrasuk, J. N. (1981). Studies in MBO effectiveness. *Academy of Management Review, 6*, 419–430.

Kowalski, T. J., & Reitzug, U. C. (1993). *Contemporary school administration: An introduction*. New York: Longman.

Levering, R. (1988). *A great place to work*. New York: Avon Books.

Levin, H. (1987). Accelerated schools for disadvantaged students. *Educational Leadership, 44*, 19–21.

Lewin, K. (1951). *Field theory in social science*. New York: Harper Torch Books.

Lovell, J. T., & Wiles, K. (1983). *Supervision for better schools*. (5th ed.). Englewood Cliffs, NJ: Prentice-Hall.

Manz, C. C., Keating, D. E., & Donnellon, A. (1990). Preparing for an organizational change to employee self-management: The managerial transition. *Organization Dynamics, 19*, 15–26.

Mayo, E. (1945). *The social problems of an industrial civilization*. Boston: Harvard Graduate School of Business.

Midas, M. T., & Devine, T. E. (1991 Summer). A look at continuous improvement at Northwest Airlines. *National Productivity Review, 10*, 374–394.

Neuhauser, P. C. (1993). *The power of storytelling as a management tool*. New York: McGraw-Hill.

Nohria, N., & Eccles, R. G. (1992). *Networks and organizations*. Cambridge, MA: Harvard University Press.

Ott, J. S. (1989). *The organizational culture perspective*. Chicago: Dorsey.

Owens, R. G. (1970). *Organizational behavior in schools*. Englewood Cliffs, NJ: Prentice-Hall.

Owens, R. G. (1995). *Organizational behavior in education*. (5th ed.). Needham Heights, MA: Allyn & Bacon.

Parsons, T. (1965). Suggestions for a sociological approach to the theory of organizations. *Administrative Science Quarterly, 1,* 63–85.

Peters, T. J., & Waterman, R. H. (1982). *In search of excellence: Lessons from America's best-run companies.* New York: Harper & Row.

Pfeiffer, I. L., & Dunlap, J. B. (1982). *Supervision of teachers: A guide to improving instruction.* Phoenix: Oryx Press.

Purkey, S. C., & Smith, M. S. (1981/1982 December/January). Too soon to cheer? Synthesis of research on effective schools. *Educational Leadership, 40,* 64–69.

Purkey, S. C., & Smith, M. S. (1985). School reform: The district policy implications of the effective schools literature. *Elementary School Journal, 85,* 353–389.

Roethlisberger, F., & Dickson, W. (1939). *Management and the worker.* Cambridge, MA: Harvard University Press.

Rogers, C. (1958 September). Characteristics of a helping relationship. *Personnel and Guidance Journal, 37,* 6–16.

Saphier, J., & King, M. (1985 March). Good seeds grow in strong cultures. *Educational Leadership, 42,* 67–74.

Schein, E. H. (1991). *Organizational culture and leadership.* San Francisco: Jossey-Bass Publishers.

Schultz, D. P., & Schultz, S. E. (1998). *Psychology and work today.* (7th ed.). Upper Saddle River, NJ: Prentice-Hall.

Sergiovanni, T. J. (1991). *The principalship: A reflective practice perspective.* Boston, MA: Allyn & Bacon.

Sergiovanni, T. J., Burlingame, M., Combs, F. S., & Thurston, P. W. (1992). *Educational governance and administration.* (3rd ed.). Boston: Allyn & Bacon.

Sizer, T. (1992). *Horace's compromise: The dilemma of the American high school.* Boston: Houghton Mifflin.

Smylie, M. A. (1995). Teacher learning in the workplace: Implications for school reform. In *Professional development in education: New paradigms & practices.* Guskey, T. R., & Haberman, M. (eds.). New York: Teachers College Press.

Stacey, R. D. (1993). *Strategic management and organizational dynamics.* London: Pitman.

Stacey, R. D. (1996). *Complexity and creativity in organizations.* San Francisco: Berrett-Koehler Publishers.

Taylor, F. W. (1911). *The principles of scientific management.* New York: Harper & Row.

Taylor, F. W. (1947). *Scientific management.* New York: Harper & Row.

Townsend, R. (1984). *Further up the organization.* New York: Alfred A. Knopf.

Weber, M. (1947). *The theory of social and economic organizations.* Trans. A. M. Henderson & T. Parsons. New York: Free Press.

Wiles, J., & Bondi, J. (1986). *Supervision: A guide to practice.* (2nd ed.). Columbus, OH: Charles E. Merrill.

Wohlstetter, P., & Smyer, R. (1994). Models of high-performance schools. In *School-based management: Organizing for high performance.* S. A. Mohrman, P. Wohlstetter, and Associates (eds.). San Francisco: Jossey-Bass Publishers.

Zigarelli, M. A. (1996 November/December). An empirical test of conclusions from effective schools research. *Journal of Educational Research, 90,* 103–110.

4 Supervisors as Leaders

OBJECTIVES

The objectives of this chapter are:

- Define leadership and describe various views of leadership behavior.
- Distinguish between leadership behavior and manager behavior.
- Identify and describe essential qualities of effective leadership.
- Describe several theoretical models of leadership.
- Discuss the characteristics of common leadership styles.
- Apply principles of leadership to school supervisory situations.
- Discuss the use of power and authority in leadership situations.

While the previous chapter described the school organization as the workplace or professional setting for supervisors, it is the quality of leadership behavior that occurs within schools that influences the overall effectiveness of the school organization. Fielder (1974) warns that, without leadership, organizations are in serious trouble because they become lifeless and ineffective; Sheppard (1996) notes that leadership and school effectiveness are "inextricably interwoven" (p. 325). It is no wonder, then, that the study of leadership is crucial to understanding organizational and school effectiveness. For supervisors, leadership is essential to promoting student achievement and creating a vision of success for the total educational program. The research of the last two decades has promoted strong support for linking successful organizations with strong leadership (Bolman and Deal, 1994; Boyan, 1988; Griffiths, 1988; Sergiovanni, 1995).

The impact of leadership on school effectiveness has been the central focus of a number of studies and part of the Effective Schools movement. Andrews (1987) observed "a powerful relationship between the leadership of the principal and student outcomes" (p. 15). In fact, within the school organization, leadership affects the way teachers perceive their work environment, and it ultimately produces a measurable gain in student achievement. In another study, Mortimore and Sammons (1987) identified 12 factors that distinguish effective elementary schools from less effective ones; most of the factors that contribute to effectiveness are related to "purposeful leadership." For Mortimore and Sammons (1987), purposeful leadership happens when the leader "understands the needs of the school and is actively involved in the school's work without exerting total control over the staff" (p. 7). Schomoker (1996) draws upon the work of Wheatley (1994) and suggests that leaders must articulate a vision and create a spirit within the school organization that unites the "particles" to form a "field—prevailing and evolving thoughts and conversations that occur in thousands of situations" (p. 106). Sorenson and Machell (1996) note that "Educational leadership today requires skills, knowledge, and attitudes that are remarkably different than those required only a few decades ago. [The leader] should be the facilitator of school improvement and the keeper of the collective covenant, rather than the custodian of the status quo" (p. 12).

An individual who accepts a supervisory position takes on leadership responsibilities; for Wiles and Bondi (1980), the relationship of leadership to supervision is enhanced when the process is viewed as a function that links administration, curriculum, and teaching. Leadership, then, is integral to the supervision process because it is seen as the "direct or indirect behaviors that significantly affect teacher and instruction and, as a result, student learning" (Liu, 1984, p. 33). Daresh and Playko (1995) describe supervisory leadership as "a product of [one's]...personalized instructional philosophy" (p. 134).

Leadership is a critical component of effective organizations, and this chapter will present a discussion concerning leadership behavior that will draw upon the research and scholarship available. Included in this discussion of leadership will be a comparison of the views and definitions of managers and leaders, the essential qualities of leaders, theoretical models, leadership styles, principles of leadership, the use of power and authority; it concludes with a scenario of the supervisor as leader.

Leadership: Views and Definitions

Leadership is seen as an important component of the supervision process, but what does it involve? Clearly, there are individuals within school organizations who are expected to demonstrate leadership abilities. For instance, superintendents, principals, and elementary and secondary coordinators are examples of various school leaders, but their position and/or title alone does not ensure leadership capability. What, then, is leadership, and what are the characteristics of leaders who are effective? These are important questions for supervisors to pursue as they work with teachers in continuously improving the teaching–learning process.

Like the term supervision, leadership has many definitions based on historical circumstances and the views of theorists and researchers. For Greenberg and Baron (1997), "leadership resembles love: it is something most people believe they can recognize but often find difficult to define" (p. 433). It is sometimes used synonymously with administration and management (McPherson, Crowson, and Pitner, 1986). Jewell (1998), however, suggests that leadership involves the art of inducing compliance through the use of influence or persuasion. Leadership has also been viewed in terms of personal traits and behavior, influence and interaction patterns, roles and positions, and the perceptions of others (Yukl, 1994). Bennis and Nanus (1997) have written that leadership is "the most studied and least understood topic" (p. 19); Wiles and Bondi (1986) have noted that there are over 130 definitions of leadership found in the educational literature. Terry (1993) cautions that leadership is not "techniques, quick fixes, or heroics" but rather a "mode of engagement with life, requiring a lifelong commitment to growing toward human fulfillment" (pp. 14–15). Lambert (1998) says that leadership involves

> learning together and constructing meaning and knowledge collectively and collaboratively—to reflect on and make sense of work in the light of shared beliefs and create actions that grow out of these new understandings (pp. 5–6).

A sample of other definitions of leadership that have appeared in the literature include:

- Behaviors of an individual as he or she directs the activities of a group toward a common goal (Hemphill and Coons, 1950)
- Creating a vision that gives an organization an identity and putting that vision into action through interaction with members as they seek to do the right things (Bennis and Nanus, 1997)
- Behaviors associated with creating and managing organizational culture (Schein, 1985)
- Behaviors associated with moving a group or organization toward a higher level of achievement (Hitt, 1988)

- Process whereby one person influences others to attain group or organizational goals (Yukl, 1994)
- Group members modifying the motivation or competence of others in the group (Bass and Avolio, 1994)

As these definitions indicate, leadership is a complex, multifaceted concept with many nuances involved in the application of the process (Rudnitski, 1996).

Of all the definitions of leadership presented, most can be classified according to one or two basic perspectives. One perspective, *structure,* refers to how the leader organizes and influences people to behave in ways that result in the attainment of goals. The second perspective, *consideration,* examines the ways leaders influence people regarding their feelings of importance, dignity, and commitment. In discussing the importance of structure and consideration as they relate to leadership, Fleishman and Harris (1962) state: "Structures include behavior in which the supervisor organizes and defines group activities and his [or her] relation to the group" (p. 43). The role each member is to assume is defined along with the task(s) members are to achieve. According to these authors, "Consideration includes behavior indicating mutual trust, respect, and a certain warmth and rapport between the supervisor and his [or her] group" (p. 44). The emphasis of this perspective is on a deeper concern for people and their needs and for encouraging them to participate in the decision-making process.

Halpin (1966), who conducted studies concerning structure and consideration with regard to leadership in schools, explains the concepts in the following way: Initiating structure refers to the supervisor's ability to define the relationship between himself or herself and the members with whom he or she works in well-defined patterns of organization and channels of communication, as well as methods and procedures to follow. Greenberg and Baron (1997) note that initiating structure activities is designed to enhance productivity or performance; leaders who employ this perspective are generally task-oriented. Consideration refers to the supervisor's ability to establish a warm, caring relationship with the members of the work group based on mutual respect and trust. Greenberg and Baron (1997) describe consideration as those actions that demonstrate a concern for the welfare of others; leaders who employ this perspective are generally people-oriented. Clearly, leadership is a function of organization and relationships within a group. A comprehensive, people-oriented definition is provided by Knezevich (1984), who says:

> Leadership is a process of stimulating, developing, and working with people within an organization. It is a human-oriented process and focuses upon personnel motivation, human relationships or social interactions, interpersonal communications, organizational climate, interpersonal conflicts, personal growth and development, and enhancement of the productivity of human factors in general. (p. 60)

Putting all of these definitions together, we see a common thread that suggests action. Leaders inspire other people to do things, to take action, or to respond in some way. Therefore, we see *supervisory leadership as the ability to motivate teachers and other educators to perform tasks and/or take actions that help the campus and/or school district achieve their goals and fulfill their mission.*

Leaders and Managers

Frequently in organizations, the terms leader and manager or leadership and management are used interchangeably, but for Greenberg and Baron (1997), the "two need to be clearly distinguished" (p. 434). Kotter (1990) says that leaders create the essence or mission of an organization—its reason for being—while managers are responsible for helping achieve the mission or vision. There are many authors who make a distinction between leading and managing; Bennis (1989) says that "leaders...do the right thing; managers...do things right" (p. 18). Covey (1989) adds, "Leadership is not management" (p. 101); before you can manage, you have to lead because leadership comes first. ASCD (1988) describes management as handling tasks, analyzing data, weighing alternatives, and making decisions by applying established principles or "doing it by the book" (p. 6). Leadership, on the other hand, "involves reaching the emotions of people through effective communication and making one's presence felt through example" (p. 6); it is a process that involves obtaining cooperation from others to achieve shared goals and objectives.

Bennis and Nanus (1997) view managers differently from leaders. Managers are in charge of things, solve problems, use procedures for finding solutions, and make sure that things are done properly. They know how to get the job done using a process orientation and tend to continue or maintain what is already in place. Leaders, on the other hand, have a vision of what can be, and what the organization can become. They have the ability to analyze and synthesize information, to see the whole rather than the parts, and to build commitment to the shared vision or mission.

In the beginning of Glasser's *The Quality School* (1990), Uroff makes a distinction between "boss managers" and "lead managers." When implementing a "boss manager" style, behaviors include driving people, relying on authority, saying "I" or "me," creating fear, knowing how, creating resentment, fixing blame, making work a drudgery, and ordering people to do their job. Conversely, the "lead manager" relies on cooperation, says we, creates confidence, shows how, generates enthusiasm, fixes mistakes, makes work interesting, calls for and recognizes group achievement, and helps people do their job better. When framing these behaviors within the context of supervisory management and supervisory leadership, several qualities surface. These qualities include:

Supervisory Management	*Supervisory Leadership*
Implementing a vision for an organization	Creating a vision—mission— and building commitment to organization goals

Supervisory Management	*Supervisory Leadership*
Identifying who to blame	Determining the problem and working to find answers/solutions
Focusing attention on doing things right	Focusing on the big picture and common goals
Reinforcing rewards for individual performance	Recognizing the group and team effort
Taking charge and telling people how and what to do better	Fostering cooperation and posing the question, How can I be of assistance?

From this list, supervisory leadership qualities include creating a vision, examining the process to prevent future problems, and fostering cooperation. Supervisors must strive to incorporate these qualities into their leadership behavior as they work with teachers in school improvement efforts.

Essential Leadership Qualities

Throughout this chapter, leadership has been described in general terms, but in this section, qualities of leadership will be discussed in some detail. According to the literature, leaders have the following qualities (Greenleaf, 1991; Costa and Garmston, 1994; Goldhammer, Anderson, and Krajewski, 1993; Bennis and Nanus, 1997; Greenberg and Baron, 1997):

- A vision with high but realistic goals that create a culture that guides the organization and its members
- Trust in people and prompt, frequent, and concrete feedback to them as they use their interpersonal skills to work effectively with others
- An ability to communicate with teachers and others
- Integrity—characterized by honesty and a willingness to take personal responsibility for their behavior and actions (a willingness to be a servant first)
- An ability to diagnose, select appropriate processes and procedures, and take risks
- An ability to unite effort with purpose

Supervisors as leaders build a following because they recognize the role of the organization's history—where the organization has been and where it wants to go. By reviewing the organization's past through talking with people as well as reading the vision and mission statements, values implicit in the vision are shared with its members. A culture develops around the history of the organization, which reinvigorates the rituals, heroes/heroines, and ceremonies. The culture helps to build an informal network among the organization's members. Ackerman, Donaldson, and Van der Bogert (1996) have found that "leaders who embrace open inquiry, the sharing of problems and solutions, and collective responsibility will foster creativity, resourcefulness, and collaboration in the work of staff and the learning of children" (p. 3).

A Vision That Guides the Organization.   One of the key qualities of leadership identified by Carr (1995) is vision. Vision suggests the mental picture of some desirable future of the organization (Bennis and Nanus, 1997). In fact, Lashway (1997) says that the "experts continue to regard it [vision] as a make-or-break task for the leader" (p. 1). Not only must leaders have a clear vision of the organization, they must be able to communicate that vision to all members of the organization (Carr, 1995). As leaders create a vision, they seek agreement on the values, beliefs, purposes, and goals that serve to focus action and shape the behavior of teachers and others in the school (Conley, 1996). Sergiovanni (1994) says that vision creates a community of purpose or mind and establishes the norms for action. It is frequently easier said than done, however, because supervisors are altering "thinking patterns, belief systems, and mind sets" (Glanz, 1994, p. 582).

Visionary leadership establishes a tension between the real and ideal which causes people to work together to close the gap (Fritz, 1996). This struggle with what is and what might be becomes the dynamic between the mission and vision. The mission is the action plan to make the vision a reality. For Calebrese and Zepeda (1997), each supervisor must answer the question, "What is my vision?" in a "personal, professional, and organizational sense" (p. 12). They further note that "A supervisor without a vision cannot have an effective mission" while "a supervisor with a vision and no mission will accomplish little" (pp. 13–14). The ability of supervisors to create an effective vision may ultimately provide the mechanism for reconnecting schools to a public that is often disenfranchised and alienated (Mathews, 1996). Finally, Hong (1996) suggests vision is an evolutionary process based on a leader's continuous reflection, action, and reevaluation.

Trust and the Use of Interpersonal Skills to Work with Others.   Of all these qualities, trust is one of the most important in order for leaders to be effective. Trust has a direct bearing on supervisory effectiveness because it is key to developing high-quality relationships. Many would assert that trust building is the single most important quality for supervisors. Supervisors must work to establish a trust account with teachers and others; without trust, they are limited as effective leaders because in the leadership game, trust is the ante, the toll, or the initial deposit. Supervisors play an important, influential role in building trust among faculty and staff in a school. The importance of building trust cannot be overstated because, without trust, "neither the supervisor nor the teacher will grow from classroom experiences" (Arrendondo, et al., 1995, p. 76).

With the quality of trust critical to effective leadership, the Association for Supervision and Curriculum Development (1988) identified the following seven suggestions that supervisors can use to establish a climate of trust in a school culture: (1) Follow through on commitments and obligations and keep your word; (2) ensure what you say is accurate and, when appropriate, maintain confidentiality;

(3) provide praise for group and individual achievement and share credit when it is due; (4) be accessible and available to discuss ideas and issues with others; (5) attend to how you say something and never correct in public; (6) solicit feedback from others and delegate responsibilities; and (7) recognize that conflict is inevitable and use it to strengthen relationships in the organization.

Covey (1989) also emphasizes the importance of trust by saying that it "is the highest form of human motivation. It brings out the very best in people" (p. 178). Covey (1990) further elaborates on the nature of trust by calling it "the emotional bank account between two people that enables them to have a win-win...agreement...and is the root of success or failure in...business, industry, education, and government" (p. 31). Supervisors can perform many tasks more effectively than others, but the key is that you want to empower teachers to do it. Building trust takes time and requires a commitment to training and development, but the payoff comes later.

The impact of trust on relationships can also be seen in communication. "When the trust account is high, communication is easy, instant, and effective" (Covey, 1989, p. 188). When the trust level is low, there is an atmosphere of tension and politicking, resulting in the tendency to protect one's vulnerable side. Most relationships, if they are to be satisfying and productive, require constant nurturing. Supervisors—as they work in leadership roles with other educators, parents, and community members—must be on the constant lookout for opportunities to build trust and make deposits in the trust account. Likewise, supervisors must be vigilant in removing conditions that destroy trust. Opening lines of communication and developing interpersonal relationships can offset the negative conditions and provide numerous benefits.

An Ability to Communicate.   Another key quality of an effective supervisor is the ability to communicate. Since Chapter 5 is devoted to this important process, suffice it to say here that communication influences leadership behavior and can be a barrier as supervisors and teachers use language in different ways, based on their knowledge and prior experience. Even though the same language is used, supervisors and teachers do not always get the same meaning from the same words. These nuances of the communication process will be explored in greater detail in the next chapter.

Personal Integrity and Responsibility.   Being supportive and respectful and having personal integrity are also part of the foundation of supervisor leadership. These qualities demonstrate an expression of personal regard, which helps to establish rapport. As Costa and Garmston (1994) note, "rapport is comfort with and confidence in someone during a specific interaction such as a teacher, parent, student, or colleague" (p. 42). Personal integrity embodies three components: self-knowledge, honesty of thought and action, and professional maturity. Having an awareness of one's strengths and weaknesses (as discussed in Chapter 11) enhances the supervisor's professional growth and development. Supervisors should be candid and straightforward, not deceitful, when dealing with others.

In their interactions with teachers and others, supervisors need to be genuine in their comments and make people feel intelligent and competent regarding their abilities. A businesslike relationship, which focuses on professional goals and objectives, often characterizes this interaction. Integrity is also enhanced by professional maturity. Supervisors have psychological needs within the school workplace environment, which include: ministration—the need for closeness, support, and guidance; maturation—the need for professional growth and development; and mastery—the need to feel in control of situations (Levinson, 1968). Having once served as teachers, supervisors can draw on these experiences as they support and encourage teachers in their professional journey of lifelong learning. Greenleaf (1991) further suggests that effective leaders are servants first, who "make sure that other people's highest priority needs are...served" (p. 13).

Diagnose, Select Procedures, and Take Risks.   The leadership qualities of diagnosing and selecting appropriate procedures and taking risks based on a vision are fundamental to functioning as a supervisor within a school organization. The selection of the appropriate supervision processes and data collection procedures to use in addressing instructional concerns are described in greater detail in Chapters 6 and 7. By incorporating these models and skills into their professional repertoire, supervisors have a framework that can guide their professional decisions. Chapter 12 investigates the supervisor's role as a risk taker and change agent. The ability to both formulate a vision and take action on that vision is central to implementing the change process in schools and to being an effective supervisor. These qualities of leadership, for us, form a key to transforming schools from places of isolation and rote learning to centers of learning where teachers make meaningful connections with others.

Unite Effort with Purpose.   Perhaps the capstone leadership quality is what Schomoker (1996) says is the ability to unite effort with purpose, which he notes is the key to school improvement. The goal of improved student learning is realized when teachers work together in an environment in which there is regular praise and celebration (Little, 1987). Praise and support from supervisors is a source of good feelings, and celebration of accomplishments is the prime ingredient in results-oriented leadership (Blase and Kirby, 1992; Schomoker, 1996). In Frederick County (Maryland) schools, these celebrations include an end-of-year dinner.

As leaders, supervisors have a responsibility for reinforcing collective effort and individual contributions. One manifestation of leadership is establishing goals, which comes from a results-oriented framework as well as a results-oriented leadership approach in a social context (Schomoker, 1996). Without goals, schools would not be able to maintain their momentum for making changes. Data-driven successes mean that leadership should seek "short-term results" and thus "spread hope" (Chang, Labovitz, and Rosansky, 1992, pp. 101–102). Leadership has to synthesize effort and people to create a unified, purposeful culture of confidence, which enables groups and individuals to accomplish goals.

For leaders to be more focused, positive, and supportive in their efforts with faculty, they have to incorporate some of the following strategies in their repertoire: (a) writing notes complimenting teachers on their successful teaching, their interactions with students, and their sponsorship of before- and after-school clubs; (b) giving small mementos to recognize individuals and/or group achievements; (c) taking a moment to praise during faculty and/or PTA meetings; (d) providing opportunities for teachers to share their accomplishments; and (e) writing a short column in the school and/or district newsletter to highlight campus activities and events (Wheatley, 1994). These strategies, when implemented by supervisors, help to promote a sense of efficacy among the teachers as they gain confidence and develop a belief in causes beyond themselves—the students.

Effective leadership also involves recognizing and capturing the energy in an organization rather than evoking fear and imposing solutions and structures (Bridges, 1992; Fullan and Hargreaves, 1991; Senge, 1990). Effective leaders help people to capitalize on their potential and get involved. Sorenson and Machell (1996) have observed that "successful educational leaders must understand their own belief system, learn about and understand the collectively held beliefs of members of the organization and facilitate the examination of the organizational covenant and lead others to work toward accomplishing goals which are developed consensually" (p. 4). The end result is a feeling that leaders count on their members. In such a system, workers enjoy a feeling that they are important, and that they have someone they can rely on who is willing and capable of taking risks and being honest in all dealings with them. Implicit in leadership is the concern for the personal and professional growth of others.

Theoretical Models of Leadership

Interest in leadership behavior seems ageless. As long as people have worked together in groups, leadership has been a factor in human history. One of the oldest perspectives or models of leadership can be found in the writings of Machiavelli (*The Prince*, 1952) from the early sixteenth century. Machiavelli viewed people as uncooperative, greedy, self-centered, and rebellious individuals; therefore, his recommendations on how to lead or govern emphasized the need to control people using whatever means necessary, including lying, cheating, and stealing, in order to establish order and maintain power.

Centuries later, theories of leadership behavior were based on Darwin's law of natural selection. Spencer (1927) universalized the concept of evolution by applying the principle of the survival of the fittest to human endeavors. In such a view of leadership, the fittest or ablest leaders are "characterized by aggressiveness, the urge to dominate, and a desire to acquire material possessions; all of which makes conflict within organizations unavoidable" (Knezevich, 1984, p. 56). Ethnologists Lorenz (1952) and Bowlby (1980) have noted the similarity of animal behavior to human activity in such phenomena as pecking orders, the struggle for dominance, the establishment of territory, and the expression of aggression as examples of a leader's behavior within an organizational setting.

These theories of leadership have been based on the belief that humans are motivated by strong emotions and selfish desires rather than by rational or social concerns. As indicated in the previous chapter, scientific management and Weber's view of the bureaucracy were organizational structures designed to compensate for the workers' limitations of self-centeredness and lack of motivation. McGregor (1960), however, coupled this limited view of human behavior with an opposing view and proposed two leadership theories based on differing patterns of behavior, which are manifested by individuals and leaders in an organization. His Theory X and Theory Y help to explain the contrasting views of motivation and other aspects of human behavior. Theory X focuses on human behavior that is typically characterized by the following traits. In the view of the leader:

- Individuals are basically lazy; they generally dislike to work and try to avoid it.
- Most individuals, because of their dislike for work, have to be coerced or threatened with punishment to get them to work toward the goals set by the organization.
- Because individuals tend to avoid responsibility, they need direction and the security of being told what to do.
- Individuals are not very bright and lack creativity.

Theory Y provides a completely different view of people's behavior and is characterized by the following traits. In the leader's view:

- Individuals seek work; the workplace and even work itself are pleasing and satisfying.
- Once committed to the organizational goals, individuals are self-directed and demonstrate self-control.
- Job-related rewards are based on a sense of satisfaction and self-actualization.
- Individuals seek and accept responsibility rather than avoid it.
- Individuals are creative and have ingenuity and imagination.

Depending on whether leaders adopt Theory X or Y, their view determines how they will respond to situations and people. Theory X leaders, who view members with distrust, tend to coerce and threaten in order to accomplish the task. Leaders who view individuals with this frame of reference tend to be autocratic or a boss manager in their approach to decisions and their interactions with others. Theory Y leaders, on the other hand, tend to view individuals as contributing members of the organization who continue to grow and develop in their capacities. Leaders with this frame of reference often work to create a vision for the group and demonstrate behaviors that build commitment to organizational goals.

Covey (1989) describes another theoretical model of leadership style and characteristics based on his six paradigms of human interaction. The Win/Win paradigm has five alternative paradigms—Win/Lose, Lose/Win, Lose/Lose, Win, and Win/Win or No deal. These styles and characteristics are presented in Figure 4.1. In analyzing the categories and behaviors associated with Figure 4.1, Covey (1989) suggests that

> The principle of Win/Win is fundamental to success in all our interactions…. It begins with *character* and moves toward *relationships*, out of which flow *agreements*. It is nurtured in an environment where *structure and systems* are based on Win/ Win. And it involves *process*; we cannot achieve Win/Win ends with Win/Lose or Lose/Win means. (p. 216)

If leaders are to be successful in implementing the Win/Win, they must have integrity and a commitment to mutuality and interpersonal leadership (Covey, 1989). Jaworski (1996) emphasizes the mutuality and interpersonal aspects of leadership and sees it as "the release of human possibilities…the capacity to inspire people…[and] communicating to people that you believe they matter" (p. 66).

FIGURE 4.1   Six Characteristics of Leadership Styles

Leadership Styles	Characteristics
Win/Win	Leaders constantly seek solutions that are mutually beneficial and satisfying to all stakeholders who are confident in and committed to the action plan.
Win/Lose	Leaders win at the expense of others and view the leadership process as the use of position and power to get their way. Competition and independent behavior are the norm, and cooperation and interdependence are not valued.
Lose/Win	Leaders tend to avoid confrontation and seek to appease. They frequently abdicate their responsibility to standards or success in anticipation of losing and therefore have few, if any, expectations or a vision of success.
Lose/Lose	Leaders who have lost in a win/lose situation may seek vindication although all parties may lose. Interactions are often adversarial, and others are seen as a potential enemy.
Win	Leaders seek to get what they want and think in terms of securing their own success. Each person is left to find ways to get what he or she wants.
Win/Win or No Deal	Leaders seek a solution that is agreeable to all parties, but if such a solution cannot be reached, then no deal; parties agree to disagree and no further interaction occurs.

Covey (1990) also describes "principle-centered leaders" as continuously learning, especially from their experiences. They also look for the best in others while demonstrating enthusiasm and being concerned for the needs of their members. These principle-centered leaders have lives that exhibit a balance in interests, including familial, social, intellectual, and work-related; in the process, they view the changes that occur in their lives as an adventure. They are also synergistic as they link talent and resources to be more productive. Finally, they seek self-renewal as they continue to grow and develop. Again, Jaworski (1996) sees leadership as synchronicity, or "creating the conditions for 'predictable miracles'" (p. ix).

A grid leadership model (Blake and McCanse, 1991; Blake and Mouton, 1985) suggests that in an organizational setting, leadership consists primarily of two attitudinal factors: concern for task or production and concern for people. The emphasis placed on each factor ultimately determines the kind of leadership behavior that results. Blake and Mouton (1985) note that individuals tend to have a dominant leadership style that they use most often, but when that orientation does not achieve the desired results, they then shift into a backup leadership style. These two factors—production and people—form the parameters of a leadership grid, which identifies five general kinds of managerial or leadership behaviors. Rather than a grid, we prefer to place each factor on a continuum so that when placed in such a way that they intersect at their midpoints, four quadrants are formed, as seen in Figure 4.2.

The quadrants represent the leadership styles that result from the intersection of concern for production and concern for people. In quadrant I, there is a low concern for task and a low concern for people. People with this leadership style are basically caretakers; they do just enough work to hold their positions. Leadership behavior in this quadrant might be seen as the leader approaches retirement. Some would refer to this behavior as laissez-faire leadership. In quadrant II, there is a high concern for task but a low concern for people. Leaders in this quadrant are often called taskmasters; their primary objective is to get the job done. This orientation to leadership, when carried to an extreme, is considered authoritarian or autocratic; the leader may use the behavior in this quadrant when a group must attain a goal within a limited time frame.

Quadrant III illustrates a high concern for people and a low concern for task. Leaders in this quadrant are people-oriented, and this style is referred to as human relations or human resources leadership. The primary focus is on creating an environment where people feel comfortable in their work, and the workplace becomes like a family. This human relations view of leadership employs behaviors that are designed to reduce stress and anxiety and improve morale. Quadrant IV leaders have both a high concern for task and a high concern for people. This style represents the participative or team leader, one who Maccoby (1981) says does not want to boss or be bossed. This leader works with people to get the resources to be successful in accomplishing the goals while also meeting the needs of group members. When properly employed, this style becomes collegial in nature.

Where the two lines intersect, a fifth leadership style is formed, resulting in a moderate concern for people and task. This leadership style is one of compromise

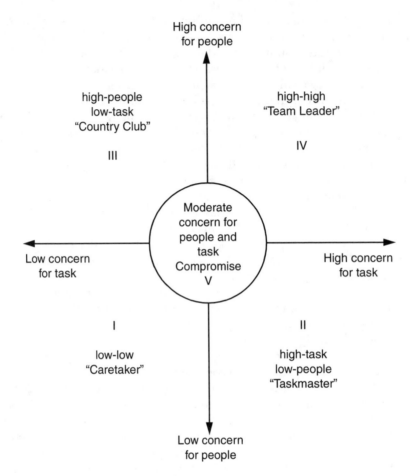

FIGURE 4.2   Leadership Styles

and negotiation, as the leader constantly seeks to balance the needs of people with the need to achieve results. Many middle-level supervisors often adopt this style as they seek to accomplish the goals and objectives of the organization and yet keep morale high in the process. To do this, they continuously make compromises to keep the peace and get results.

For many years, this grid model has been used to analyze various styles of leadership. As Daresh and Playko (1995) note, "its implications about the relative effectiveness of certain behaviors provide useful directions for any individual seeking to perform as an effective educational leader" (p. 126).

Successful leaders recognize the need to maintain a balance between a task orientation and a people orientation. Nearly two decades ago, Naisbitt (1982) observed that leaders must be both "high tech" and "high touch" if they are to be successful in any modern organization, especially schools. Maccoby (1981), in his book *The Leader,* provides another view of leadership that he suggests is important for today's leader. The leadership characteristics of this new leader are similar to those of the team leader or participative leader and have the following seven traits: (1) tolerance of strangers and flexibility in social arrangements; (2) willingness to experiment with different roles at work and in the family; (3) orientation toward lifelong learning and self-development; (4) orientation toward the continuous development of others and a willingness to support such development; (5) lack of loyalty, submission, and self-sacrifice to the organization in the traditional sense; (6) unwillingness to follow orders blindly and insistence on valid reasons for orders or directions; and (7) willingness to be productively involved in organizations that foster cooperation, demonstrate equity, and show concern for human dignity.

The leader, as envisioned by Maccoby, has a good sense of self, personal integrity, and commitment to productive relationships within both the family and the organization. As Gardner (1990) further elaborates, "If one is leading…or engaged in any other activity that involves influencing, directing, guiding, helping, or nurturing, the whole tone of the relationship is conditioned by one's faith in human possibilities. That is the generative element…that gives life to the relationship" (p. 199).

Another theoretical model of leadership suggests that environmental factors or situations determine the behavior of the leader. The proponents of this theory do not recommend a single approach to leadership; rather, they believe that the situation dictates the kind of behavior to be exhibited by the leader (Hershey and Blanchard, 1993; Yukl, 1994). According to Gorton (1987), there are situations or contexts that prompt different types of leadership, such as the task or problem, obstacles or constraints, characteristics of the members of the organization, and the qualities of the organizations themselves.

In recent years, situational leadership has gained prominence as school leaders are selected, based on their personality and professional expertise, to deal with specific school tasks. As circumstances change, these leaders can move on to other supervisory positions that best utilize their skills. The situational theory of leadership maintains that the leader is matched to the demands of the task, but there are problems as well. It may not be economically feasible to bring in leaders whose professional qualities best meet the demands of the immediate context that needs attention. If movement is not possible, it may become unreasonable to expect supervisors to change their dominant leadership style, personality, and disposition to have a better fit with the demands of the situation (Gorton, 1987).

Sergiovanni (1990) presents a more contemporary model of leadership, which he labels value-based. He identifies stages of leadership and school improvement in which he describes two general leadership types, four specific leadership styles, stages of school improvement, leadership conceptions, the type of involvement by followers, the needs being satisfied, and the end results or effects. *Bartering* is the first leadership style. The leader exchanges human needs and interests for getting the followers to agree with the organizational objectives. The second category of leadership style that is part of the value-added or transformational leadership is *building*. This style involves setting expectations for both the leader and the followers to motivate them to higher levels of commitment and performance. Leadership as *bonding* means there is a breakthrough in which the leader and the followers share a moral commitment and covenant, which bond them. In doing so, there is an increased level of awareness and consciousness, which raises the organizational goals and purposes to a higher level. The last style of leadership is *banking*, which occurs when the improvements become routinized and occur without great effort.

Finally, a new theoretical model of leadership has emerged that is an extension of the transactional leadership strategy proposed by Bass (1981). The transactional model focused on the interactions or exchanges that occurred between and among leaders, colleagues, and others as they discussed the agreements that shaped their behavior. For Bass and Avolio (1994), transformational leadership occurs as leaders: (a) encourage others to view their work from different perspectives; (b) create an awareness of the purpose or mission of the group; (c) foster the development of higher levels of ability and success in others; and (d) motivate others to transcend their own interests so that the group will benefit. As Bass and Avolio (1994) observe, "Transformational leaders motivate others to do more than they originally intended and often more than they thought possible" (p. 3). Avolio, Waldman, and Yammarino (1991) suggest that transformational leaders employ one or more of the "Four I's" to achieve superior results. The Four I's are:

1. *Idealized influence*—Transformational leaders serve as role models for others, especially followers, and are admired, respected, and trusted. They can be counted on to do the right thing and maintain high standards.

2. *Inspirational motivation*—Transformational leaders motivate and inspire others by providing a challenge and meaning to their work. Team morale, enthusiasm, and positive outlook are enhanced and evident. The leader involves others in thinking about attractive future outcomes or states.

3. *Intellectual stimulation*—Transformational leaders encourage and prompt others to be innovative and think of alternatives by questioning, rethinking problems, and examining their work in new and different ways. When people engage in creative problem solving, their ideas and mistakes are not criticized, and they are encouraged to try their ideas.

4. *Individualized consideration*—Transformational leaders serve as coaches and mentors in the professional growth and development of their members and acknowledge each person's need to be successful. They listen to others and delegate tasks to provide opportunities for success. They monitor progress and provide additional encouragement as needed in a supportive environment.

Sheppard (1996) notes that the trend in leadership is away from the technological, rational planning models "toward cultural, collaborative approaches in which teachers are viewed as partners" (p. 328). He agrees with Larocque and

Coleman (1991), who suggest that the creation of a school ethos that emphasizes a shared vision and collaboration is more in keeping with transformational leadership. Leithwood (1992, 1994) says that transformational leadership is important in meeting the challenges facing schools today. In the transformational leadership model, the leader pays attention to individuals and provides opportunities for them to achieve and grow in a supportive environment. Such a leader interacts freely in a two-way dialogue that can be characterized as more personalized. In such a model, the members are intended to be involved and to develop tasks based on their needs and desires (Evans, 1996).

As our understanding of people and the way they behave in organizations increases over time, so too will our understanding of leadership behavior. From the historical perspectives on leadership models, it is evident that certain behaviors and styles are more appropriate than others. These theoretical models can provide supervisors with a wide range of qualities and behaviors from which to choose as they attempt to develop their personal leadership profile.

Supervisory Leadership Styles

Supervisory leadership can be classified from a variety of perspectives. The first classification is the broadest and includes laissez-faire, autocratic, and democratic. These three styles have been described by Giammatteo (1975) and referred to in the previous section. Another classification, proposed by Glickman (1990), includes directive, collaborative, and nondirective. The third classification of styles (Blake and McCanse, 1991; Blake and Mouton, 1985), which was discussed earlier in this chapter, includes caretaker, country club leader, taskmaster, compromiser, and team leader. While it should be clear that one style is not inherently superior to another, there are distinct advantages and disadvantages associated with each, based on several constructs—vision, motivation, conflict management, decision making, communication, change, and fellowship (Carr, 1995).

Since the grid styles (Blake and McCanse, 1991; Blake and Mouton, 1985) were discussed earlier in this chapter and Glickman's styles will be discussed in Chapter 6, Giammatteo's traditional styles are presented here. A *laissez-faire* leadership style is just what the term suggests—to do little or nothing as a leader, and let others do as they choose. In implementing the laissez-faire leadership style, members go their own way. The greatest advantage of this style is that there is little work for the leader, and when group members are self-starters, the leader has to do very little to look good. There might be rare occasions when it would be advisable for the leader to adopt this style, but only for a short period when it is necessary to wait and see. Some of the disadvantages of this style include lower productivity or task accomplishment, poorer quality of work, and less satisfaction with work.

An *autocratic* leadership style is a directive approach in which the leader tells others what to do; all or most decisions are made by the leader, generally without considering the needs or wishes of group members. Distinct advantages of this leadership approach are that decisions can be made quickly and productivity tends to be higher—but only while the leader is present. Disadvantages include greater hostility from group members, more dependence on the leader, increased apathy, and a decrease in productivity when the leader is absent.

A *democratic* leadership style involves a participative approach to leadership, with individuals having input into decisions affecting programs and operations and the leader serving to help the group meet its needs and goals. The leader shows respect for group members; he or she offers direction but does not take total control. Generally, the advantages outweigh the disadvantages. Benefits include greater individual responsibility, more motivation and individual growth, higher morale, and more efficient implementation. One significant disadvantage is the length of time it can take to make a decision or arrive at a clear consensus.

Carr (1995) has summarized the various styles of leadership and suggests that they can be expressed along a continuum that ranges from autocratic to transactional to participative and finally to transformational. The traits or constructs that define leadership style include vision, motivation, conflict management, decision making, communication, change, and fellowship. Depending on the situation, the leader may need to assume an autocratic style if a task needs to be completed quickly. Generally, the democratic style would result in a greater sense of collaboration, accomplishment, and ownership. Each style, however, could be viable in specific situations. Figure 4.3 provides a summary of the basic leadership styles (autocratic, democratic, and laissez-faire) and includes characteristic behaviors related to mission and goals (vision), motivation, decision making, and change. As Figure 4.3 illustrates, each style has a set of leader behaviors that guide and shape what is done to get results in an organization. Although no single style is best, the democratic style clearly produces the greatest amount of collegiality and cooperation.

Leadership Principles

Instructional leaders, to be effective as they interact with teachers and others, should be knowledgeable about the general guiding practices of leadership as reflected in the literature. The list provided is a compilation of research from a variety of sources (Alfonso, Firth, and Neville, 1981; ASCD, 1988; Bennis and Nanus, 1997; Carr, 1995; Goldhammer, Anderson, and Krajewski, 1993; Lovell and Wiles, 1983). These 10 guiding principles provide insights into the individual, group, and organizational dimensions of leadership:

1. Leadership is not the result of any single personality trait or combination of traits.

2. Leadership is widespread and diffuse throughout an organization; it is a group role and is largely determined by the expectations of the group.

3. Leadership is a function of the frequency of interaction with members of the group; it determines the flow of information in the organization and whether communication is effective.

FIGURE 4.3   **Basic Leadership Styles**

Selected Traits	Autocratic	Democratic	Lassez-Faire
Vision (Mission and Goals)	Mission and goal identified at the top and communicated from the top down to the members of the organization	Mission and goals commonly developed and shared throughout the organization	Mission and goals usually missing; members follow their own personal and professional goals
Motivation	Reward structure and interest developed extrinsically; individuals seek affirmation from leader	Rewards and interest generated intrinsically; individuals and group members affirm each other	Rewards and interest may or may not be present; members must motivate themselves
Decision Making	Centralized decision making from the top down; little, if any, input from teachers and staff; decisions made in response to a situation or to prevent a problem	Decision making is a group function accomplished through a collaborative process occurring proactively; input provided by members when the situation warrants	Decision making is haphazard, sometimes alone and sometimes with others; decisions often made on an as-needed basis
Change	Change facilitated through mandates initiated by those in power when deemed necessary	Change involves stakeholders (teachers and staff); group input and feedback considered in the process; change is reached through consensus	Change may or may not occur; change depends on individual teachers and staff members and their level of satisfaction

4. Status and position do not necessarily guarantee leadership, but leadership will be enhanced if the leader has status and power in the organization.

5. Leadership can be enhanced by maintaining some degree of psychological distance from members of the group.

6. Leadership styles generate different and predictable responses and patterns of achievement among group members, and the leader should be aware of his or her dominant leadership style.

7. Leadership effectiveness is impacted by the feelings individuals have about the leaders, norms of the group, organizational conditions, ability to perform needed group functions, and gender of the leader and members of the group.

8. Leadership behavior is perceived differently by subordinates (group members) and superiors (bosses) and treats conflict as an opportunity for growth.

9. Leadership is enhanced when leaders are visionary and can identify what motivates their members.

10. Leadership is strengthened when it provides for active participation in decision making and involves members' mental and emotional states.

These 10 principles form a conceptual framework that supervisors can use as they consider appropriate behaviors for a particular school/educational situation.

Power and Authority: Their Use in School Organizations

As leaders, supervisors have at their disposal and may use various kinds of power and authority. The intent of both is to ensure that schools are effective in carrying out their mission. Power has been examined in many different educational contexts and across numerous subject areas (O'Hare and Blase, 1992). Power has been defined by Bennis and Nanus (1997) as "the basic energy needed to initiate and sustain action or,…the *capacity to translate intention into reality and sustain it*" (p. 16). Greenberg and Baron (1997) see power as "the ability to change the behavior or attitudes of others in a desired manner" (p. 402). Alfonso, Firth, and Neville (1981) describe the importance of authority by suggesting that it "can be expressed by various members of a formal organization and is not restricted to those holding formal offices" (p. 65). The purpose of power and authority, then, is to obtain from individuals voluntary compliance with requests. "Most teachers do what…[is] ask[ed] of them because they feel that [supervisors] have a legitimate right to make demands" (Tye and Tye, 1984, p. 321). Therefore, a supervisor's power and authority are inherent in the position or associated with the responsibilities assigned and the expression of leadership.

The use of power in organizations, or the micro-politics of schools is designed to achieve organizational goals, influence others, and protect oneself; it determines how effective supervisors ultimately are in carrying out their responsibilities (O'Hare and Blase, 1992). To get others to carry out their assignments or responsibilities, leaders may use different types of power. What types of power have been identified? To help answer this question, descriptions of the kinds of power used by supervisors when working with teachers and peers seems appropriate. These definitions come from qualitative and quantitative research studies; the various types of power are explained in the following section.

Supervisors use various kinds of power to foster or obtain compliance with organizational rules and goals. Etzioni (1965) was one of the earliest to describe the types of power, which include coercive, utilitarian, and identitive, that leaders can use. The use of force or the threat of force is considered *coercive power*. In schools, the threat of nonrenewal of a contract or job is an example of the use of coercive power. Providing rewards of a material or service nature is an illustration of *utilitarian power*. This kind of power is often used when the supervisor views the organization from a political perspective. For example, granting an extra planning period, providing a teacher's aide, or giving a pay bonus is using utilitarian power, which is often employed within the structural view of organizations. The use of symbols and prestige would represent *identitive power*. For a teacher to be selected to teach an honors course or to be recognized as the "Teacher of the Year" would be an example of identitive power. This type of power is often a tool for supervisors who view the school organization from a symbolic perspective. All three types of power are designed to shape behavior in ways that meet the school mission and accomplish the goals and objectives of the school organization.

French and Raven (1959) and Greenberg and Baron (1997) have proposed eight different types of power available to leaders. While some differ from those described above, there are common elements in both sets. The eight kinds of power are:

1. *Position power*—Based on the individual's formal position in the organization (organizational chart). This power comes from the specific job assignment and is given to anyone who holds that position. The superintendent of schools has power as a result of the office he or she holds.

2. *Legitimate power*—Based on the recognition and acceptance by others of one's authority within the organization and as an extension of position. The use of legitimate power is illustrated in the following statement: "As principal of this school, I have decided to name you as…"

3. *Reward power*—Based on the ability to provide members with valued rewards. Examples of reward power would be statements like: "From reading the results of the survey I distributed, I see that you are interested in…" "Maybe we can obtain additional release time so you can implement that idea." Inherent in this dialogue is a willingness to accommodate the person by providing a valued reward.

4. *Coercive power*—Based on the capacity to punish, or to threaten to punish, by such means as dismissal, lower evaluation ratings, or less desirable teaching assignments. For example, a statement such as, "You have conducted yourself in an unacceptable manner; if you don't change your behavior, you will leave me no choice but to…" illustrates coercive power. Coercive power is normally used when data indicate that there are problems or concerns with an individual and a decision regarding the status of continued employment needs to be made.

5. *Information power*—Based on access to or specific detailed information about the organization. The idea that "knowledge is power" illustrates this method. For example, the supervisor might have inside information and say, "I know how the organizational chart will be drawn and which positions will be eliminated so…"

6. *Personal power*—Based on one's individual qualities or characteristics and often viewed as charisma. Power generally comes from making others feel good about themselves and inspires trust and loyalty. For example, a supervisor using personal power might tell others, "You are a valued member of this school. I applaud you on a job well done!"

7. *Expert power*—Based on an individual's specialized knowledge or skill, such as computer programming capabilities, that benefits the organization. Using this example, expert power is communicated by saying, "I have the data system in the computer for correlating grades and attendance and can identify potential strengths and weaknesses in the instructional program."

8. *Referent power*—Based on the degree to which one is liked and admired by others and the association individuals have with other people in leadership positions. The use of referent power is seen in the following: "You have trusted me in the past and I would like you to continue to do so now." Another example would be when a teacher works closely with a supervisor and takes on extra duties, and this teacher is perceived to have power because of his or her association with the supervisor. Supervisors increase their referent power when they become advocates for teachers and students.

The supervisor's total power is the sum of these eight forms; the only power actually conferred on the supervisor in the organization is positional power. The supervisor's total power can be strengthened or weakened by the use or nonuse of the various kinds of power. Using this formula as an example, supervisors with little formal, positional, or legitimate power might still have significant authority through friendships, respect from the teachers, or expertise in an area. According to Terry (1993), "The underlying fact…is that no one person or group is totally powerful or powerless. There are always options and consequences" (p. 204). Position power, which comes from the official position in the organization, is only one element, and its effectiveness might be determined by the presence or absence of the seven other types of power.

Covey (1990) also suggests that supervisors have a choice of the power they wish to use; these powers include coercion, utility, and principle-centered. *Coercive power* is based on fear and is used to get people to comply with requests. Covey (1990) continues by saying, "It is relatively easy when push comes to shove and the pressures are on,…to force someone else to follow[;]…it is almost impossible not to resort to force when a leader is in the middle of a crisis" (p. 105). Supervisors who attempt to control through coercion and fear will find that compliance is temporary, and such an approach can ultimately result in alienation, suspicion, and deceit.

In discussing the ways that organizations function, Covey notes that *utility power* holds most organizations together by offering members something they want. He says that supervisors "are followed because it is functional for the followers" (p. 103). Supervisors can multiply their influence and reduce alienation by opting to use utility power to promote people to new positions, provide additional resources, and/or encourage and reward new responsibilities and relationships.

Covey (1990) describes the third kind as *principle-centered power,* and it is rare because it is based on honor between supervisors and members of the organization as well as the overlap of values, which results in sustained and proactive influence. In such a situation, supervisors have the respect and loyalty of their group members, and supervisors' behavior is based on a sense of self-control, purpose, vision, and ethics. The supervisor who chooses principle-centered power must invest in a long-term commitment by building trust and demonstrating sincerity. As Covey (1990) explains, what supervisors do beyond what they provide for teachers "ultimately determines the depth of principle-centered power" (p. 105).

Closely associated with authority and power is the feeling of intimidation. Supervisors may feel intimidated when dealing with powerful individuals, or they may fail to take action because they are afraid of peers, superiors, and/or subordinates. The best shield against intimidation is competence, confidence, and following procedures that have been established. By knowing their jobs, carrying out their assignments with confidence, and following district procedures and implementing them, supervisors should not feel threatened by others and should be better at asserting themselves. Likewise, they must guard against using intimidating tactics with others because such behavior undermines trust.

Others offer a different interpretation of power. Gorton (1987) suggests that influence, rather than power, might be a better term. In recent years, researchers have identified techniques that supervisors use to influence others in the organization (Schriesheim and Hinkin, 1990; Yukl and Tracey, 1992; Yukl, Falbe, and Youn, 1993). These techniques include using arguments and facts (rational persuasion), appealing to values and ideas (inspirational appeal), asking for involvement in planning and decision making (consultation), putting others in a good mood or getting them to like you (integration), appealing to others' feelings of loyalty or friendship (personal appeal), and asking for support or involvement of others (coalition building). Since power is implicit in many supervisory situations, it seems unlikely that a teacher who does not want to comply will do so because of the power of the supervisor, but rather due to the influence techniques employed.

In reality, the whole issue of power becomes less important in the context of supervision as presented in this text. Since supervision is described as a collaborative process, there is a partnership established for achieving instructional effectiveness. In this contextual situation, there is less need for power because the emphasis is on establishing a trusting, collaborative relationship and avoiding punishing while enhancing members' intrinsic desire to improve. Nevertheless, it is important for supervisors to understand the concept of power and its implications when dealing with diverse groups within the school organization.

A View from the Field

After serving as superintendent of a large suburban district for five years, Mrs. Samuels is ready to retire. She takes a few moments to answer the following six questions in an interview with a reporter from the local paper. As she responds, she draws upon not only her recent experience in supervisory positions but the accumulated wisdom of over 20 years as a school leader.

> REPORTER: What supervisory qualities contributed to your success in the district, given the financial conditions and the low morale of the teachers and staff when you arrived?

SUPERINTENDENT: I am a good analyzer; I see the big picture. Because of the severity of the situation, I wanted to be honest with people. I moved quickly in conducting an analysis of the situation. I want to be clear that I certainly have not been successful alone. I have had help—help from others. But I am good at recognizing the barriers; with the help of my staff, we developed a strategy for creating an environment for dialogue and consensus building. I believe that working together is the only way problems can be solved. A superintendent can't do it alone; it takes a team of committed individuals who are concerned for and committed to the children.

REPORTER: During your tenure in this district, what was your vision for the school district when you arrived and now five years later?

SUPERINTENDENT: When I arrived here, I saw a dedicated and hardworking staff who were confronted with a lack of resources to do their jobs effectively. My vision became one of locating resources that would allow them to continue to serve the education community in their extraordinary way. It was evident to me that just working harder when they were already overworked was not the answer, so working smarter with more resources was an important part of my vision. For me, if the teachers and staff members are content and happy, it transfers to the children as well. Also, I worked hard in getting the district to establish a strong relationship with the community.

REPORTER: Women administrators and how they have overcome the "glass ceiling" have been in the news a lot lately. As the first female superintendent of this district, do you think your job has been harder? Did you have to prove yourself? Do you think that women's supervisory styles are different from men's?

SUPERINTENDENT: By serving as the first female superintendent of this district, I hope that girls, as well as boys, see that as long as they have the drive, desire, and commitment, they can be whatever they choose to be; for them, I hope I have been a role model to be emulated. And as far as the glass ceiling is concerned, I remember being asked during the interview, Do you think you can make the tough decisions? The implication was that women are soft, but my answer was, I have made all types of decisions and I am committed to making any decision that is in the best interests of the students in this district.

I think there are differing leadership styles among all supervisors; the styles do not have to be confrontational but can be complementary. As I view the question globally, supervisors are taking on qualities that strengthen their abilities. Some men in leadership positions are taking on what has been called the "soft approaches" that are often used to characterize female leaders. Likewise, women are taking on the more traditional leadership styles. In an article by Nelton (1991), Judith Hoy comments on this topic when she notes that "female leadership traits can help companies solve three major problems—the need for better customer service, the demand for higher quality, and the need for leadership itself" (p. 16); I agree with Ms. Hoy.

REPORTER: What leadership qualities have you looked for in others who work with you?

SUPERINTENDENT: Foremost is the ability to listen. When you are in the education business, listening is three-fourths of the job. A leader needs to be clear about what the issues are before the next steps can be taken. Coupled with listening is the ability to communicate a message that is supportive yet shows concern for the welfare of the children of the district. It may seem trite, but trust is essential. All leaders need to be trustworthy and have integrity; they need to be models that children, parents, teachers, and staff look up to. Knowledge and experience in instructional strategies, curriculum design, and implementation are important, too. To borrow a phrase, I look for those who not only walk the walk but talk the talk. Finally, I look for people who are visionaries themselves, who think in terms of what might be possible, and who then work to create an environment in which their vision can become a reality.

REPORTER: During your time as superintendent, you have been recognized as a successful leader as you moved the district to solvency, initiated the use of computers as classroom instructional tools, provided necessary staff development, and implemented pay raises, especially for teachers. However, there have been moments in the last year when your leadership was questioned or challenged. What has been your reaction, and how have you addressed the concerns?

SUPERINTENDENT: I have been single-minded about what I felt needed to be done. The members of the community, the teachers, the school board members, and even some of the students shared freely what they thought I should do. I have worked hard to meet these challenges, but I think the one thing that has worked for me over the past 20 years is to seek open and honest feedback from those who question what is done. I tried to involve the critics, to make them a part of the solution, which freed me from defending future actions. As stakeholders, they become the defenders of the policy. For the most part, this collaborative strategy has worked. There is still more to be done. In the last 8 months, my critics have questioned some of my decisions regarding emotionally charged issues; given time, I think that this strategy would work again. But at this point in my life, I am ready to take some time off and be with my family.

REPORTER: Any final thoughts?

SUPERINTENDENT: I feel good about the progress we have made with regard to student success, not only on standardized tests and performance measures but in areas of their lives that are often difficult to measure. I also think the morale in the district is the highest it has been in years, and people who feel good about themselves and their work are more productive. It has been challenging over the past five years, but I will have many memories to take away with me and cherish in the years ahead.

Summary

This chapter focused on leadership theory as it applies to supervisors. By becoming supervisors, individuals also accept leadership roles within the school organization. It is leadership that links the administrative and managerial functions with curriculum and teaching functions with the goal of effective instruction. Leadership is a critical component in promoting school effectiveness, and the research is clear in linking strong leadership with successful schools.

The chapter began with a discussion of various views and definitions of leadership. There are many definitions of leadership; in fact, Wiles and Bondi (1986) suggest that there are over 130 different definitions. This chapter provided several important definitions for instructional leaders/supervisors to consider as they examine their own understanding of the leadership process. Often, the way leadership is defined is determined by the roles and responsibilities of the leader. As our understanding of people and the way they behave in organizational settings has grown, so too has our understanding of leadership behavior. Two perspectives of leadership focus on structure, or the way the leader organizes people to accomplish a task, and consideration, which examines the leader's relationship with others. In the section on leaders and managers, it is clear that their roles are perceived differently, and they often perform different tasks.

Next, the chapter discussed various leadership qualities considered essential to being successful. They include having a vision that creates a culture of success, establishing trust, communicating effectively, demonstrating personal integrity, diagnosing situations to establish processes and procedures, and creating unity of purpose. Leaders understand the beliefs and needs of their members and work to accomplish goals that have been developed consensually.

Various theoretical models were examined next. The concepts and theories of leadership proposed by Machiavelli, Spencer, McGregor, Covey, Blake and Mouton, Maccoby, and others illustrate how leadership is the result of patterns of behavior and responses from members within an organization. It is evident that there is no one best theory of leadership, but it is also true that, under particular circumstances, some theories are more appropriate than others. By being aware of the range of leadership views and theories, instructional leaders/supervisors will be able to develop their own leadership behavior.

In understanding leadership behavior, it is also important to discuss leadership styles. Common leadership styles identified in the literature include laissez-faire, autocratic, and democratic. Each of these styles is briefly described, and each may be appropriate for a given situation. Next, the chapter synthesized the research done on leadership and presented a list of leadership principles to guide and direct the behavior of supervisors. These principles provide insights into the individual, group, and organizational dimensions of leadership behavior.

As supervisors interact with teachers and others within the school organization, they wield power and authority. The various kinds of power often employed by supervisors were discussed. It is important for supervisors to understand the uses of power in order to use it well. The intent of the use of power is to have individuals voluntarily comply with the rules and regulations of the organization.

Finally, in A View From the Field, a set of interview questions was posed to a superintendent. It is evident from her responses that trust building is an essential leadership quality. She goes on to say that building trust may be the single most important quality, since all else may hinge on the trust level in the schools. In her five years as superintendent, she has found that other essential qualities of leaders include: communication, modeling, integrity, diagnosis, selection of appropriate processes and procedures, and sometimes even some risk taking.

YOUR TURN

4.1. You may be curious about which leadership behaviors you possess and exhibit; these may be evident after engaging in the following exercise. If you had to design a coat of arms for yourself, what would you include that would describe you and communicate to others what is important to you? Use any shape for your coat of arms, being sure to have four places to write information. Take a few minutes to jot down several of your ideas or adjectives that best describe you; then put these in visual form (review the list and several leadership qualities as presented in the chapter).

4.2. Audiotape a role-playing situation—a meeting between a teacher and you, with you playing the supervisor. The focus of the mock meeting is a disagreement regarding a change in the teacher's assignment. After the meeting, analyze the dialogue using French and Raven's list of types of power. How many times did you [supervisor] use reward, coercive, or other types of power statements? How many ways did you communicate the idea that you are in charge and therefore said "you must" as opposed to providing reasons for the change in his or her teaching assignment?

4.3. Role-play the three leadership styles: laissez-faire, autocratic, and democratic. Have three groups construct a building using straws and masking tape. Have one participant role-play one specific leadership style in each group. The participant role playing the laissez-faire style, for example, takes on those qualities of that leader: Participants assuming autocratic and democratic styles role-play in their respective group. Each group should work in a different location so that there is no opportunity for hearing or sharing ideas. The objective of the exercise is to move the group members along to construct a building that is pleasant to view, free-standing, and tall with a leader exhibiting a specific style. After 20 minutes, the groups come back together again and describe the role of the leader and what transpired during the group activity. Finally, the building that meets all three criteria, judged by a neutral person, wins. A discussion should follow regarding what style of leadership was used and why, whether it helped, and why, etc.

4.4. How would you respond to this quotation: "Leadership style is an extension of one's view of people, task, power, and authority"? Do you agree or disagree with this statement? Why?

4.5. Several theoretical models of leadership are presented in the chapter. Taking the ideas of Bennis and Nanus, how would you characterize a leader and a manager? How do these authors view failure, success, and learning? For more information, see *Leaders*. It might be interesting to contrast their ideas regarding leadership with those of Stephen Covey in *The 7 Habits of Highly Effective People*.

4.6. You are in a situation in which you have neither a budget nor a staff that is responsible to you. Your title is sufficiently vague to encourage a variety of interpretations of your supervisory role. Yet, as an instructional supervisor, you are expected to improve the overall climate for teaching and learning in a school district. You are told after you accept the position that about the only real power you have is "the power of persuasion." How will you meet the expectations of your assignment with this type of power and authority? As you develop short-range and long-range plans, use the principles of leadership outlined in the chapter to guide you.

4.7. You and several of the teachers in the school district attended classes together at a local university. Over the years, you have all become good friends. In fact, many of the teachers have developed the practice of playing pranks on each other. You are concerned because you have recently been promoted to a supervisory position and the other teachers have continued to play practical jokes on you. In an effort to maintain a cordial relationship with these teachers and at the same time establish your position and authority, what course of action will you take when you discuss this matter with your friends/professional colleagues?

REFERENCES

Ackerman, R. H., Donaldson, G. A., & Van der Bogert, R. (1996). *Making sense as a school leader.* San Francisco: Jossey-Bass Publishers.

Alfonso, R. J., Firth, G. R., & Neville, R. F. (1981). *Instructional supervision: A behavior system.* (2nd ed.). Boston: Allyn & Bacon.

Andrews, R. (1987). On leadership and student achievement: A conversation with Richard Andrews. *Educational Leadership, 45,* 1, 9–16. [Interview with Ron Brandt, editor of *Educational Leadership.*]

Arrendondo, D. E., Brody, J. E., Zimmerman, D. P., & Moffett, C. A. (1995). Pushing the envelope in supervision. *Educational Leadership, 53,* 3, 74–78.

Association for Supervision and Curriculum Development (ASCD). (1988). *Educational administrator effectiveness profile: Self-development guide.* Plymouth, MI: Human Synergistics.

Avolio, B. J., Waldman, D. A., & Yammarino, F. J. (1991). Leading in the 1990s: The four I's of transformational leadership. *Journal of European Industrial Training, 15,* 4, 9–16.

Bass, B. (1981). *Stogdill's handbook of leadership.* New York: Free Press.

Bass, B. M., & Avolio, B. J. (1994). *Improving organizational effectiveness through transformational leadership.* Thousand Oaks, CA: Sage Publications.

Bennis, W. (1989). *Why leaders can't lead: The unconscious conspiracy continues.* San Francisco: Jossey-Bass Publishers.

Bennis, W., & Nanus, B. (1997). *Leaders: The strategies for taking charge.* New York: HarperCollins Publishers.

Blake, R. R., & McCanse, A. A. (1991). *Leadership dilemmas—Grid solutions.* Houston: Gulf Publishing Co.

Blake, R., & Mouton, J. S. (1985). *The new managerial grid III: The key to leadership excellence.* Houston: Gulf Publishing.

Blase, J. L., & Kirby, P. C. (1992 December). The power of praise—A strategy for effective principals. *NASSP Bulletin, 76,* 69–77.

Bolman, L., & Deal, T. (1994). Looking for leadership: Another search party's report. *Educational Administration Quarterly, 30,* 1, 77–96.

Bowlby, J. (1980). *Attachment and loss.* (vol. 3). New York: Basic Books.

Boyan, N. J. (1988). Describing and explaining administrative behavior. In *Handbook of research on educational administration.* N. J. Boyan (ed.). New York: Longman.

Bridges, E. M. (1992). *Problem-based learning for administrators.* Eugene, OR: Education Resources Information Center.

Calebrese, R. L., & Zepeda, S. J. (1997). *The reflective supervisor.* Larchmont, NY: Eye on Education.

Carr, A. A. (1995). Performance technologist preparation: The role of leadership theory. *Performance Improvement Quarterly, 8,* 50–74.

Chang, Y. S, Labovitz, G., & Rosansky, V. (1992). *Making quality work: A leadership guide for the results-driven manager.* Essex Junction, VT: Omneo.

Conley, D. T. (1996). *Are you ready to restructure? A guidebook for educators, parents, and community members.* Thousand Oaks, CA: Corwin Press.

Costa, A., & Garmston, R. (1994). *Cognitive coaching: A foundation for renaissance schools.* Norwood, MA: Christopher-Gordon Publishers.

Covey, S. K. (1989). *The 7 habits of highly effective people.* New York: Simon & Schuster.

Covey, S. K. (1990). *Principle-centered leadership.* New York: Simon & Schuster.

Daresh, J. C., & Playko, M. A. (1995). *Supervision as a proactive process: Concepts and cases.* (2nd ed.). Prospect Heights, IL: Waveland Press.

Etzioni, A. (1965). Organizational control structure. In *Handbook of organizations.* J. G. March (ed.). Chicago: Rand McNally.

Evans, T. J. (1996). Elementary teachers' and principals' perceptions of principal leadership style and school social organization. Ed.D. dissertation. Kalamazoo, Western Michigan University.

Fielder, F. E. (1974). *Leadership and effective management.* Glenview, IL.: Scott, Foresman.

Fleishman, E. A., & Harris, E. F. (1962). Patterns of leadership behavior related to employee grievances and turnover. *Personnel Psychology, 15,* 1, 43–44.

French, J. R., & Raven, R. (1959). The bases of social power. In *Studies in social power.* D. Cartwright (ed.). Ann Arbor: University of Michigan Press.

Fritz, R. (1996). *Corporate tides: The inescapable laws of organizational structure.* San Francisco: Berrett-Koehler Publishers.

Fullan, M. G., & Hargreaves, A. (1991). *What's worth fighting for? Working together for your school.* Andover, MA: Regional Laboratory for Educational Improvement of the Northeast, and Islands, Toronto: Ontario Public School Teachers' Federation.

Gardner, J. (1990). *On leadership.* New York: Free Press.

Giammatteo, M. C. (1975). Training package for a model city staff. Field paper no. 15. Portland, OR: Northwest Regional Educational Laboratory.

Glanz, J. (1994 September). Dilemmas of assistant principals in their supervisory role: Reflections of an assistant principal. *Journal of School Leadership, 4,* 577–593.

Glasser, W. (1990). *The quality school.* New York: Harper & Row.

Glickman, C. D. (1990). *Supervision of instruction: A developmental approach.* (2nd ed.). Boston: Allyn & Bacon.

Goldhammer, R., Anderson, R. H., & Krajewski, R. J. (1993). *Clinical supervision: Special methods for the supervisor.* Fort Worth: Harcourt Brace Jovanovich.

Gorton, R. A. (1987). *School leadership and administration.* (3rd ed.). Dubuque, IA: C. Brown Publishers.

Greenberg, J., & Baron, R. A. (1997). *Behavior in organizations.* (6th ed.). Upper Saddle River, NJ: Prentice-Hall.

Greenleaf, R. K. (1991). *Servant leadership: A journey into the nature of legitimate power and greatness.* New York: Paulist Press.

Griffiths, D. (1988). Administrative theory. In *Handbook of research on educational administration.* N. J. Boyan (ed.). New York: Longman.

Halpin, A. W. (1966). *Theory and research in administration.* New York: Macmillan.

Hemphill, J. K., & Coons, A. E. (1950). *Leader behavior description.* Columbus: Personnel Research Board, Ohio State University.

Hershey, P., & Blanchard, K. H. (1993). *Management of organizational behavior.* Englewood Cliffs, NJ: Prentice-Hall.

Hitt, W. D. (1988). *The leader-manager.* Columbus, OH: Battelle Press.

Hong, L. (1996). *Surveying school reform. A year in the life of one school.* New York: Teachers College Press.

Jaworski, J. (1996). *Synchronicity: The inner path of leader.* San Francisco: Berrett-Koehler Publishers.

Jewell, L. N. (1998). *Contemporary industrial/organizational psychology.* (3rd ed.). Pacific Grove, CA: Brooks/Cole Publishing Co.

Knezevich, S. J. (1984). *Administration of public education.* (4th ed.). New York: Harper & Row.

Kotter, J. P. (1990). *A face for change: How leadership differs from management.* New York: Free Press.

Lambert, L. (1998). *Building leadership capacity in schools.* Alexandria, VA: Association for Supervision and Curriculum Development.

Larocque, L., & Coleman, P. (1991). Negotiating the master contract: Transformational leadership and school district quality. In *Understanding school system administration studies of the contemporary chief education officer.* K. Leithwood and D. Musella (eds.). New York: Falmer.

Lashway, L. (1997 January). Visionary leadership. *ERIC Digest,* No. 100, 1–2. Report #EDD-EA-92-2.

Leithwood, K. (1992). The move toward transformational leadership. *Educational Leadership, 49,* 8–12.

Leithwood, K. (1994). Leadership for school structuring. *Educational Administration Quarterly, 30,* 498–518.

Levinson, H. (1968). *The exceptional executive: A psychological conception.* Cambridge, MA: Harvard University Press.

Little, J. W. (1987). Teachers as colleagues. In *Educator's handbook.* V. Richardson-Koehler, ed. White Plains, NY: Longman.

Liu, Ching-Jen. (1984). An identification of principals' instructional leadership in effective high schools. Unpublished Ed.D. dissertation. Cincinnati: University of Cincinnati.

Lorenz, K. (1952). *King Solomon's ring.* New York: Crowell.

Lovell, J., & Wiles, K. (1983). *Supervision for better schools.* (5th ed.). Englewood Cliffs, NJ: Prentice-Hall.

Maccoby, M. (1981). *The leader.* New York: Simon & Schuster.

Machiavelli, N. (1952). *The prince.* New York: NAL Penguin.

Mathews, D. (1996). *Is there a public for public schools?* Dayton, OH: Kettering Foundation Press.

McGregor, D. (1960). *The human side of enterprise.* New York: McGraw-Hill.

McPherson, R. B., Crowson, R. L., & Pitner, N. J. (1986). *Managing uncertainty: Administrative theory and practice in education.* Columbus, OH: Charles E. Merrill.

Mortimore, P., & Sammons, P. (1987). New evidence on effective elementary schools. *Educational Leadership, 45,* 4–8.

Naisbitt, J. (1982). *Megatrends.* New York: Warner Books.

Nelton, S. (1991 May). Men, women & leadership. *Nation's Business, 79,* 16–22.

O'Hare, M., & Blase, J. (1992). Power and politics in the classroom: Implications for teacher education. *Action in Teacher Education, 14,* 10–17.

Rudnitski, R. A. (1996). Global leadership theory: Theoretical roots, principles, and possibilities for the future. *Gifted Educational International, 11,* 80–85.

Schein, E. H. (1985). *Organizational culture and leadership.* San Francisco: Jossey-Bass Publishers.

Schomoker, M. (1996). *Results: The key to continuous school improvement.* Alexandria, VA: Association for Supervision and Curriculum Development.

Schriesheim, C. A., & Hinkin, T. R. (1990). Influence tactics used by subordinates: An empirical analysis and refinement of the Kipnis, Schmidt, and Wilkinson subscales. *Journal of Applied Psychology, 75,* 246–257.

Senge, P. M. (1990). *The fifth discipline: The art and practice of the learning organization.* New York: Doubleday.

Sergiovanni, T. J. (1990). *Value-added leadership: How to get extraordinary performance in schools.* San Diego: Harcourt Brace Jovanovich.

Sergiovanni, T. J. (1994). *Building community in schools.* San Francisco: Jossey-Bass Publishers.

Sergiovanni, T. J. (1995). *The principalship: A reflective practice perspective.* Boston: Allyn & Bacon.

Sheppard, B. (1996). Exploring the transformational nature of instructional leadership. *Alberta Journal of Educational Research, 42,* 325–344.

Sorenson, D., & Machell, J. (1996). Quality schools through quality leadership. Paper presented at the fifth annual National Conference on Creating the Quality School, Oklahoma City, OK. March 27–30.

Spencer, H. (1927). *Education: Intellectual, moral and physical.* New York: Appleton-Century-Crofts.

Terry, R. W. (1993). *Authentic leadership: Courage in action.* San Francisco: Jossey-Bass Publishers.

Tye, K. A., & Tye, B. B. (1984). Teacher isolation and school reform. *Phi Delta Kappan, 65,* 319–322.

Wheatley, M. (1994). *Leadership and the new science.* San Francisco: Berrett-Koehler Publishers.

Wiles, J., & Bondi, J. (1980). *Supervision: A guide to practice.* Columbus, OH: Charles E. Merrill.

Wiles, J., & Bondi, J. (1986). *Supervision: A guide to practice.* (2nd ed.). Columbus, OH: Charles E. Merrill.

Yukl, G. A. (1994). *Leadership in organizations.* (3rd ed.). Englewood Cliffs, NJ: Prentice-Hall.

Yukl, G., Falbe, C. M., & Youn, J. Y. (1993). Patterns of influence behavior for managers. *Group and Organization Management, 18,* 5–28.

Yukl, G., & Tracey, J. B. (1992). Consequences of influence tactics used with subordinates, peers, and the boss. *Journal of Applied Psychology, 77,* 525–535.

5 Communicating Effectively

A Critical Component for Supervisors

OBJECTIVES

The objectives of this chapter are:

- Identify and discuss the definitions and characteristics of communication.
- Describe the communication model and explain the importance of a response in the process.
- Identify and apply responses that promote effective communication.
- Identify and describe responses that create barriers to effective communication.
- Explain the importance of communicating in descriptive, nonjudgmental ways.
- Identify forms of communication other than spoken dialogue/conversation.
- Identify and apply principles of effective communication.

Knowledge of organizational structure and the ability to provide leadership are important components of supervision, but the ability to communicate may ultimately determine the degree of success supervisors have as they interact with others and seek to improve instruction. For Tracy and MacNaughton (1993), skill in communication is the most important of all the skills of supervision; Oliva and Pawlas (1997) say that the ability to communicate is the primary tool of the supervisor. Raiola (1995) elaborates by saying that the art of communicating is a vital tool for the transformational leader. Lysaught (1984) has observed that the problems associated with transmitting ideas and meaning are persistent in organizations, and when there are failures in communication, problems will result in goal setting as well as productivity and assessment. Jewell (1998) puts this in a contemporary context by saying that "given the importance of influence, cooperation, imitation, and leadership, it is clear that communication is the means by which things get done in organizations" (p. 448).

Communication as Hamilton and Parker (1993) define it—"the process of people sharing thoughts, ideas, and feelings with each other in commonly understandable ways" (p. 5)—is a part of all organizations, including corporations, families, and schools. The ability to communicate ideas and information effectively to others is vital to the success of any endeavor. Levering (1988) notes that ongoing communication is the mark of effective workplaces. Because of their various leadership positions in schools, supervisors communicate with a wide variety of people, including students, teachers, parents, and other school personnel, as well as members of the community. Barr, Elmes, and Walker (1980) suggest that "without clear, direct communication...[the supervisor] could not possibly build with teachers the type of nonthreatening, healthy and fruitful relationship necessary to facilitate the teacher's growth as a professional" (p. 15).

Floyd and Jacobs (1992) suggest that the most important component in educational organizations is communication; it is the all-pervasive variable at the center of organizational reform. Jacobs (1992) further suggests that by understanding school communication instructional supervisors can help teachers bridge the theory and practice gap. Gorton (1987) believes that to be successful, supervisors must possess effective communication skills. Pfeiffer and Dunlap (1982) observe that the supervisor must be knowledgeable about the many aspects of the communication process, "since the supervisor deals with human relationships—working with an individual, a small group, or a large group to change behavior which results in the improvement of instruction" (p. 179).

Recognizing the importance of communication skills, this chapter will (a) examine some definitions of communication and describe various characteristics of the communication process; (b) discuss supervisor responses that encourage and/or inhibit effective communication; (c) look at ways of communicating in behavioral language; (d) examine other forms of communication; and (e) identify principles of effective communication.

Definitions and Characteristics of Communication

The term *communication* comes from the Latin word *communicatus,* which means to impart, to share, or to make common. The communication process, therefore, becomes *a way of establishing common understandings, meanings, or purposes.* According to Knezevich (1984):

> The many definitions of communication consider it (1) imparting or exchanging attitudes, ideas, and information through the use of human abilities or technology; (2) transmission and reception of ideas; (3) the broad field of interchange of thoughts and opinions among humans; or (4) a process of giving and receiving facts, feelings and ideas. (p. 75)

Perhaps one of the most commonly used definitions has been offered by Kelly and Rasey (1952), who define communication as "the process by which one individual can to a degree know what another thinks, feels or believes" (p. 78). This early definition is reinforced by Jewell (1998), who says that, in an organizational setting, "communication is the exchange of information, ideas, or feelings between two or more individuals or groups" (p. 448). Floyd and Jacobs (1993) define school communication as "that family of related concepts identifying the process transpiring in school organizations wherein human beings produce and exchange signs about personally and socially significant knowledge, skills, and values" (p. ii). Floyd (1993) continues by suggesting a theoretical construct of "symbolic interactionism" that transforms the elements of communication into symbols that convey meaning.

Clearly there are similarities in all of these definitions that emphasize a common or mutual understanding and a sharing of information. Mortensen (1980) identifies five characteristics of communication that will prove helpful to supervisors. These include:

1. *Communication is dynamic.* Change occurs during the communication process involving ideas or behaviors of those involved. The dynamic or change-oriented aspect of communication is influenced by a number of factors that include the teacher's physical and emotional state, visual and auditory stimuli, previous associations and experiences, and interpersonal dynamics.

2. *Communication is irreversible.* Words cannot be erased or called back once uttered. The supervisor and teacher cannot take back their words, once they have uttered them. This reinforces the need to think through what we are going to say and realize that conversations with individuals and groups have a cumulative effect. What we said last week cannot be retracted, so today what we say either adds to, refutes, or explains previous conversations.

3. *Communication is proactive.* The intra- and interpersonal nature of communication includes a sense of self or identity and a psychological involvement of the individuals. Self-esteem and identity are involved in messages as well as the communication process. Energy is also expended as those involved must listen as well as speak.

4. *Communication is contextual.* Verbal interactions take place within a space or setting, and the characteristics of the environment are critical to the communication process. For example, reprimanding an individual in a public setting or forum has an impact on the communication process that perhaps a private conversation would not have.

5. *Communication is interactive.* It is difficult—if not impossible—to leave a conversation, even if one-sided, and be unaffected. Even if not an equal partner in the communication process, one is drawn into or involved in the process, and communication becomes a reciprocal process that influences all parties.

Jacobs (1993) suggests that school communication is the process that binds the educational system together. To aid in understanding the various avenues of communication, he proposes a communication atlas that identifies five ways (road maps) through which communication travels in schools. These communication road maps include (1) cause and effect, (2) psychological, (3) interactive, (4) pragmatic, and (5) semiotic.

The first way or road map of communication is *cause and effect* and is made up of links that are connected to form a communication chain, which is viewed as a linear channel. Sometimes the message becomes distorted as it moves from link to link along the chain (in the channel), and to improve the communication process, one must reduce the "noise" in the channel. When interacting with teachers, the supervisor tries to send a clear message using a variety of data-collection techniques (scripting, anecdotal record, audio/video recordings). When a teacher fails to understand the message, the cause–effect road map suggests that the lack of understanding is due to the presence of "noise" in the channel. The supervisor must diagnose what is causing the "noise" and making it difficult for the teacher to understand. The supervisor knows that communication is successful when the teacher begins to recognize the patterns presented in the data and discussions take place to address the issue.

The second communication road map is *psychological,* which views communication as an intrinsic process within the mind as sensory data are entered, stored, and then used to evaluate new data as they are processed. In this road map, communication is a series of stimuli that bombard an individual; the person must rely on previously stored data and experience to interpret and make sense of the new information in order to formulate an appropriate response. In working with a teacher to improve instruction, the supervisor would have to shift his or her focus from the "noise" in the channel to how the teacher is receiving and responding to the data or sensory stimuli and processing the information. The supervisor will be successful when the data can be interpreted in a way that connects with the teacher's prior experience or mind-set.

The third road map is *interactive*, which suggests that communication is a by-product of actions that symbolize meaning and is a result of interactions between and among people. It involves rehearsing our next response, mentally testing alternatives, and anticipating reactions. Within this construct, the setting of communication is much like a stage, and individuals act toward each other in ways that are designed to convey meanings. As supervisors interact with teachers, each plays a role and uses symbols during these interactions. Both the supervisor and teacher simultaneously experience and interpret meaning. Supervisors will sense success when teachers can interpret meaning from the interaction and articulate that meaning.

The fourth road map, *pragmatic*, likens communication to a system that incorporates each person's actions and utterances and their interdependence. The pragmatic view focuses on redundant patterns of behavior within the system, how people respond to these patterns, and the anticipation of communication outcomes. As supervisors interact with teachers during the year, they define their relationships and established patterns of behaviors. Instead of focusing on individual interactions between teacher and students in the classroom, the pragmatic road map examines the recurring patterns of the teacher's behavior within the classroom and notes that such behavior is predictable. Regardless of student involvement, for example, the teacher demonstrates a predictable, redundant, recurrent response. It also examines the recurrent patterns of behavior as supervisors and teachers interact within the school system. Even supervisors develop "stock" responses as they interact with teachers.

The fifth road map is the *semiotic* type of communication, which is a product of words spoken and actions taken to convey meaning. In such a view, there is a difference between what was said and what was meant; our spoken words do not always signify our deepest thoughts or even our best interests. This road map to communication highlights the impact of symbolic forces that shape who we are and help us conceptualize how students, teachers, and instructional supervisors produce meaning in their lives. When working with teachers using the semiotic road map, the language used is not as important as what the language signifies. The ideology and cultural values that lie beneath the surface of the dialogue between teachers and supervisors ultimately determine what the teachers and supervisors really hear and believe to be true and valuable.

Effective communication can be a tool for promoting learning and growth and can serve as a means of influencing the instructional behavior of teachers. Berlo (1960) and Seiler and colleagues (1982) have identified some basic components or aspects of the communication process, which include the following:

- The purpose to be achieved by the message
- The source of the communication or person(s) sending the message
- The encoding of the message and the ways or channels for sending the message
- The information or content of the message or the message itself
- The receiver(s) or person(s) to whom the message is sent

- The decoding or translating of the message
- The need for a response to or feedback about the message

As noted from these different components, communication is clearly more than talk; more than words or sounds are communicated. Costa and Garmston (1994) suggest that the communication process is so complex because "each person engages in dialogue from the perspectives of their own identity [which is]...constructed from both consciously and unconsciously held beliefs" (p. 212). They continue by saying, "an individual's sense of identity is tied to the moment-to-moment intentions of what one wants to communicate" (p. 212). These moment-to-moment intentions create metamessages that reside primarily at the unconscious level, and "it is the metamessages that cause the most difficulties in communication" (p. 213). For example, in a faculty meeting, men often take the initiative to speak because they have grown up in a culture that encouraged them to demonstrate that they are knowledgeable and are expected to propose viable solutions. The unconscious message that the men may send is that they want to control the dialogue. Women speak most often when called upon and when given opportunities. If, however, a woman's identity picks up on the unconscious metamessage of the men (control), she is likely to respond by negating the input from them and proposing an alternative solution or what she sees as a better idea.

As individuals communicate with each other, feelings and purposes are also communicated through expressions, gestures, posture, and overall physical attitudes. Raiola (1995) says that "communication means building relationships" (p. 13). Communication, then, occurs in different ways at multiple levels. Covey (1989) describes the importance of communication when he says:

> If I were to summarize in one sentence the single most important principle I have learned in the field of interpersonal relations, it would be this: Seek first to understand, then to be understood. This principle is the key to effective interpersonal communication. (p. 237)

In addition to these basic characteristics or components of communication, external factors, such as ideas, feelings, suggestions, and descriptions, help to shape and give meaning to the message. The person communicating the message has a need to share such ideas and feelings in a form that will transfer a common meaning to the receiver. Therefore, the information and related factors must be encoded into a message through the use of symbols (oral language or printed words). The channel is the medium or method for transferring the message, which must then be decoded to the original meaning(s) by the receiver.

Communication Model.   Although we often treat the communication process as perfect, it is important to note that it is seldom, if ever, 100 percent accurate. This false assumption is most often seen when we think that because we have told someone something that they have heard what we said. However, when the receiver has an opportunity to make a response to the message, the sender has a chance to verify that the receiver has accurately decoded the message and checked the accuracy of the message. Champy (1997) suggests that "What's required is conversation, not just communication.... It's in the give and take that people will discover the truth" (p. 15). Figure 5.1 represents a model of communication with a response or feedback component. It is important to note that, throughout life, the receptive aspect of language—what we read and hear—is greater than our expressive language—what we speak and write. We use both as we encode and decode messages.

As Figure 5.1 shows, the response mechanism provides a means of clarifying the message and of validating its accuracy. Supervisors may sometimes encounter situations in which the listener, or the receiver of the message, simply does not hear the message being sent. Without a response, it is difficult, if not impossible, to determine what has been heard. This results in what Barr, Elmes, and Walker (1980) refer to as a "problem in communication" (p. 16). Many individuals may recall the famous line in the movie *Cool Hand Luke* in which the prison warden, after severely punishing Luke for continuing to disobey, says to the inmate, "What we have here is a failure to communicate." What supervisors must carefully guard against is a failure to communicate with the teachers and others with whom they work.

Tracy and MacNaughton (1993) have identified four barriers that contribute to communication failure. These include: (1) barriers of self, where a supervisor's personal characteristics and sense of self cause mixed or multiple messages to be sent; (2) barriers of the relationship, where the view that teachers and supervisors

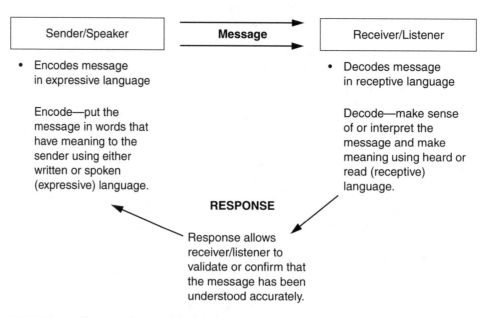

FIGURE 5.1   **Communication Model**

have of each other and their professional competence create distortions and create inaccuracies in the sending and receiving of messages; (3) barriers in the message, which involve words we do not understand (jargon or letters), insufficient information, and conflicting or double messages; and (4) organizational barriers, which include the structure of the organization, the flow of information, the norms of the organization, and the value of dialogue within the organization. As Hamilton and Parker (1993) have observed, "Everyone's communication style is affected by the work environment" (p. 67). Furthermore, the language itself is a barrier. There is a propensity to use language as a "straitjacket" that is often biased against girls and women. This gender bias in our language—the use of pronouns, the way relationships are expressed, and the vocabulary itself—helps to shape perceptions of girls/women and boys/men (Reinhartz and King, 1993).

For supervisors, communicating effectively involves the application of the five Cs of language usage: clarity, concreteness, correctness, conciseness, and cultural sensitivity (Osborn and Osborn, 1994). Clarity emphasizes the need to deliver a clear and simple message that the listeners can relate to and comprehend. As Hanaka and Hawkins (1997) note, too often supervisors provide information overload. "Effective communication for the future, if it is to be efficient…will be timely and have an appropriate level of detail" (p. 175). Concreteness illustrates the importance of using precise or pictorial words rather than abstract terms, which can create confusion and result in disinterest. Correctness involves the appropriate use of grammar while also selecting words that convey the intended meaning. Conciseness is related to clarity in that the points need to be presented quickly and efficiently so that the message communicated is simple and direct.

Culturally sensitive language communicates respect for the audience by avoiding any allusions to negative stereotypes and/or racist and sexist inferences. A common difficulty in cross-cultural communication is selecting a response that is most appropriate to both the people and the situation, considering "the mix of cultural differences in the situation—age, race, [gender], values, positional authority, and socioeconomic class" (Costa and Garmston, 1994, p. 212). Language for supervisors is a powerful communication tool that helps them to share perceptions, feelings, and best practices with teachers and other educators. As Osborn and Osborn (1994) note, "Words can promote togetherness [collegiality] and help launch programs of action to accomplish worthy goals [vision/mission].… [Furthermore], words may also preserve memories of our heritage and help stabilize our [school] culture" (p. 286).

Supervisor Responses That Promote Effective Communication

In order to overcome barriers in communication and enhance the accuracy of the message, the supervisor should not only provide an opportunity for a response, as seen in Figure 5.1, but should encourage responses from the listener/receiver.

Barr, Elmes, and Walker (1980), Boyan and Copeland (1978), Raiola (1995) suggest various types of responses that supervisors can use to help ensure effective, clear communication. These responses are designed for the supervisor to use in encouraging teachers and others to communicate openly and freely, to not only enhance the accuracy of the message but to also verify the degree of understanding. The six response modes are: (1) asking clarifying questions, (2) paraphrasing and summarizing, (3) perception checking, (4) offering information, (5) active attentive listening, and (6) encouraging the heart (Minor, 1995, p. 197).

1. *Asking clarifying questions.* The intent of this type of response is to verify the meaning of the teacher's message and probe for accuracy of information. As the supervisor listens to what the teacher says, the message may appear to be vague or overly generalized and to have multiple meanings. The supervisor's response should be to ask the teacher to repeat or clarify what was said. For example, the supervisor might say to the teacher, "I'm not sure I know what you mean when you say that Jerry is an active student. Is he disruptive?" Or the supervisor might respond by saying, "I'm not sure I understand the situation completely. Could you describe her behavior again for me?" In using responses like these, the supervisor is asking the teacher to provide more information to improve the degree of clarity.

2. *Paraphrasing and summarizing.* This kind of response helps the supervisor avoid making assumptions about the situation and the message. By paraphrasing, the supervisor repeats the message in his or her own words; thus, the teacher has an opportunity to verify the supervisor's understanding. For example, the teacher might say, "I can't get Sally to do what I ask her to do." From what the teacher says, the supervisor might assume that Sally is a discipline problem. In paraphrasing, the supervisor might say, "No matter what you do, Sally is a discipline problem because she won't mind you in class." Now the teacher can respond either, "Yes, that is what I mean," or "No, she just sits quietly and daydreams and won't complete her assignments." The goal of paraphrasing is for supervisors to put the message in their own words so that teachers can correct or modify the content and verify the degree of accuracy of the communication. As they engage in conversation with teachers, supervisors must also be able to summarize the content, feelings, themes, or proposed actions regarding issues discussed.

3. *Perception checking.* Use of this kind of response allows the supervisor to explore the meanings behind the message and to verify the feelings incorporated in the teacher's message. Often misunderstandings occur because the supervisor misinterprets the feelings behind the message; perception checking can help prevent this. For example, the teacher might say very little during the initial moments of an after-school conference the supervisor had requested. The supervisor might misinterpret the teacher's reticence as "pouting" or a way of showing displeasure about attending the conference. If these perceptions are not checked or verified, they could lead to serious misunderstandings. Therefore, the supervisor might state, "I have the feeling or impression that you are upset at having to meet with me this afternoon. Am I right?" The supervisor's question gives the teacher the chance to say

either "Yes, I am very unhappy that I had to meet with you today when I had other plans," or "No, I'm not upset. I'm just tired and was thinking of all the work I have to get done between now and tomorrow." Such an interchange clears the air, and the supervisor can proceed with the intent or purpose of the conference.

Kreps (1990) also indicates that perception checking can help clarify misunderstandings about expectations because many of our "expectations remain unspoken until they are violated" (p. 150). These misunderstandings occur because supervisors assume others know what is expected of them. For example, the supervisor might assume that all teachers know and feel comfortable with providing input about campus decisions and becomes impatient with teachers who tend to allow others to provide input into the decision-making process. It is not until a pattern of noninvolvement emerges that the supervisor realizes that an expectation has been violated because it was not clearly stated and perceptions checked.

4. *Offering information.* In this type of exchange, the supervisor can react to the teacher's message by offering relevant information. The teacher can then analyze the information to determine if it applies to the original message. The supervisor might say, "From what you have told me about the student, it appears that we have two choices. Either we could begin the diagnostic process to determine if the student will qualify for the special program, or we could implement immediate intervention strategies to help overcome the academic deficiencies." A word of caution must be sounded, however, concerning the use of such a response. Often supervisors want to "tell" or offer information before they have given the teacher a chance to fully explain the problem; if not used sparingly and in conjunction with the four other types of responses listed here, offering information can actually become a hindrance to clear communication. The purpose of this response is to provide enough relevant information from the supervisor's perspective to enable the teacher to weigh the information and determine its appropriateness for a given situation.

5. *Active attentive listening.* This type of response may be the most critical in fostering open and free communication with others. It is often difficult for the supervisor to stay "tuned in" when, at the end of a long day, a teacher schedules an appointment to talk about an instructional problem. The key to developing good listening skills is to attend to the speaker by "using eye contact and demonstrating an open body posture" (Minor, 1995, p. 65). Active, attentive listening is responsive listening and requires a response to the message that is being sent. For example, the supervisor might respond with "Yes," "I see," "Go on," "I understand what you are saying," or "Uh-huh." The supervisor can convey interest in the message through alert facial expressions and helpful spoken responses.

6. *Encouraging the heart.* Supervisors must be able to convey a clear message to participants that their contributions to the discussion or issue are welcome. Supervisors must be genuine in their encouragement of others in the exchange of communication. As teachers make inquiries, disclose information, or share feelings, the supervisor must be able to recognize contributions, celebrate accomplishments, be open and honest, and invite continued participation or interaction.

Covey (1989) suggests that you, as a supervisor, engage in empathic listening where you not only listen with your ears, "but you also...listen with your eyes and your heart...for feeling, for meaning,...for behavior [so that] you're focused on receiving the deep communication of another human soul" (p. 241).

These response modes are called freeing responses because they are designed to promote free, open communication. As the supervisor interacts with teachers, these responses can be used to facilitate communication as conversation and to increase understanding by keeping the dialogue or discussion going rather than ending it. In the next section, we will examine some communication behaviors that restrict dialogue and discussion.

Responses That Create Barriers to Communication

Not all the responses supervisors employ are as helpful as the freeing responses in promoting effective communication. Other types of responses often serve to restrict or inhibit communication with teachers. Barr, Elmes, and Walker (1980) and Boyan and Copeland (1978) have identified six response models that supervisors frequently use that result in discouraging communication or providing barriers to clear and open communication. These six responses are (1) changing the subject, (2) explaining the teacher's behavior, (3) giving directions, (4) leveling the teacher's expectations, (5) denying the teacher's feelings, and (6) giving commands or orders.

1. *Changing the subject.* A response of this type serves to inhibit clear communication because it draws attention away from the teacher's message. The teacher might say, for example, "I really need help in motivating my low math group." But in changing the subject, and therefore the focus of the communication, the supervisor might respond by saying, "I'm so glad you came by. I needed to talk about your class achievement tests that are scheduled for next week." By not addressing the teacher's concern of motivating her or his low math group, the supervisor has cut off communication with the teacher and has not dealt with the teacher's concern but focused only on the achievement tests.

2. *Explaining the teacher's behavior.* Supervisors using this kind of response tell the teacher why he or she feels a certain way. For example, the supervisor might say, "I know that you are upset about the low test scores, but remember you have been ill this past week. I'm sure you will see things differently when you feel better." A response like this communicates to teachers that there is more to the situation than the spoken word, and that the supervisor provides a reasonable explanation; therefore, the teacher's message was not significant and time will take care of things.

3. *Giving directions.* This response pattern is related to offering information. A supervisor who asks a teacher to do something, without first exploring all dimensions of the message, does not encourage the teacher to discuss the matter further. For instance, after hearing only a few moments of the teacher's concerns or message, the supervisor may respond with a list: "Well, what you need to do to solve your problem is to develop a seating chart, post your classroom rules, and prepare more detailed lesson plans." Such a response by the supervisor communicates that the subject is not open for discussion. The supervisor has figured things out *without* teacher input. Such a response will probably inhibit the teacher from continuing the conversation.

4. *Leveling the teacher's expectations.* Such a response can really serve to deflate a teacher and shut off open communication. A supervisor's statement such as "I hope you don't have any concerns about the new computer-assisted spelling program," or "I hope you won't disappoint me by being one of the last to review the new history textbook" only serves to commit the teacher to the supervisor's level of expectation. The teacher may not feel comfortable with such a level of performance. Such statements do not encourage additional dialogue on the situation, often escalating the teacher's level of anxiety.

5. *Denying the teacher's feelings.* A response of this sort communicates to teachers that their feelings are not important. For example, a supervisor says, "Surely you don't feel that way about the block schedule, uniforms, and the year-round school concept; that's nothing to get upset over." The message conveyed is that the teacher's feelings do not count. Supervisors need to make time for teachers to share their feelings and to vent their frustrations; otherwise, such statements discourage teachers from further discussing how they really feel, which in turn inhibits the communication process.

6. *Giving commands or orders.* A response of this nature clearly limits further communication. When the supervisor says, "You will standardize the scope and sequence of the science curriculum for sixth grade by the end of the week," the teacher's autonomy has been undermined, and the communication process is curtailed. The teacher is likely to feel that the supervisor would rather issue orders—regardless of their appropriateness to the teacher's classroom needs—than listen to and think about a description of the particular problems the teacher may be facing. Such communication behaviors prevent teachers from developing ownership or feeling like a member of a team.

Supervisors—in their attempts to facilitate communication, encourage conversation, and promote a clear understanding of the message—should avoid using the restricting responses and employ the freeing responses in their place. As supervisors work with teachers, the goal of the interaction should be open and honest dialogue or discussion, which leads to mutual understanding and continued professional development.

As supervisors speak with teachers, they need to be aware of the role their voice plays in communicating the meaning of the message. Each supervisor's voice has personal qualities, but attention should be given to pitch, rate, volume, and variety. When speaking, pitch refers to the high and low sounds of your voice; the most effective range is one that is comfortable for the speaker as well as listener(s). The rate (speed) of the speaker and the volume (loudness) help to determine the level of success. Supervisors should monitor not only how fast or slow they speak but the loudness and softness as well. Variety suggests that supervisors should avoid speaking in a monotone and use varying degrees of pitch, rate, and volume to send clearer messages (Osborn and Osborn, 1994).

By focusing on freeing responses and eliminating binding responses, supervisors can develop communication skills that foster collaboration—the sharing of ideas and attitudes that lead to a degree of understanding between the sender and receiver. It is also important to note that supervisors receive messages as well as send messages, and they must practice attentive listening as well as perception checking during the process.

Giving teachers feedback has been effective in developing desirable pedagogical skills. The use of feedback has its roots in communication theory. Within this communication model, the supervisor is both the communicator and encoder. The teacher is often the receiver and decoder. The supervisor must have the encoding skills to enable the teachers to receive the message as it was intended. As supervisors receive information, they alter their communication behavior so as to ensure that the message from the teachers is clear. Supervisors should strive to avoid the dilemma in which there is a discrepancy between what is said and what is actually received.

Communicating in Descriptive, Nonjudgmental Language

When communicating with teachers, instructional supervisors should understand the following prerequisites of communication. First, the supervisor should avoid making judgmental statements when describing classroom events and teaching behaviors. Second, the supervisor must communicate with the teacher in accurate and precise terms (Goldhammer, Anderson, and Krajewski, 1993). The teacher must be able to comprehend the supervisor's meaning, and the supervisor must likewise understand the teacher's meaning. Only through a "mutual understanding will a healthy supervisory relationship grow" (Barr, Elmes, and Walker, 1980, p. 32). Finally, the teacher's area of instructional concern must be identified in precise and specific terms. As Barr, Elmes, and Walker (1980) add, "To sum up, effective instructional supervision requires use of a language with three main characteristics. It must be (1) non-judgmental, (2) easily understood, and (3) specific" (pp. 32–33).

The tool used for helping the supervisor meet all three of these criteria is called *behavioral language,* which is communication that describes classroom behavior impartially and factually rather than evaluatively; it is communication that is precise, clear, and unambiguous. In developing a behavioral vocabulary, the supervisor should focus on observable behaviors that occur within the teaching–

learning process. For example, when observing an English class, the supervisor might note that the teacher called on only 3 of 22 students during the lesson, but that those 3 students responded 18 times. Instead of saying to the teacher, "I don't think you did a very good job of questioning because you only called on 3 students," a nonjudgmental response would be, "I noted that you asked 18 questions during the English lesson, and John, Julie, and Sam were the students who responded to them." This second statement simply describes what happened in the classroom and makes no attempt to judge or evaluate the actions.

In another situation, the supervisor might observe that "During a 20-minute lesson, 15 students (65 percent) were on task, 6 students (26 percent) were passively off task, and 2 students (9 percent) were actively off task." Such a statement is called a behavioral statement and focuses on specific behaviors and interactions in the classroom. It is important that these statements are accurate, specific, and precise descriptions of observable behaviors. Such behavioral statements contain information related to measurable quantities and observable events. There is no judgment made; it is simply a statement or report of what happened. Nonbehavioral statements contain a high degree of ambiguity or vagueness and may send a message to the teacher that sounds judgmental and that is easily misunderstood or misinterpreted. For example, if the supervisor, at the conclusion of an observation, is forced to comment, "That was a good lesson" is often used. This comment is general and vague, and the word "good" can be misleading and misinterpreted by the teacher. Figure 5.2 provides examples of nonbehavioral and behavioral statements.

To communicate effectively with teachers, supervisors must learn to develop a behavioral language vocabulary. This will help in communicating clearly and concisely and is designed to influence teachers' instructional behavior.

Other Forms of Communication

Most of the discussion to this point has dealt with spoken or verbal communication. As indicated earlier in the chapter, communication is a multifaceted process that occurs on a variety of levels, with the sender using different methods or channels to convey messages. Gorton (1987) identifies various channels of communication that can be used to transmit messages. These include writing (notes, letters, memos, and newsletters), oral face-to-face (conferences, group meetings, and social functions), and oral electronic/visual (telephone, E-mail, announcements, overheads, and videotape) methods.

Two prevalent forms of communication that are used either by themselves or in conjunction with spoken messages are written communication and nonverbal communication. Both of these forms can be effective tools for the instructional supervisor in working with teachers and others in schools.

Written Communication. Nearly all organizations seem to have an affinity for written communication, especially in the form of memos and reports. Because of

FIGURE 5.2   **Nonbehavioral and Behavioral Language**

Nonbehavioral Language	Behavioral Language
"There was no depth to your lesson on writing a research paper."	"After spending the first 5 minutes asking the students about the 3Gs of writing a research paper, 25 minutes remained with no student engaged in the lesson."
"Your lesson was over their heads."	"During the lesson, you asked 13 questions. Only 1 student answered two correctly, and when assigned guided practice (questions to answer), 18 of 25 students could not accomplish the task."
"You had a lot of student activity during your lesson."	"Although you used cooperative learning as a teaching strategy, five students moved from group to group interrupting the learning task, and nine students were observed disrupting other members of their groups by hiding materials, arguing over answers, and pushing and shoving to go first to the table to get supplies."
"You used a lot of instructional strategies."	"During the lesson on Drawing Conclusions, you introduced and modeled the process, practiced the process with a visual example, and had students apply the process in an activity."

the various titles and positions instructional supervisors have and the administrative functions and duties they perform, it is often necessary to construct a "paper trail" of documents, especially when dealing with personnel matters, which can be referred to at a later date. A paper trail verifies that important messages concerning specific behaviors have been communicated to the necessary teachers. In addition, written messages can provide specific advantages over oral or other forms of communication. Pfeiffer and Dunlap (1982) consider the following to be the four major advantages of written communication:

1. Communication (words) on paper provide a relatively permanent record.

2. Communication in written form contains valuable data that may be necessary for legal and/or political judgments.

3. Communication in written form can be affirmative, descriptive, and informative and can be distributed to infinite numbers of people in order to generate support or action.

4. Written communications often have a greater impact on the reader/receiver than spoken messages do, since written messages tend to be taken more seriously.

Clearly, there are times when the supervisor, in working with teachers, will find that a conversation will suffice. Frequently, a conversation will be preferable because it allows the teacher the opportunity to respond immediately. However, there are times, as noted above, when written communication is not only preferable but is called for because of the nature of the situation. Finally, written communication provides teachers with something to refer to when they reflect on a given situation; it sets the stage for rethinking, reassessing, and reviewing the event.

When preparing written communications, supervisors must guard against what Pfeiffer and Dunlap (1982) refer to as the tendency to "use words creatively" (p. 190) or engage in the kind of "wordsmanship" tactics that often plague organizations. In using the "wordsmanship" strategy, supervisors and other education professionals may construct sophisticated phrases that are, in fact, virtually meaningless. Supervisors must resist the creativity of word games and provide forms of written communication that use clear and precise language.

In his book *Art of Plain Talk*, Flesch (1946) criticizes the use of "gobbledygook," or wordy and confusing jargon, and calls for forthright communication. The following guidelines, based in part on Flesch's ideas, should be considered by anyone preparing written communications:

- Avoid writing up or down to the audience. Choose your vocabulary carefully, remembering that the *receptive vocabulary*—the one that is used in reading and listening—is several times larger than the *expressive*—or written—*vocabulary* (Burmeister, 1984).
- Do not use sarcasm or irony in written communications. Memos and reports are not the place to convey unfriendly remarks.
- Use concrete words and illustrations. Avoid vague or abstract terms that might require lengthy elaboration.
- Communicate in a direct and forthright fashion. Simply stated, do not beat around the bush; get to the point.
- If possible, compose a draft of the communication for review before sending. Make sure the message you are sending is the one you want communicated.

These guidelines can help the supervisor communicate more effectively with teachers and others when written communication is called for.

Nonverbal Communication.   Another form of communication that supervisors need to be aware of is nonverbal communication. Gorton (1987), in citing the work of Lipham and Francke (1966), states, "Whether we realize it or not, we communicate nonverbally through our facial expressions, our gestures, our dress, our tone of voice and the physical environment in which we communicate" (p. 40). Supervisors should be careful to match their body language, or nonverbal communication, with their verbal communication. Mixed messages and unclear communication can result when, for instance, the supervisor smiles while delivering unpleasant information or frowns when delivering good news. Six broad categories of nonverbal behavior include haptic, optic, proxemic, labic, pedic, and chromic communication (Osborn and Osborn, 1994; Pfeiffer and Dunlap, 1982).

1. *Haptic communication.* This form of nonverbal communication focuses on hand motion as a way of transferring a message or meaning. Clearly, the handshake is the most universally accepted form of haptic communication; when speaking, gestures and movements should be natural and spontaneous.

2. *Optic communication.* This type of nonverbal communication uses the eyes to send a message to the receiver. Through the use of optic communication, the sender conveys a message that words cannot impart. In the United States, eye contact, especially during a conversation conveys honesty and respect.

3. *Proxemic communication.* Nonverbal communication of this type is concerned with personal territory or personal space. Proxemic communication relates to the placement or positioning of individuals in a social setting, normally while they are talking. Associated with proxemic communication is the physical layout of a room or the placement of furniture. Because such factors may determine how individuals position themselves within the space, supervisors should be aware of how they structure their offices or conference rooms.

4. *Labic communication.* This form of nonverbal communication involves messages, other than words, sent by the mouth. Smiles, frowns, and pouts are some common examples of labic communication and serve to reinforce the meanings of words and/or feelings.

5. *Pedic communication.* This type of nonverbal communication involves messages sent through the feet. Such behaviors as tapping the foot, swinging one foot while sitting, and even positioning the body on one foot and then the other communicate messages to others.

6. *Chromic communication.* This form of nonverbal communication involves the use of color. Color is such an integral part of our environment that we often take it for granted. Supervisors can use color to their advantage in the communication process in items ranging from personal clothing to colors of ink on paper (such as red marks to indicate a particular kind of response or comment).

These examples of nonverbal communication are included to help supervisors in their interactions with teachers. With an awareness of the various types of nonverbal communication, supervisors may be able to increase their effectiveness when they work with teachers in improving classroom instruction.

Communication Principles

As a way of highlighting what is known about effective communication practices, the following propositions provide a synthesis of research summaries cited in Alfonso, Firth, and Neville (1981), Berelson and Steiner (1964), Lovell and Wiles (1983), Osborn and Osborn (1994), and Raiola (1995). The following list can guide supervisors as they communicate with teachers about classroom instruction:

1. Communication is never 100 percent accurate because of the nuances associated with the communication process. The process involves a sender, a receiver, and other variables, and problems may arise in any of these stages in the process.
2. Effectiveness in communication can be increased by completing the communication circuit with immediate feedback; that comes from two-way (oral or spoken) rather than one-way (written) communication.
3. Communication is affected by the positions the sender and receiver hold in an organization, and the message is more likely to be precise and accurate if it progresses in a downward direction (based on authority) than if it progresses in an upward direction within the organization.
4. The experience, expertise, and credibility of an individual affect the frequency of interaction and the degree of acceptance of the message (information) by others.
5. The message communicated is distorted by the types of personality (superiority/inferiority) of the sender and the receiver involved.
6. Communication is more effective when the sender and the receiver share common views and experiences as well as when the message is compatible with these views and is considered reasonable.
7. Communication verifies group norms, and the communication patterns affect accuracy, group leadership, satisfaction of members, and the efficiency with which the group carries out its tasks.
8. Communication is most effective when it is consistent with an individual's views.
9. Communication of factual information is not always the most effective in changing others' opinions; the stronger the emotional and psychological factors, the less impact the factual information may have on the individual.
10. Communication effectiveness is increased when the sender considers his or her personality and style and then communicates the message, using channels (written, verbal, or mass media) that are consistent with the expectations of the group.
11. Communication effectiveness can be improved if the sender organizes the content of the message, determines the appropriate vocabulary for the receiver(s), and matches verbal messages with nonverbal cues.

Communication is an important part of what supervisors do as they confer with teachers, visit with parents, consult with other educators, write memos, talk on the phone, and have meetings. In each situation throughout the day, messages are being sent and received through oral and/or written methods as well as through nonverbal gestures and visual cues. According to Hoy and Miskel (1991), supervisors spend as much as 70 percent of their time communicating with others and are involved in as many as 200 interactions during the school day (Morris et al., 1984). Hoy and Miskel (1991) emphasize the importance of good communication by suggesting that it is the basis for virtually all organizational decisions and is critical to decision making and effective leadership.

In many of the illustrations throughout this chapter, the emphasis has been on communication as it occurs on a day-to-day level in schools. This emphasis has provided supervisors with the technical information to be an effective communicator. These technical skills, over time, have a cumulative effect that helps to establish the tone, shape attitudes, and build commitment to a vision within the school organization. Supervisors must recognize that effective communication is more than nuts and bolts and that words alone are not enough. Ultimately, effective communication contributes to the supervisor's ability to articulate a vision that is clear and shared by both members of the organization and various constituencies; it is building a sense of community and ownership, which serves to guide all aspects of organizational behavior, that leads to change.

Summary

Effective communication practices are essential in working with others in school organizations. This chapter emphasized the technical skills supervisors need to communicate in ways that are clear and concise to achieve the goal of improved instruction. Communication is more than talk; more than words or sounds is communicated. Most definitions of communication recognize some aspect of a common or mutual understanding and/or the sharing of information. Factors for supervisors to consider in the communication process include the sender, encoding of the message, the message, the channel(s) of communication, decoding of the message, and the receiver. To improve the accuracy of the communication process, an opportunity should be provided for the receiver to respond to the message. This form of two-way communication is usually preferable to one-way communication because it provides opportunities for interaction.

There are several responses that supervisors can use to encourage and promote open and free communication. These freeing responses include (1) asking clarifying questions, (2) paraphrasing and summarizing, (3) perception checking, (4) offering information, (5) active attentive listening, and (6) encouraging the heart. In addition to these freeing responses, supervisors may sometimes find themselves employing responses that discourage open, clear communication. These restricting responses include (1) changing the subject, (2) explaining the teacher's behavior, (3) giving directions, (4) leveling the teacher's expectations, (5) denying the teacher's feelings, and (6) giving commands. To develop open and clear communication practices, supervisors should focus on the freeing responses and avoid using the restricting responses. To be effective communicators, supervisors must use their voice effectively and learn to use descriptive, nonjudgmental language.

Supervisors may also employ other forms of communication, especially written and nonverbal. Written communications are often necessary to document that a message has been delivered. Guidelines were provided that supervisors can follow to improve the quality of memos and reports. Categories of nonverbal communication were also listed to help the supervisor be aware of the role and impact that facial gestures, movement, eye contact, and other behaviors have on communication. Finally, communication principles were cited as a guide to help supervisors as they work with teachers and others in schools. These principles can serve as benchmarks for supervisors to use in their interaction with others.

YOUR TURN

5.1. Compose a memo to teachers describing the professional development opportunities that your school district has developed for the year. In this memo, identify any state and local district policies concerning teachers' personal and professional growth and development, the titles of the programs, and the procedures (if any) for registering for the sessions. Develop a rubric for writing routine memos.

5.2. A teacher has stopped you in the hall and wants to discuss his plans for a class field trip. On the basis of a few statements, you have concerns about the trip and feel that perhaps not enough advanced planning has been done to be a successful learning experience for the students. You do not want to say no automatically, but you feel that this is neither the time nor the place to discuss the matter. You would, however, like to keep the lines of communication open. How can you indicate a willingness to discuss the matter further and at the same time express your concerns that the planning may be inadequate and that the matter should be discussed in a more suitable setting? Write out your response, and then role-play this scenario with a colleague/peer.

5.3. Communicating in behavioral language is very important for the supervisor when working with teachers. This form of communication not only adds precision to descriptions of teaching–learning behaviors, but it also helps supervisors avoid making judgmental statements. After observing in a classroom for several minutes (at least 15), develop at least five statements in behavioral language that reflect your observations and then discuss them with the teacher.

5.4. The Association for Supervision and Curriculum Development (ASCD, 1988) has offered 10 suggestions to improve communication. These include:

1. Ask rather than tell
2. Listen more and talk less
3. Explain the reasons
4. Talk as one adult to another
5. Recognize both verbal and nonverbal cues
6. Check for understanding of both oral and written communication
7. Establish trust with staff members
8. Consider employees' feelings
9. Provide feedback in a nonjudgmental way to reduce resistance and defensiveness
10. Try to keep calm and cool

Tape-record a grade level or department meeting, and analyze the discussion according to the suggestions for improved communication listed above. Before listening to the tape, take each of these items and rewrite each as a question. Under each question, place a tally mark if the discussion during the meeting answered these questions and how many times. For example, Do the members of the group ask rather than tell as they make contributions during the meeting? (1), or Are the feelings of the employees considered? If so, to what degree? (8)

5.5. Your school district has a practice of taking turns highlighting special or unique programs at school board meetings during the year. As a central office supervisor in charge of a special program in the district (choose one, such as talented and gifted, resource/special education, developmental reading, or adult education), it is your turn to make a presentation at the meeting this month. What will you communicate to the board about your program in less than three minutes? How will you communicate this information? What prior review or approval will you need for your presentation? What kind of response do you want the board to make? Outline your presentation and have a brief synopsis of your program to distribute to board members. In your outline, indicate the visuals you will use in communicating the information.

REFERENCES

Alfonso, R. J., Firth, G. R., & Neville, R. F. (1981). *Instructional supervision: A behavior system.* (2nd ed.). Boston: Allyn & Bacon.

Association for Supervision and Curriculum Development. (1988). *Educational administrator effectiveness profile: Self-development guide.* Alexandria, VA: Association for Supervision and Curriculum Development.

Barr, D., Elmes, R., & Walker, B. (1980). *Educational leadership for inservice administrators: Participant's manual for an experimental training program.* Omaha: Center for Urban Education.

Berelson, B., & Steiner, G. A. (1964). *Human behavior. An inventory of scientific findings.* New York: Harcourt Brace Jovanovich.

Berlo, D. K. (1960). *The process of communication.* New York: Holt, Rinehart & Winston.

Boyan, N. J., & Copeland, W. D. (1978). *Instructional supervision training program.* Columbus, OH: Charles E. Merrill.

Burmeister, L. E. (1984). *Reading strategies for secondary school teachers.* Reading, MA: Addison-Wesley.

Champy, J. A. (1997). *Preparing for organizational change.* In *The organization of the future.* F. Hesselbein, M. Goldsmith, & R. Beckhard (eds.). San Francisco: Jossey-Bass Publishers.

Costa, A. L., & Garmston, R. J. (1994). *Cognitive coaching: A foundation for renaissance schools.* Norword, MA: Christopher-Gordon Publishers.

Covey, S. R. (1989). *The 7 habits of highly effective people.* New York: Simon & Schuster.

Flesch, R. (1946). *Art of plain talk.* New York: Harper & Row.

Floyd, K. (1993). Symbolic interactionism: Some reflections about leadership and school organization. *Journal of Management Systems, 5,* 32–38.

Floyd, K., & Jacobs, R. M. (1992 August). The discipline of communication: A practical paradigm for educational leadership? Paper presented at the 10th annual meeting of the Association of Management, Las Vegas, NV.

Floyd, K., & Jacobs, R. M. (1993). School communication—An elusive variable? *Journal of Management Systems, 5,* i–iv.

Goldhammer, R., Anderson, R. H., & Krajewski, R. J. (1993). *Clinical supervision: Special methods for the supervision of teachers* (3rd ed.). New York: Holt, Rinehart & Winston

Gorton, R. A. (1987). *School leadership and administration.* (3rd ed.). Dubuque, IA: Wm. C. Brown.

Hamilton, C., & Parker, C. (1993). *Communicating for results: A guide for business and the professions.* (4th ed.). Belmont, CA: Wadsworth.

Hanaka, M., & Hawkins, B. (1997). Organizing for endless winning. In *The organization of the future.* F. Hesselbein, M. Goldsmith, & R. Beckhard (eds.). San Francisco: Jossey-Bass Publishers.

Hoy, W. K., & Miskel, C. G. (1991). *Educational administration: Theory, research and practice.* (4th ed.). New York: McGraw-Hill.

Jacobs, R. M. (1992). Hermeneutics: Probing the nature and logic of school communication. *The Association of Management Proceedings, 10,* 102–107.

Jacobs, R. M. (1993). Road maps to understand school communication. *Journal of Management Systems, 5,* 1–15.

Jewell, L. N. (1998). *Contemporary industrial/organizational psychology.* (3rd ed.). Pacific Grove, CA: Brooks/Cole Publishing Co.

Kelly, E. C., & Rasey, M. I. (1952). *Education and the nature of man.* New York: Harper & Row.

Knezevich, S. J. (1984). *Administration of public education.* (4th ed.). New York: Harper & Row.

Kreps, G. (1990). *Organizational communication.* (2nd ed.). New York: Longman.

Levering, R. (1988). *A great place to work.* New York: Random House.

Lipham, J. M., & Francke, D. (1966). Nonverbal behaviors of administrators. *Educational Administration Quarterly, 2,* 101–109.

Lovell, J. T., & Wiles, K. (1983). *Supervision for better schools.* (5th ed.). Englewood Cliffs, NJ: Prentice-Hall.

Lysaught, J. P. (1984). Toward a comprehensive theory of communication: A review of selected contributions. *Educational Administration Quarterly, 20,* 101–127.

Minor, M. (1995). *Coaching for development: Skills for managers and team leaders.* Menlo, CA: Crisp Publications.

Morris, V., Crowson, R. L., Porter-Gehrie, C., & Hurwitz, E. (1984). *Principals in action: The reality of managing schools.* Columbus, OH: Merrill.

Mortensen, C. D. (1980). Communication postulates. In *Messages: A reader in human communication.* (3rd ed.). S. Weinberg (ed.). New York: Random House.

Oliva, P. F., & Pawlas, G. E. (1997). *Supervision for today's schools.* (5th ed.). New York: Longman.

Osborn, M., & Osborn, S. (1994). *Public speaking.* (3rd ed.). Boston: Houghton Mifflin.

Pfeiffer, I. L., & Dunlap, J. B. (1982). *Supervision of teachers: A guide to improving instruction.* Phoenix: Oryx Press.

Raiola, E. O. (1995). Building relationships: Communication skills for transformational leadership. *The Journal of Adventure Education and Outdoor Leadership, 12,* 13–15.

Reinhartz, J., & King, F. L. (1993). Rethinking the paradigm: Women in leadership roles. In *Women as school executives: A powerful paradigm.* G. Brown & B. Irby (eds.), Texas Council of Women School Executives.

Seiler, W. J., Baudhuin, S. E., & Schuelke, D. L. (1982). *Communication in business and professional organizations.* Reading, MA: Addison-Wesley.

Tracy, S. J., & MacNaughton, R. (1993). *Assisting and assessing educational personnel: The impact of clinical supervision.* Needham Heights, MA: Allyn & Bacon.

Models and Mechanics of Supervision

Chapter 6: Supervision Processes: A Framework for Action
Chapter 7: Classroom Observation: Collecting Information
            about Teaching and Learning

Part Two emphasizes the implementation of effective supervisory practices by providing various models of supervision while also describing various tools and skills to use when conducting classroom observation. Chapter 6 provides a framework for supervisory practice by discussing various models, including clinical and developmental supervision, collegial and collaborative supervision, mentoring, and self-assessment supervision. These models give supervisors options as they implement and apply specific skills when working with various constituencies in schools. Chapter 7 details technical and procedural skills for supervisors as they capture classroom data during observations of teaching and learning episodes. Included in this chapter are suggested guidelines and procedures for collecting information and, perhaps most importantly, tips concerning interacting with teachers as the data from the observations are retrieved. Chapter 7 also provides a wealth of suggested data-capture forms.

6 Supervision Processes

A Framework for Action

OBJECTIVES

The objectives of this chapter are:

- Identify and describe the steps involved in clinical supervision.
- Explain the guidelines for the use of clinical supervision.
- Explain how the Instructional Supervision Training Program (ISTP) is an extension of clinical supervision.
- Identify and describe the components of developmental supervision.
- Describe how clinical and developmental processes work together.
- Discuss the cognitive coaching and mentoring processes as they relate to supervision.
- Describe the self-assessment process and how to apply it personally.

Working to improve the quality of instruction depends on the efforts of both teachers and the supervisory staff. Supervisors as well as other educational leaders have the responsibility for facilitating professional development, building teams of teachers or cohorts and empowering teachers to make decisions regarding their instructional performance. These activities not only involve collecting information and providing feedback but include a variety of ways and contexts for teachers to work together in collegial relationships. What an awesome responsibility! The challenge for supervisors is to integrate what is known about supervision into a process that helps remove obstacles in working with teachers to foster their professional growth and promote quality teaching and learning. The supervisor helps to reshape the school workplace environment so that it is conducive to reflection and dialogue and encourages "greater involvement, autonomous thinking, and collective action" among all members (Glickman, Gordon, and Ross-Gordon, 1998, p. 46). Mastering a repertoire of supervisory skills, as part of the supervisory process, involves promoting collaboration, encouraging dialogue, and achieving the mission established for a school campus. These skills must be applied within a coherent framework to produce the best possible results.

Many of the skills of supervision are acquired as supervisors grow and develop as effective teachers, and as they engage in on-the-job activities. We believe that sufficient theory and knowledge have been generated to assist supervisors in developing a knowledge base and a coherent set of supervisory practices to function effectively. The development of supervisory practices, particularly clinical and developmental ones, provides a framework for implementing and applying specific skills as supervisors work with various constituencies. Coaching and mentoring provide an ongoing process that "encourages sustained reflection on experience, and permits rich opportunities for personal and professional growth" (Reiman and Thies-Sprinthall, 1998, p. 8).

Goldsberry (1988) looks at supervision in a different way. For him, there are three ways of viewing supervision, which include nominal (to maintain status quo), prescriptive (to promote uniform practices), and reflective (to promote reflective adaptation). Of these views, the reflective is least often used because it is difficult to imagine. Goldsberry (1988), like others, views supervision as a complex process with many teacher variables, such as varying backgrounds and past experiences, to consider.

For supervisors to be successful in their role of promoting instructional effectiveness, with the goal of ultimately increasing student achievement, a framework for practice is needed. Such a framework or process should encourage a dialogue and interactions between the supervisor and teacher, which result in agreement about what steps to take and how to proceed. In implementing a framework for action, supervisors should recognize that each teacher is an individual with unique levels of cognitive and professional functioning and with specific degrees of commitment to his or her position and teaching. Therefore, different supervisory processes as well as supervisory styles are required. In this chapter, we will use the term process to describe the various approaches or models that supervisors can use; it connotes an ongoing, continuous professional growth and development.

Within the context of professional growth, supervision processes should take into consideration what is known about teacher development as it relates to supervisory styles and procedures. Clinical supervision, for example, gives the supervisor or teacher mentor a way to begin the dialogue and plan strategies for addressing issues and concerns of the teacher. Developmental supervision integrates the salient attributes of adult development with supervisory styles and suggests that individuals will vary in their backgrounds and relationships.

Supervisors can enhance this supervision process by using a repertoire of supervisory strategies with different teachers, just as teachers must employ a variety of methods to reach all their students. The literature is clear: Teachers have different backgrounds and experiences, different abilities in abstract thinking, and different levels of concern for others (Bents and Harvey, 1981; Christensen, 1985; Glickman, 1981, 1990; Hopkins, 1990; Wilsey and Killion, 1982). Supervisors must employ a framework that most appropriately matches the strategies to the situation or context and the unique characteristics of each teacher.

The primary objective for supervisors is to provide the context for analysis and reflection about classroom teaching behaviors so that courses of action can be developed to assist teachers, as individuals or in teams. This chapter examines the processes of clinical and developmental supervision, along with the processes of coaching and mentoring. The chapter concludes with a discussion of self-assessment supervision, an approach that provides for greater teacher autonomy in the supervisory process. Each process has distinct qualities that can contribute to teachers' growth and development as they seek to improve instruction.

Clinical Supervision

Clinical supervision is a long-term, field-based cyclical process that Reavis (1976, 1977) calls supervision up close because it brings clarity to the classroom and seeks to upgrade the quality of instruction. The use of clinical supervision encourages supervisors and teachers to study and practice the craft of teaching and involves the observation of teachers as they interact with students. Clinical supervision is based on the work of Cogan in the 1950s. Cogan (1973) and Goldhammer (1969) were early advocates of the clinical supervision process. Goldhammer (1969) describes clinical supervision as

> that phase of instructional supervision which draws its data from first-hand observation of actual teaching events, and involves face-to-face...interaction between the supervisor and the teacher in the analysis of teaching behaviors and activities for instructional improvement. (pp. 19–20)

For Cogan (1973), clinical supervision is professional "colleagueship" that takes place between supervisors and teachers and results in the development of teachers who are professionally responsible and who can analyze their own performance while being self-directing and open to input from others. Seager (1992) states that, for himself, Cogan, and Goldhammer, "[clinical] supervision is a form of teaching and that the process goals [are] the same as for any other form of teaching…shared problem solving to empower teachers to manage the resources made available to them in instruction" (p. 2). Anderson (1997) summarizes the definitions of clinical supervision by saying that it is "a hands-on, classroom centered, supportive or developmental activity in which the supervisor…plays essentially a teaching/helping/coaching role and does not engage…in making personnel decisions" (p. 226).

Five-Step Cycle

As clinical supervision is often practiced, it sometimes falls short of its potential because the skills required in the process are underdeveloped or undeveloped in both supervisors and teachers. Goldhammer's (1969) five-step clinical supervision process provides a structure that includes preobservation conference, classroom observation, analysis and strategy, supervision conference, and postconference analysis. In the following section, each step of the five-step cycle is discussed in more detail. Although reference is made to the supervisor, teachers—as they work together in coaching teams either as cognitive coaches or mentors—perform similar functions.

1. Preobservation Conference.   For Kosmoski (1997), the preobservation conference occurs before any classroom observation and "is…the most important stage of the clinical supervision cycle" (p. 184). The purpose of this step is to establish the guidelines and procedures for the activities that will follow. It provides the mental and procedural framework for conducting classroom observations and implementing the rest of the cycle (Goldhammer, Anderson, and Krajewski, 1993). The supervisor and the teacher discuss issues or areas of focus for the observation and the procedures for collecting classroom data relative to these areas; they agree on the basis of this dialogue which teaching–learning behaviors will be examined during the observation period. It is during the preobservation conference that a "contract" is agreed upon; both parties—supervisor and teacher—explicitly buy in to the reasons for the observation, the behaviors to be observed, and the kinds of data to be collected.

Throughout the initial conference, the supervisor and the teacher strive for open and honest communication. For Goldhammer, Anderson, and Krajewski (1993), the preobservation conference serves to (a) confirm and nurture the relationship between the supervisor and teacher, (b) provide an opportunity for the teacher to present his or her lesson plan in its most polished version, (c) give the teacher the opportunity to mentally rehearse the lesson in discussing the proposed teaching–learning episode, (d) give the teacher the opportunity to revise the lesson based on the discussion with the supervisor, and (e) secure agreement on the reasons for the observation and protocol to be followed.

2. Classroom Observation.   During this step, the supervisor observes in the classroom and collects data about the teaching–learning episode. The instructional supervisor acts as another pair of eyes in gathering the information. This step of viewing an actual classroom puts the observer in close proximity to the teacher and students in a specific instructional setting. For Reiman and Thies-Sprinthall (1998), observations serve to capture data about classroom activities and "form the basis for future planning, coaching, and supervision" (p. 196). Information collected about the teaching act is codified by the observer in a systematic way.

Because observational data can be used to resolve problematic issues, it is essential for the supervisor to make careful and detailed notes while observing. Manatt (1981) emphasizes the need for accurate notes when he says that a particular behavior or incident cannot be said to have happened if the observer did not write it down; if it was not written down, the supervisor cannot use it. Other data-collection procedures are described in Chapter 7; such techniques as audiotaping and videotaping may be helpful but are not essential to the process. The classroom observation step is designed to capture as accurately as possible the behaviors of both the teacher and students during a given lesson—to hold up a mirror on the classroom. The essence of this step is to record the behaviors in the classroom such that the notes reflect what actually happened during the lesson.

3. Analysis and Strategy.   The purpose of this step is to make sense out of the data collected and to put the information in some format that can be easily interpreted and understood. Using tallies, the supervisor may convert these to percentages or represent behaviors on charts, graphs, or diagrams; then the teacher can draw his or her own conclusions.

Analysis is the heart of clinical supervision; it assists the supervisor, and ultimately the teacher, in "thinking analytically about what was observed and coming to an understanding of the issues, questions, and principles that are involved" (Goldhammer, Anderson, Krajewski, 1993, p. 45). The analysis step moves the results of the observation from what could be an arbitrary and, in some cases, punitive view to a more accurate and objective interpretation. After the data have been analyzed, a plan of action (strategy) is developed to determine future sequences of instruction and the focus of future observations (if needed). The analysis of the observational data and the subsequent development of strategies provide the basis for discussion and decisions about what comes next.

4. Supervision Conference.   For Goldhammer (1969), "All roads lead to the conference" (p. 67). During the postobservation conference, the information collected during the observation along with the analysis is presented to the teacher for review, discussion, and recommendations (Glenn, 1993). The postobservation conference provides the supervisor and the teacher with the opportunity to review the behaviors that were initially agreed upon initially in step one, to assess the data collected regarding the instructional sequence, to reinforce or commend effective behaviors, to discuss future observation times, and/or to redefine the observation agreement.

Another benefit of the supervision conference is that it gives the supervisor the opportunity to discuss with the teacher possible solutions and techniques of self-supervision. In the most ideal situations, the supervisor and the teacher work collaboratively to resolve any problem areas and to stimulate interest in long-term professional growth and development. The "critical moment...comes when the teacher acknowledges that the procedure has yielded an accurate assessment of existing...professional attributes" (Beach and Reinhartz, 1982, p. 9).

5. *Postconference analysis.* During this stage, supervisory techniques, assumptions, emotional variables, and goals are analyzed by the supervisor. For Goldhammer, Anderson, and Krajewski (1993), it is the conscience of clinical supervision. In this step, the supervisor reflects on his or her behavior to determine if the best agreement with the teacher was developed and if the teacher was helped. When the teacher acknowledges that the data collected are valid and accurate, then the supervisor, working cooperatively with the teacher, can formulate recommendations for change in classroom instructional behaviors. The postconference analysis helps the supervisor find an answer to the question, "How effective was I?"

Figure 6.1 provides an overview of the steps in the clinical supervision process within the context of what is known about effective teaching (see Chapter 9 on teaching).

Seager (1992) summarizes the circumstances and motivation for clinical supervision when he says that "Bob [Goldhammer] address[ed] those who believe that clinical supervision can follow a model that exists independently, i.e., apart from the individual supervisor and teacher engaged in the process" (p. 2). Seager (1992) continues by citing Goldhammer on the subject of clinical supervision and the need to be independent in the process:

> In large part, we avoid the pretentiousness of supervision that is armed with *a priori* values and that is satisfied only when it has remade teachers in its own image. In spite of our limitations, there is no question that we have been genuinely helpful to many...teachers [because] we have...been able to work from within their frames of reference and to engage them in producing...changes which generate new satisfactions. (p. 2)

Guidelines for Use of Clinical Supervision

Renewed interest in clinical supervision has resulted in several new perspectives that provide additional guidelines for its use. Goldhammer, Anderson, and Krajewski (1993) have conceptualized clinical supervision as a technology to improve instruction. Glatthorn (1984), while cautioning against the use of "reliable generalizations," does offer tentative research findings about the effectiveness of clinical supervision. Supervisors may find the following results helpful:

■ Most teachers and administrators agree with the basic assumptions of clinical supervision (Eaker, 1972).

■ Teachers tend to favor a supervisor who is close and supportive (Gordon, 1976).

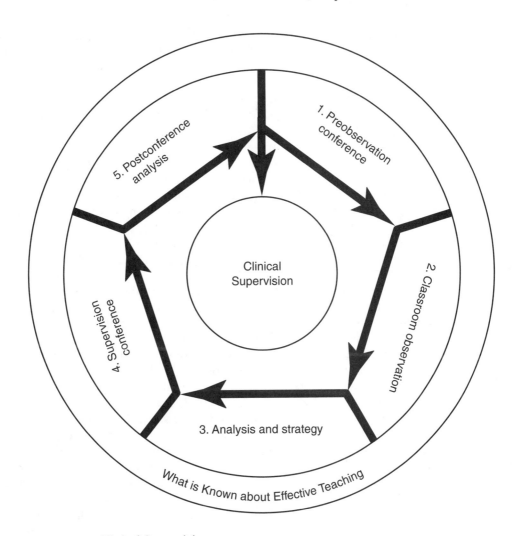

FIGURE 6.1   **Clinical Supervision**

■ Teachers seem to prefer clinical supervision to traditional supervision and believe that the techniques of clinical supervision are worthwhile (Reavis, 1977; Shinn, 1976).

■ Clinical supervision can provide a mechanism for assisting teachers in changing behavior in a desired direction (Garman, 1971; Gordon, 1992; Kerr, 1976; Krajewski, 1976; Shuma, 1973).

■ Supervisors using a clinical supervision process seem more open and accepting in postobservation conferences than those using a traditional approach (Reavis, 1977).

■ Teachers differ in the type of supervisory interactions they prefer; there is some evidence that experienced teachers prefer nondirective supervision while beginning teachers seem to prefer a more direct style (Glickman, 1985).

For clinical supervision to be effective, there are some common themes that are evident. These themes include (a) teachers and supervisors develop a collegial relationship characterized by trust, respect, and reciprocity; (b) teachers control which aspects of their teaching–learning process will be focused on and reported back during the follow-up conferences; (c) teachers retain control over decisions that impact their teaching practices; (d) the clinical supervision process continues over an extended period lasting from three months to several academic semesters; (e) supervisors provide teachers with nonjudgmental observational data that focus on interactions of interest to the teacher; and (f) both teachers and supervisors engage in reflective practice (Nolan, Hawkes, and Francis, 1993).

Supervisors, as they employ clinical supervision, should be aware of the perceptions of teachers. For example, teachers tend to favor individualized, close, and supportive supervision, which addresses their individual needs. Teachers also agree on the basic assumptions and worthwhileness of clinical supervision and are willing to accept recommendations for change. Finally, teachers believe that change in their classroom behavior is possible.

Clinical supervision is not a panacea for supervisors. For Tanner and Tanner (1987), clinical supervision focuses "on actual class practices…which…ensures that the process is of practical significance to the teacher" (p. 183). It is a way of promoting teacher growth in self-direction and self-confidence by encouraging teachers to make instructional decisions. The supervisor supports the teacher as the decision maker and asks him or her to consider options based on a knowledge of sound instructional practices, as well as the feedback from observational data when appropriate; the supervisor "can pinpoint inappropriate teaching decisions and behaviors, then offer productive alternatives" (Hunter, 1985, p. 58). Yet, at the same time, clinical supervision places much of the responsibility for identifying and solving instructional problems on the teacher (Pellicer, 1982). Clinical supervision is more than a teacher inspection model (Snyder, 1981); it is a framework for observing and interacting with teachers. Clinical supervision equips the instructional supervisor and the teacher with the knowledge and skills to improve instructional performance.

The Instructional Supervision Training Program

An expanded version of clinical supervision has been developed by Boyan and Copeland (1978). The Instructional Supervision Training Program (ISTP) is a 5-stage, 10-step sequential process that the instructional supervisor and the teacher can use as they focus on classroom instructional interactions. A description of the 5 stages of the process is presented in Figure 6.2.

In stage I, the preobservation conference, the teacher and supervisor identify, in behavioral terms, the area or issues of instructional concern and discuss a base rate, which represents the frequency of the behavior(s). They also select or create an observation instrument for the supervisor to use in collecting data during the classroom observation.

In stage II, the supervisor observes the teacher's class and collects data, using the observation instrument. In stage III, the supervisor analyzes the data from the observation and puts them in a visual form for the teacher to interpret and analyze. The supervisor also analyzes the data and determines which teaching behaviors should be maintained and which ones should be modified (for discussion in the postobservation conference).

Stage IV involves the postobservation conference, where the supervisor provides the teacher with the results of the observation in a visual form and, together

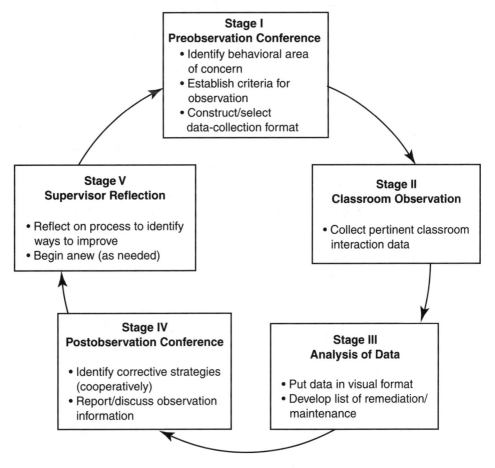

FIGURE 6.2   Instructional Supervision Training Program

with the teacher, determines specific strategies to implement to correct the identified instructional problem(s).

We have added stage V where the supervisor engages in reflection concerning the process and seeks to determine ways to improve the process by asking: How accurate were the data? Was the visual feedback to the teacher useful in analyzing what occurred? How could I have been more effective? Did I establish a trusting, collegial relationship? Were we able to develop possible solutions?

An underlying assumption of the ISTP process is the belief that as teachers become more directly involved in initiating, altering, or modifying specific instructional behaviors, and as they analyze the data presented by the supervisor, instructional issues will be addressed and/or solved. Close cooperation between the supervisor and the teacher is critical in the ISTP process; if it is to work effectively, it must be characterized by trusting, collegial, and collaborative relationships.

A word of caution is in order, however. When clinical supervision is used as the primary means of evaluating personnel, it makes such a collegial relationship extremely difficult, if not impossible. The ISTP process should be perceived more as a supportive system, with the instructional supervisor focusing on the collective action of those involved within the school environment. In such an environment, the commitment to professional growth is strengthened.

Clinical supervision, as seen in the ISTP process, links the growth phase of professional development with everyday classroom events and provides supervisors and teachers with the framework for improving teaching when "characterized as a partnership...targeted on discovering and refining ways to enhance learning" (Goldsberry, 1984, p. 14). If such a partnership is nurtured, supervision as inspection gives way to supervision as problem solving.

When supervisors and teachers become proficient in the use of clinical supervision, either the five-step process or the expanded ISTP version, they become better at reflecting on the teaching–learning behaviors and developing strategies for change. Supervisors can serve as catalysts in promoting instructional effectiveness as they establish cohort groups of teachers or peer coaching teams that utilize the steps of clinical supervision as a comprehensive professional growth and development process. It is encouraging that Holifield and Cline (1997) found that "teachers...assigned a high value to...clinical supervision [and its]...inherent practices and intended outcomes" (p. 112). The clinical supervision process can be helpful in identifying, collecting, and interpreting information germane to the school's, teacher's, and sometimes the supervisor's mission and goals.

Pajak (1993) summarizes by describing four families of clinical supervision. The first, the original clinical process (Cogan, 1973; Goldhammer, 1969; Mosher and Purpel, 1972), represents an eclectic view. It draws upon contemporary psychological theory while emphasizing collegiality, mutual discovery, and problem solving. The second in the clinical family is the humanistic/artistic approach (Blumberg, 1974, 1980; Eisner, 1979, 1982). This view of supervision emphasizes the interpersonal relationships that occur as supervisors work with teachers while recognizing the importance of intuition, artistry, and idiosyncrasy in the holistic analysis of classrooms. The third view in the clinical family is technical/didactic

(Acheson and Gall, 1992; Hunter, 1980, 1985; Joyce and Showers, 1982, 1988). This approach emphasizes supervisor behavior in sequencing and applying discrete skills in planning, observing, and conferencing. It also utilizes the application of effective teaching practices as a framework for observation. The fourth view in the clinical supervision family is developmental/reflective (Glickman, 1985, 1990; Glickman, Gordon, and Ross-Gordon, 1998). It focuses on the developmental characteristics of teachers; by fostering reflection and introspection, teachers become aware of their own behaviors and motivations.

Clinical supervision has enjoyed a long history, and it has endured several decades of reform and restructuring. Yet, it continues to be a viable process for supervisors and teachers to employ as they both strive to improve student achievement.

Developmental Supervision

Another process of supervision is called developmental supervision (Glickman, 1981, 1985, 1992; Glickman, Gordon, and Ross-Gordon, 1998). This model recognizes teachers as individuals who are at various stages of growth and development. Within this framework, supervisors (as they interact with teachers) seek to foster thinking skills, which help in the analysis of classroom instruction and make teachers more aware of the many options for change. In this process, effective instruction requires autonomous and flexible-thinking teachers, yet many school systems fail to encourage autonomy or provide ways to stimulate teachers' thinking about teaching. For many teachers, change means simplifying and deadening the classroom environment by disregarding student differences and establishing and maintaining routines that result in a sterility of sameness.

In such a bleak environment, teachers strive just to get through the day. Studies (Oja, 1981; Sprinthall and Thies-Sprinthall, 1982; Thies-Sprinthall, 1980) suggest that in a supportive and stimulating environment where teachers' developmental characteristics are recognized, teachers can think at higher abstract levels. For Glickman, Gordon, and Ross-Gordon (1998), "Instructional improvement takes place when teachers improve their decision making about students' learning… and…improving teacher decision making is largely a process of adult learning" (p. 51). Developmental supervision is built on the premise that "human development is the aim of education" (Glickman, 1985, p. 85). As supervisors work with teachers in an educational setting, they "should match their assistance to teachers' conceptual levels, but with the ultimate goal of teachers taking charge of their own improvement" (Glickman and Gordon, 1987, p. 64). In addition, supervisors must be knowledgeable about and responsive to the developmental stages and life transitions of teachers. The implications of personal and professional development will be discussed more fully in Chapter 11.

Glickman, Gordon, and Ross-Gordon (1998), in describing the developmental process, identify four styles supervisors may employ: (1) directive control, (2) directive informational, (3) collaborative, and (4) nondirective. The *directive control style* includes the following kinds of supervisory behaviors: directing, standardizing, and reinforcing consequences; it results in a mutually agreed-upon plan of action. In the *directive informational style,* the supervisor standardizes and restricts choices, and the plan of action is supervisor-suggested. The *collaborative style* includes the following behaviors: listening, presenting, problem solving, and negotiating; the result is a mutually agreed-upon plan of action. A *nondirective style* views teachers as capable of analyzing and solving their own instructional problems; the outcome is generated by the teacher, who determines the plan of action. Behaviors associated with the nondirective approach include listening, clarifying, encouraging, and reflecting.

Developmental supervision is also influenced by two teacher variables that change over time and are related to instruction: level of commitment and level of conceptual thinking. Commitment is the willingness of teachers to expend time and energy in their work. It appears that, over time, teachers move developmentally from a concern for self to a concern for their students to, finally, a concern for other students and other teachers. This concern is expressed in the teachers' willingness to devote their time and energy to helping others.

This aspect of teacher development, level of commitment, can be viewed as occurring along a continuum:

Low Commitment   High Commitment

As Glickman (1981, 1990) suggests, teachers who are at the low commitment end tend to be centered on their own personal and professional goals and exert time and energy to ensure their survival in the classroom. These teachers, whose concern is for their own success and/or survival, demonstrate less concern for students and others. Supervisors, in working with these teachers, generally employ a directive style to achieve some movement in a positive direction along the continuum. At the opposite end of the continuum are teachers who have a high level of commitment, which is shown in their concern not only for their students but for other students and teachers as well. These teachers are willing to expend extra time and energy in activities in an effort to help others. Supervisors most often use a nondirective style in working with these teachers. In the mid-range of the continuum are teachers at various stages of development; because of a wide variance in levels of commitment in this area, supervisors frequently use a collaborative style in working with these teachers.

Conceptual levels can also be viewed as a continuum, as Glickman (1981, 1990) and Glickman, Gordon, and Ross-Gordon (1998) suggest. Teachers at high conceptual levels would be at one end, those with moderate ability in the mid-range, and teachers with low conceptual levels at the opposite end.

Low Conceptual Thinking (Concrete)	Moderate Conceptual Thinking (Moderately Abstract)	High Conceptual Thinking (Abstract)

Teachers at the high end of the continuum have the ability to conceptualize a problem from many perspectives, formulate several alternative plans, select a plan, and follow through with each step. These teachers tend to be "independent, self-actualizing, resourceful, [and] flexible" (Glickman, Gordon, and Ross-Gordon, 1998, p. 58). In working with teachers who can think abstractly, the supervisor encourages and reassures them as they experiment with new ideas and teaching methods and secures appropriate resources for successful lesson implementation. Teachers who are comfortable with the supervisory style that matches their developmental stage and that is appropriate to their needs—the nondirective approach—tend to be less rigid, more independent, more perceptive, and task-effective; they adapt easily to problem-solving situations.

Teachers who are capable of a moderate level of abstract thinking can define the problem but are limited in their ability to generate several possibilities, formulate a plan, and then follow through. They "have difficulty formulating a comprehensive plan" (Glickman, Gordon, and Ross-Gordon, 1998, p. 58). Supervisors most often use a collaborative style of supervision in working with these teachers, encouraging them to reflect on what they are doing—their decisions about planning, teaching, and interacting with their students.

Teachers who have low conceptual thinking levels may be unclear about the problem and unable to conceptualize what should be done. They frequently assess the situation in simple terms and respond in habitual ways that have worked in the past. In working with teachers who have a limited ability to think abstractly, the supervisor is usually more directive. Working collaboratively with teachers, the supervisor emphasizes the importance of preparing detailed plans and provides these five types of assistance: (1) simple, clear statements and explanations; (2) many opportunities to practice what is discussed; (3) support in developing a sequence of instructional skills; (4) concrete guidance during frequent conferences; and (5) consistent and regular feedback and reinforcement.

In the developmental process, the role of the supervisor is to give more responsibility for instructional improvement to the teachers, within a cooperative problem-solving framework. Supervisors and teachers (or teachers and teachers when using a peer coaching or cognitive coaching approach) make joint decisions and collectively work out solutions to instructional issues that have been identified. Motivation for continued instructional improvement comes from the action of the teacher as well as from the supervisor or other teachers. In such an environment, teachers become empowered by taking greater control of their own professional development.

The Clinical and Developmental
Models Working Together

The clinical and developmental models give supervisors and teachers choices about how classroom instruction is viewed and analyzed. Clinical supervision provides the structure and steps to follow or a framework for working with teachers. Developmental supervision provides the supervisor with a way to connect the teacher's level of professional development with an appropriate supervisory style. The two approaches, while unique in their views of the supervision process, are not mutually exclusive and can often be employed together. A supervisor, for example, might use a directive style, which has its roots in developmental supervision, when giving a teacher experiencing instructional difficulty specific suggestions about what to do to correct a problem. In the preobservation conference, the supervisor would request the following information: a seating chart, a list of rules for classroom conduct, a list of instructional objectives, lesson plans, and a list of resources used in the preparation of the lesson. When giving the teacher precise instructions, the supervisor uses a directive control style. The preobservation conference and data collection take place within the context of clinical supervision. In this example, the characteristics of clinical supervision are not violated even though modifications have been made and a directive supervisory style used. In fact, the clinical and developmental models of supervision can complement each other and enhance the supervisor's effectiveness.

Sparks-Langer and Colton (1991) have developed a self-directed practice, which includes coaching, and a developmental supervision continuum, beginning with a directive approach and moving to a nondirective approach, with collaboration generally occurring in the middle. The essence of the directive approach employs the clinical supervision cycle of starting with a preobservation conference, collecting data with the help of a coach, and concluding with a postobservation conference (using an added dimension of reflective journal writing). When the collaborative approach is employed, the emphasis, according to Sparks-Langer and Colton (1991), is to problem-solve using action research, interactive journals, modeling/teaming, goal setting, analysis of ideas, and reciprocal conferences. The last position on the continuum, nondirective, is peer or cognitive coaching that includes a modified version of clinical supervision, with the preobservation conference and data collection followed by a postobservation conference. The purpose of the nondirective approach is self-assessment and self-reflection.

Whatever the style used (directive, collaborative, or nondirective), the process involves a coach who asks questions, which in turns leads to action. However, it is still the teacher who makes key decisions about the plan of action and the way the plan can be achieved. For Sparks-Langer and Colton (1991), reflection is important to the overall process and has several implications. Teachers' reflective thinking can:

1. Be fostered through micro-teaching, journal writing, self-analysis, and discussion of student learning

2. Be promoted through an examination of cases that focuses on context, content, and pedagogy

3. Provide them with opportunities to construct their own meaning from research and other sources of information

4. Encourage them to analyze their "preconceptions of teaching, learning and the purposes of schooling" to allow for a thoughtful approach to teaching (p. 43)

Getting teachers to think about their teaching behavior by employing both clinical and developmental supervision brings to the forefront the special qualities of each model. Supervisors using the clinical process have a structure to follow and very specific tasks to accomplish. When the developmental model is used in conjunction with clinical supervision, the human dimensions are added, including information about the developmental levels and needs of teachers. By recognizing that each teacher is at a specific point in his or her professional career, supervisory support will vary; thus, supervisory behaviors will vary from teacher to teacher as well.

Collegial and Collaborative Supervision

Partnerships, collegial and collaborative relationships, coaching, and mentoring are names that are also given to the supervision process in which learning, growing, and changing are the mutual focus for supervisors and teachers. Such names are designed to make "supervision more collaborative, and the culture of teaching less isolating and hierarchical" (Arredondo, Brody, Zimmerman, and Moffett, 1995, p. 74). For Kirby and Meza (1997), in the collegial perspective, "The school is seen as a center of shared expertise in which experimentation, discovery and risk taking are encouraged and mistakes are considered learning opportunities" (p. 81).

Peer Coaching

One collaborative approach involves the development of peer coaching (Joyce, 1987; Joyce and Showers, 1982; Showers, 1984; Showers and Joyce, 1996). Peer coaching utilizes teams of teachers—across grades and subjects—who provide daily support and encouragement to each other. The role of the supervisor is one of facilitator as he or she works with small groups of teachers. The coaching approach uses cohorts and is often coupled with clinical supervision; it emphasizes professional action by peers. As teachers participate in small-group sessions, their focus is on asking questions, which serve to clarify their own perceptions about schooling and learning. Through analysis and feedback, supervisors (along with cohort members) find out the reasons for a teacher's decision and coach the teacher on the job by translating research on effective planning and teaching into classroom practice. Showers and Joyce (1996) have found that "teachers who had a coaching relationship—that is who shared aspects of teaching, planned together, and pooled their experiences—applied new skills more frequently and appropriately" (p. 14).

The question often asked about coaching is, How do you start? For Showers (1990), it begins with a school philosophy or mission that is supportive of collaboration among teachers. Such collaboration means having time to develop plans and talk about instructional strategies, so it is important for entire faculties to decide if they want to be part of the peer coaching process (Showers and Joyce, 1996). In addition, there is a commitment among faculty members to lifelong learning and growing. Such an environment is ripe for coaching. The next concern is the selection of partners or team members. When selecting partners, it is important to consider pairing teachers who get along personally, have similar schedules (common planning times), have learning styles that match, and are from different grade levels or disciplines. In establishing peer coaching teams, Showers and Joyce (1996) have found "attention to the social organization is extremely important" (p. 14). The development of coaching skills usually focuses on three areas: observation, communication, and problem solving.

In examining the evolution of peer coaching, Showers and Joyce (1996) have established four principles to guide the process. These principles are:

1. Teachers must collectively agree to be part of the peer coaching teams and support one another.

2. Verbal feedback is not necessary and can be omitted as a coaching component.

3. In the coaching teams, the person teaching is the coach and the person observing is being coached.

4. The collaboration that occurs in coaching teams is more than observing and conferencing; it includes planning, developing, thinking, and working together.

Kirby and Meza (1997) discovered that, despite some barriers, "coaching... has been remarkably successful" (p. 89). They also found that peer coaching can be instrumental in school restructuring efforts.

Cognitive Coaching

According to Costa and Garmston (1994), "cognitive coaching is a nonjudgmental process built around a planning conference, observation, and a reflecting conference" (p. 2). It also involves the application of specific strategies to enhance a colleague's perceptions, decisions, and intellectual functions with the intent to improve student learning. Or, as Pajak (1993) suggests, it "is a process of mediating, nurturing, and enhancing the intellectual functions, perceptions, and decision making processes of teaching" (p. 264). It is the improvement of these inner thought processes of teachers, which are precursors to the improved teaching behaviors, that leads to increased student learning. For Reiman and Thies-Sprinthall (1998), "Coaching encourages persons to perform in more complex ways as they undertake their new roles" (p. 240).

Cognitive coaching may pair teacher with teacher, teacher with supervisor, or supervisor with supervisor, but when two educators in similar roles or positions are linked, the process is also called peer coaching. For Costa and Garmston (1994), the three major goals of cognitive coaching include: (1) developing and maintaining a trusting relationship; (2) promoting learning through a coaching relationship; and (3) fostering growth toward both autonomous and interdependent behavior (holonomy).

The cognitive coaching process is built on a foundation of trust, which is fundamental to success. Therefore, trust must be nurtured and maintained as the participants interact with each other, especially when the interaction involves supervisor and teacher. Trust is built over time and, as noted by Pajak (1993), supervisors help to establish trust "most directly through demonstrations of their own competence, consistency, personal availability, and confidentiality" (p. 266). As teachers work with teachers or supervisors in a coaching relationship, learning is the ultimate goal of the interaction. Costa and Garmston (1994) view learning as the rearrangement and restructuring of mental processes. As supervisors and teachers interact, opportunities are presented for them to learn more about themselves, each other, and the teaching–learning process as they conduct a dialogue about the decisions made prior to, during, and after instruction. Teachers and supervisors are encouraged to move beyond their current abilities into new or enhanced behaviors and skills.

As a result of the coaching process, teachers are encouraged to become more autonomous, self-assured, and self-modifying individuals in their classrooms. At the same time, teachers also realize that they are interdependent, a part of a greater whole within their school or district. This interplay between autonomy and interdependence Costa and Garmston (1994) call holonomy.

The coaching process has three components: the planning conference, the lesson observation, and the reflecting conference. The planning conference provides an opportunity to build trust, to focus on the teacher's goals, to mentally rehearse the lesson, and to establish the parameters of the reflecting conference. The following questions, which can be asked during a planning conference, illustrate how a coach mediates by having the teacher address the questions listed:

Coach	*Teacher*
What do you want the students to learn from this lesson?	Clarify student outcome(s) for the lesson
How will the students learn what you want them to learn?	Clarify the plan for the lesson and the teaching strategy
What will you have students do to demonstrate they have learned?	Clarify methods for gathering evidence of student learning
What would you want me to observe while you teach? What data would be important for me to collect?	Identify the coach's data-gathering focus and procedures

The lesson observation provides the context for the coach to employ one or more of a variety of data-collection strategies agreed upon in the planning conference. The reflecting conference is normally conducted after a period of time has elapsed so that the teacher can think about the lesson before participating in the conference. During the reflecting conference, the coach encourages the teacher to describe and discuss impressions about the lesson and to compare what was discussed during the planning conference with what actually happened. The teacher describes what might be done in future lessons and what insights have been gained as a result of the process. Finally, the teacher comments on the success of the coaching process.

For coaching to be successful, sufficient time must be made available to enable the individuals involved to work together. Making time means providing a forum for professional dialogue—freeing up teachers to team with fellow teachers so they can work with each other, examine topics they are not familiar with, and observe each other. Coaching provides another way to support professional growth and change in teachers. Inherent in the process is the notion that, in the end, all students will benefit because all faculty are sharing ideas as they work toward the goal of learning for all.

Mentoring

Recently, the process of mentoring has been viewed as another collaborative approach to supervision. In fact, Reiman and Thies-Sprinthall (1998) have entitled their book *Mentoring and Supervision for Teacher Development* to reinforce this linkage. Elliott (1995) has also noted that "Mentoring as a practice…has been adopted at a rate which has exceeded the conceptual development itself" (p. 246).

Mentoring, as described in the literature, involves interacting with a protégé in order to transmit the lessons of experience or a professional legacy (Healy and Welchert, 1990). Anderson and Lucasse-Shannon (1988) emphasize the relationship between the key figures by citing five mentoring functions: teaching, sponsoring, encouraging, counseling, and befriending. Turner (1993) stresses the importance of the relationship by pointing out that the personality of each is important to successful interaction. Elliott and Calderhead (1993) also emphasize the relationship aspect of mentors and their protégés. In his landmark book, *Effective Teaching and Mentoring*, Laurent Daloz (1986) describes mentors as guides who

> lead us along the journey of our lives. We trust them because they have been there before. They embody our hopes, cast light on the way ahead, interpret…signs, warn us of…dangers, and point out unexpected delights along the way. (p. 17)

The Commission on the Role and Preparation of Mentor Teachers (1991) of the Association of Teacher Educators describes mentoring as a complex process or function that involves support, assistance, and guidance, but not evaluation of the protégés. It also requires time and communication in order to facilitate self-reliance in protégés. The complexity of the mentoring process requires that mentors recognize the importance of their function if effective mentoring is to occur. To illustrate this, Head, Reiman, and Thies-Sprinthall (1992) suggest that at "the heart…of mentoring is [the]…belief in the value and worth of people" (p. 5).

As mentors work with protégés, they perform several roles or functions. First, the mentor provides guidance by helping the protégé to negotiate the complexities of the institutional culture and to understand the policies and procedures that govern behavior (Little, 1990; Reiman and Edelfelt, 1990). Next, the mentor provides coaching regarding professional practice and helps with professional development through cycles of assistance (Bey, 1990). The mentor also serves as a trusted advisor or colleague who lends an attentive ear and helps identify, analyze, and solve problems (Daloz, 1986). Finally, mentors also serve as encouragers and developers both by praising and celebrating successes and by causing their protégés to think about their teaching and other professional experiences (Reiman, 1988).

Mentoring models have proven to be effective for adults in that they help to shorten the learning curve and improve initial performance. Mentoring also serves to increase collegiality and retention in the profession. Finally, it helps to establish a professional legacy as experienced educators and mentors recognize that their own professional growth is linked to that of their protégés (Daloz, 1986).

Gillman and Rickert (1991) have noted that for the mentoring process to be successful, mentors who are role models must be recruited and provided with training. In addition, the ground rules for the process must be established and clarified at the onset of the mentoring relationship in a one-to-one situation. As the mentor and protégé interact, they develop and agree on an agenda or outline of goals for the relationship. Finally, mentors must work to establish a rapport with their protégés that facilitates good communication and destroys any biases or prejudices. As Odell (1990) has observed, the essence of mentoring is found in its assistance functions such as supporting, sponsoring, guiding, counseling, advising, encouraging, befriending, and protecting. These functions can serve as a type of supervision, using a formative approach, which can guide the professional growth and development of teachers.

Self-Assessment Supervision

Another process of supervision involving teachers is called self-assessment supervision. As Reiman and Thies-Sprinthall (1998) note, "The most important dimension of self-assessment is the ability to reflect on one's experience as a teacher" (p. 284). To improve instructionally, teachers learn to analyze their own classroom behavior. Although supervisors may be involved as they collect classroom data, assessment of classroom performance begins with teachers who are developmentally ready. Teachers, therefore, need to have self-analysis skills to examine the various aspects of their instructional delivery system. Such skills assist teachers in making appropriate decisions about their teaching (Reinhartz and Beach, 1983).

Self-assessment is the process of reflection that engages teachers in a variety of activities (e.g., inventories, reflective journals, and portfolios) for the purpose of instructional improvement by rethinking past instructional episodes and generating alternatives. But as Reiman and Thies-Sprinthall observe, "Unfortunately for many…self-analysis may not be automatic" (p. 284). Therefore, to begin the process, teachers may work with supervisors or in peer groups, responding to oral or written prompts or engaging in conversations about their teaching profile (their instructional selves).

As a part of the site-based management movement, self-assessment seems appropriate with the focus being the school, the individual teachers becoming the unit of measure, and self-governance being the goal (Glickman, 1992). Self-assessment supervision shifts the responsibility for change from the supervisor to the teacher. Even though the supervisor is involved, he or she plays a different role—one who assists the teacher in developing an accurate instructional profile. In addition, the supervisor is invited to participate in the self-assessment process and works with the teacher to optimize resources. Self-assessment helps teachers be the best they can be, and the new attitude becomes one of continuous improvement.

During self-assessment, teachers are called upon to evaluate their own performance so they will be more aware of the strengths and weaknesses associated with their classroom instruction. As teachers begin the process, they can start to compare their teaching–learning profile with the characteristics of effective instruction. Goldhammer (1969) feels that teachers should "confront" their teaching. Smyth (1991) says of Goldhammer's attitude that teachers need to come "face-to-face with the realities of their own teaching" (p. 345). Smyth suggests that teachers "confront themselves…[and] move beyond the habitual, the unquestionable, and the ritualistic in a way that enables them to better see the social and historical nature of those practices" (pp. 345–346). Figure 6.3 shows the sequence of seven steps in the self-assessment process that helps teachers confront the realities of their instructional selves.

The first step in self-assessment supervision is for teachers to analyze and reflect on their teaching performances. Self-diagnosis and self-awareness are the keys to this process. As they reflect on their performances, teachers may choose to use inventories that are based on behaviors associated with effective instruction (cited in Chapter 9) or other inventories that would describe their classroom and instructional behavior. The inventories should be specific enough to encourage teachers to make critical decisions regarding their instructional efficacy. The results generated from this step give teachers a beginning database for developing an instructional profile. Keeping a journal is also critical in step one; it provides teachers with opportunities to record what occurs daily and how they feel about each occurrence. Reflection time is key to self-assessment. Reflection becomes time devoted to personal and professional thinking, and the journal writings represent the past as well as the present and help to shape the future. Teachers consider how they feel by tapping into their deepest feelings.

In the second step of the self-assessment process, teachers use the information from their journals and from the completed inventories to answer the question, "How effective have I been in assessing my own performance?" As they analyze their own recorded perceptions, they begin to get a sense of their professional selves. Taken together, these images help to form a picture or profile for the teacher.

The third step in self-assessment involves feedback from other sources. Feedback can be solicited from supervisors, peers, and/or students. The inventories are normally designed to gather information about teachers' classroom behavior. As they work together, supervisors and teachers can modify these inventories

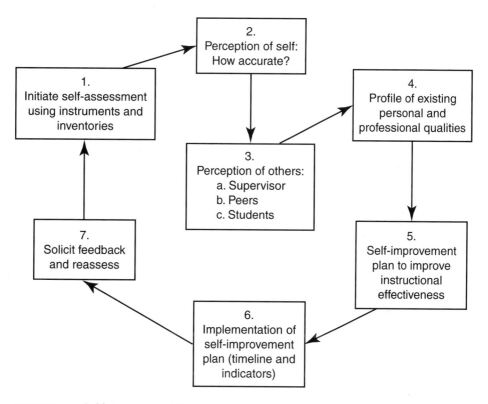

FIGURE 6.3   Self-Assessment Process

or develop other inventories that parallel the objectives of their own school and district or speak to other identified needs. The perceptions of others also help the teacher in constructing a professional profile.

In addition to inventories and journals, videotaping and audiotaping can be useful tools for the teacher in building a teaching portfolio or profile. These techniques provide a more objective database for analyzing classroom behaviors and give teachers the opportunity to see how they look and/or sound. Teachers can view or listen to these tapes in private, which is also less threatening. Teachers may ask their peers and/or the supervisor to observe a lesson, complete an inventory, or assist them in the process of cognitive coaching.

The fourth step in self-assessment is most important in determining the accuracy of the information from other sources. The critical moment in the self-assessment comes when the teacher acknowledges that the process has yielded an accurate picture or profile of existing personal and professional attributes. A common reaction teachers need to guard against is the rationalizing or explaining away of ineffective classroom behaviors. At this point, teachers may believe that the perceptions of others are inaccurate and feel that no one knows them well enough to provide pertinent data. For the process of self-assessment to be effective, teachers should make an honest commitment to analyze their classroom behaviors and, when appropriate, to make changes. Additionally, teachers must have confidence in the process and in themselves. If these two factors are objectively addressed, the original goal of the model—that of self-improvement—can be achieved.

If the data collected on the inventories or the feedback from others is inconsistent with the teacher's own assessment or perception, then there is a misconception concerning classroom effectiveness. In such cases, it is necessary to work toward reconciling the teacher's self-perception with the results of the other measures. For example, in an extreme mismatch, the teacher may perceive himself or herself as fair, student-oriented, and committed to the school's philosophy; supervisors, peers, or students may view the teacher as inflexible, demanding, and too content-oriented. For the self-assessment model to work, the teacher must be prepared to objectively compare the responses from all sources. The goal of self-assessment is not necessarily to have the teacher's responses match those of others. It is essential, however, for the teacher to acknowledge possible differences in perceptions, work with the supervisor to put the discrepancies in perspective, and then brainstorm possible causes for the differences.

A discrepancy may be the result of a teacher's lack of candidness when completing the self-assessment inventory. Or, the teacher may be unaware of the perception of the class during instruction and sincerely believe that everything concerning classroom performance is progressing satisfactorily. In step four, teachers who are genuinely interested in self-improvement will want to constructively deal with the different perceptions as presented by inventory results. When there are few or minimal discrepancies, the teacher will want to examine the feedback closely and think of potential growth areas.

The fifth step involves developing possible strategies for initiating improvement. With the focus on self-assessment, the teacher takes the lead in generating possible instructional changes that would facilitate professional growth and development while also enhancing instruction. The supervisor may be asked to provide input regarding the recommendations as well as to make some suggestions. The sixth step in self-assessment comes as teachers implement the agreed-upon changes in their own instructional behavior. As teachers implement the recommendations, they are thinking about the teaching act and consequently behave differently. Self-assessment comes to a close at step seven when the teacher reassesses the effectiveness of the change or changes and decides if additional modifications are needed. For Reiman and Thies-Sprinthall (1998), "ongoing self-assessment and documentation are essential elements of any true profession" (p. 284).

As noted by Joyce and Showers (1980), instructional improvement relies on five components: theory, demonstrations, practice, feedback, and classroom application. These five components often require changes in a teacher's behavior, but the magnitude of change may depend on each teacher's willingness and ability to accept feedback. Supervisors can help increase the teachers' acceptance of feedback by establishing a collegial, nonthreatening environment in the school. Teachers, as they work in small teams or groups, can demonstrate and practice teaching skills in front of each other. Team members then provide teachers with feedback about the content presented and the effectiveness of the teaching method selected. After experiencing the process of self-assessment and receiving nonthreatening feedback and support from others, teachers are more willing and more likely to utilize in their classrooms the skills they have practiced in the small group.

As mentioned earlier in the chapter, the concept of peer or cognitive coaching can be a useful strategy for improving instruction, reconciling perceptions, and sharing mutual feelings or problems with other educators (Costa and Garmston, 1994; Joyce and Showers, 1982). Coaching, when linked with self-assessment, provides the needed support system for teachers attempting to make changes in their instructional behavior. Additionally, it contributes an element of companionship and collegiality that encourages teachers to share their successes and frustrations and to work out problems that may have surfaced during small-group sessions. By adding the coaching dimension to self-assessment, teachers can receive assistance, which is given in an acceptable and nonthreatening manner, from experienced peers.

The steps outlined for self-assessment are most effective if conducted several times during the school year as part of ongoing staff development. The key to successful self-assessment supervision on a districtwide basis is to connect effective teaching behaviors with the needs and perceptions of teachers. The undergirding philosophy of the self-assessment process becomes one of formulating an objective perception and analysis of the instructional self, using what is known about effective teaching and learning.

The ambiguities and uncertainties often associated with current and past supervisory practices must give way to more clearly defined roles and responsibilities, based on the recognition of individual differences in both supervisors and teachers. To be effective in their roles, supervisors must begin to utilize various processes of supervision that provide a consistent pattern of interaction with teachers. The currently employed practice—a supervisor making one or two visits a year and calling this effective supervision—has proven to be unacceptable and ineffective. Second, the current approach—a supervisor observes a class, completes an evaluation—and discusses the evaluation, should be modified. How many supervisors, when they were teachers, found this series of events helpful? Most will admit that such an approach was not (Shanker, 1985). Yet, many supervisors continue to conduct classroom observations in this manner.

Thus, supervisors must become committed to a long-term process of initiating and sustaining instructional growth and change for teachers. Supervisors, as they work with teachers, can provide support through implementing the most appropriate supervisory process and by formulating strategies for professional growth and development, which result in improved classroom performance.

Summary

The continuous improvement of instruction is a complex, challenging task for both supervisors and teachers. This chapter highlighted four specific processes and approaches of supervision: (1) clinical, with the Instructional Supervision Training Program (ISTP) presented as an expanded clinical version; (2) developmental; (3) collegial and collaborative; and (4) self-assessment. Supervision was discussed in light of fostering professional development among teachers; the intent is not to put the processes in competition with each other but rather to encourage supervisors and teachers to use each one in a way that will be most effective in meeting a specific need. The supervisory process selected depends on a number of classroom and teacher variables.

The clinical supervision process is perhaps the oldest; the five steps include (1) preobservation conference, (2) classroom observation, (3) analysis and strategy, (4) supervision conference, and (5) postconference analysis. Supervisors, as they implement clinical supervision, should be aware that teachers: favor individualized, close, and supportive interactions; agree on the basic assumptions and worthwhileness of the process; are willing to accept recommendations; and believe that change in classroom behavior is possible.

The Instructional Supervision Training Program (ISTP) is a 5-stage, 10-step expanded version of clinical supervision in which the supervisor assists the teacher in addressing instructional concerns. The basic premise of this process is the belief that an observer in the classroom can objectively collect data that serve as a mirror on the classroom and that help teachers "see" the teaching–learning behaviors; then, working together, they determine a course of action. Clinical supervision, as implemented in ISTP, provides an opportunity for supervisors and teachers to work together in a partnership designed to discover and refine ways to enhance teaching and learning.

Supervisors who employ developmental supervision treat teachers as individuals who are at various stages of growth and development. This process is based on the premise that teacher development is greatly impacted by human development. There are four supervisory styles (directive control, directive informational, collaborative, and nondirective); supervisors select a style that is most compatible with two key developmental characteristics related to teacher effectiveness (level of commitment and level of conceptual thinking).

Collegial and collaborative processes focus on partnerships between and among supervisors and teachers. Peer coaching and cognitive coaching are included as ways of using cohort groups, with the role of the supervisor being that of a facilitator. As a result of the coaching process, teachers not only become more autonomous, but they also recognize they are part of a larger whole, called holonomy. Mentoring is also included as part of the collegial and collaborative processes. Mentoring involves working with a protégé while serving as a professional guide. It is a complex process or function and is built on trust. The heart and soul of mentoring is the belief in the worth of people.

Self-assessment supervision encourages teachers to become aware of their own instructional performance. This process asks the teacher to seek input and then compare data collected from self-assessment inventories with feedback from other sources. The primary aim of self-assessment supervision is to involve the teacher in reflection and the development of an instructional profile. Self-assessment supervision offers teachers a positive, nonthreatening approach to self-improvement. Competency in self-assessment comes with practice and requires a willingness on the part of the teacher to engage in systematic analysis on a regular basis so that continuing instructional improvement and change may occur.

The processes of supervision presented in this chapter provided a variety of ways for supervisors to work with teachers to improve their instructional effectiveness and thereby increase student achievement. Supervisors and teachers have choices about how classroom instruction is viewed and analyzed. Time invested in teacher instructional improvement is time well spent as teachers engage in coaching and begin to make decisions about their teaching.

YOUR TURN

6.1. Read the following case study of Mr. Johnson, a middle school teacher, and then complete the task.

The case study. As students enter the classroom, Mr. Johnson usually greets them at the door, identifying each one by name. He begins each life science class with a lecture, which includes a general overview of the concepts to be presented that day, listing on the chalkboard the major vocabulary words that will be encountered during the lesson. In each lesson, he stresses content. Mr. Johnson plans activities for the students to be completed during the lesson, particularly laboratory activities. He has a minimum of one lab activity a week but usually at least two.

During the lesson, Mr. Johnson periodically stops to ask if students have any questions before he moves on to the next topic or concept. Students seldom respond to opportunities to elaborate on the material and rarely volunteer information or ask questions. Mr. Johnson clearly communicates to the class what he expects in the way of classroom conduct. He often discusses proper classroom conduct and consistently enforces class rules. The class atmosphere can be described as orderly and cooperative; misbehavior is minimal.

As he begins a lesson, Mr. Johnson usually stands behind the laboratory demonstration table. During his overview and lecture, he seldom moves more than a few feet from the demonstration table or away from the chalkboard. Not only does he remain in one area during the lesson, but his students also seldom move once the bell rings. Students move about only when laboratory activities are planned, at which time their movements are restricted to getting equipment and supplies.

Due to the nature of his subject, Mr. Johnson feels that there is not enough student–teacher interaction. After his brief lecture, he would like his students to discuss the concepts presented. He is frustrated when they do not respond to his invitation to clarify the content when he asks, "Are there any questions?" He is not convinced that he has an adequate understanding of how well students know the information until he gives them a test. By that time, it is often too late.

Student reluctance to participate in discussions, volunteer answers, and/or initiate questions is creating a problem for Mr. Johnson. Consequently, he is beginning to question his effectiveness as a middle school teacher. While several students seem to do well in his classes, he concludes that most students could be doing much better. If he could get them to open up and talk about what they are studying, he thinks he would have a better indication of what they know. He is very concerned that his students do not appear to be motivated, are not responsive, and take a passive role in classroom activities. Mr. Johnson would like his students to demonstrate some excitement about what they are studying.

The task. Determined to do something about the situation, Mr. Johnson decides to seek help from his instructional supervisor (select a specific supervisory position). Following a brief discussion after school one day, the instructional leader suggests that Mr. Johnson use a combination of coaching and self-assessment to analyze his instructional performance. As the instructional leader, what overall plan would you develop to assist Mr. Johnson? How would you initiate coaching and the self-assessment process of supervision with him? Identify the actions or steps you would take to complete the seven steps in self-assessment (see Figure 6.3). Do you think there are elementary and secondary teachers who have perceptions like Mr. Johnson? If so, what are the perceptions? If not, why not?

6.2. Read each of the following situations and respond to the questions that follow:

  a. You are a consultant and have just observed a fourth grade teacher who ignores many of her students. She does not establish the purpose of the lesson and continues to use the lab sheet as the single most important resource in her classroom. What supervisory processes would you use as you work with this teacher during the school year?

  b. You are a principal of a middle school, and the teachers, at your request, turn in lesson plans at the end of each week. How would you evaluate each plan in an effort to assist each teacher in achieving his or her instructional best?

  c. You are given a new responsibility that includes evaluating teachers' classroom performance. You have previously been serving in a helping role; now the role has been expanded to that of evaluator. You are aware that effective schools have teachers who engage in professional dialogue on a regular basis. You want teachers to talk to each other in your school. How could you encourage teachers to talk about their expectations, teaching strategies, curriculum resources, use of time, and so on? What steps would you take to increase teacher talk so that the effective instructional practices of master teachers reach the less effective teachers?

  d. You are working with a secondary teacher who refuses to write a supervisory contract during the preobservation conference. Yet, this teacher (on the whole) is quite effective with his students. What do you do as his instructional leader? Where do you turn for help? You are caught between your desire to show him who is in charge and the need to implement aspects of successful supervisory practices. Which supervisory process(es) would help you resolve this dilemma? How? In what ways?

  e. You have completed your observation of a 10-year veteran elementary teacher, but you do not have anything positive to offer during the supervision conference. She constantly yells at students, she rarely moves from sitting on her stool, she ignores student questions, students are seldom on task, and their assignments appear to be more busywork than constructive activities. What action would you take with this teacher? How could the processes of supervision help you be honest yet caring with this teacher, especially if she becomes defensive or belligerent? How could you show concern for her professional growth and still inform her of areas that may need to be modified?

6.3. Sometimes supervisors who espouse a preference for self-assessment supervision do not use that approach when working with teachers. Read the following brief exchange between a teacher and a supervisor:

TEACHER: I really felt that the questions were coming easier today. After many weeks of struggling, the task of formulating questions became natural for me. Even the students responded enthusiastically. They hadn't been this active before. Rather than responding with short yes-or-no answers, the students seemed to be ready to discuss each comment offered.

SUPERVISOR: So you thought the questioning part of the lesson was greatly improved today in comparison to previous days?

TEACHER (eagerly responds): Yes!

SUPERVISOR (after a long pause): Um-hm.

Rewrite the dialogue in such a way as to indicate that the supervisor supports self-assessment supervision for teachers.

6.4. Under what circumstances would you suggest that teachers use student and parent questionnaires in building a professional profile for teacher evaluation?

REFERENCES

Acheson, A. A., & Gall, M. D. (1992). *Techniques on the clinical supervision of teachers* (3rd ed.). New York: Longman.

Anderson, E. M., & Lucasse-Shannon, A. (1988). Toward a conceptualization of mentoring. *Journal of Teacher Education, 34,* 38–42.

Anderson, R. H. (1997). Is clinical supervision a viable model for use in the public schools? Yes. In *Educational supervision: Perspectives, issues, and controversies.* J. Glanz and R. Neville (eds.). Norwood, MA: Christopher-Gordon Publishers.

Arredondo, D. E., Brody, J. L., Zimmerman, D. P., & Moffett, C. A. (1995). Pushing the envelope in supervision. *Educational Leadership, 53,* 74–78.

Beach, D. M., & Reinhartz, J. (1982). Improving instructional effectiveness: A self-assessment procedure. *Illinois School Research and Development Journal, 19,* 5–12.

Bents, R. H., & Harvey, K. R. (1981). Staff development: Change in the individual. In *Staff development/organization development.* B. Dillon-Peterson (ed.). Alexandria, VA: Association for Supervision and Curriculum Development.

Bey, T. M. (1990). A new knowledge base for an old practice. In *Mentoring: Developing successful new teachers.* T. M. Bey & C. T. Holmes (eds.). Reston, VA: Association of Teacher Educators.

Blumberg, A. (1974). *Supervision and teachers: A private cold war.* (2nd ed.). Berkeley, CA: McCutchan Publishing Co.

Blumberg, A. (1980). *Supervision and teachers: A private cold war.* (2nd ed.). Berkeley, CA: McCutchan Publishing Co.

Boyan, N. J., & Copeland, W. D. (1978). *Instructional supervision training program.* Columbus, OH: Charles E. Merrill.

Christensen, J. C. (1985). Adult learning and teacher career stage development. In *Career long teacher education.* P. J. Beuke & R. G. Heideman (eds.). Springfield, IL: Charles C. Thomas.

Cogan, M. L. (1973). *Clinical supervision.* Boston: Houghton Mifflin.

Commission on the Role and Preparation of Mentor Teachers. (1991). *Principles of mentoring.* Reston, VA: Association of Teacher Educators.

Costa, A. L., & Garmston, R. J. (1994). *Cognitive coaching: A foundation for renaissance schools.* Norwood, MA: Christopher-Gordon Publishers.

Daloz, L. A. (1986). *Effective teaching and mentoring.* San Francisco: Jossey-Bass Publishers.

Eaker, R. E. (1972). An analysis of the clinical supervision process as perceived by selected teachers and administrators. Doctoral dissertation, University of Tennessee.

Eisner, E. W. (1979). *The educational imagination: On the design and evaluation of educational programs.* (2nd ed.). New York: Macmillan.

Eisner, E. W. (1982). An artistic approach to supervision. In *Supervision of teaching.* T. J. Sergiovanni (ed.). 1982 yearbook. Alexandria, VA: Association for Supervision and Curriculum Development.

Elliott, B. (1995). Developing relationships: Episodes in professional development. *Teachers and Teaching: Journal of the International Study Association on Teacher Thinking, 1,* 247–264.

Elliott, R., & Calderhead, J. (1993). Mentoring for teacher development: Possibilities and caveats. In *Mentoring perspectives on school based teacher education.* D. McIntyre, H. Hagger, & M. Wilkin (eds.). London: Kagan Page.

Garman, N. B. (1971). A study of clinical supervision as a resource of college teachers of English. Doctoral dissertation, University of Pittsburgh.

Gillman, J. N., & Rickert, S. R. (1991). The mentoring spiral: Mentoring is life. Paper presented at the conference of the Association of Management, Atlantic City, NJ. [Mimeograph.]

Glatthorn, A. A. (1984). *Differentiated supervision.* Alexandria, VA: Association for Supervision and Curriculum Development.

Glenn, S. A. (1993). Supervision and evaluation of teachers. In *Educational administration.* (2nd ed.). J. Kaiser (ed.). Mequon, WI: Stylex Publishing.

Glickman, C. D. (1981). *Developmental supervision: Alternative practices for helping teachers improve instruction.* Alexandria, VA: Association for Supervision and Curriculum Development.

Glickman, C. D. (1985). *Supervision of instruction: A developmental approach.* Boston: Allyn & Bacon.

Glickman, C. D. (1990). *Supervision of instruction: A developmental approach.* (2nd ed.). Boston: Allyn & Bacon.

Glickman, C. D. (1992). The essence of school renewal: The prose has begun. *Educational Leadership, 50,* 24–27.

Glickman, C. D., & Gordon, S. P. (1987). Clarifying developmental supervision. *Educational Leadership, 44,* 64–68.

Glickman, C. D., Gordon, S. P., & Ross-Gordon, J. M. (1998). *Supervision of instruction: A developmental approach.* (4th ed.). Boston: Allyn & Bacon.

Goldhammer, R. (1969). *Clinical supervision.* New York: Holt, Rinehart & Winston.

Goldhammer, R., Anderson, R. H., & Krajewski, R. J. (1993). *Clinical supervision: Special methods for the supervision of teachers.* (3rd ed.). New York: Holt, Rinehart & Winston.

Goldsberry, L. F. (1984). The realities of clinical supervision. *Educational Leadership, 41,* 12–15.

Goldsberry, L. F. (1988). Three functional methods of supervision. *Action in Teacher Education, 10,* 1–10.

Gordon, B. G. (1976). Teachers evaluate supervisory behavior in the individual conference. *The Clearing House, 49,* 231–238.

Gordon, B. G. (1992 March). Making clinical supervision a reality: Steps toward implementation. *NASSP Bulletin, 76,* 46–57.

Head, F. A., Reiman, A. J., & Thies-Sprinthall, L. (1992). The reality of mentoring: Complexity in its process and function. In *Mentoring: Contemporary principles and issues.* T. M. Bey & C. T. Holmes (eds.). Reston, VA: Association of Teacher Educators.

Healy, C. C., & Welchert, A. J. (1990). Mentoring relations: A definition to advance research and practice. *Educational Researcher, 19,* 17–21.

Holifield, M., & Cline, D. (1997). Clinical supervision and its outcomes: Teachers and principals report. *NASSP Bulletin, 81,* 109–113.

Hopkins, D. (1990). Integrating staff development and school improvement: A study of teacher personality and school climate. In *Changing school culture through staff development*. B. Joyce (ed.). *The 1990 ASCD Yearbook*. Alexandria, VA: Association for Supervision and Curriculum Development.

Hunter, M. (1980). Six types of supervisory conferences. *Educational Leadership, 37*, 408–412.

Hunter, M. (1985). What's wrong with Madeline Hunter? *Educational Leadership, 42*, 57–60.

Joyce, B. (1987 February). On teachers coaching teachers: A conversation with Bruce Joyce. *Educational Leadership, 44*, 12–17. [Interview with Ron Brandt, editor of *Educational Leadership*.]

Joyce, B., & Showers, B. (1980). Improving inservice training: The messages of research. *Educational Leadership, 37*, 379–384.

Joyce, B., & Showers, B. (1982). The coaching of teaching. *Educational Leadership, 40*, 4–10.

Joyce, B., & Showers, B. (1988). *Student achievement through staff development*. White Plains, NY: Longman.

Kerr, B. J. (1976). An investigation of the process of using feedback data within the clinical supervision cycle to facilitate teachers' individualization of instruction. Doctoral dissertation, University of Pittsburgh.

Kirby, P. C., & Meza, J., Jr. (1997). Changing roles: Coaching models for restructuring schools. *NASSP Bulletin, 81*, 590, 80–90.

Kosmoski, G. J. (1997). *Supervision*. Mequon, WI: Stylex Publishing.

Krajewski, R. J. (1976). Clinical supervision to facilitate teacher self-improvement. *Journal of Research and Development, 9*, 58–66.

Little, J. W. (1990). The mentor phenomenon and the social organization of teaching. C. B. Cazden (ed.). *Review of Research in Education, 16*, 297–351.

Manatt, R. P. (1981). Evaluating teacher performance. Alexandria, VA: Association for Supervision and Curriculum Development. [Videotape.]

Mosher, R. L., & Purpel, D. E. (1972). *Supervision: The reluctant profession*. Boston: Houghton Mifflin.

Nolan, J., Hawkes, B., & Francis, P. (1993 October). Case studies: Windows onto clinical supervision. *Educational Leadership, 51*, 52–56.

Odell, S. J. (1990). Support for new teachers. In *Mentoring: Developing successful new teachers*. T. M. Bey & C. T. Holmes (eds.). Reston, VA: Association of Teacher Educators.

Oja, S. N. (1981 April). Deriving teacher educational objectives from cognitive-developmental theories and applying them to the practice of teacher education. Paper presented at the annual meeting of the American Educational Research Association, Los Angeles.

Pajak, E. (1993). *Approaches to clinical supervision: Alternatives for improving instruction*. Norwood, MA: Christopher-Gordon Publishers.

Pellicer, L. O. (1982). Providing instructional leadership—a principal challenge. *NASSP Bulletin, 66*, 27–31.

Reavis, C. A. (1976). Clinical supervision: A timely approach. *Educational Leadership, 33*, 360–363.

Reavis, C. A. (1977). A test of the clinical supervision model. *Journal of Educational Research, 70*, 311–315.

Reiman, A. J. (1988). An intervention study of long-term mentor training: Relationships between cognitive-developmental theory and reflection. Unpublished doctoral dissertation, North Carolina State University, Raleigh, NC.

Reiman, A. J., & Edelfelt, R. (1990). School-based mentoring programs: Untangling the tensions between theory and research. Research report No. 90–7. Raleigh: Department of Curriculum and Instruction, North Carolina State University.

Reiman, A. J., & Thies-Sprinthall, L. (1998). *Mentoring and supervision for teacher development*. New York: Longman.

Reinhartz, J., & Beach, D. M. (1983). *Improving middle school instruction: A research-based self-assessment system*. Washington, DC: National Education Association.

Seager, G. B. (1992). Bob Goldhammer in retrospect. In *The Robert Goldhammer papers. Early writing of a distinguished educator*. Tampa, FL: Council of Professors of Instructional Supervision. Pedamorphasis, Inc.

Shanker, A. (1985). The revolution that's overdue. *Phi Delta Kappan, 66*, 311–315.

Shinn, J. L. (1976). Teacher perception of ideal and actual supervisory training programs sponsored by the Association of California School Administrators. Doctoral dissertation, University of Oregon.

Showers, B. (1984). *Peer coaching: A strategy for facilitating transfer of training.* Eugene, OR: Center for Educational Policy and Management.

Showers, B. (1990). Aiming for superior classroom instruction for all children: A comprehensive staff development model. *Remedial and Special Education, 11,* 35–39.

Showers, B., & Joyce, B. (1996 March). The evolution of peer coaching. *Educational Leadership, 53,* 12–16.

Shuma, K. Y. (1973). Changes effectuated by a clinical supervisor relationship which emphasizes a helping relationship and a conference format made congruent with the establishment and maintenance of this helping relationship. Doctoral dissertation, University of Pittsburgh.

Smyth, J. (1991 Fall). Problematisizing teaching through a "critical" approach to clinical supervision. *Curriculum Inquiry, 21,* 321–352.

Snyder, K. (1981). Clinical supervision in the 1980's. *Educational Leadership, 38,* 521–525.

Sparks-Langer, G. M., & Colton, A. B. (1991 March). Synthesis of research on teachers' reflective thinking. *Educational Leadership, 48,* 37–44.

Sprinthall, N. A., & Thies-Sprinthall, L. (1982). Career development of teachers: A cognitive developmental perspective. In *Encyclopedia of Educational Research.* (5th ed.). H. Mitzel (ed.). New York: Free Press.

Tanner, D., & Tanner, L. (1987). *Supervision in education: Problems and practices.* New York: Macmillan.

Thies-Sprinthall, L. (1980). Promoting the conceptual and principled thinking level of the supervising teacher. Doctoral dissertation, St. Cloud State University.

Turner, M. (1993). The role of mentors and teacher tutors in school-based teacher education and induction. *British Journal of In-Service Education, 19,* 36–45.

Wilsey, C., & Killion, J. (1982). Making staff development programs work. *Educational Leadership, 40,* 36–43.

7 Classroom Observation

Collecting Information about Teaching and Learning

OBJECTIVES

The objectives of this chapter are:

- Describe the nature and purpose of classroom observations.
- Identify general guidelines for conducting observations.
- Name and describe at least five procedures for collecting data and use at least one while observing in a classroom.
- Using data collected in an observation, analyze the data and put in a form for feedback to a teacher.
- Discuss the components for conducting an effective postobservation conference with teachers.

Classroom observation procedures are common components of the supervision process and are used to objectively identify and describe the teaching and learning behaviors that occur during instruction. For Calebrese and Zepeda (1997), "The classroom is the heart of the school. In the classroom students and teachers come together for the purpose of learning" (p. 213). They continue by saying that as supervisors conduct classroom observations, they are providing "a baseline of data to assist teachers" (p. 213), especially as supervisors and teachers conduct a dialogue in postobservation conferences.

Knowing which procedures or techniques to employ in various instructional settings contributes to the supervisor's overall effectiveness. However, as supervisors prepare for what to observe, how to observe, how to record and analyze or interpret, and how to present the data, they begin to realize the complexities involved in conducting classroom observations. As Oliva and Pawlas (1997) note, classroom observations require the use of highly specialized technical and analytical skills, and classroom observations are made more difficult by the fact that every instructional episode is unique, and "every observation is a new situation" (p. 415). Garman (1990) further elaborates on the complexity of classroom observation by noting that there are various modes of observation, different methods of collecting data, and different treatments in analyzing the qualitative and quantitative data. With this challenge in mind, supervisors must constantly adapt classroom observation procedures so that the teacher–pupil behaviors and classroom interactions are objectively recorded. The purpose of data collection is to provide feedback about what happened in the classroom during instruction.

While the primary focus of this chapter is the role of the supervisor in conducting observations and collecting data, it should be noted that teachers who coach or mentor other teachers (as described in the previous chapter) also work with colleagues and collect data about the teaching–learning process. The techniques that apply to supervisors would also apply to cognitive coaches and mentors as well. Networking promotes sharing ideas, information, and actual activities that take place in classrooms; such sharing is "...a powerful [aid] to learning" (Woolsey and Bellany, 1997, p. 389). In addition, classroom observations may not be convenient because distance may be a barrier. McDevitt (1996) offers a suggestion: the use of telecommunications networks to promote meaningful communication among and between teachers and with supervisors. Such technology links can improve the quality of interactions because "the voices of good teachers...[are] included in discussions of teaching" (Hilty, 1993, p. 104).

This chapter assists supervisors in developing classroom observation skills by: (a) discussing what supervisors should consider as they prepare to observe, (b) providing some general guidelines for conducting classroom observations, (c) outlining data-collection and data-analysis procedures, and (d) discussing procedures for conferencing with teachers about the observations. By examining some of the fundamental aspects of classroom observation, especially techniques related to data collection, supervisors can be more effective in recording and analyzing teacher–pupil interactions and presenting the information to teachers.

Preparing to Observe in Classrooms

To be effective as observers in classrooms, supervisors should be aware of several factors that can impact the observation process and limit their ability to be objective and accurate in data collection. Observing or "seeing in classrooms," as described by Good and Brophy (1997), is a complex process that is often influenced by our past experiences, attitudes, and prejudices. It is exceedingly difficult to be impartial in conducting observations, to not add our personal interpretations. Simply put, as we observe a teaching episode, we see things that we would have done differently because of our background and experiences, but that should not color our objectivity in recording classroom events.

Doyle (1986) calls attention to five factors that supervisors must be cognizant of as they prepare for classroom observations. First, classrooms are multidimensional, with many different tasks and events occurring during instruction. In addition to the many events that occur, several occur simultaneously. There is often an immediacy as the pace is rapid and students are engaged in learning. The classroom is also an unpredictable place with many spontaneous actions. Finally, classrooms have norms in behavior and conduct that are based on a history of the class members being together over time.

As supervisors conduct classroom observations, they should confine their activities to collecting and coding information pertinent to classroom interactions. Only after classroom behaviors have been observed and recorded is it appropriate for the supervisor to formulate hypotheses about the teaching episode. At that time, supervisors should be cautioned to let the data suggest the hypotheses rather than letting their own perceptions, intuitions, and interpretations influence the analysis of the data. To avoid misinterpretation of classroom behavior, supervisors need to be aware of their perceptual blinders (Good and Brophy, 1997). For some supervisors, for instance, highly verbal teachers are often perceived as more effective, while more soft-spoken teachers, who listen a great deal to their students, may be perceived as less effective. Such conclusions, based on a general perception of teacher style, can be inaccurate. Such perceptual blinders hinder a supervisor's ability to objectively "see" classroom interactions. Therefore, when gathering information about teaching and learning in classrooms, supervisors must recognize and guard against personal biases that can influence the kinds of data they collect during an observation.

Supervisors should also be cautioned against having a list of personal likes and dislikes that is universally applied to all teaching situations. Calebrese and Zepeda (1997) note that a common mistake supervisors make is to "project their idealized version of good teaching on others" (p. 215). These personal interpretations fail to recognize the complexities and contextual nature of teaching and learning and often lead to erroneous analyses, hypotheses, and recommendations, which then can lead to mistrust between supervisors and teachers.

Another element to consider when preparing for classroom observations is the level of teacher confidence, trust, and anxiety. Teachers who are less confident and feel threatened or who are insecure while being observed will behave differently during the instructional episode (da Costa, 1995; da Costa and Riordan, 1996). Their lack of ease will also influence the behavior of their students. Teacher anxiety and level of trust, then, can distort instructional interactions; supervisors should be cognizant of this distortion (Coates and Thoresen, 1976). Teachers who are uncomfortable during in-class observations often have a more difficult time interacting with students; as a result, the quality of a teacher's instructional efficacy may be masked (da Costa and Riordan, 1996). "The result: the teacher executes a lesson…feeling basically insecure. The lesson is stilted and unnatural" (Goldhammer, Anderson, and Krajewski, 1993, p. 81). It becomes the supervisor's responsibility to foster the necessary self-confidence and level of trust in teachers so that they can demonstrate their instructional ability during the observation of a lesson. Peer coaching and mentoring, discussed in Chapter 6, provide ways of building trust as teachers work with teachers in the collection of data. This collegiality can reduce the fear and anxiety associated with classroom observations.

General Guidelines for Classroom Observation

It is important to note that observation is *not* assessment. The primary goal of observation is to collect information that is pertinent to the specific teaching episode. To accomplish this goal and make observations less threatening, "talk and trust-building…need to be at the core of any teacher observation model" (Sahakian and Stockton, 1996, p. 50). Sahakian and Stockton (1996) further note that as teachers go through several cycles of observation, they become more confident in their abilities and less threatened by the process. Observations also serve to initiate an instructional dialogue between the observer and the teacher (Glickman, Gordon, and Ross-Gordon, 1996).

The following six general guidelines are related to the observation process. Although classrooms vary, as do teachers, these guidelines are presented for supervisors to follow as they observe instructional episodes. The first guideline of observation is to *focus on student behavior.* Although the first thought of some supervisors may be to watch teacher behaviors, Good and Brophy (1997) suggest that the key to observations is to observe student behavior because student engagement reveals much about what the teacher is doing. Wheeler (1994) suggests that supervisors can improve the quality and quantity of their observation data by focusing on instructional activities during classroom observations. By looking at the effects of teacher behavior on student behavior, supervisors are less tempted to view the teaching episode through their own personal-bias lens. Watching how students respond to and interact with the teacher in the learning situation produces a more objective observation. This is not to say that the supervisor should ignore teacher behaviors; the important point to remember is that the observer should concentrate on the dynamics of the classroom.

A second guideline of observation is to *limit the number of specific instructional variables to be observed.* Classroom instructional variables often include such components as: on-task/off-task behaviors; lesson transitions; pacing; general class climate; attitudes of the students toward class activities and assignments; and other aspects of teacher–student interactions. To collect accurate information, the supervisor should limit the number of variables recorded or tallied during a given teaching episode.

The third guideline is to *avoid disturbing the natural setting* of the classroom environment. This guideline may seem obvious, but it is important to mention because when supervisors enter a classroom, they often impact the nature and quality of interactions in the classroom. Manatt (1981) refers to this as "observer effect" and notes that praise and criticism ratios are often impacted. To maintain a balance, supervisors should be as unobtrusive as possible. This can be done by avoiding eye contact with the students and the teacher, by refraining from talking to or helping students at their desks, and by finding a quiet place in the room to sit and take notes. By attempting to blend in, supervisors convey a message to teachers and students that they are to carry on as usual. Supervisors soon discover that this is often difficult to do even under the best observation conditions. Having equipment to record the event may also have an impact the observation; it may prove helpful to have the equipment left in the classroom over a period of time so it is viewed as routine.

The fourth guideline for an observation is to *take complete, clear, and accurate notes* during classroom observations. As Manatt (1981) has noted, teachers expect supervisors to take notes during an observation. It is also important to remember that an incident cannot be said to have happened if the supervisor didn't write it down. Therefore, note taking is a skill that supervisors need to develop in order to accurately capture instructional behaviors, to minimize interpolation of what is viewed, and to maximize reliability of what was observed. Supervisors should take detailed notes and not rely on their memory with regard to what happened. To facilitate note taking, supervisors can use a personal shorthand with symbols representing common words, student responses to teacher, and instructional transitions. Scripting or what some supervisors call yellow pad observations are described in greater detail later in this chapter.

Following an observation, the fifth general guideline is for supervisors to *conduct a detailed analysis* of the data collected during the observation. After systematically reviewing all the information, the supervisor should then look for patterns, correlations, and/or inconsistencies in behaviors. Careful analysis of the data may help the supervisor answer such questions as: "Are there identifiable relationships in teacher–student interactions?" "Are there recurring patterns of behaviors?" "What additional information is needed?" Taking time to comb through the notes can help prevent drawing unwarranted conclusions. By taking time to analyze the data and putting them in a visual form (e.g., a chart, graph, and/or diagram) also give greater credibility to the information when it is presented to the teacher.

The sixth and last guideline of observation is to *provide feedback to the teacher.* Reporting the results of the observation to the teacher during the postobservation conference requires the supervisor to organize and present the information in such a way that the teacher can easily understand and readily acknowledge it as accurate and valid. The purpose here is to validate the classroom observation—that what was seen was recorded and is accepted by the teacher as a reflection of what actually happened.

Supervisors and teachers are presently reformulating the traditional classroom observation model to include colleagues not only in the actual classroom observations but in the postobservation conferences as well. As a result, supervisors may be part of a team that includes other teachers in the classroom observation process. Sahakian and Stockton (1996) describe this process: Teachers from the same department work in triads or teams to observe each other (peer coaching) twice a week over a four-week period each semester; the supervisor observes three times, for 30 minutes each time, over a four-week period each semester; and the culminating activity is a 90-minute team postobservation conference. By involving other members of the department in the observation process, teachers engage in dialogues about instruction; perhaps just as important, they develop common perspectives on the curriculum and a greater sense of collegiality. As one of the participants described the peer observation process, it "allows teachers to learn more about themselves; thus they become better teachers, bringing more knowledge to the classroom" (Sahakian and Stockton, 1996, p. 53). At this point, the purpose of the classroom observations is to address formative instructional issues.

These six general guidelines, if followed, can help the supervisor be more effective in conducting classroom observations and reporting results to teachers. It should be emphasized that the observation process is primarily designed to yield the most accurate and objective information possible that is relevant to teachers' professional growth and development.

Procedures for Collecting Data

By using a variety of data-collection procedures, supervisors can focus on specific student behaviors during a classroom observation. Acheson and Gall (1997) suggest using several data-collection procedures that include verbatim records, observations based on seating charts (e.g., on-task behavior, verbal flow, and movement), and descriptive records. These procedures become the starting point for studying instructional episodes and help to break down the complexities of the classroom. Although data-collection procedures do not provide total objectivity, they do establish a record of instructional behaviors that is descriptive and less judgmental. The data-collection procedures that are discussed in detail in the sections that follow may prove helpful as supervisors record information during classroom observations. These data-collection procedures include: timelines; topical data capture chart; on-task and off-task checklists; records of transitions and lesson pacing; teacher mobility, classroom management, and teacher–student interaction maps; and verbal interaction codes using the FIAC System.

Timelines.   Timelines are one of the most common forms of data-collection procedures used in the classroom. This procedure involves writing down what was seen and/or heard in the instructional episode and keeping a running time log (usually every three to five minutes) in the left margin (Hunter, 1983; Manatt, 1981). This procedure has also been described as scripting or yellow pad notes. As supervisors observe teaching–learning interactions in the classroom, they record anecdotal or verbatim notes, while keeping track of the time along the left-hand margin. Over a decade ago, Kuralt (1987) suggested using a laptop computer as a tool for scripting classroom observations. This use of technology in the supervision process helps to "produce a complete transcript of classroom interaction[s]" (p. 71).

In recording observations, anecdotal notes are narrative descriptions of events that occur in the classroom that relate to who, what, when, where, or under what circumstances (McNeely, 1997). For example, the supervisor might record that the teacher called on volunteers to work their problems on the board and that all eight students worked their problems correctly. These notes describe something that happened in the classroom: who did what, when it occurred, what happened as a result, and what circumstances or conditions were present. Verbatim notes are exact statements of what was said by the teacher and/or students—a script of the lesson (McNeely, 1997). For example, the supervisor records: T, "Who can give me one cause of World War II?" In using a timeline, it is common practice for supervisors to record both anecdotal and verbatim kinds of data in their observational notes. Anecdotal notes are most often used at the beginning and end of class, when there are changes in content, when there are changes in methods or strategies, or when the teacher or students change activities or behaviors. Scripting is often used to record lesson introduction or engagement, learning expectations, questions, teacher feedback or comments, probes, directions, and summaries or closure. In using a timeline, it is important to record changes in content or methodology as well as the times when changes occur; be sure the notes reflect what is seen, not what is felt.

Topical Data Capture Chart. Another data-collection procedure recommended by Manatt (1981) is the construction of a topical data capture chart. A topical data capture chart is a more focused form than scripting and timelines. The chart has three components: The first two are identified by the supervisor and teacher in the preobservation conference and may include such issues as classroom management, question types and interactions, lesson presentation (input and modeling), and information relative to specific student behavior in the classroom (e.g., blurting out answers); the third part provides a place for the observer to record teacher behaviors that are distractions or that interfere with the lesson (e.g., false starts and repeated "OKs" or "uhs"). The supervisor records relevant verbatim and anecdotal notes in each segment of the chart during the classroom observation. This data-collection procedure is similar to scripting but is often easier to use because the supervisor limits the focus and collects data relative to only one or two identified areas rather than recording all classroom interactions. Figure 7.1 provides an example of a topical data capture chart.

Using the chart in Figure 7.1 to collect data during a classroom observation, the supervisor records both verbatim and anecdotal notes that describe interactions

Teacher–Student Behavior #1:
(e.g., Classroom Management)

Teacher–Student Behavior #2:
(e.g., Questions—Number and Cognitive Level)

Distracting Behaviors That Interfere with Teaching & Learning:

FIGURE 7.1   **Topical Data Capture Chart**

or behaviors relevant to the areas identified in each area of the figure. These quotations and narrative descriptions construct a picture of what happened during the
lesson as they relate to the identified issues.

On-Task and Off-Task Behavior Checklists.   When conducting classroom observations, supervisors may find it helpful or necessary to use a checklist to record
student on-task/off-task behavior. Using a checklist to mark at two- to-five-
minute intervals, supervisors note student behavior and the time it is occurring.
Glickman (1985) suggests randomly selecting three to five boys and three to five
girls to observe during the period and scanning the room every five minutes to
code the behavior of these students. Often when discussing what to focus on
during a classroom observation, the teacher may request that the supervisor track
the on-task/off-task behavior of specific students who have a pattern of disrupt-
ing the class. Acheson and Gall (1997) note that "before an observer can use this
technique, he or she must be acquainted with what the teacher expects the stu-

dents to be doing [the task]" (p. 90). Figure 7.2 provides an example of an on-task/off-task behavior checklist.

Using Figure 7.2, if at 1:15 P.M. a student is listening, doing assigned work, or engaging in class discussion, the supervisor records a check in the Attentive to Task column for this time period. If, on the other hand, a student at 1:30 P.M. is reading a book, that student is considered to be passively off task, and a check is placed in the Inattentive/Passive column.

Another type of off-task behavior is labeled Inattentive/Active, and a check is placed in this column when students are out of their seats, wandering around the room, or talking to others about noninstructional matters. After the observation, the results are tallied, analyzed, and then presented to the teacher during the postconference for analysis, discussion, and reflection.

Stallings and Freiberg (1991) provide a variation to the model of coding on-task/off-task behaviors. They recommend using a seating chart or grid to represent the seats of students in a classroom and scanning the class every five minutes, indicating each time which students are on or off task. An observer's job is made easier by having a seating chart with student pictures as well as names on it. A

Class Time	Attentive to Task	Inattentive/ Passive	Inattentive/ Active

FIGURE 7.2   **Record of Student On-Task Off-Task Behavior**

digital camera can be used to take student pictures; these can be printed out and arranged on a seating chart. Keeping several sets of these pictures available can be helpful in placing students in groups as well. At the end of the observation period, tallies from the chart are totaled. When the sum of the number of off-task students for each observation is divided by the number of students in class times the number of observations, a picture emerges of the percentage of off-task behavior in the classroom. For example:

$$\frac{\text{Total number of off-task tallies}}{\text{Total number of students}} = \text{Percentage of off-task behavior}$$

Topic of lesson: _____

Type of lesson: _____

Date and time of observation: _____

Class size: _____

Directions: Record the time and the nature of each transition in the lesson as the teacher moves from one topic to another or from one activity to another.

Time	Nature of Transition

FIGURE 7.3   **Record of Lesson Transitions and Pacing**

Transitions and Lesson-Pacing Records. Instruments can also be used to gather information about lesson transitions as the teacher moves from one concept or topic to another and the pacing and/or time involved with each during in-class observations. These data-collection procedures are also modifications of the time-line. The supervisor records the nature and type of each transition that takes place during a single class period. With each transition entry, it is important to record the time, the topic or concept, and nature of the transition (such as moving from large-group instruction to small cooperative-learning groups). The dialogue and descriptive notes (what the teacher says or does and/or what the students say or do) are recorded and provide information not only about the nature of the transi-tion but also about the pacing of the lesson. Figure 7.3 may prove helpful to the su-pervisor in monitoring lesson transitions and pacing, as both aspects can be charted and analyzed.

When focusing on lesson transitions, supervisors can also use a timeline sim-ilar to that shown in Figure 7.4. In addition to a brief description of teacher/student behaviors, an x is placed on the timeline when transitions are made and a zero (0) when a transition is needed but not presented. This modified timeline can be used to examine methodology or various instructional strategies.

For example, Mrs. Cassandras plans to use the following instructional se-quence when teaching a unit on the biomes of Australia. The geographic address of Australia is the first in a series of lessons from the unit. She decides to use an activity designed to capture the attention of the entire group of sixth-graders,

Description of Classroom Behaviors:

| Time | 1:00 | 1:15 | 1:30 | 1:45 | 1:55 |

X = transition made
O = transition needed but not present

FIGURE 7.4 **Lesson Transitions Timeline**

followed by cooperative learning tasks; then she will bring the class back together to report and to close the lesson.

The observer in the preobservation conference has determined what Mrs. Cassandras wants from the first and last parts of the lesson concerning which specific students she is interacting with. The observer constructs a seating chart as described and uses tallies next to the picture of the student being asked a question, being invited to respond, and/or being reinforced. A circle can be drawn around the picture if he or she initiates a comment, volunteers a response, and/or asks a question.

During the cooperative learning tasks, a chart with students' pictures arranged in a group should be prepared. The goal is to record—using a check mark—every minute the teacher and the students interact with a general comment of encouragement, a rhetorical question, and/or some form of touch or reassurance.

At the conclusion of the lesson, there is a review of the opening and close of the lesson, which provides the teacher with information regarding whom the teacher is interacting with and those students who have been ignored or who have had very little contact. Using this information, Mrs. Cassandras can begin to deliberately involve students who have not been engaged during whole-class activities and group work as she monitors the activities.

A descriptive note is made when the teacher changes from one strategy to another or from one activity to another (e.g., cooperative learning groups to individual work).

Teacher Mobility, Classroom Management, and Teacher–Student Interaction Maps.   Behaviors associated with teacher mobility or movement in the classroom, location of classroom management or behavior problems, and locations of teacher–student interactions can also be recorded by using a representative seating chart to code such data. The supervisor can make a sketch of the classroom arrangement by using Xs to mark the students' desks and sketch the location of materials, computer equipment, and other pertinent resources. Acheson and Gall (1997) state that these classroom sketches can be used as a record of what occurred and can be analyzed for verbal flow and movement patterns of both teachers and students. An example of such a chart is provided in Figure 7.5 and illustrates how the supervisor sketches the desks in the classroom and then maps the teacher's movement in the room.

Using a diagram like the one in Figure 7.5, the supervisor records the location of the teacher in the classroom at five-minute intervals or any time there is movement from one area of the class to another (Fifer, 1980). This sketch can also be used to code incidents of teacher–student interactions (e.g., questions/answers or reinforcement) and/or the location of student behavioral problems. This mobility map provides the basis for posing the following questions about a teacher's instructional behavior as the supervisor analyzes the data and provides feedback during the conference with the teacher:

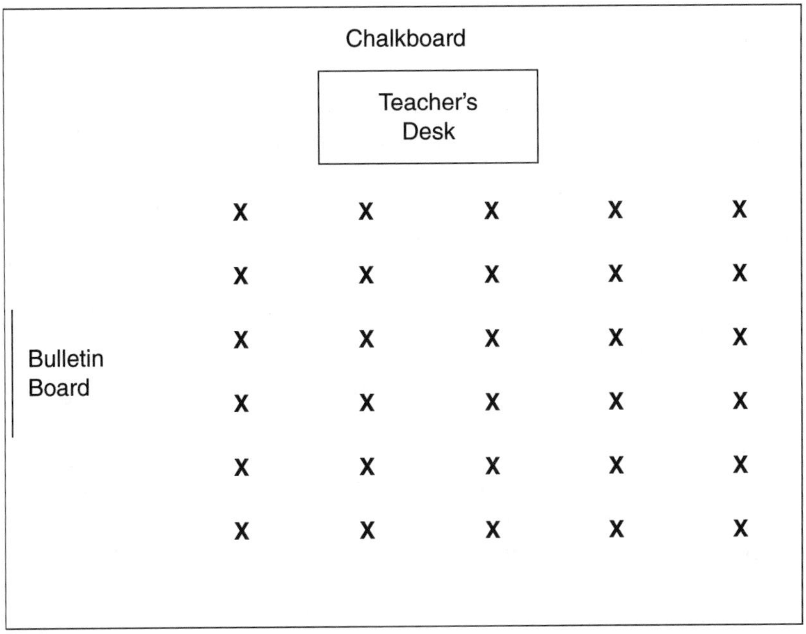

```
                    Chalkboard

                   ┌──────────────┐
                   │  Teacher's   │
                   │    Desk      │
                   └──────────────┘

        X       X       X       X       X

        X       X       X       X       X

        X       X       X       X       X
Bulletin
Board   X       X       X       X       X

        X       X       X       X       X

        X       X       X       X       X
```

FIGURE 7.5   Mobility Map

1. Can you recall where you were standing at the beginning, middle, and end of the lesson?

2. In which general area of the room did student behavior problems (if any) develop?

3. How do you think proximity to students influences their behavior?

4. What changes in movement might you plan to make tomorrow?

When using the seating chart to record where there are student behavior problems, the supervisor notes every time a student misbehaves or is actively off task and records a mark or tally by the X that represents that student's desk. At the end of the observation period, the supervisor and teacher will have a better indication of where off-task misbehavior or classroom management problems exist. Overhead transparencies can be made of the teacher's mobility that can overlay the grid of behavioral problems.

Finally, when using the same configuration of Xs to represent desks in the classroom, the supervisor can note those students who are called upon in class or who volunteer contributions to the discussion by circling the X every time the students respond or make a contribution. This grid provides a picture of the number and kinds of teacher–student interactions in the class and can also be made into a transparency to overlay the maps of the other two categories (mobility and behavior problems).

Verbal Interaction Codes.   Lastly, one tool that has been used in the past to collect data about specific dimensions of classroom interactions is an observation procedure called the Flanders Interaction Analysis Category System, or FIAC (Flanders, 1967). Dunkin and Biddle (1974) believe that this system is an important tool for supervisors to use in describing verbal classroom interactions. For them, "Flanders' contribution to research in classrooms has been important and pervasive," and they go on to say that the FIAC procedure may be the "single most-often-used instrument for observing [and coding] classroom behaviors" (p. 100).

The FIAC System can prove helpful in contemporary classrooms because it describes and codes common verbal patterns that teachers and students follow in the classroom. It not only contains seven categories for coding teachers' direct and indirect verbal behavior, but it includes two categories for student verbal behavior (either response or initiation) and another category for silence or confusion.

Teacher talk is divided into two major headings: indirect influence and direct influence. According to Flanders (1967), "Indirect influence consists of soliciting the opinions or ideas of the pupils, applying or enlarging on those opinions or ideas, praising or encouraging the participation of pupils, or clarifying and accepting their feelings" (p. 109). Teacher verbal interactions that are indirect influence are coded according to four categories: (1) accepts feelings, (2) praises or encourages, (3) accepts or uses ideas of students, and (4) asks questions. Teacher talk that is coded as indirect influence encourages students to respond more freely.

Teacher statements that are designed to provide information or restrict or limit student responses are coded as direct influence by the teacher. Flanders (1967) describes direct influence as behavior associated with "stating the teacher's own opinion or ideas, directing the pupil's action, criticizing…[pupil] behavior, or justifying the teacher's authority or use of that authority" (p. 109). Teacher talk that is considered direct influence is coded according to three categories: (5) lectures, (6) gives directions, and (7) criticizes or justifies authority.

Student talk includes two categories: (8) student talk response and (9) student talk initiation. The first category involves students responding to the teacher (that is, answering a question); the second involves talk initiated by the students. The last category (10) consists of periods of silence or confusion. During this period, there is no talking, or the communication, if spoken, cannot be understood by the observer. Taken together, there are 10 categories, with each category assigned a specific number (as indicated in parentheses above). The numbers do not imply a particular value on a scale; they simply identify a verbal behavior.

When using the FIAC, supervisors should spend the first 5 to 10 minutes of a class sitting and observing without coding any interactions. This period of time allows the supervisor to get a feel for the total classroom environment and diminishes the effect of an outside observer on teacher–student behavior. Before beginning to record numbers or encode data, the supervisor should write a brief narrative description of the class and activities. Once this has been accomplished, the recording process begins.

The supervisor observes teacher and/or student interactions and records the appropriate number of the behavior for every three seconds that the behavior occurs or until there is a change in the behavior. For example, in a sixth-grade science class, the teacher might begin the session by asking questions about the previous day's lesson (4s); as each student responds to a question (8s), the teacher acknowledges and praises the response (2s) and sometimes uses the response to formulate a comment about the lesson (3s). The teacher then begins to lecture on the topic for today (5s). When students initiate questions about the lesson (9s), the teacher elaborates (5s) and praises their questions (2s). Only once or twice does the teacher have to call on students to get them back on task (7s). The numbers are recorded in a column; for every minute of observation, there will be approximately 20 numbers recorded. At the conclusion of a 15- or 20-minute observation, the supervisor will have recorded several columns of numbers. It is essential for the supervisor to be accurate in coding the behavior and to develop a consistent tempo when recording numbers. Not only are the total numbers important, but the patterns of the numbers is also important.

When the class activity is no longer teacher-directed and students work in groups, work at their desks individually, or read silently, the supervisor stops recording numbers. A line is drawn under the last number recorded, and notes are made concerning the new activity. It is not unusual for supervisors, as they code behaviors, to make notes that further explain and interpret what they have observed. The coding system developed by Flanders aids the supervisor in recording behaviors quickly and efficiently. As in the case of other data–collection procedures cited earlier, the next step for the supervisor is to analyze the data and information that have been recorded.

Although not used as frequently as it once was, the Flanders Interaction Analysis Category System can be used by teachers without the direct involvement of an observer. Teachers can conduct their own analysis of classroom interactions by making an audiotape of the lesson and then scoring it as they play back the lesson. In this way, the FIAC can be a tool for teachers to use as they gain information about their classroom.

Data Analysis

Following the classroom observation and the collection of relevant information, the supervisor begins the process of examining the data and tries to reconstruct the information so that it will provide an accurate picture of what occurred in the instructional episode. The information should be arranged in such a way that it can be easily communicated to and understood by the teacher. Goldhammer, Anderson, and Krajewski (1993) suggest that in analyzing the data, "you begin to formulate some initial impressions of the kinds of patterns characterizing a teacher's work.... Think back to what you observed...to see whether certain ways of dealing with problems or talking or reacting to the students or moving around represents a persistent pattern" (p. 113). One way to begin this process is to write a descriptive narrative or transcript citing specific observed behaviors and communicating in an objective, nonjudgmental way (Clements and Evertson, 1980). The advantage of preparing a transcript of the lesson is that it provides a holistic perspective of what took place. The narrative includes major categories that reflect the focus of the observation, such as off-task behavior and the number and kind of teacher–student interactions, along with specific examples of questions asked, student responses, and other appropriate behaviors.

In organizing the data, Goldhammer, Anderson, and Krajewski (1993) suggest that the supervisor: (a) consolidate the information and put the information in a visual format (chart, graph, diagram); (b) look for recurring patterns; (c) isolate behaviors, based on empirical data, before presenting them to the teacher; and (d) look for relationships between behaviors and consequences. In addition to preparing a narrative, supervisors are encouraged to develop visuals that clarify items addressed in the narrative. As the adage goes, a picture, chart, diagram, and/or graph may be worth a thousand words. It is at this point that diagramming the teacher's mobility in the classroom, charting transitions from one topic to the next, and/or preparing a graph of the time the teacher spent in different types of dialogue with students can be useful. The narrative, charts, and graphs form the basis for initiating the conversation about the lesson and provide a way to engage teachers in an in-depth dialogue about their teaching. The information in the narrative, along with the visual charts and diagrams, give the supervisor a wealth of information to share with the teacher by holding up a mirror to the classroom. As Pajak (1993) describes Goldhammer's original intent, the analysis process provides a way for the supervisor to engage the teacher in a process of discovery as the data are presented.

During the data-analysis phase, the supervisor may seek answers to the following four questions:

1. Based on what has been recorded, did major patterns of teacher and/or student behavior emerge?

2. What strategies did the teacher use to involve students in the lesson and keep them engaged and on task?

3. What approaches were used to monitor behavior, and did the teacher recognize and redirect off-task behavior?

4. What instructional strategies did the teacher employ throughout the lesson, and were the materials relevant, with real-world situations, and appropriate for the learners?

For example, as the supervisor presents verbatim statements made by the teacher to the students, areas such as praise or the lack of it, prejudicial comments, or content presentation or input may emerge for discussion. These verbatim statements help teachers examine the messages they send to students. The information regarding the verbal classroom interaction patterns generated by the FIAC data-collection procedure can also be used as a visual format for the postobservation conference. Figure 7.6 shows how the results obtained during a 55-minute world history class have been compiled by the supervisor and expressed as a graph. In analyzing the results, the supervisor plots the percentage of total time in the class for each of the 10 verbal interaction categories.

Once the data have been put in a graphic form, analysis continues. An interpretation of Figure 7.6 indicates that the teacher lectured 79.67 percent of the time, or nearly 44 minutes of the period. In addition, the teacher spent 3.26 percent of the time giving directions and 6.23 percent of the time asking questions, leaving only 8 percent of the time for student responses or student talk. With a graphic representation of the data, the teacher should find it easier to identify the types of behavior that occurred during the lesson and realize whether he or she was engaged in the majority of the verbal interactions during this class period. The graph also shows the teacher that student involvement was limited during this world history class. If the teacher's objective was to have a class discussion, the data

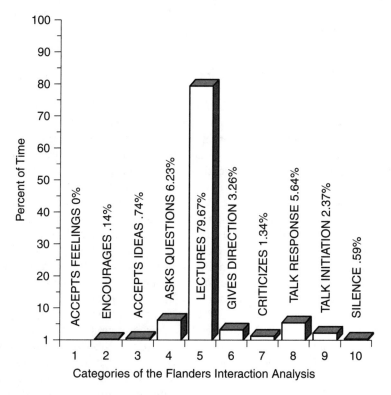

FIGURE 7.6 Analysis of Time Spent per Category

would indicate that such interaction did not occur. Graphs like the one presented here serve as a picture of the teaching–learning behaviors during the instructional episode and represent a true-to-life view of what happened during the lesson.

Supervisors and others serving in a coaching or mentoring role conduct classroom observations for two primary reasons. The first is to provide specific and valid feedback to the teacher about the teaching–learning process with the intent to establish a dialogue about continued professional growth and development. The second reason supervisors conduct classroom observations is to collect information about teaching–learning behaviors in order to both identify successful teaching practices and assess the effectiveness of teaching strategies and techniques. In Chapter 10, the assessment process is presented, with observation as a part of that system. There is no single procedure that is most appropriate for one purpose or the other. The timeline with scripting is the most comprehensive in that it attempts to record all of what was said and done in the classroom. However, timelines in isolation may not yield the necessary data to plan professional development or assess a teacher's level of performance. Observing is not the only way to provide relevant information to teachers. The use of audio and/or video recordings may prove helpful as well as the supervisor's notes taken during an observation. Observations must also consider the context of the lessons; teachers and supervisors should realize that, at best, observations are just snapshots of teaching–learning behaviors that occur throughout the year and over time.

Interacting and Conversing with Teachers

Once the information collected during the classroom observation has been analyzed and translated into a form that can be presented to the teacher, the supervisor is ready to conduct a postobservation conference. The goal of the supervisor in the conference is to use language "that enhances rather than inhibits thought and productive thinking" (Texas Education Agency, 1991, p. 42). In planning for the conference, there are general guidelines that supervisors should consider as they prepare to meet with the teacher. For Griffin (1973), a good conference is like a good lesson: It has to be well planned, well organized, and then evaluated.

Before the conference can occur, it is important for the supervisor to spend time building trust and rapport with teachers. "Trust is a basic condition which must be created, nurtured, and maintained in order for the goals of the [conference] to be achieved" (Texas Education Agency, 1991, p. 40). Trust provides the foundation for establishing rapport and producing effective conferences with teachers. Effective supervisors build trust by actively listening with precision and empathy and read signals that reflect a teacher's unconscious thinking processes. These signals include posture, breathing, gestures, voice tone, and language. Supervisors maintain rapport by knowing how and when to match these responses with their own behavior. "Skillful supervisors help teachers gain access to their own inner resources of confidence, knowledge, empathy, and personal self-esteem" (Texas Education Agency, 1991, p. 40). It is during formal and informal

FIGURE 7.7   Postobservation Conference Form

	Comments
1. Did you begin the conference in a manner that encouraged the teacher to feel comfortable?	
2. Did you establish goals for the conference?	
3. Would you describe the type of conference as cooperative? Confrontational? Passive?	
4. Did you present information in a format that fostered understanding?	
5. Did you use a format that included a graph? Chart? Continuum?	
6. Did you prepare a narrative?	
7. Did the teacher understand what you presented and your interpretation of the facts? Did you check for understanding?	
8. Was the general tone of the conference positive? Constructive? Negative?	
9. Did you close the conference with a description of what was observed? With modifiable items? By making plans for another observation?	
10. Were the instruments you used appropriate?	List each: a. b. c. d.

conferences that the communication skills discussed earlier in Chapter 5 are put to use as supervisors seek to employ freeing responses rather than restricting responses.

A good place for the supervisor to begin preparing for a meeting with the teacher is a quick review of the postobservation conference form as presented in Figure 7.7. Although designed to be completed after the conference, the questions on this form can assist the supervisor in preparing for the conference by noting the kinds of information and interactions that are important in conferencing with teachers.

Dubois (1994) has suggested four essential components for a successful conference: preparation, human relations, communication, and a plan of action. First, *preparation* is the component in which "the supervisor plans a road map for moving through the conference as well as [determines] the desired destination at the end of the conference…like any other well-designed adult activity it has a beginning, a productive give-and-take discussion, and a good closing" (Tracy and MacNaughton, 1993, p. 194). The supervisor must plan an agenda, think ahead, and anticipate any potential problems. Second, *human relations* involves the interpersonal skills used to conduct the conference; these include such behaviors as problem solving, spontaneity, and empathy. Human relations involves behavior and practices that help people to obtain knowledge about and understand themselves and others and then use that information to improve performance and/or interact more effectively with others. *Communication*, the third essential element, was discussed in Chapter 5; it involves the use of freeing responses to encourage two-way communication and limiting restricting responses, which serve to discourage two-way communication. "Supervisors need to be aware of presuppositions that impede openness…[as] they…strive for language that promotes mental rehearsal and precise thinking" (Texas Education Agency, 1991, p. 42). A primary consideration in planning for the postobservation conference is to give teachers accurate, specific data obtained from classroom observations. Since one of the primary functions of the conference is to provide feedback to the teacher, it is important to focus on actual occurrences. At this point, the narrative and the visual representations of the data can be used to reference specific teaching–learning behaviors that were observed.

Communication, an important part of the postobservation conference, is highly variable and complex. When supervisors send a message, they communicate not only facts gathered but feelings, perceptions, and innuendoes. As supervisors participate in the conference, they should be aware that they communicate messages through gestures, physical posture, facial expressions, tone of voice, and by what is said as well as how it is said. A supervisor's communication style, then, becomes a part of the message; it refers to the total range of verbal and nonverbal behaviors the supervisor displays. In addition, the same message may carry both an intentional and an unintentional meaning. Double meanings can often pose unusual difficulties for both the supervisor and the teacher. Supervisors should always be conscious of what they communicate and the manner in which they communicate it.

Another consideration that the supervisor must be cognizant of during the postobservation conference is the selection of words that are used. Words that convey a value of "good and bad" or "appropriate and not appropriate" should be avoided. An extreme example would be for the supervisor, in showing the teacher the data represented in Figure 7.6, to say, "Looking at the data, what do you conclude—that you dominated the classroom interaction and students were not involved in a meaningful way?" The intent is to let the data "speak" in an objective way so that the teacher can recognize areas that need to be changed or improved.

It is also important for the supervisor to avoid making assumptions and drawing hasty conclusions from inferences. During the postobservation conference, supervisors may need to ask questions that seek additional information and/or insight into the instructional environment. For example, the supervisor should be cautious about assuming that the teacher talked a great deal during the lesson because the students were not adequately prepared to respond in class. The supervisor should stick to the data and ask the teacher, "Is this a typical pattern for your classroom interactions?" or "Were you aware of this pattern during the lesson?" If the supervisor does offer an "outside, objective" interpretation, the teacher should be encouraged to respond to the interpretation or offer an alternative explanation. Even though there is often a temptation to make judgments and offer advice, the supervisor must guard against such temptations, which can emotionally charge the dialogue. As Dubois (1994) notes, the language for the conference should be descriptive, focused, specific, brief, and simple.

Throughout the postobservation conference, the supervisor not only sends messages but receives them. As indicated earlier, listening is not only crucial to establishing trust and rapport but is a critical component of the communication process; supervisors should strive to "really hear" what teachers are saying. Good listening includes the following verbal skills: acknowledging, reflecting, paraphrasing, summarizing, clarifying, and elaborating on what is said (Conoley and Conoley, 1982). Skilled supervisors "ask questions to determine if what is being discussed is understood [and they] ask for feedback or have the teacher summarize" (Texas Education Agency, 1991, p. 51). Agreement precedes change, and checking for agreement involves verifying if the teacher agrees with the feedback and analysis. The supervisor can informally check for agreement by asking questions like, "What do you think about…?"

As the conference comes to an end, the teacher and supervisor should come to the fourth essential element—a mutually agreed-upon *plan of action*. The plan of action identifies what is to be done in the future as a result of the feedback. By focusing on and stressing teaching–learning behaviors that can be modified, the supervisor offers the teacher a place to begin. The objective is to promote ownership after the teacher has analyzed the lesson and indicated a receptivity to change. The supervisor should focus on the modification behaviors discussed and ask, "Is that something you want to work on?" The supervisor might also indicate what he or she will do to assist the teacher. At the conclusion of the conference, the supervisor should review the postobservation conference reflection form again. This time, the checklist should help the supervisor evaluate his or her own performance during the conference.

A major purpose of the postobservation conference is for supervisors to establish a dialogue with teachers about the creation of short-term as well as long-term professional development goals. Setting goals requires teachers to make a commitment to some course of action. It becomes the supervisor's task to distill and clarify the essential elements discussed during the conference. The supervisor should ask questions that encourage the teacher to think about what he or she will do in the future. For example, the supervisor might ask one or more of the following questions:

- "What will you do tomorrow if the same students are disruptive?"

- "What preventive measures will you take to ensure that these students' behaviors will not occur next week?"

- "How can you involve reluctant learners in the class discussion?"

- "What instructional priorities are you going to set for yourself?"

The entire discussion during the postobservation conference should be directed toward having teachers problem-solve as they process information about their instructional performance. Using E-mail and interactive (synchronous) computer conferencing would allow for continuing dialogue and idea exchange (Andrews and Herschel, 1996).

Summary

This chapter described procedures that supervisors can use when conducting classroom observations and interacting with teachers. The specific procedures identified can be useful to supervisors as they plan for in-class observations and then prepare and discuss this information with teachers. The data-collection and -analysis procedures provide supervisors with tools that facilitate a dialogue about what happened during the instructional episode that was observed.

The first section of the chapter began by cautioning supervisors against biases that can influence what they view. Areas that supervisors should strive to avoid include: making personal interpretations about the lesson; observing with perceptual blinders; applying a set of personal likes and dislikes; and misinterpreting teacher behaviors.

The general guidelines for classroom observation help to prepare supervisors for conducting and reporting to teachers about the in-class observation. The six guidelines of observation are: (1) focusing on teacher–student behaviors, (2) limiting the number of instructional variables to observe at one time, (3) minimizing classroom disruptions caused by the observer, (4) developing good note-taking skills, (5) analyzing the data collected, and (6) providing feedback to the teacher.

In addition to these general guidelines, the chapter provided examples of specific data-collection procedures that can be used when observing in classrooms. The data-collection procedures discussed include: timelines (scripting); topical data capture charts; records of on-task and off-task behaviors; records of transitions and lesson pacing; maps or charts of teacher mobility, classroom management, and teacher–student interactions; and coded verbal interactions (Flander's Interaction Analysis Categories). Supervisors may follow these procedures or modify them to meet specific or unique classroom situations. Depending on the nature of the instructional behaviors to be observed, the supervisor may want to create an observation or data-collection procedure that is more compatible with the purpose of the observation.

After the raw data have been collected, supervisors must analyze the information objectively and accurately. In preparing for the postobservation conference, the supervisor can present the results of the observation both as a descriptive narrative and in a visual form. Supervisors, in working with the data obtained from the observation, are cautioned to be nonjudgmental as they look for patterns of behavior and the effects of those behaviors. The purpose of analysis is to reconstruct what happened so that the teacher accepts the results as accurate and valid.

At the postobservation conference, the supervisor should convey the findings in a visual, objective format. In planning for a conference with the teacher to present the information, the supervisor should prepare the feedback materials, use interpersonal skills that facilitate dialogue, utilize effective communication skills, and then cooperatively determine a plan of action. At the end of the conference, the supervisor should guide the teacher to higher-order thinking about his or her teaching behaviors in the classroom and develop a plan of action. Taken together, the cautions as well as the guidelines presented in the chapter give supervisors the mechanics or tools for conducting objective observations, which in turn provide supervisors with the foundation for accurately communicating information to teachers.

YOUR TURN

7.1. You have been working with a secondary art teacher, Mr. Avales, for the past month, and he would like you (the supervisor) to observe him. He has admitted, and you concur, that he is not "coming across" to his students. For whatever reason, during the past several weeks as you talked with him, Mr. Avales had difficulty describing his concern.

   a. How will you script? Longhand? Computer?

   b. What observational procedures would you suggest to him before you observe (during the preobservation conference)? Why have you recommended these data-capturing procedures? What type of data will be generated that can be used, and what form will you use to share with Mr. Avales?

7.2. You have observed a mathematics class. You developed the following chart of the teacher's behavior as you observed. The Xs mark the students' desks and the circles around the Xs represent students who are off task talking. The T represents the location of the teacher at various times during the lesson. Look at the diagram below.

   a. What teacher mobility and student behavior patterns seem to be present?

b. After analyzing this visual, what questions would you ask during the post-observation conference?

T (leaning on wall)	T (seated at desk)
First 15 minutes	Remainder of period

X X X X X X X X X X

X X X X (X) X X X (X) X

X X X (X) X X X (X)(X) X

7.3. The following is a verbatim transcript obtained from a classroom observation. After reading the transcript, code it using the numbers of the FIAC. You may assume that each complete printed line of a sentence is a student or teacher statement and is three seconds in duration.

[T = Teacher statement; S = Student statement]

T: Who can tell me what a microscope is? What is it used for?

S: It is something scientists use; it gives a picture of something small. I've used it before; it's neat.

T: Now, what else can you say about the microscope?

S: It is heavy.

T: How many of you think so too?

S: Me, and some are really powerful.

T: Good. What does that mean?

S: You can see a lot more.

T: More in terms of number?

S: Yes, but also in terms of size and detail.

T: Good for you. Terry has the right idea—that a microscope is a tool that makes organisms and objects larger. It magnifies them. OK, why is magnification so important?

S: Well, it makes things big.

T: But why is making something big so important?

7.4. You are planning to observe an English/language teacher. Before the observation, it was decided that you would focus on the types of questions asked during the period. At the completion of the class period/session, you had the following categories of data:

5   rhetorical questions

3   probing (analysis/synthesis/evaluation) questions (according to Bloom's cognitive domain)

10   recall questions

12   comprehension questions

Before the visit, the teacher convinced you that she asks a variety of questions. When you started the observation, there was an expectation that her repertoire included many different types of questions, but your observation record did not confirm what this teacher shared with you.

Now you have to present the results to the teacher. Was this a typical lesson for this teacher? Outline the steps you will take during the postobservation conference, and describe the way you plan to present this information to the teacher. Also, what questions would you ask to get this teacher to recognize that her perceptions regarding types of questions asked were not accurate during the lesson observed?

7.5. You are ready to begin the postobservation conference with a teacher who, on the whole, is very good. But you want to help this teacher be even better. You conclude, based on the data collected from many in-class observations, that at the beginning of the school year the teacher was exceptionally accommodating to students; this had a positive effect on the classroom climate. But now, with three months of school left, the teacher is getting to be more controlling, disagreeable, unpredictable, and often harsh in interacting with the students. You feel that this teacher will agree with you about the situation and that ways will be identified to correct this more negative spiral, which is having an effect on classroom climate. Your attitude coming into the conference is one of hopeful anticipation.

However, when you present the results from the observations, the teacher totally rejects the data and what you say and becomes highly defensive. What do you do? What overall strategy will you use? What techniques will you employ? What steps will you take to communicate your findings and help the teacher "hear" what you are saying?

REFERENCES

Acheson, K. A., & Gall, M. D. (1997). *Techniques in the clinical supervision of teachers: Preservice and inservice applications.* (3rd ed.). New York: Longman.

Andrews, P. H., & Herschel, R. T. (1996). *Organizational communication: Empowerment in a technological society.* Boston: Houghton Mifflin.

Calebrese, R. L., & Zepeda, S. J. (1997). *The reflective supervisor: A practical guide for educators.* Larchmont, NY: Eye on Education.

Clements, B., & Evertson, C. (1980). *Developing an effective research team for classroom observation.* R & D Report No. 6103. R & D Center for Teacher Education. Austin: University of Texas.

Coates, T., & Thoresen, C. (1976). Teacher anxiety: A review with recommendations. *Review of Educational Research, 46,* 159–184.

Conoley, J. C., & Conoley, C. W. (1982). *School consultation: A guide to practice and training.* New York: Pergamon.

da Costa, J. L. (1995). Teacher collaboration: The roles of trust and respect. Educational Document Retrieval Service, ED 384 607.

da Costa, J. L., & Riordan, G. (1996). Teacher efficacy and the capacity to trust. Educational Document Retrieval Service, ED 397 010.

Doyle, W. (1986). Classroom organization and management. In *Handbook of research on teaching.* (3rd ed.). M. Wittrock (ed.). New York: Macmillan.

Dubois, D. J. (1994 August 9). Mentoring, conferencing, and supervisory skills. Marriott Hotel, Arlington, TX. [Mimeograph.]

Dunkin, M. J., & Biddle, B. J. (1974). *The study of teaching.* New York: University Press of America.

Fifer, F. (1980). Teacher in-class observation form. Dallas: University of Texas at Dallas. [Mimeograph.]

Flanders, N. A. (1967). Teacher influence in the classroom. In *Interaction analysis: Theory, research and application.* E. J. Amidon & J. B. Hough (eds.). Reading, MA: Addison-Wesley.

Garman, N. B. (1990). Theories embedded in the events of clinical supervision. *Journal of Curriculum and Supervision, 5,* 209–210.

Glickman, C. D. (1985). *Supervision of instruction.* Boston: Allyn & Bacon.

Glickman, C. D., Gordon, S. P., & Ross-Gordon, J. M. (1995). *Supervision of instruction: A developmental approach.* (3rd ed.). Boston: Allyn & Bacon.

Goldhammer, R., Anderson, R. H., & Krajewski, R. J. (1993). *Clinical supervision: Special methods for the clinical supervision of teachers.* (3rd ed.). Fort Worth, TX: Harcourt Brace Jovanovich.

Good, T. L., & Brophy, J. E. (1997). *Looking in classrooms.* (5th ed.). New York: Addison-Wesley.

Griffin, F. (1973). *A handbook for the observation of teaching and learning.* Midland, MI: Pendell.

Hilty, E. B. (1993). Teacher education: What is good teaching, and how do we teach people to be good teachers? In *Thirteen questions.* J. L. Kinchelol & S. R. Steinberg (eds.). New York: Peter Lang.

Hunter, M. (1983). Script taping: An essential tool. *Educational Leadership, 41,* 43.

Kuralt, R. C. (1987). The computer as a supervisory tool. *Educational Leadership, 44,* 71–72.

Manatt, R. (1981). Evaluating teacher performance. Alexandra, VA: Association for Supervision and Curriculum Development. (Videotape.)

McDevitt, M. A. (1996). A virtual view: Classroom observations at a distance. *Journal of Teacher Education, 47,* 191–195.

McNeely, S. L. (1997). *Observing students and teachers through objective strategies.* Boston: Allyn & Bacon.

Oliva, P. R., & Pawlas, G. E. (1997). *Supervision for today's schools.* (5th ed.). New York: Longman.

Pajak, E. (1993). *Approaches to clinical supervision: Alternatives for improving instruction.* Norwood, MA: Christopher-Gordon Publishers.

Sahakian, P., & Stockton, J. (1996). Opening doors: Teacher-guided observations. *Educational Leadership, 53,* 50–53.

Stallings, J., & Freiberg, H. J. (1991). Observation for the improvement of teaching. In *Effective teaching: Current research.* H. C. Waxman and H. J. Walberg (eds.). Berkeley, CA: McCutchan Publishing Co.

Texas Education Agency. (1991). *Conferencing skills: An instructional module to enhance professional development.* Austin: Texas Education Agency.

Tracy, S. J., & MacNaughton, R. (1993). *Assisting and assessing educational personnel: The impact of clinical supervision.* Boston: Allyn & Bacon.

Wheeler, P. (1994). *Improving classroom observation skills: Guidelines for teacher evaluation.* Educational Document Retrieval System, ED 364 961.

Woolsey, K., & Bellamy, R. (1997). Science education and technology: Opportunities to enhance student learning. *Elementary School Journal, 97,* 385–399.

The Instructional Dimension of Supervision

Chapter 8:   Curriculum Development: The Role of the Supervisor
Chapter 9:   Teaching: A Complex Process
Chapter 10:   Assessing the Complexity of Teaching: Characteristics
              and Components

Part Three elaborates on the roles of the supervisor in the overall instructional process, including curriculum development, teaching, and assessing of teaching. Chapter 8 describes how supervisors interact with others in the curriculum development process by emphasizing the importance of the development of a philosophy and elaborating on the use of curriculum models, designs, and resources. The complexities of teaching are the focus of Chapter 9. Various definitions and views of teaching, along with common concerns of classroom teaching, provide a backdrop for analyzing instruction. Historically, teaching behaviors identified through process–product research have served as the primary lens for assessing effective teaching. More recent research on effective teaching has moved beyond the process–product emphasis to one that includes analysis of the dynamics of teaching and learning within the context of classrooms, the nature of both student learning and subject-matter teaching, and new data-collection procedures. Chapter 10 describes the performance assessment process as a means not only of assessing teaching but of promoting continuous professional development. Components of assessment systems, such as portfolios and case-based methods, are presented as tools supervisors can use in conducting comprehensive assessments.

8

Curriculum Development

The Role of the Supervisor

OBJECTIVES

The objectives of this chapter are:

- Define and describe various views of curriculum.
- Discuss the role of a philosophy in the curriculum development process.
- Identify and describe three major philosophical perspectives and their impact on curriculum development.
- Analyze mission statements and determine the dominant educational philosophy.
- Describe the curriculum development process advocated by the Tyler model.
- Identify and describe the sources of the curriculum.
- Explain how a theory of learning shapes the development of curriculum.
- Reduce a general goal to an instructional objective.
- Describe the role of taxonomies of objectives in developing curriculum.
- Identify and give examples of each kind of curriculum design.
- Identify and describe the steps in the curriculum development process.

Perhaps in looking at the title of this chapter, you wonder, "What does curriculum development have to do with supervision?" Glickman, Gordon, and Ross-Gordon (1995) say that the school's curriculum is defined by those within the school organization and becomes the foundation for effective teaching. As supervisors work with teachers in planning for teaching and learning, they can be more effective as helpers when they are knowledgeable about the curriculum development process.

Supervisors also play an important role as they assist teachers in continually refining and expanding the overall school curriculum and the grade-level instructional program. As Tanner and Tanner (1987) have noted, "The need for the professional staff to engage in curriculum development as a central responsibility and as a continuous process…becomes evident when one considers that the curriculum is always in danger of…subject matter being added" (p. 42).

Many teachers as well as supervisors accept the curriculum just as they accept the air they breathe, without thinking about it. Teachers seldom question its development or content; for many, the curriculum is a given in the teaching–learning process. It is often seen as something developed by someone else, and those in supervisory positions have often been considered the guardians of curriculum (Tanner and Tanner, 1980). Rather than being static, the curriculum is dynamic and changing and is modified as the needs, interests, and goals of the students and school change.

According to Reinhartz and Beach (1997), curriculum is built on an infrastructure that includes four elements: (1) the historical roots that have shaped the present K–12 school curriculum; (2) the contemporary organization patterns of the elementary and secondary schools; (3) the social, political, and economic climate and forces; and (4) the developmental characteristics of students. These authors continue by saying that "These four areas of study are crucial, not only in helping teachers understand the underlying issues of the curriculum development process, but more importantly, in structuring teaching and learning so that the results are appropriate and meaningful" (p. 99).

In addition to these four areas of study, a philosophy of education provides a way of understanding the roots and educational belief system (Reinhartz and Beach, 1997). These areas of study help to provide answers to the following questions: Why do teachers teach? What are the instructional strategies they use? Why do they teach the way they do? Why is the school year based on a nine- to ten-month calendar? Why are the instructional programs tailored to the needs and interests of students?

Curriculum development has been referred to as integrated, fused, correlated, individualized, and humanized, but it is generally agreed that curriculum development has two parts—a process part and a content part. Frazee and Rudnitski (1995) have observed that "Curriculum development is a process…like the writing process in that one retraces one's steps in re-reading, editing and revising" the content of what has been written (p. 120). This chapter will focus on the process of developing curriculum rather than discussing the specific content to be included. In examining the curriculum development process, the chapter will provide several definitions of curriculum, describe the role of a philosophy in developing curriculum, provide a model that can be used as a template in developing curriculum, discuss several curriculum designs, operationalize the curriculum development process, and suggest resources for curriculum development.

Definitions and Views of Curriculum

Before examining the complexities of the curriculum development process, it is important to understand what is meant by the term *curriculum*. Schubert (1993) notes that "the term curriculum is shrouded in definitional controversy"; definitions continue to evolve, based on educational conditions at a given time in history and our understanding of the teaching–learning process. One of the earliest meanings of curriculum was derived from the Latin root of the word, which means a racecourse or a prescribed course to follow. Later, the term was adapted to refer to a prescribed series of courses to complete a program of studies. The first modern definition of the term appeared in the 1920s and viewed curriculum as a process, not a product (Wiles and Bondi, 1984, 1993). Bobbitt (1924) defined curriculum as all the organized and unorganized educational experiences students encounter. Other definitions, including more recent ones, are:

- All that is planned and directed by teachers to achieve the educational goals (Tyler, 1957)

- Plans for guiding teaching and learning (Glatthorn, 1987)

- A work plan that includes both the content and the strategies for teaching and learning (English, 1992)

- The reconstruction of knowledge and experience under the guidance of the school, which fosters learning (Tanner and Tanner, 1995)

- A flexible plan for teaching that meets the needs of students as well as provides opportunities for teachable moments (Reinhartz and Beach, 1997)

The role of the student in mastering or learning some prescribed or planned body of knowledge is a common theme in many definitions of curriculum. For us, *curriculum development includes careful planning, with the ultimate goal of increasing student achievement and is not only the written plan or construct but the content, learning experiences, and results.*

Before describing the models used in the curriculum development process, it is essential to answer the questions, "What is the curriculum?" and "Where does the curriculum come from?" Supervisors should be prepared to answer these questions and empower teachers to take ownership of what is taught in their classrooms—their curriculum. By becoming stakeholders in the curriculum development process, teachers begin to recognize it as one of the vital ingredients of the instructional life of schools and individual classrooms.

The Role of Philosophy
in Developing Curriculum

For Berliner (1996), the process of developing a curriculum is undergirded by a belief system or ideology that provides a context for teaching and learning. Whatever the curricular focus—mainstreaming, inclusion, use of cooperative learning, or programs for the gifted and talented or for those students whose first language is not English—a teacher's views or beliefs play a major role in determining which curriculum is supported and which is not. In the bigger picture, these views or beliefs are referred to as philosophies of education, which represent the theoretical and intellectual underpinnings of the curriculum building process (Reinhartz and Beach, 1997).

Supervisors should provide an environment for teachers (as a part of the overall process of their growth and development) in which they feel supported and have opportunities to reflect on and think about what they are teaching and why they teach the way they do. Knight (1989) stresses that when teachers come face-to-face with their philosophies, they come to understand the meaning and mission underlying education by reflecting on what and why they teach, and they "develop a clear vision regarding the purpose of education" and the curriculum (p. 3).

"Having a professional belief system guides the development of a personal vision for teaching [and] this vision embodies both the means and ends of curriculum development" (Reinhartz and Beach, 1997, p. 101). Teachers' belief systems are shaped by their culture, past experiences, religious and moral principles, and values. How teachers handle specific situations in a classroom also reveals their educational philosophy (Ornstein and Levine, 1984). If teachers are not aware of the impact of their educational philosophy on teaching and learning, they may be vulnerable to externally imposed societal pressures, which may be fashionable at a given time but which are not necessarily educationally sound.

Entire books and courses examine the development and implications of educational philosophies in great detail. Our purpose here is to briefly describe three major philosophies and to show how they give direction and focus to the general goals and objectives of the curriculum. Figure 8.1 presents these educational philosophies along with the corresponding purposes of education, the nature of the curriculum and the learner, and the type of teaching strategies. These philosophies of education—essentialism, progressivism, and existentialism—will be described in the following pages.

The *essentialist philosophy,* a combination of idealism and realism, has several basic tenets, including support for the liberal arts—English, history, foreign languages, mathematics, science, and other core subjects (see Figure 8.2). Essentialists believe that the curriculum is timeless and that, in the pursuit of basic truths, the intellect should be cultivated through the study of great ideas as well as the study of nature and natural laws. According to Pasch and colleagues (1995), essentialists

FIGURE 8.1   Three Philosophies of Education: An Overview

Philosophy	Instructional Focus	Curriculum	Methodology	Nature of Learner
Essentialism	The world of ideas, cultivation of knowledge, and pursuit of academic excellence	Content of the academic disciplines (the liberal arts, math, science, etc.)	Drill and practice, memorization, and writing essays or term papers	Thinking, rational individual who gains insights
Progressivism	Cooperative learning and problem solving, which emphasize experience	Comprehensive core (interdisciplinary and problem-focused)	Interactive groups, reflective thinking, and group projects	Responsible, socially oriented individual interested in solving problems of humankind
Existentialism	Search for personal meaning and personal development	Individual choice of content selection and mode of learning (based on a moral philosophy)	Learning centers and individualized instruction or learning plan	Highly individualistic choice maker who creates own view of truth and knowledge

As an English teacher, I feel it is extremely important for students to read the classics, which stress the great ideas of authors from each of the major periods of literature. The argument is often made that the classics are difficult to read because they are in the vernacular of a different time and place and, therefore, should not be taught. This argument is sometimes supported by data showing that some students are reading on a sixth-grade level and cannot comprehend these great pieces of literature. It is my belief, however, that I am not wasting my time or the time of my students by having them vicariously experience different cultures in different times and places of the globe. I believe it is essential that students be exposed to the literature of the ages so they can more fully understand the great ideas of past civilizations, cultures, and customs. For me, these essentials represent the basic foundation for comprehending more recent literary genres and contemporary writing. This study of great works provides basic models that serve as building blocks for helping my students develop more effective written and oral communication skills.

FIGURE 8.2   Essentialism

believe that "because it has been examined, refined, and revised over the centuries, the knowledge gained from disciplinary study is more valuable than knowledge gained from any other source of educational content" (p. 17). The performing arts, industrial arts, vocational studies, and physical education are often considered nonessentials. Educators holding the essentialist view believe that the school's main purpose is to equip students with intellectual powers and skills. For them, the students' interests are secondary to the pursuit of academic excellence because the purpose of school is to teach basic skills through a uniform curriculum. Learning is measured by rigorous testing; as a result, students are frequently tracked or ability-grouped based on test scores.

Progressivism, the second philosophy, has a basis in experimentalism and pragmatism; it views people as thinking beings who are capable of solving social problems (see Figure 8.3). Progressivism is an action-oriented philosophy that "sees thought as intrinsically connected with action. The value of an idea is measured by the consequences [results] produced when it is translated into action" (Rosen, 1968, p. 67). The architect of progressivism in schools was John Dewey (1902, 1916), who defined experience as the students' interaction with the environment and believed that the purpose of education is to develop problem-solving skills. According to Dewey (1916), "The scheme of a curriculum must take account of the adaptation of studies to the needs of existing community life; it must select with the intention of improving the life we live in common so that the future shall be better than the past" (p. 125). According to this philosophy, schools—like society—require social interaction. For the progressives, learning is thus an active process in which all students participate. And most favor "curriculum experimentation and flexibility rather than a prescribed program for the transmission of subject matter" (Pasch et al., 1995, p. 16). Following the precepts of progressivism, the learning environment is child-centered; the teacher serves as a guide or project director. Thus, the progressive teacher tends to use an inductive approach to learning, and education involves a

At our school, teachers use cooperative learning and problem-solving strategies as an integral part of the teaching–learning process. Whether the students are in language arts, mathematics, science, or social studies, we encourage them to work in groups and to interact with materials and data as they address a problem or situation they are given. The group arrives at a decision and offers suggestions for ways to solve the problem—be it scientific or technological (environmental, health), social (policies, programs, conditions), and/or governmental (drugs). Stressing a hands-on, collaborative, learner-centered approach when dealing with hypothetical real-world situations provides students with the skills they need to solve problems they will encounter as they become adults and assume their roles as responsible citizens.

FIGURE 8.3   Progressivism

series of process-oriented experiences in which students find themselves using problem-solving strategies to generate practical solutions.

The third philosophy is *existentialism;* see the example in Figure 8.4. Tenets of this philosophy include the view that individuals exist in a world in which they are required to make choices within the context of the "anguish of freedom." It is through the choices individuals make that they give meaning to their lives and discover their personal worth and capabilities. Individuals determine their destiny through the choices they make. For the existentialist, the purpose of school is to help students identify their strengths and weaknesses and to make appropriate choices in learning. The goal of education is to help each student achieve self-development and self-fulfillment. The existentialists oppose a structured core curriculum because their attention is focused on individual student learning. The arts, literature, and social studies become the basis for the curriculum, and they do not exist in isolation from each other. When existentialist ideas are implemented in a school, they take various forms—from totally student-run programs, such as A. S. Neill's (1960) Summerhill School, to the use of individualized programs, which include learning packets, computer-assisted instruction (CAI), and learning centers. The teacher functions as a facilitator who guides students in making choices, thereby helping them to develop the confidence to think for themselves. Existential thought allows the student to search for personal identity and meaningfulness.

Tanner and Tanner (1987) summarize the influence of educational philosophy on the curriculum when they state that "the philosophy one subscribes to determines the uses to which the behavioral sciences are put in connection with (1) the nature of the learner, (2) the nature of society, and (3) the design of the curriculum" (p. 344). Using the philosophical tenets identified in this chapter and summarized in Figure 8.1, supervisors and teachers can examine the instructional goals in light of their own educational philosophy. They can then seek to determine any conflicting views and, based on their findings, establish the type of curriculum they should provide. In the final analysis, teachers may embrace a philosophy that is multifaceted and has aspects of each of these three philosophies.

Our school follows a philosophy that recognizes the uniqueness of each student and treats each student as "a lamp to be lighted, not a vessel to be filled." In our school, students have opportunities to improve their self-concept and to learn about their strengths and weaknesses as they interact with peers and adult role models. The principals and teachers plan school projects and activities directed toward helping each student experience success. The "I am special" and "I can do" attitudes develop over time as students, in their day-to-day activities, experience personal satisfaction and growth along with academic success. Teachers plan instructional activities that are based on self-improvement plans for students and that are designed to provide a sense of worth and accomplishment.

FIGURE 8.4 Existentialism

A Curriculum Development Model

In working with teachers to plan for teaching and learning, supervisors can follow one of several models to guide the curriculum development process. For us, the process described by Tyler (1949) has been a most helpful framework in working with teachers in conceptualizing the curriculum development process. It is more global in nature and therefore is used to view the big picture of a school or grade-level curriculum.

Goals of Education.   As a planning tool, the Tyler model can assist teachers in systematically identifying the overall content of the curriculum. It can also serve as a beginning point for supervisors as they work with teachers to identify general educational goals and then translate those goals into specific instructional objectives. It is through the process of curriculum development that teachers formulate learner behaviors and develop ways to provide students with appropriate and effective learning experiences.

Tyler (1949) identified four basic questions that supervisors and teachers should address when developing curriculum. These questions are:

1. What educational purposes should the school seek to promote?
2. What educational experiences can be implemented that are likely to achieve these purposes?
3. How can these educational experiences be effectively organized?
4. How can we determine whether the purposes are being achieved? (pp. 1–2)

These questions form the basis of a curriculum development process that helps teachers identify learning outcomes, develop learning strategies, and establish assessment criteria and procedures.

Sources of Curriculum.   According to the model, the three main sources of the curriculum are society's values, students' needs, and input from subject-matter specialists. These sources provide data and help determine the educational purposes schools should pursue. In addition, the sources suggest looking at the broader context that impacts the curriculum and offer possible answers to the following five questions:

1. What educational goals should the schools hope to achieve through the curriculum?

2. What knowledge and skills are needed to prepare students for jobs today and in the future?

3. How can schools provide an educational program (curriculum) for students who have different interests, skills, learning styles, and abilities?

4. Is the subject hierarchical, sequential, and/or spiral in nature, and how can knowledge and skills across areas of study be integrated?

5. How can a thematic approach help students to see the interrelatedness of knowledge?

The answers to these questions are complex, but using a model such as Tyler's is a first step toward determining the scope of the school curriculum and the general goals of education. The general goals of education ultimately determine what should be taught in school, how it should be taught, and how it should be assessed. These general goals are usually expressed as part of state and school district mission statements.

Two Screens.   In implementing the general goal statements generated from the three sources of curriculum, teachers apply two screens: their educational philosophy, discussed in an earlier section (see Figure 8.1), and their understanding of a psychology of learning. Teachers use their philosophy and views of learning to construct instructional objectives and describe student learning in precise terms. A teacher's philosophy of education and view of learning influence what will be included in the curriculum (ends) and how it will be taught (means). The philosophy screen is important because it gives meaning and direction to actions taken by teachers regarding the curriculum.

Many, if not most, of the things teachers do in their classrooms can be traced to a specific theory of learning. This second screen helps answer the questions, "How do students learn best?" and "Are the goals appropriate for the level of the students?" While space does not allow for a complete overview of learning theories, two major theories of learning are presented as examples of how this screen operates in the Tyler model. These major fields of study regarding how students learn are behaviorism or the S-R (stimulus-response) theory and the cognitive-field or Gestalt theory.

According to the *behaviorism* or *S-R theory*, people learn through a conditioning process in which correct or approximately correct responses are reinforced. The reinforcement strengthens the bond between the stimulus (question or problem) and the response (answer or solution). As students practice or learn the task, each correct response they make is followed by reinforcement, so that appropriate behavior is encouraged or rewarded. In many classrooms, learning follows this model, and many activities tend to be confined to the lower end of what has become known as Bloom's (1956) taxonomy of the cognitive domain (recall and comprehension). According to Hohn (1995), within the behaviorism/S-R theory, "Learning consists of new stimulus-response connections, gradually acquired through practice and strengthened through associations with external rewards" (p. 110). For Bigge (1982), in behaviorism "the nature of the learning process is centered in a study of the relationships of…stimuli and responses and what occurs between them" (p. 89). Examples of classroom applications of the behaviorist/S-R learning theory include use of the following:

- Assertive discipline (reinforcing or rewarding appropriate behavior with treats or free time)

- Behavior modification techniques (reinforcing appropriate behavior with praise)

- Questioning techniques (using many recall questions—informational or factual—that have a high degree of success)

- Token economies (earning tokens or points for desired behavior, which can be exchanged for rewards later)

- Computer-assisted instruction, or CAI (using computers to provide questions, verifications of responses, and sometimes reinforcement)

- Motivational strategies (using rewards for students who complete instructional tasks)

- Contingency contracts (written statements that specify rewards or reinforcement for desired behavior)

The *cognitive-field or Gestalt theory* of learning is another view of how students learn. This approach to learning takes into account the learner's attitudes, values, prior experiences, and interests; it proceeds from the whole to the part. For Bigge (1982), "the key word of the Gestalt-field psychologists in describing learning is *insight*." Hohn (1995) notes that in the cognitive-field theory, "learning consists of the formation of new perceptions when the learner is confronted with problem situations" (p. 25). Learning, then, is a process of developing new insights and is influenced by the sum total of what each person brings to the learning situation.

There are certainly classroom applications for the cognitive-field or Gestalt theory of learning: Problem-solving teaching strategies are emphasized; mistakes are seen as opportunities to learn; integrated thematic planning is encouraged; self-concept activities are included; and teacher questions focus on higher-order cognitive skills (such as application, analysis, synthesis, and evaluation). Teachers can provide mnemonic devices as a way to provide encoding, elaboration, organization, and imagery as students process information. Conceptual models or mind maps that are diagrams and words help students build mental constructs of the concepts studied (Hohn, 1995).

After studying the general goals of education, the three sources of curriculum, and the two screens through which these goals are viewed, supervisors and teachers arrive at the final step in the Tyler model—the identification of specific instructional objectives. Supervisors, as they work with teachers individually or in planning teams, facilitate the curriculum development process as they suggest ways to translate school and district goals into classroom instructional objectives.

Reduction of Goals to Instructional Objectives.   Selecting and writing instructional objectives is the final step in the Tyler curriculum development model. The formulation of specific objectives, often called *instructional* or *behavioral objec-*

tives, clarifies and gives direction to the general goals of education. Within the Tyler curriculum framework, the general goals are translated into specific learning outcomes, which become the central focus for planning instructional units and daily lessons, selecting strategies and activities, and developing assessment or evaluation procedures.

It is during this final step that teachers are most directly involved in the curriculum development process as they write precise instructional objectives for their classrooms, based on the general goals. For Mager (1962), a pioneer in the field, instructional objectives are designed to describe observable or measurable student behaviors and should be clearly stated. As Reinhartz and Beach (1992) note, "It is the responsibility of the classroom teacher to write instructional objectives in such a way that the specific behavior students will be expected to exhibit ...will be clearly articulated" (p. 186). Reducing goals to precise instructional objectives is a complex process that requires knowledge not only about the goals but also about the concepts or subject matter and the learners.

An initial decision a teacher makes in reducing goals to instructional objectives concerns what students will be expected to learn during each day of instruction. The fundamental question that the teacher must answer is, "What do I want the students to know or be able to do following instruction?" To make this decision, the teacher needs to decide on the scope and sequence for the course by determining the essential concept and skills to be learned and the order of their presentation. By writing instructional objectives, the teacher articulates, in great detail, the specific behaviors students will be expected to exhibit or demonstrate and can develop an appropriate sequence, or order, for the objectives.

In addition to behaviors that are observable or measurable, instructional objectives include a condition under which the behavior will occur, such as on an exam or in the lab. A third criterion to include when writing instructional objectives is a minimum level of performance, which is often expressed as "correctly" or as a percentage correct (for instance, 80 percent correct). Using the Magerian technique, listing the precise measurable or observable behavior, the condition under which the behavior will take place, and a level of acceptable performance ensures that the teacher has a clear understanding of what the student is expected to do, what the teacher will need to do to help the student accomplish the objective, and how the learning will be ensured.

Taxonomies of Objectives.   Once instructional objectives are written, they can be classified according to specific levels and domains of learning. The classification system, or taxonomy, provides a way to categorize or evaluate instructional objectives. The learning outcomes can be classified into three domains of learning: cognitive, affective, and psychomotor.

Objectives written in the *cognitive domain* involve intellectual skills that range from remembering or reproducing material that has been learned to higher-order thinking skills, such as reasoning, problem solving, and synthesizing or evaluating ideas and materials. According to the *Taxonomy of Educational Objectives: Handbook I: Cognitive Domain* (Bloom et al., 1956), cognitive objectives can be assessed by moving from simple behaviors to more complex behaviors using the following six levels:

1. Knowledge—recalling previously learned material or factual information

2. Comprehension—translating information from one form to another without fully understanding implications

3. Application—using information or abstractions (rules, laws, principles, theories) in new or concrete situations

4. Analysis—dissecting or breaking down information or material into smaller component parts so that structure and relationships can be seen

5. Synthesis—putting elements or components together to form or create a new entity (such as a book, speech, painting, musical score)

6. Evaluation—judging material or information according to external criteria that are provided or internal criteria that the individual derives

The *affective domain* emphasizes values, feelings, and attitudes; relevant behavior ranges from simply paying attention to personal actions that are consistent with a set of values. According to Krathwohl and others (1964), the affective domain can be assessed using the following five-step hierarchy:

1. Receiving—is sensitive to external stimuli and pays attention to the stimuli

2. Responding—is involved with, and reacts or responds to, the stimuli

3. Valuing—appreciates or values a particular object, phenomenon, or behavior

4. Organizing—internalizes values and develops a value system that helps guide or shape behavior

5. Being characterized by a value—consistently operates or behaves according to a value system

The *psychomotor domain* stresses muscular or motor skills that require neuromuscular coordination. Bloom, Krathwohl, and their associates developed an early version of the levels of this domain; Harrow (1972) revised the earlier work and developed the following six levels:

1. Reflex movements—involuntary movements that begin at birth and continue to maturation and include such behaviors as flinching or ducking when an object is thrown

2. Fundamental movements—inherent movement patterns, such as crawling or swaying, which become part of more specialized and complex movements

3. Perceptual abilities—integration of physical and mental abilities, such as the neuromuscular response of catching a ball

4. Physical abilities—behaviors, such as strength, endurance, and agility, that (as they develop) can provide a sound, efficient body to conduct skilled movements

5. Skilled movements—movements, such as dance steps or sports skills, that are complex and require learning through practice

6. Nondiscursive communication—behaviors that range from facial expressions to dance choreographies and that incorporate all previously learned behaviors to communicate

These domains of learning and the levels within each domain provide supervisors and teachers with a framework for examining instructional objectives. For Smith (1975), every lesson should have objectives in each of the three domains, and these objectives should be written for different levels of the domains. Instructional supervisors can assist teachers in planning instruction by encouraging them to incorporate multiple levels and different domains of learning within their curriculum.

Curriculum Designs

Tyler provided the infrastructure for organizing, identifying, and selecting information for elementary and secondary students that is consistent with goals and objectives from the community and academic specialists, as well as appropriate for the students themselves. Using a series of screens, the model helps in the development of learning objectives for a specific population of students.

The way the learning objectives are organized for teaching and learning is shaped by a variety of curriculum designs: the K–12 subjects, the students, broad fields, problem-solving dilemmas, and/or integrative themes. A *subject-centered or discipline-based* curriculum design focuses on a separate subject orientation with little or no integration of information or skills shared with other curriculum areas. As Frazee and Rudnitski (1995) state, "Most instruction in schools, from kindergarten to grade 12, is based in the disciplines—the separate subject areas" (p. 138). This design reflects Bruner's (1960) view that subjects form the basis for what is taught in school and are made up of concepts, generalizations, and facts. These form the heart of curriculum development.

Another curriculum design is *student-* or *learner-centered;* it focuses on the developmental levels as well as the needs and interests of the students. Knowledge of child growth and development comes into play as the curriculum is planned. According to Morrison (1993), "whatever happens to children in school—what they are taught, the activities they participate in, and how they are taught— should be appropriate to their physical, emotional, social, and cognitive levels of development" (p. 88). The progressive educators advocated that school learning activities be centered around the characteristics of the child. From the existentialist's view, each learner should have a unique instructional program, which takes the learner-centered curriculum design one step further.

A third curriculum design is *broad fields*. The broad-field design takes disciplines that are related—such as history, economics, sociology, political science (civics, government), geography, and anthropology—and considers them as one field of study, such as social studies. As Ornstein and Hunkins (1993) note, "It [is] an attempt to integrate content that appear[s] to fit together logically" (p. 245). In elementary school, for example, social studies would be listed on the schedule of classes, whereas in high school, the broad-field design gives way to individual, separate areas, such as world history, U.S. government, and geography, that (upon closer examination) is really the subject-centered curriculum design. In the broad-field curriculum design, the solving or addressing of social problems is most compatible with the progressive philosophy.

The *problem-solving* design organizes the curriculum around individual and group activities and projects that engage learners in seeking solutions to various problems. These situations provide a context for thinking about and identifying the problem, generating options, making decisions, and developing action plans for carrying out the agreed-upon strategies. Ornstein and Hunkins (1993) suggest that "the numerous curricula for teaching critical thinking exemplify this procedural design" (p. 247). A teacher in science class, for example, wants to get students to think about ways of celebrating Earth Day. She poses the question, "What can we do as a class to help celebrate Earth Day in a constructive way?" Students working in cooperative groups will generate at least three ideas to share with the class, and together the students will decide on the best project to pursue. Another idea might be to have students identify ways to celebrate a state's anniversary of statehood and list ways to spread the word (such as E-mail, TV, newspapers, grocery bag designs, radio show, etc.).

The *integrated or thematic* curriculum design is organized around a topic or theme and involves the content and skills from several subjects. Wolfinger and Stockard (1997) describe an integrated curriculum as one

> in which the lines separating subject matter areas from one another are erased...and utilizes a conceptual or life-problem-oriented approach to organization. (p. 5)

For Frazee and Rudnitski (1995), in integrating the curriculum, "subjects [are] integrated conceptually, through skills, and through relationships; they are essentially interdisciplinary" (p. 141). Take, for example, what high school students are doing to protect the Little White River in central South Dakota from pollution. The Little White River feeds into the well that supplies water to the entire community as well as the Rosebud Sioux Indian Reservation. The theme is "Save the River." In science, the students are engaged in a number of activities (taking water samples regularly and analyzing them for dissolved oxygen, nitrates, phosphates, and levels of acid). In communications class, the students prepare and deliver public talks at the state water board and at environmental conferences; in addition, the students plan and videotape segments showing how fragile the river is and how important it is to the communities. In geography, students learn about the river's location; its history; the natural terrain that contributes to its drainage; the average rainfall each year; and the times of light and heavy flow (in order to predict times of potential trouble that could impact on the quality of the water and ultimately the water table) (*NEA Today*, 1996). In this example, several subjects are woven into a fabric of study focusing on an ecological topic, "Save the River."

It should be evident that rarely is one design used exclusively; in practice, teachers implement a number of designs simultaneously, depending on the unit or lesson objectives and the overall mission and philosophy of the school. Regardless of the design used to guide the development of the curriculum, it is essential that the instructional goals and objectives, teaching strategies, and assessment procedures are aligned. With such alignment, the curriculum is considered coherent, meaning that all the parts work together in harmony, which gives the curriculum its cohesiveness (Beane, 1995; Ornstein and Hunkins, 1993). Eggebrecht et al. (1996) and Kosmoski (1990) recount how, without integration, a curriculum becomes fragmented and compartmentalized. When the curriculum focuses exclusively on content and is driven by state-mandated tests, there are serious deficiencies—those of transfer and connectedness of knowledge (going beyond the classroom) and transfer of authority (the degree to which students take ownership of learning).

Operationalizing the Curriculum Development Process

Once the instructional objectives have been developed (based on the goals and a review of the content) and a curriculum design has been selected, then it is time to operationalize the curriculum development process with a focus on classroom instruction. The three key steps in the classroom curriculum development process are: (1) planning for teaching and learning, (2) implementing the plan, and (3) assessing teaching and learning (the effectiveness of the plan and student achievement). These three steps provide a framework for supervisors to use in working with teachers in groups or individually as they develop a blueprint for teaching and learning in classrooms and schools. Figure 8.5 illustrates the three steps of the curriculum development process. These steps are portrayed as a cycle, demonstrating that the process begins and ends with planning, which provides opportunities to modify the unit or lesson and reteach.

Step one, *planning for teaching and learning,* involves determining prior knowledge and skills of learners, establishing instructional outcomes, and reviewing appropriate resources and materials. Planning the curriculum also means reviewing the sources of curriculum, as recommended in the Tyler model. The planning step is a rehearsal for what will occur or take place during the second step, teaching. Eggen and Kauchak (1994) define planning as the process of organizing content, identifying and sequencing learning tasks, selecting assignments, and determining assessment and classroom management procedures. For us,

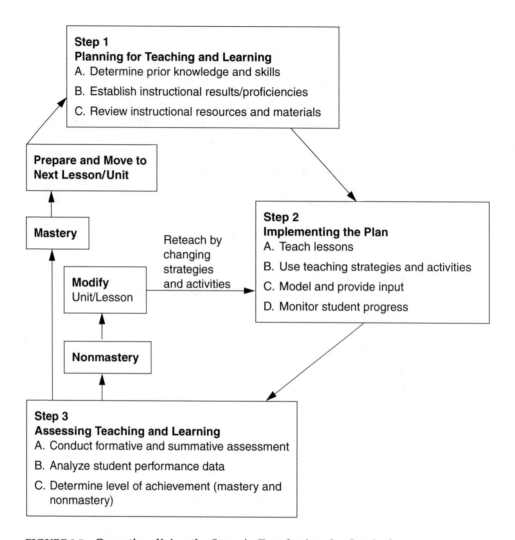

FIGURE 8.5   Operationalizing the Steps in Developing the Curriculum

planning means that teachers think about and reflect on the teaching and learning process and then write their instructional intentions. These plans become a blue-print for the teacher to follow but can be modified as they are implemented with students.

Many veteran teachers view planning as very personal and indicate there is no single best way to plan. Not every teacher begins with learning or instructional objectives; some start by thinking about strategies and activities. Reinhartz and Beach (1997) have identified the following six items that teachers should consider when planning: (1) teaching strategies/activities, (2) the students, (3) assessment procedures, (4) goals and objectives, (5) resources and materials, and (6) content or subject areas. It is important to point out that the order in which a teacher selects these items often depends on the teacher's personal preferences, past experience, and views about teaching and learning. Take, for example, resources and materials. A teacher may consider many different sources, curriculum guides, and reading materials (literature), as well as consult with colleagues or use educational technology. This teacher may decide to use the Global Explorer, which is a computer globe, to display full-color maps of the world on the computer rather than using wall maps. The advantage of this resource over maps is that the projections can be magnified through 15 levels in order to see topographic features such as wetlands, glaciers, and oil fields (Delorme Mapping, 1994).

For us, supervisors have the opportunity to review written plans with teachers for the what of the lesson (the scope of the curriculum) and the when (the sequence). In addition, teachers need to consider (a) the complexity and concreteness or abstractness of the content to ensure developmental level appropriateness; (b) prerequisite knowledge and skills to build on as new knowledge is constructed; (c) characteristics of deductive learning (general to particular) and inductive learning (particular to general); and (d) the sequence or chronology of the concepts presented. Consideration of these elements is not a linear process (Reinhartz and Beach, 1997).

Supervisors play a key role in curriculum development as they prompt teachers to reflect on key questions and select appropriate content and activities. Secondly, as supervisors and teachers examine the planning process along with the specific steps, they have opportunities to better understand the complexities involved in planning and how these complexities impact teaching and learning. Implicit in planning is decision making (Sardo Brown, 1988). Ultimately, the success of the curriculum depends on the quality of planning and the decisions that teachers make as they prepare for instruction.

Implementing the plan is the second step in the curriculum development process. Curriculum plans are implemented either as parts of a unit or as daily lesson plans. Implementing the plan involves teaching the lesson, using various strategies and activities, modeling and providing content input, and monitoring student progress during the lesson. Too often, curriculum and teaching are used interchangeably; for many, curriculum involves outcomes (the ends) and teaching is the means to attain these ends. For us, there is indeed a relationship between curriculum and teaching: "curriculum [is not] just ends, isolated from teaching or means; together they create a whole that is greater than the sum of their parts" (Reinhartz and Beach, 1997, p. 113).

Thus, the curriculum is not only the written plan or mental construct, but the results, content, and learning experiences. Teaching becomes an action or implementation of the curriculum. As Pasch and others (1995) describe the process, "Implementation is usually accomplished in face-to-face contact with...students" (p. 6). In the final analysis, curriculum and teaching are interdependent, not mutually exclusive. During the implementation step (teaching), the teacher presents the lesson, models skills, provides input, monitors student progress, and delivers the content using a variety of strategies; when necessary, the teacher modifies the plans to meet the developmental and cognitive abilities of the students. Specific variables associated with effective teaching are discussed in greater detail in Chapter 9.

The third step, *assessing teaching and learning,* provides a measure of success for instruction. Throughout this step, teachers use a variety of formative and summative procedures to determine if the benchmarks established during the planning step are achieved. For Pasch and colleagues (1995), "When we assess, we determine what students know about some content and/or their level of skill in performing some task" (p. 82). If students show limited success in learning, the curriculum development process requires modifying the plan and reteaching the concepts with different instructional strategies.

Supervisors can assist teachers in designing and using a variety of assessment procedures that will more accurately portray what students have learned. Teachers are often required to use tests as the major criteria for determining student achievement, but supervisors can help them expand their assessment repertoire by using a holistic approach to assess learning. Such an approach would include the following alternative assessment procedures:

- Products developed and presented orally to the class
- Written work samples of stories, poems, and science laboratory sheets
- Demonstration of skills that can be observed
- Journals to provide a reflective commentary
- Production of audio and/or video materials
- Portfolios, including samples of student work

Resources for Curriculum Development

As indicated earlier in the chapter, teachers make several decisions in the curriculum development process; one significant decision is determining the scope and sequence of the series of lessons or units. In writing about the earliest understanding of these terms, Saylor and Alexander (1954) say that "scope...may be thought of as the 'what' of the curriculum.... Sequence refers to the 'when' in curriculum planning" (pp. 248–249). Scope and sequence charts are often available from the district, the state department of education, or the textbook publisher. Such charts vary in degree of specificity but do provide a framework that can be useful in curriculum development and planning. At the appropriate time in the planning step, supervisors can discuss with teachers their proposed scope and sequence outline and time allotted for the various lessons or units.

Curriculum guides are another helpful tool in the curriculum development process. A curriculum guide, sometimes called a course syllabus, is a document that describes in detail the material to be covered for specific areas of study for a specific grade level. Curriculum guides may also include the objectives that are to be mastered within each subject area and grade level. Often, the curriculum guides are written by the local school district or by teachers in the state department of education to assist teachers in planning for teaching.

A resource guide is another planning aid that supervisors have available to them as they work with teachers. The resource guide is a collection of suggested materials, activities, procedures, and (sometimes) objectives that have been suggested by teachers, which can be used in planning to teach a given series of lessons or units. This collection of ideas may be developed at the local district level by supervisors and teachers, but it most often takes the form of the teacher's edition of the textbook. Many textbook publishers provide a wealth of information and suggestions for teaching different units or topics; this resource should not be overlooked.

A View from the Field

At a recent department meeting of social studies teachers at Swift Middle School, teachers decided to consider adopting supplementary material to their textbook series. As they examined the standardized test scores from the last three years and looked at their campus improvement plan and school mission statement, they felt that their textbook underrepresented many groups. Many voiced a concern regarding this omission because their students may not have the understanding needed to address several sociocultural issues that will be presented during the course of the year.

The district social studies specialist, Jerome Miller, has been invited to the first of several meetings that will focus on both selecting materials and resources that more accurately address the campus mission, the social studies curriculum goals, and student academic needs and integrating technology in the social studies curriculum (e.g., Internet research, E-mail, and data-based student profiles). These are two lofty objectives for the members of the social studies department to undertake this year.

The teachers at Swift Middle School have asked Mr. Miller to help them use the resources of the Internet to add another dimension to the social studies program by being able to tap into firsthand accounts of events, speeches, presentations, and interviews. One teacher offered the following example: I would model the use of the Internet and then incorporate Dr. Martin Luther King's "I Have a Dream" speech when providing the context for the 1960s in the United States. Since Mr. Miller has just returned from a series of workshops on technology, he has not only many materials to share with the group but suggestions about how to integrate them into the social studies curriculum.

Mr. Miller, as a supervisor, views his role as one of supporting teachers as they expand their teaching repertoire and ensure that the curriculum is representative of the diverse nature of American society.

The role of the instructional supervisor is critical in the curriculum development process. Supervisors—using the Tyler model, the various curriculum designs, and the resources identified in this chapter—can be more effective in promoting comprehensive planning prior to teaching. Throughout the curriculum development process, supervisors need to talk with teachers and encourage them to take the time to reflect on the steps in the process and the decisions they make. Such reflection provides teachers with the opportunity to analyze their plans and take the necessary steps to refine the curriculum for improved teaching and learning.

Summary

Curriculum development is a dynamic and complex process and the foundation of effective teaching. The chapter began with several definitions and views of curriculum, including the view that curriculum involves careful planning for the presentation of content and concepts. Effective teaching and learning require comprehensive and detailed planning; the Tyler model was presented as a traditional way to systematically promote curriculum development. In this chapter, the Tyler model provided a basis for supervisors and teachers to answer the question, "Where does curriculum come from?" Curriculum decisions that directly impact students are made at the classroom level, so there is a need for teachers to understand what the curriculum is, where it comes from, and how it affects teaching and learning. The Tyler model provides a schema for determining the sources of the curriculum and making decisions about the purposes of education, and then translating those purposes into curriculum goals and instructional objectives that ultimately guide daily instruction.

The Tyler model considers the purposes and goals within the philosophical and psychological screens that address how students learn, what content should be presented, and how it should be taught. These screens provide a vehicle for identifying and writing precise instructional objectives and encourage supervisors and teachers to examine the relationship that exists among the steps of the curriculum development process—planning, teaching, and assessing.

The values of society regarding what to teach and how to teach it provide the first data source. Two other data sources, students' needs and recommendations from subject-matter specialists, also help determine what is taught in school and how it is taught. All three sources have a profound effect on determining the goals and mission of the school.

Philosophies of education and psychologies of learning serve as screens that supervisors and teachers use in filtering the goals of education and interpreting them for implementation in the classroom. Educational philosophies help to guide the creation of mission statements and the selection of goals that seem most viable, as well as the implementation process to attain those goals. Supervisors and teachers must be aware that a philosophical view ultimately determines what happens instructionally in the classroom. Psychologies of learning also provide a framework for developing goals and selecting teaching strategies.

The curriculum designs presented included subject-centered, student-centered, broad field, problem solving, and integrated or thematic. The most common design is the subject-centered, which focuses on the content and skills of a single subject. As supervisors work with teachers, they should encourage teachers to consider other curriculum designs, especially the integrated or thematic that links several areas of study with a theme and helps students make connections among the various concepts taught.

The steps in the curriculum development process that were presented include planning, implementing, and assessing. In the planning step, teachers (after consulting various resources and determining prior student learning and skills) establish instructional objectives. In implementing the plans (teaching), teachers select teaching strategies and activities, model and provide input, and monitor student progress. In the final step, teachers assess teaching and learning by determining what students have learned using a variety of assessment procedures and decide if students have achieved the objectives in the area of study.

The chapter concluded by discussing other resources that can be used in the curriculum development process. These include scope and sequence charts, curriculum guides, and resource guides. These materials can be valuable tools for the supervisor to use with teachers who are having difficulty either articulating learner behaviors or planning appropriate activities to accomplish the objectives.

YOUR TURN

8.1. You are working with a new teacher who is assigned to four government classes. One of the goals of schools is to foster the development of good citizenship. The school district is trying to emphasize being a good citizen in light of the many newspaper stories, court cases, investigations involving insider trading on Wall Street, and abuses of power that have occurred in business and government. The goal of good citizenship, when incorporated into the school curriculum, is to strengthen a student's sense of civic responsibility. This novice teacher does not have any notion of how to incorporate this goal into the curriculum and is in fact nervous about the potentially controversial nature of the topic. What steps could you, as an instructional supervisor, take to assist this teacher in incorporating this goal into his social studies curriculum? What would you suggest first? (*Hint:* Begin with the Tyler curriculum model—the students, community, and subject-matter specialists.)

8.2. You are working with a teacher who is excellent but who views the curriculum as only what is defined in the district's curriculum guide and included in the textbook. You have asked this teacher to expand her curriculum, but she does not feel comfortable and is reluctant to participate. You suggest that the teacher think about her beliefs and attitudes regarding what she teaches and how. You may want to prepare an example, using the topic of health education, following the three steps in the curriculum development process.

8.3. According to author J. Abner Pediwell (*Saber-Tooth Curriculum*, 1939), "the first school was established in Paleolithic times to teach fish-grabbing, tiger-scaring, and horse-clubbing. Paleolithic society believed that the essence of true education is timelessness. Such an education is something that endures through changing conditions like a solid rock standing squarely and firmly in the middle of a raging torrent. You must know there are some *Eternal Verities*, and the Saber-Tooth Curriculum is one of them" (pp. 43–44).

a. Do you believe there are eternal truths in education? Why or why not? If you believe there are, what do you consider them to be?

b. What philosophy of education does your response to question a. support?

8.4. You are the elementary/secondary supervisor in mathematics, and you have been appointed to the districtwide curriculum committee. The charge to the committee is to write a mathematics curriculum guide for the primary grades (K–3 if elementary) or grades 7 and 8 (if secondary). Before you begin this task, you examine several other guides (certainly at least one in detail) to be sure that your new guide will include all the essential elements of a mathematics curriculum, especially a manipulative approach to mathematics instruction. Your task is to become an expert in evaluating curriculum guides so that you will be more proficient at writing one for your own district. As you go through the review process, here are some questions to answer:

a. Can you ascertain the educational philosophy that permeates the objectives and activities? If so, what is it?

b. Was the guide written for the appropriate student population or grade level? Give reasons for your response.

c. What political, social, economic, and local community forces (if any) seem to have influenced the scope and sequence of the curriculum guide?

d. Are objectives included? If so, are they clearly stated? Are the objectives for the math curriculum appropriate and comprehensive? Give reasons for your response.

e. Are teaching–learning strategies or activities listed? Does the curriculum guide emphasize direct experiences and purposeful learning activities? Explain your answer.

f. Are evaluation procedures to help assess student learning and progress toward accomplishment of objectives listed?

8.5. Based on the following descriptions of three school programs, determine the dominant philosophy operating in each school and write a brief rationale for your choice.

a. At the Strawberry Hill School, we view each student as "a lamp to be lighted, not a vessel to be filled." We realize that each student is an individual. Therefore, the primary objectives at Strawberry Hill are self-development, self-fulfillment, and self-realization.

b. At the University Academy, we stress the great ideas from literature and history. We have few frills here in the way of sports competitions or vocational programs. We take great pride in our students' abilities, motivation, and communication skills (spoken and written), as well as their admission to the finest universities.

c. At Webster School, we stress the practical nature of an education to equip students to solve problems, particularly social problems. Therefore, we emphasize the scientific method and those areas of the curriculum that encourage students to analyze situations and find solutions to problems.

REFERENCES

Beane, J. A. (ed.). (1995). *Toward a coherent curriculum: The 1995 ASCD yearbook.* Alexandra, VA: Association for Supervision and Curriculum Development.

Berliner, D. (1996 February). Research and social justice. Presentation at the 76th annual meeting of the Association of Teacher Educators, St. Louis, MO.

Bigge, M. L. (1982). *Learning theories for teachers.* New York: Harper & Row.

Bloom, B. S., Engelhart, M. D., Furst, E. J., Hill, W. H., & Krathwohl, D. R. (1956). *Taxonomy of educational objectives: Handbook I: Cognitive domain.* New York: McKay.

Bobbitt, F. (1924). *How to make a curriculum.* New York: McGraw-Hill.

Bruner, J. (1960). *The process of education.* Cambridge, MA: Harvard University Press.

Delorme Mapping. (1994 September). Reader service no. 77. *Syllabus, Technology for Education, 8.*

Dewey, J. (1902). *The child and the curriculum.* Chicago: University of Chicago Press.

Dewey, J. (1916). *Democracy and education.* New York: Macmillan.

Eggebrecht, J., Dagenais, R., Dosch, D., Merczak, N. J., Park, M. N., Styer, S. C., & Workman, D., et al. (1996 May). Reconnecting the sciences. *Educational Leadership, 53,* 4–8.

Eggen, P., & Kauchak, D. (1994). *Educational psychology: Classroom* connections. (2nd ed.). New York: Merrill Publishers.

English, F. W. (1992). *Deciding what to teach and test: Developing, aligning and auditing the curriculum.* Newbury Park, CA: Corwin Press.

Frazee, B., & Rudnitski, R. A. (1995). *Integrated teaching methods: Theory, classroom applications, and field-based connections.* Albany, NY: Delmar Publishers.

Glatthorn, A. A. (1987). *Curriculum leadership.* Glenview, IL: Scott, Foresman.

Glickman, C., Gordon, S. P., & Ross-Gordon, J. M. (1995). *Supervision of instruction: A developmental approach.* (3rd ed.). Boston: Allyn & Bacon.

Harrow, A. J. (1972). *Taxonomy of the psychomotor domain: A guide for developing behavioral objectives.* New York: McKay.

Hohn, R. L. (1995). *Classroom learning and teaching.* White Plains, NY: Longman.

Knight, G. R. (1989). *Issues and alternatives in educational philosophy.* Berrien Springs, MI: Andrews University Press.

Kosmoski, P. K. (1990 February). Needed: A whole-curriculum approach. *Educational Leadership, 47,* 72–77.

Krathwohl, D. R., Bloom, B. S., & Masia, B. B. (1964). *Taxonomy of educational objectives: Handbook II: Affective domain.* New York: McKay.

Mager, R. F. (1962). *Preparing instructional objectives.* Palo Alto, CA: Fearon.

Morrison, G. S. (1993). *Contemporary curriculum K–8.* Boston: Allyn & Bacon.

National Education Association (1996 May). Save the river. *NEA Today, 14,* 22.

Neill, A. S. (1960). *Summerhill.* New York: Hart.

Ornstein, A. C., & Hunkins, F. P. (1993). *Curriculum: Foundations, principles, and issues.* Englewood Cliffs, NJ: Prentice-Hall.

Ornstein, A. C., & Levine, D. U. (1984). *An introduction to the foundations of education.* (2nd ed.). Boston: Houghton Mifflin.

Pasch, M., Langer, G., Gardner, T. G., Starko, A. J., & Moody, C. D. (1995). *Teaching as decision making.* (2nd ed.). White Plains, NY: Longman.

Pediwell, J. A. (1939). *Saber-Tooth Curriculum.* New York: McGraw-Hill.

Reinhartz, J., & Beach, D. M. (1992). *Secondary education: Focus on curriculum.* New York: Harper-Collins Publishers.

Reinhartz, J., & Beach, D. M. (1997). *Teaching and learning in the elementary school: Focus on curriculum.* Upper Saddle River, NJ: Merrill Publishers.

Rosen, B. (1968). *Philosophic systems and education.* Columbus, OH: Charles E. Merrill.

Sardo Brown, D. (1988). Twelve middle-school teachers' planning. *The Elementary School Journal, 89,* 69–87.

Saylor, J. G., & Alexander, W. M. (1954). *Curriculum planning for better teaching and learning.* New York: Holt, Rinehart & Winston.

Schubert, W. H. (1993). Curriculum reform. In *Challenges and achievements of American education: The 1993 ASCD yearbook.* Washington, DC: Association for Supervision and Curriculum Development.

Smith, M. D. (1975). *Educational psychology and its classroom applications.* Boston: Allyn & Bacon.

Tanner, D., & Tanner, L. (1980). *Curriculum development: Theory into practice.* New York: Macmillan.

Tanner, D., & Tanner, L. (1987). *Supervision in education: Problems and practices.* New York: Macmillan.

Tanner, D., & Tanner, L. (1995). *Curriculum development: Theory into practice.* (3rd ed.). Upper Saddle River, NJ: Merrill Publishers.

Tyler, R. (1949). *Basic principles of curriculum and instruction.* Chicago: University of Chicago Press.

Tyler, R. (1957). The curriculum then and now. In *Proceedings of the 1956 conference of testing problems.* Princeton, NJ: Educational Testing Service.

Wiles, J., & Bondi, J. C. (1984). *Curriculum development: A guide to practice.* (2nd ed.). Upper Saddle River, NJ: Merrill Publishers.

Wiles, J., & Bondi, J. C. (1993). *Curriculum development: A guide to practice.* (4th ed.). Columbus, OH: Merrill Publishers.

Wolfinger, D. M. & Stockard, J. W., Jr. (1997). *Elementary Methods: An integrated curriculum.* White Plains, NY: Longman.

CHAPTER

9

Teaching

A Complex Process

OBJECTIVES

The objectives of this chapter are:

- Define teaching and discuss various ways of viewing the teaching process.
- Describe the various elements of the art and science of teaching.
- Identify and describe common concerns related to teaching.
- Discuss the effective teaching practices derived from the process–product focus.
- Explain the new views of teaching, which move beyond the process–product focus.
- Discuss the role of the supervisor in the continuous improvement of teaching and learning.

As supervisors work with teachers to enhance the teaching and learning in their classrooms, a continuous series of decisions are made. As indicated in the previous chapter, the hallmark of good teaching is planning and as teachers plan for instruction, they make macro-decisions regarding what content or concept to cover, how much time to spend on the topic, what assignments will be made, and how learning will be assessed. These teacher decisions link objectives, content, and strategies; as the plans are carried out in teaching, teachers engage in micro-decisions, such as which concept should be taught first, which students in the class should be called on, what praise words should be used for correct responses, and/or what corrective feedback is needed when students don't understand. These micro-decisions involve the application of effective teaching practices moment by moment, as teachers implement curriculum plans and interact with students within the context of the classroom. As teachers and supervisors discuss these macro- and micro-decisions related to effective teaching practices, they are engaging in a process that Shulman (1987) refers to as sharing the wisdom of practice.

As teachers continuously engage in professional growth and development, taking time to reflect on their teaching is essential. The degree to which teachers think about prior teaching experiences plays a significant role in their ability to modify instruction in their classroom. Reflection leads teachers to view the realities of the classroom from a variety of perspectives as they recognize the nuances of the classroom and interact with the students more effectively. By encouraging teachers to become more reflective, supervisors help them become more like orchestra conductors in their classrooms, giving the "piccolos" a chance while saving space for the "brasses" (Eisner, 1983).

As teachers reflect about teaching and learning practices, they take the time to "rehearse mentally and on paper what will take place when they teach" (Reinhartz and Beach, 1997, p. 125). Supervisors, using their knowledge of curriculum development and effective instructional practices, can assist teachers not only in planning for teaching but in carrying out those curriculum plans with a variety of learners in the classroom.

This chapter begins by defining teaching and presents various elements that reflect either an art or science orientation to teaching. Next, the chapter presents several common concerns of teachers that are related to classroom teaching and learning and includes suggested ways that teachers can address these concerns. The next section discusses effective teaching and learning from a process–product research focus. To elaborate on this view, a general teaching sequence or framework is presented that incorporates various teaching behaviors and strategies. The chapter then looks beyond the process–product research and describes new research on teaching, which includes the context of teaching and learning, new views of learning, new ways of teaching subject matter, and new classroom data-collection procedures. The chapter concludes with a discussion of the role of the supervisor in addressing those teacher concerns in their continuous improvement of teaching and learning.

Definitions and Views of Teaching

The implementation of instructional plans is more commonly known as *teaching*. Teaching is an activity that involves thinking about ends and means, as well as consequences, and puts into action the collective information generated in planning. As for supervision, there are many definitions for teaching. Zeuli and Buchmann (1987) view teaching as a moral activity that involves thinking about ends, means, and their consequences. Hunter (1984) defines teaching "as the constant stream of professional decisions that affects the probability of learning: decisions that are made and implemented before, during, and after interaction with the students" (p. 169). Hunter further suggests that "Teaching is an applied science derived from research in human behavior: an applied science that utilizes the findings from psychology, neurology, sociology, and anthropology" (p. 170).

Dawe (1984), Eisner (1983, 1994), and Rubin (1985) view teaching as more of an artistic or creative endeavor. Rubin (1985) captures the creative essence of this view of teaching by noting that it involves "skill, originality, flair, dexterity, ingenuity,…which, together, engender exceptional performance" (p. 15). Aoki (1992) sees teaching as "pedagogical thoughtfulness [which] embod[ies]…doing and being…and the study of teaching involves…the measure of the immeasurable" (pp. 26–27).

Eby and Kujawa (1994) see teaching as "a common and natural occurrence" (p. 168); Lefrançois (1994) is more specific by noting that it is an arrangement of activities in a context that facilitates learning, retention, and transfer. Shulman (1992) says teaching involves "a fundamental tension between ideas [concepts/content] as they are understood by…[teachers] and as they might be grasped by school children" (p. 27).

As teachers implement their plans, the art and science of teaching come together. For Rubin (1985), the art and science of teaching merge when teachers use proven strategies while exhibiting qualities of being flexible, spontaneous, and creative. Figure 9.1 provides an example of the elements of the art and science of teaching from a classroom teacher's view, represented in a Venn diagram. The art of teaching is reflected in the teacher's values, style, life experiences, commitment, level of abstract thinking, and climate of classroom interactions. The science of teaching is seen in the teaching strategies, management and assessment procedures, communication skills, lesson plans, and knowledge of theories and models of teaching and learning. As these elements come together and overlap, they strengthen the teacher's effectiveness. As supervisors and teachers discuss teaching, they need to examine the characteristics teachers exhibit that are related to both the art and science of teaching and then construct their own Venn diagram of effective teaching.

According to Eisner (1983), teachers are less like technicians and more like orchestra conductors when they apply their art and craft in the classroom. More than

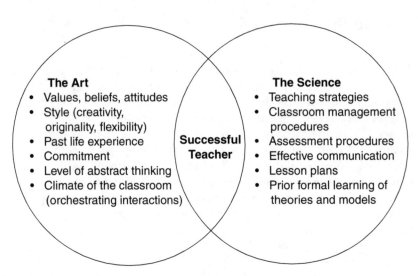

FIGURE 9.1   The Art and Science of Teaching

scientific prescriptions, they use a series of guidelines and their educational imagination to initiate a dialogue that involves all students in classroom experiences. Salomon (1992) concurs with Eisner's orchestra conductor analogy. Whether teaching is an art, a science, or both, we view it as a complex and complicated endeavor that puts into practice the information generated during planning. It takes many forms that may include all or some of the following: telling, explaining, defining, providing examples and nonexamples, stressing critical attributes, modeling, questioning, demonstrating, and assessing.

Concerns Related to Classroom Teaching

Drawing upon their own knowledge and experience related to teaching and learning, supervisors should also be aware of several concerns that studies have shown are common to teachers, especially when they are beginning teachers or when they are new to an assignment. These eight concerns are: (1) establishing goals and direction; (2) conducting student assessment; (3) developing and following a scope and sequence; (4) selecting teaching strategies; (5) recognizing and dealing with instructional constraints; (6) functioning in a school culture; (7) assuming/performing multiple responsibilities; and (8) achieving success as a teacher (Cunningham and Gresso, 1993; Davis, Alexander, and Yelon, 1974; Mager, 1962; Raines and Shadiow, 1995; Schultz, 1996). The degree to which teachers are affected by these concerns can impact the teaching and learning process.

The first of these concerns, *establishing goals and direction,* occurs during a lesson if the teacher fails to provide a "map" for student learning by establishing expectations and responsibilities. Students are at a disadvantage when the teacher does not communicate the goals, objectives, and learning tasks for the day, the week, or even the semester. Without describing or modeling expected behaviors and skills, students are unsure of what they are to demonstrate in order to show they have learned. Assistance from the supervisor in writing and communicating goals and objectives can result in greater instructional clarity.

The second area is *conducting student assessment*. Feedback about performance can serve as a prime motivator for learning, and students need information concerning their progress in class. Teachers should develop assessment procedures that provide both oral and written feedback to students so they can monitor their own success. The assessment procedures for feedback on daily, weekly, or unit activities are an important part of successful teaching; supervisors and teachers in partnership can generate a variety of procedures to use, such as portfolios, authentic assessment, daily work, projects, and tests. Assessing students in a variety of ways helps them to gain knowledge about their academic performance and provides an awareness of the results. By developing a comprehensive assessment plan, teachers will have performance results that can be communicated to students and parents.

The third instructional concern is *developing and following a scope and sequence* that are developmentally appropriate for the students. This third concern surfaces when there is an apparent lack of either content or organization in the presentation of that content. In feeling the pressure to cover "everything in the book," teachers may present information in bits and pieces so that it lacks sufficient depth or a logical sequence, which makes the lessons seem fragmented and disjointed. Teachers, in attempting to cover a breadth of information, may fail to provide the necessary depth to promote understanding. The role of the supervisor is to provide guidance and serve as a sounding board for teachers as they address these issues of scope and sequence and think through the material they will present. This supervisory role is often performed by mentor teachers or department leaders. It is often helpful for new teachers to begin with an outline of the semester and then divide it into parts, such as reporting periods of six or nine weeks.

Tied closely to content and organization are concerns dealing with the *selection of teaching strategies*. The strategies used in presenting the material help to determine the degree to which the students become involved and motivated to learn. Teachers should have in their instructional repertoire a cafeteria of alternatives available from which to choose (Joyce and Weil, 1996). Among the strategies, the use of educational technology (including audiovisual materials and computers) to respond to varying learning styles is increasingly becoming part of how information is presented and learned in elementary and secondary classrooms. Beach and Reinhartz (1989) suggest that supervisors and teachers work to find ways to align strategies with content and learning objectives. As supervisors and teachers discuss the lesson, supervisors can start brainstorming by offering a wide range of options, from telling to discovery, as they attempt to match content with the appropriate strategies. When teachers rely solely on one strategy, regardless of what that strategy is, they fail to take advantage of what is known about effective practices in teaching and learning.

The next four concerns, although not directly tied to the interactive dynamics of teaching, nevertheless influence the teaching and learning process. Supervisors often assist teachers in *recognizing and dealing with instructional constraints* experienced when implementing the lesson. For example, teachers who try to teach a lesson using laboratory equipment in a space that is not appropriately designed may experience difficulty and limited success. Instructional constraints are those resources that, when absent or insufficient, can negatively impact learning. The use of instructional technology is increasing at a rapid pace, but the funds for purchase and repairs are often difficult to obtain. Supervisors may be involved in generating ideas in cooperation with teachers, identifying alternatives or securing needed resources, and training teachers in the use of technology through district funding or grants from other public and private agencies.

Functioning within the school culture also causes concerns for teachers. When the philosophy and mission of the school are not consistent with the views of a teacher, then conflicts may develop. For example, if the prevailing belief in the school is that quiet classrooms are learning classrooms and the teacher believes that effective teaching and learning occur in a classroom environment that fosters social interaction as students discuss their ideas with each other, then there is the potential for disagreement. The role of the supervisor becomes one of providing an atmosphere where teachers can be empowered individuals while also assisting them in accommodating and assimilating the tenets of the school culture. Playing such a supervisory role is a difficult task as individuals don't easily change their thinking, beliefs, and values about teaching; most importantly, learning takes time.

Teachers also have to *assume multiple responsibilities* within the school organization, which is the seventh concern. These responsibilities are not limited to planning and teaching but may also include taking lunch count, meeting with parents or colleagues, and performing hall or bus duty. Carrying out any one of these responsibilities individually can be cause for concern; the concern is compounded when many of these responsibilities occur almost simultaneously (e.g., teaching while dismissing certain students to special programs or events). When partnering with teachers, supervisors need to provide opportunities for them to feel confident and competent in meeting these multiple responsibilities and yet limiting the amount of out of-classroom tasks.

Finally, a common concern, especially for beginning teachers or those new to a school, is *achieving success as a teacher* and answering the question, "Am I going to survive?" Teachers often begin by being concerned with helping their students learn and "make it." But as they encounter the culture of the school and the multiple responsibilities of their job, they may begin to have doubts about their ability to be a teacher and their capacity to learn on the job. The role of the supervisor is to "coach" and guide while providing recognition and celebration for small as well as major successes.

If each of these concerns is not consciously considered, problems may occur during teaching. Supervisors, as they interact with teachers, can help them anticipate many of these concerns and begin to think about ways to address them. As teachers reflect on their teaching, they become aware of their options and begin to "demonstrate their expertise in a myriad of ways" (Henderson, 1992, p. 1). Reinhartz and Beach (1997) observe that as teachers "become more confident in their teaching, they expand their repertoire of teaching strategies/skills," and many of the early concerns related to teaching and learning diminish (p. 153).

Effective Teaching Behaviors: Process-Product Focus

Historically, research on effective teaching has sought to identify those teaching behaviors that increase student achievement (Eggan and Kauchak, 1994). Researchers (Gage, 1985; Gage and Giaconia, 1981; Good and Brophy, 1987, 1991) have found that higher-achieving classes were taught differently than classes that had lower-achieving students. In attempting to identify those teaching practices that promote greater student achievement, Hirsche (1996) notes that a consensus on the reasons has emerged from two independent sources: "(1) small-scale pairings of different teaching methods; [and] (2) basic research in cognition, learning, memory, psycholinguistics, and other areas of cognitive psychology" (p. 35). The research findings generated by these studies identified "the behavior[s] of teachers whose students scored high on standardized tests...[and] when other teachers were trained in these behaviors, their students, too, scored higher" (Brandt, 1992a, p. 3). The various lists of discrete teaching behaviors is known as process–product research; student performance on tests is the primary criterion for judging teaching effectiveness.

The process–product research studies have identified a core of technical teaching behaviors, sometimes called effective teaching practices (ETPs), that have served as a foundation to guide supervisors and teachers in their quest to improve student achievement. This core of technical behaviors from the process–product research focuses on teacher characteristics that correlate positively with student learning or achievement gains (Berliner, 1984; Gage and Berliner, 1984; Greenblatt, Cooper, and Muth, 1984; Manatt, 1981a, 1981b, 1987; Rosenshine, 1983; Rosenshine and Furst, 1971; Ryan, 1960; Walberg, Schiller, and Haertel, 1979; Wang, Haertel, and Walberg, 1993/1994; Weinert, Helmke, and Schrader, 1992). Using this core of technical teaching behaviors, effective teaching, as seen in a snapshot of the classroom, involves specific, observable, and job-related behaviors, which have as their goal student achievement.

Our purpose here is to provide supervisors with an overview of some of the technical teacher behaviors commonly described in the process–product research. Here is a list of 10 specific teaching behaviors generated from the research that have been consistently shown to foster student achievement:

1. *Focus or set induction and review of previous day's work.* Teacher prepares students for the day's lesson by capturing their attention and reviewing the previous day's lesson or work (Good and Grouws, 1979; Medley, 1977; Rosenshine, 1986).

2. *Statement of instructional goals and objectives.* Teacher communicates to students in written or oral form regarding what they are to accomplish (objectives) as well as the learning behaviors expected (Brophy, 1981; Good, 1987; Good and Brophy, 1986; Manatt, 1981a, 1981b; Purkey and Smith, 1983).

3. *Teacher input and modeling.* Teacher presents information clearly, stressing important points and dimensions of content; illustrates a cognitive skill or demonstrates procedures for handling equipment and materials (Evertson, Emmer, and Brophy, 1980; Good and Grouws, 1979; Peterson, 1979; Rosenshine, 1979, 1986; Rosenshine and Furst, 1971; Walberg, Schiller, and Haertel, 1979)

4. *Instructional clarity.* Teacher presents information and skills in a clear and organized sequence of steps and paces the lesson content to match students' abilities and interests (Hines, Cruickshank, and Kennedy, 1985; Rosenshine, 1983, 1986; Rosenshine and Furst, 1971; Walberg, Schiller, and Haertel, 1979).

5. *Check of understanding/asking questions.* Teacher uses a variety of techniques to determine the level of student understanding, asks a large number of questions with high success rate, uses wait time, and asks higher-order questions (Barell, 1985; Barnes, 1981; Rosenshine and Furst, 1971; Rowe, 1974).

6. *Guided and independent practice.* Teacher provides opportunities for students to practice content and skills before having them apply the information or skills independently beyond the examples and context of the lesson (Coker, Lorentz, and Coker, 1980; Fisher et al., 1981; Good and Grouws, 1979; Hunter and Russell, 1981; Rosenshine, 1983, 1986; Sharan, 1980; Slavin, 1991; Stallings and Kaskowitz, 1974).

7. *Feedback to students.* Teacher monitors students' performance during the lesson and provides feedback and/or clarifies misunderstandings (Anderson, Evertson, and Brophy, 1979; Reid, 1980; Rosenshine, 1983; Stallings, 1978; Stallings and Kaskowitz, 1974).

8. *Academic learning time.* Teacher keeps students engaged in learning activities to maximize the amount of time available for teaching and learning (Caldwell, Huitt, and Graeber, 1982; Capie, Tobin, and Boswell, 1980; Ellett, Capie, and Johnson, 1981; Emmer, 1982; Emmer, Evertson, and Anderson, 1980; Fisher, Marliave, and Filby, 1979; Good and Grouws, 1977; Rosenshine and Furst, 1971; Walberg, Schiller, and Haertel, 1979).

9. *Classroom management and organization.* Teacher specifies behavior expectations and uses techniques to prevent, redirect, or stop inappropriate behavior (Doyle, 1985; Emmer, 1982; Evertson and Emmer, 1982; Sanford and Evertson, 1980).

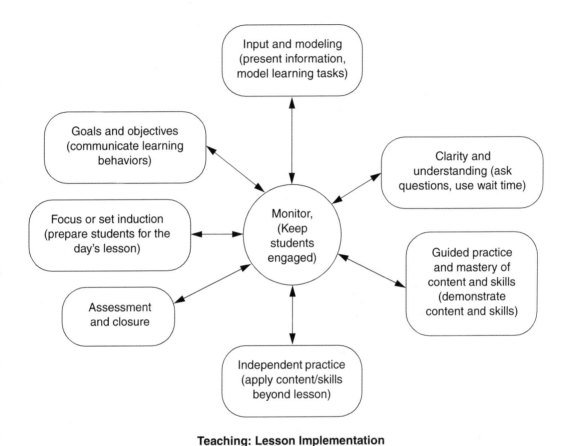

Teaching: Lesson Implementation

FIGURE 9.2   A Framework for Lesson Implementation

10. *Varied instruction.* Teacher uses different strategies, materials, and instructional tools to provide variety in instruction (Joyce and Weil, 1986, 1996; Rosenshine and Furst, 1971).

Research and practice come together in Figure 9.2 as many of these behaviors are integrated into a framework for lesson implementation. The lesson framework in Figure 9.2 illustrates the complexities of teaching, which involve making decisions; some decisions occur before instruction (during the planning stage), while other decisions are made during teaching. It is important, then, that the framework for implementation acknowledges that prior instructional decisions have been made during planning, but that the lesson actually begins with the teaching act. The lesson framework in a teacher-directed lesson incorporates many of the effective teaching practices previously identified and includes the following components:

focus or set induction; goals and objectives; input and modeling; clarity and understanding; guided practice; mastery of content and skills; independent practice; and assessment and closure. Throughout the lesson the teacher monitors the students to keep them engaged in learning to ensure time on task and maximize success.

These components of the lesson implementation framework, although listed sequentially, may occur simultaneously. A description of each component is provided to illustrate the teaching behavior as it occurs during a lesson. The following descriptions can be valuable to supervisors and teachers in identifying and labeling the teaching behaviors they model:

■ *Focus or set induction.* One of the essential components in the lesson sequence is to prepare students for the day's lesson. Focus or set induction establishes the communication link between the teacher and the students and sets the stage for learning. In this component, the teacher uses a series of attention-getting strategies to quickly involve students in the lesson. This part of the lesson should motivate and prepare students for what is to come in the remaining parts of the lesson. Some of the various ways to introduce the topic under study are to: (a) use advance organizers to outline the flow of concepts and information (Ausubel, 1960); (b) review the previous day's work with questions; (c) begin the lesson with a provocative question; (d) provide visuals and/or graphic organizers (Irvin-DeVitis, Modlo, and Bromley, 1995); and (e) discuss similarities and differences.

■ *Goals and objectives.* This component in the lesson implementation communicates the expected learning behaviors and helps students understand what they should know or be able to do as a result of instruction. As Porter and Brophy (1988) note, "Effective teachers are clear about what they intend to accomplish through their instruction" (p. 81). It provides the necessary clues for students as to what is important and expected in terms of learning and helps to eliminate guessing. In this component, the objectives may be stated throughout the lesson as the teacher moves from one concept or skill to the next. Two examples of verbalizing this teaching behavior are: "Today we will learn an important geography skill—map reading; by the end of the lesson, you will be able to find places on the globe using latitude and longitude," and "When you finish this lab, you should be able to name four common acids and bases and give the properties of each."

■ *Input and modeling.* This component of lesson implementation refers to the actual teacher-directed, or "teaching," portion of the lesson where the teacher presents information and models learning tasks. The overall purpose of this component is to identify, define, and describe the critical attributes of concepts, skills, and attitudes included in the lesson. As the critical attributes are identified, examples as well as nonexamples should be used as illustrations. The instructional strategies should be varied to promote thinking and retention, transfer previous learning to current topics under study, and involve and challenge students.

There are two basic teaching strategies teachers can use in this lesson sequence: inductive and deductive. The *inductive* strategy views the teaching and learning process from a part-to-whole perspective. For example, components or aspects of a principle are provided as experiences that engage students so that they can construct the general rule or principle from these elements. The part-to-whole approach requires students to synthesize and create a whole from pieces of data generated or given. The opposite strategy, *deductive,* begins with a definition of the principle or concept. Students analyze the principle or generalization and develop or apply examples to illustrate it. Once these two basic strategies are understood, the teacher has a multitude of methods (lecture, role play, learning packets, computer simulations) as well as resources that can be used to enhance instruction.

Modeling or demonstrating a concept, process, skill, procedure, technique, and/or attitude can be done by the teacher, through the use of media (computers, digital cameras, graphing calculators, audio- and videotapes, CD-ROM, and films), or by expert resource personnel in the school or community. Modeling aids students in remembering what was taught and provides the basis for students to replicate the essential behaviors or skills. For instance, math teachers provide examples and model, or illustrate, the process of solving mathematics problems, such as the multiplication algorithm or the derivation of the quadratic formula.

■ *Clarity and understanding.* In this component, the teacher asks questions and uses wait time for student responses. The teacher monitors student performance and checks for understanding using an informal assessment (by means of individual or choral responses, or thumbs up/down signals) to determine if what has been taught, modeled, and/or practiced is clearly understood (Oliva, 1993). Checking for understanding often relies heavily on questioning techniques. The teacher may ask students simple, factual recall questions. To verify the depth of comprehension, however, the teacher asks students to explain in their own words, provide examples and nonexamples, elaborate on critical attributes, and/or add to other responses. The teacher might ask the students at the end of the lesson or period to write on a sheet of paper the five or six main points covered. In this component of the lesson, the teacher clarifies and corrects any misunderstandings and gives students feedback on their level of proficiency. Porter and Brophy (1988) also suggest that "Effective teachers create learning situations in which their students [also]…organize information in new ways and formulate problems for themselves" (p. 81).

■ *Guided practice and mastery of content and skills.* During this part of the lesson, students demonstrate the content skills presented. Students are not left alone but are carefully monitored by the teacher to ensure that tasks are completed accurately (Lezotte, 1989). An important part of this lesson component is "feedback with guidance" (Goodlad, 1984); knowledge of results provides students with information about their progress. Generally, the purpose of practice is to help students gain command of a concept or skill. Practice gives meaning to the concept or skill by directly involving the learner in some task or operation. Before moving to independent practice, it is critical that learners have success at least once; the more success learners have, the greater the level of mastery. When different kinds of guided practice are planned, the following variables should be considered: the amount of material covered, the amount of time available, the schedule (mass or distributive practice), and the degree or level of overlearning.

- *Independent practice.* This component provides an opportunity to apply the content and skills beyond the lesson taught. It is in this part of the lesson that students are given the chance to demonstrate the skills and concepts in a real-world situation or dilemma. The independent practice may take the form of surveys and science fair projects in the elementary school and projects or term papers at the secondary level. Usually, homework or creative assignments require students to work independently and apply what they have learned. The goal of independent practice is to provide an opportunity for students to demonstrate mastery by completing an assignment on their own to show that what is learned in school can be applied to life experiences.

- *Assessment and closure.* This component may occur continuously throughout the lesson as the teacher monitors and adjusts instruction based on students' responses to questions, students' involvement in learning activities, and students' performance. Assessment can be either formative or summative. In the classroom, *formative* assessment includes an examination of the ongoing process during the lesson. The teacher asks himself or herself: "How am I doing?" "To what degree are the students learning?" Within the classroom, *summative* assessment involves making a judgment about the effectiveness of learning. At this point, the teacher decides either to continue on to a new topic, concept, or unit or to reteach the lesson based on the performance of the students. The assessment tools that teachers can use range from formal daily quizzes or weekly tests to portfolios and projects to informal summary statements.

This component brings the lesson or implementation to a logical conclusion. Closure may take many forms, which include such things as a summary by the students and/or the teacher of the main points covered in the lesson or a review of what has been discussed in the lesson. Often, teachers will combine this component with checking for clarity and understanding by asking the students to identify the main points and listing them on the board.

The effective teaching behaviors supported by research, presented in Figure 9.2, and discussed in the previous section establish a framework for supervisors and teachers to use as they seek to continuously improve the teaching and learning process. Such a frame of reference offers an opportunity to focus on specific teaching and learning skills and can be shared with elementary and secondary teachers who are striving to improve the academic performance of their students.

A word of caution, however, should be sounded against overgeneralizing these behaviors because the research studies are often situational as well as subject- and student-specific (Griffin, 1985; Lezotte, 1989). It is clear that the representative correlation studies have consistently identified many of the common elements—such as clarity of instruction, efficient use of time, and checking for understanding—as effective behaviors that teachers have used as they sought to increase student achievement, but as Griffin (1985) cautions, "the results may not be generalizable to other situations" (p. 44). These studies have produced behaviors that contribute to what Sammons and colleagues (1995) call purposeful teaching. In the next section of this chapter, newer perspectives that focus on contexts as a way of viewing effective teaching will be discussed.

Beyond Process-Product: New Views of Effective Teaching

For Senge (1990), the most exciting discoveries about teaching and learning have emerged during the last 15 years. The behaviors identified by the process–product research provide concrete images of what successful teachers do and form a "sound base for the kinds of studies now being conducted" (Brandt, 1992b, p. 3). However, new perspectives on effective teaching have focused on (a) the dynamics of teaching and learning within the overall context of the classroom, (b) the nature of student learning, (c) the nature of subject-matter teaching, and (d) new classroom data-collection procedures. There are several studies that correlate teaching and learning with school and teacher effectiveness (Sammons et al., 1995). By concentrating on the quality of teaching and learning, student achievement and individual behavior are greatly enhanced (Creemer, 1994; Mortimore, 1993; Scheeren, 1992).

Prawat (1992) describes the new research on effective teaching as examining the role of prior learning and experience, as well as the contextual (social and cultural) nature of teaching and learning, and analyzing the ways students learn both in and out of the classroom. The change in the focus of research on teaching has resulted in a change in the way educators define and view learning. There has been a shift from a focus on individual learners to an emphasis on a community of learners. This emphasis is described by Leinhardt (1992), who sees learning as involving a community of learners as they engage in an active process of sense-making and knowledge construction that takes place mostly through social participation in authentic tasks.

Context.   One new perspective of effective teaching centers on the context of the classroom, and student achievement becomes part of the total effort to improve teaching and learning within the entire school. For Sammons and colleagues (1995), "It is clear from the research literature…[that] quality teaching is at the heart of effective schooling" (p. 15). The process–product research was an attempt to identify the dots (aspects of effective teaching) while the new perspective attempts to connect the dots by examining a variety of areas beyond discrete teaching behaviors. Areas that are being considered as part of the school context, which impacts teaching and learning, include brain research, new definitions of learning, and the role of teachers as leaders.

Student Learning.   Another new view of effective teaching seeks to expand our definitions of learning by taking into consideration the fact that students "learn and retain only when knowledge has relevancy and meaning for them" (Schmoker, 1996, p. 66). Students then incorporate this new information into their knowledge base as they construct their own meaning and understanding. In this process, their learning "remain[s] 'upshifted' into the cerebrum" which houses language, symbols, and images (Grisham, 1995, p. 8). Leinhardt (1992) further suggests that research on learning extends our understanding of effective teaching when we recognize (a) that there are multiple forms of knowledge (Armstrong, 1994; Gardner, 1983, 1991); (b) that students build on prior knowledge as they construct new knowledge (Brooks and Brooks, 1993); and (c) that learning involves social interaction (Piaget, 1952, 1967; Vygotsky, 1978).

Subject Matter.   The research on subject-matter teaching has called attention to the need for students to see a more integrated picture of the various subjects in the curriculum. In the past, the learning of isolated pieces of information was the goal of instruction. In isolation, students were often unable to relate to the pieces or parts and were not motivated to learn. For Brophy (1992):

> Current research focuses on attempts to teach both the individual elements in a network of related content and the connections among them, to the point that students can explain the information in their own words and can use it appropriately in and out of school. (p. 5)

Teaching subject matter involves not only explaining the concepts but modeling the connection of knowledge and skills using "think aloud" techniques by "selecting a theme and building lessons around it" (Sadowski, 1995, p. 3). Schmoker (1996) supports Steve Hess, who suggests that "emphasizing application within the content areas is the best grounding for authentic integration within and among the disciplines" (p. 82).

Brophy (1992) further suggests that effective teaching of subject matter involves five steps: (1) identifying instructional goals that emphasize students' ability to apply content in an authentic setting; (2) selecting content and concepts that are organized around a set of principles, powerful ideas, or themes; (3) changing the teacher's role from presenting information early in the process to scaffolding and responding to students' questions; (4) incorporating activities and assignments that require critical thinking and problem-solving skills; and (5) creating a classroom that becomes a learning community where dialogue and interaction promote understanding.

Data Collection.   New data-collection procedures in the research on teaching focus on specific teaching units, take into account teachers' instructional goals, and then assess student learning based on these plans and goals. Unlike the process–product research that took numerous snapshots of the classroom with regard to discrete teaching behaviors, the new views of teaching examine the ongoing aspects of the teaching–learning process using a case study approach throughout a unit of instruction. This new research seeks to create an inventory of stories shared by teachers about the teaching of concepts and themes as well as the specific skills utilized. Through stories, teachers begin to see the strengths of their students, take greater control over their professional development, and make plans for or modifications in their teaching (Gomez, 1996). It is through case study knowledge that there is an interaction between content and pedagogy. The age-old controversy of content versus teaching becomes a moot point because these stories, as retold by teachers, provide a more comprehensive picture of the wisdom of teaching practices. "Stories capture experience...[and] provide a way to express and represent the multidimensional aspects of any teaching decision or action" (Pinnegar, 1996, p. 13).

As Porter and Brophy (1988) have observed, "Effective teachers are thoughtful about their practice; they take time for reflection and self-evaluation" (p. 82). As teachers reflect on these case studies, they find teaching–learning situations that have meaning for them at a particular point in their planning and teaching. As Shulman (as quoted by Brandt, 1992b) notes, "for most of us as teachers, the unit of instruction is not the lesson; the lesson is just a piece of something larger. The better we get as teachers the more we think about how our lessons hang together" (p. 16). The new research considers the complexity of the classroom and thought reflection regarding the wisdom of practice in the context of the classroom.

Teaching: The Role of the Supervisor

As supervisors work with teachers in the continuous improvement of teaching and learning, they should encourage teachers to engage in a reflective process that helps them move from holding a more structured or technical view of teaching to becoming reflective practitioners with a more complex view of instruction. As teachers engage in reflection about the teaching–learning process, they begin to become more aware of the decisions that are made and the nuances that make them successful. The diagram below helps to illustrate this movement from teacher as a technician or a technical practitioner to teacher as a reflective practitioner:

Teacher as   Teacher as
Technical   ————————————————————————————————→ Reflective
Practitioner   Practitioner

As teachers gain experience with the behaviors from the process–product research provided in the framework of lesson implementation (mentioned earlier), they can reflect on their teaching and begin to consider other strategies or ways to implement the lesson. By considering these other strategies, teachers move beyond the process–product view of effective teaching to a more contextual basis for classroom instruction. Other strategies that supervisors can assist teachers in considering as part of their teaching repertoire include guided discussion and reciprocal questioning, cooperative learning, learning centers or packets, and independent study (Reinhartz and Beach, 1997).

Supervisors can use the continuum above to create a dialogue with teachers about effective teaching. At one end of the effective teacher continuum is the structured, technical approach based on the process–product research, which utilizes discrete teaching behaviors. At the other end, effective teaching is represented as a complex, reflective process when viewed through the new research perspectives. These new views of effective teaching (the context of teaching and learning, a broader definition of student learning, the teaching of subject matter, and new classroom data-collection procedures) provide supervisors with new lenses for viewing their work as they coach and mentor teachers. When short-term goals and immediate instructional improvement are the focus of the supervisory relationship, the process–product view of teaching is frequently used. As teachers gain confidence in their ability to teach and develop a collegial supervisory relationship, effective teaching is viewed differently and becomes more reflective and ongoing. This movement along the continuum takes place during the lifetime of a teacher.

Using process–product research, supervisors can support teachers as they incorporate the discrete teaching behaviors into their teaching repertoire and become proficient in their use. Supervisors may also coach teachers as they develop lessons that incorporate each, if not all, of the effective teaching behaviors. As supervisors engage in classroom observation, their task becomes one of identifying and recording evidence of these behaviors and how often each behavior occurs. The process–product research provides a clear template to be used by the teacher when observed by the supervisor. When viewing teaching through the process–product lens, teaching is structured and more technical. As one experienced teacher has commented, it takes several years for professional change to take place as teachers move along the continuum. "The first year you're just becoming aware. The second year you actually start doing it. The third year you begin to build up some credibility and confidence. In the fourth year you can really start throwing out things that don't work" (Sadowski, 1995, p. 4).

As supervisors work with teachers over time, they engage in professional conversations, which offer opportunities for promoting different ways of viewing teaching effectiveness (Danielson, 1996). Such conversations help to develop common understandings of the process–product teaching behaviors as well as the contextual nature of the teaching–learning process, new views of learning, and classroom data-collection procedures. Taken together, these conversations provide a different template for not only teaching but school improvement as well. As supervisors work with teachers, the science of teaching often seems to be obvious, especially when the process–product research is applied. In the final analysis, the art of teaching still needs to be factored into the teaching process as teachers reflect on and monitor their own behaviors in the classroom.

Summary

This chapter presented the heart of the process of supervision, which is teaching. It began with a discussion on the complexities of teaching; definitions and views of teaching were included. These definitions included both the art and the science of teaching as strategies for teaching and learning intersect with the teacher's value or belief system. Eisner, Rubin, and others consider teaching to be an art, which is a creative endeavor that puts plans into action and engages students in learning. According to Hunter (1984), teaching requires the teacher to make a "constant stream" of decisions related to the teaching/learning process, which makes teaching a science.

Next, the chapter discussed some of the common concerns related to teaching that supervisors will need to address as they assist new teachers in improving their instructional effectiveness. The first four concerns (establishing goals and direction, conducting assessment, developing and following scope and sequence, and selecting teaching strategies) are directly related to classroom instruction. The other four concerns (recognizing and dealing with instructional constraints, functioning in a school culture, assuming multiple responsibilities, and achieving success) are less directly related to teaching and learning but still impact the instructional effectiveness of the teacher.

The chapter then reviewed the research on effective teaching practices from a process–product perspective. This section focused on research that identified discrete teaching behaviors that have been shown to impact student achievement. A list of behaviors were presented along with those researchers who were responsible for identifying these teaching behaviors. According to much process–product research on teaching, teachers who are described as effective or successful, based on student learning, exhibit the following 10 behaviors: (1) They provide the lesson focus and conduct daily reviews; (2) they state instructional goals and objectives; (3) they provide input and model for students what is expected; (4) they teach information in an organized sequential way; (5) they check for understanding and ask questions; (6) they provide guided and independent practice; (7) they provide feedback to students; (8) they keep students engaged in learning activities; (9) they identify behavior expectations and use classroom management techniques; and (10) they vary instruction.

A lesson sequence that incorporates these effective teaching behaviors was presented to demonstrate how these behaviors might appear during instruction. The framework offers a nine-step process for teachers and supervisors to use as a means of navigating through an individual lesson. In addition, the lesson sequence provides a structure for incorporating effective teaching practices, along with the essential lesson components, that can also contribute to successful teaching. These nine components are: (1) establishing focus, (2) communicating objectives and purposes, (3) modeling, (4) checking for understanding, (5) providing guided practice, (6) checking for mastery, (7) using independent practice, (8) assessing and closing, and (9) monitoring and engaging students.

The chapter then discussed work being done that moves our understanding of effective teaching and learning beyond the process–product paradigm. In recent years, researchers have focused on the context of teaching and the process over time rather than on isolated, discrete behaviors. The new research examines the context of the classroom, the nature of both student learning and subject-matter teaching, and data-collection procedures.

The chapter concluded with a discussion of the contexts that move the teacher from a technical practitioner to a reflective practitioner. It was the perspective of this chapter that as teachers gain confidence in their teaching ability, they become more effective in their teaching. Supervisors have the responsibility to provide a professional dialogue that links theory, or what is known about good teaching gained from the research literature, with effective instructional practice.

Y O U R   T U R N

9.1. Think of your favorite teacher and jot down all the reasons you thought of this particular teacher. Now think of a teacher whom you are less than enthusiastic about and make a parallel list of traits you found undesirable as a student in his or her class, and explain why. Now reflect on your instructional strengths and weaknesses—what will you work on as a supervisor?

9.2. Some educators perceive teaching as an art, practiced by individuals who are born with intuitive awareness; others perceive teaching as a science, practiced in a scientific manner. Still others view teaching as both an art and a science. Using the ideas presented in this chapter combined with those from your own personal experience, develop your own view of teaching. How would you explain your position to someone else? Respond in your journal.

9.3. Read the following class descriptions and indicate if the teaching strategy is inductive or deductive, and explain why.

a. The teacher writes the word "osmosis" on the board and says, "Today we are going to examine the meaning of this word. It pertains to a particular biological process that involves diffusion through a special membrane. First, you will look up some definitions of the word and find examples of where the process occurs." The students begin looking up definitions of the word while the teacher passes out a worksheet illustrating osmosis that the students are to label. The students spend the remainder of the period on this assignment.

b. As the students enter the room, a tape is playing and two slides of famous paintings are projected on two sides of the room. Students are directed to be seated, listen to the tape, and look carefully at the projected paintings. After a few minutes, the teacher calls the students together and asks them to share their observations. The teacher asks, "What did you see in the paintings?"

"What did you hear on the tape?" "Are the tape and paintings related?" The teacher helps the students recall their observations or experiences, begins to group these responses into examples, and then makes a generalization about what the students have seen and heard.

c. Each day as students enter their math class, the teacher reviews their homework with them. Sometimes, the teacher works the problems on the board; at other times, the teacher asks for student volunteers to do so. After questions regarding the homework have been answered, the teacher proceeds by putting a new theorem or math principle on the board, works some sample problems for the students in order to illustrate the principle, assigns 30 problems for homework, and allows students to spend the remainder of the period working quietly in class while moving about the room helping individual students.

9.4. Analyze the following written lesson plan and answer the questions that follow.

Lesson Plan

Objective: When shown a film that depicts the flow of blood through the heart and body (*Hemo the Magnificent*), the student will be able to identify at least two differences and two similarities between veins and arteries.

A. Explain the task to the students. Tell them to view the film and take notes about veins and arteries, recording similarities and differences.

B. Show the film.

C. Have each pupil use notes to list two similarities and two differences.

D. Discuss the similarities and differences as a class. Ask students how they felt as they watched certain parts of the film, for example, the heart pumping.

  1. What are the students supposed to learn?

  2. Does the teacher provide for individual differences? Why or why not?

  3. Does the teacher provide an opportunity for active student participation? Explain your answer.

REFERENCES

Anderson, L. M., Evertson, C. M., & Brophy, J. E. (1979). An experimental study of effective teaching in first grade reading groups. *The Elementary School Journal, 79,* 193–223.

Aoki, T. T. (1992). Layered voices of teaching: The uncannily correct and the elusively true. In *Understanding curriculum as phenomenological deconstructed text.* W. F. Pinar & W. M. Reynolds (eds.). New York: Teachers College Press.

Armstrong, T. (1994). Multiple intelligences: Seven ways to approach curriculum. *Educational Leadership, 52,* 26–28.

Ausubel, D. P. (1960). The use of advance organizers in the learning and retention of meaningful verbal material. *Journal of Educational Psychology, 51,* 267–272.

Barell, J. (1985). You ask the wrong questions. *Educational Leadership, 42,* 18–23.

Barnes, S. (1981). *Synthesis of selected research on teaching findings.* Austin: Research and Development Center for Teacher Education, University of Texas at Austin.

Beach, D. M., & Reinhartz, J. (1989). *Supervision: Focus on instruction.* New York: Harper & Row.

Berliner, D. (1984). The half-full glass: A review of research on teaching. In *Using what we know about teaching*. P. L. Hosford (ed.). Alexandria, VA: Association for Supervision and Curriculum Development.

Brandt, R. (1992a September). Overview: A more ambitious agenda. *Educational Leadership, 50,* 3.

Brandt, R. (1992b April). On research or teaching: A conversation with Lee Shulman. *Educational Leadership, 49,* 14–19.

Brooks, J. G., & Brooks, M. G. (1993). *In search of understanding: The case for constructivist classrooms*. Alexandria, VA: Association for Supervision and Curriculum Development.

Brophy, J. E. (1981 March). Teacher praise: A functional analysis. *Psychological Review, 88,* 93–134.

Brophy, J. E. (1992 April). Probing the subtleties of subject-matter teaching. *Educational Leadership, 49,* 4–8.

Caldwell, J. H., Huitt, W. G., & Graeber, A. O. (1982). Time spent in learning: Implications from research. *Elementary School Journal, 82,* 471–479.

Capie, W., Tobin, K. G., & Boswell, M. (1980). Using student achievement to validate ratings of student teacher competencies. Paper presented at the annual meeting of the American Educational Research Association, Boston.

Coker, H., Lorentz, C. W., & Coker, J. (1980). Teacher behavior and student outcomes in Georgia study. Paper presented at the annual meeting of the American Educational Research Association, Boston.

Creemer, B. P. M. (1994). The history, value and purpose of school effectiveness studies. In *Advances in school effectiveness research and practice*. D. Reynolds et al. (eds.). Oxford: Pergamon.

Cunningham, W. G., & Gresso, D. W. (1993). *Cultural leadership: The culture of excellence in education*. Boston: Allyn & Bacon.

Danielson, C. (1996). *Enhancing professional practice: A framework for teaching*. Alexandria, VA: Association for Supervision and Curriculum Development.

Davis, R. H., Alexander, L. T., & Yelon, S. L. (1974). *Learning system design: An approach to the improvement of instruction*. New York: McGraw-Hill.

Dawe, H. A. (1984). Teaching: A performing art. *Phi Delta Kappan, 65,* 548–552.

Doyle, W. (1985). Classroom organization and management. In *Handbook of research on teaching*. (3rd ed.). M. C. Wittrock (ed.). American Educational Research Association. New York: Macmillan.

Eby, J. W., & Kujawa, E. (1994). *Reflecting, planning, and evaluation*. Columbus, OH: Merrill Publishers.

Eggen, P., & Kauchak, D. (1994). *Educational psychology: Classroom connections*. (2nd ed.). Columbus, OH: Merrill Publishers.

Eisner, E. (1983). The art and craft of teaching. *Educational Leadership, 40,* 4–14.

Eisner, E. W. (1994). *The educational imagination: On the design and evaluation of school programs*. (3rd ed.). New York: Macmillan.

Ellett, C. D., Capie, W., & Johnson, C. E. (1981). *Further studies of the criterion-related validity of the teacher performance assessment instruments*. Athens, GA: Teacher Performance Assessment Project.

Emmer, E. T. (1982). *Management strategies in elementary school classrooms*. Report no. 6052. Austin: Research and Development Center for Teacher Education, University of Texas at Austin.

Emmer, E. T., Evertson, C. M., & Anderson, L. M. (1980). Effective classroom management at the beginning of the school year. *Elementary School Journal, 80,* 219–231.

Evertson, C. M., & Emmer, E. T. (1982). Effective management at the beginning of the school year in junior high classes. *Journal of Educational Psychology, 74,* 485–498.

Evertson, C. M., Emmer, E., & Brophy, J. E. (1980). Predictors of effective teaching in junior high mathematics class. *Journal of Research in Mathematics Education, 11,* 167–178.

Fisher, C., Marliave, R., & Filby, N. (1979). Improving instruction by increasing academic learning time. *Educational Leadership, 37,* 52–54.

Fisher, C. W., Berliner, D. C., Filby, N., Marliave, R., Cahen, L. S., & Dishaw, M. M. (1981 Winter). Teaching behaviors, academic learning time, and student achievement: An overview. *Journal of Classroom Interaction, 17,* 2–15.

Gage, N. L. (1985). *Hard gains in the soft sciences: The case of pedagogy.* Bloomington, IN: Phi Delta Kappa.

Gage, N. L., & Berliner, D. (1984). *Educational psychology.* (3rd ed.). Boston: Houghton Mifflin.

Gage, N. L., & Giaconia, R. (1981). Teaching practices and student achievement: Causal connections. *New York University Education Quarterly, 12,* 2–9.

Gardner, H. (1983). *Frames of mind: The theory of multiple intelligences.* New York: Basic Books, a division of HarperCollins Publishers.

Gardner, H. (1991). *The unschooled mind: How children think and how schools should teach.* New York: Basic Books.

Gomez, M. L. (1996 Fall). Telling stories of our teaching, reflecting on our practices. *Action in Teacher Education, 18,* 1–12.

Good, T. L. (1987). Two decades of research on teacher expectations: Findings and future directions. *Journal of Teacher Education, 38,* 32–37.

Good, T. L., & Brophy, J. E. (1986). School's effects. In *Handbook of research on teaching.* (3rd ed.). M. Wittrock (ed.). New York: Harper & Row.

Good, T. L., & Brophy, J. E. (1991). *Looking in classrooms.* (5th ed.). New York: Harper & Row.

Good, T. L., & Grouws, D. A. (1977). *Teacher's manual: Missouri mathematics effectiveness project.* Columbia: Center for Research in Social Behavior, University of Missouri.

Good, T. L., & Grouws, D. A. (1979). The Missouri mathematics effectiveness project. *Journal of Educational Psychology, 7,* 355–362.

Goodlad, J. I. (1984). *A place called school.* New York: McGraw-Hill.

Greenblatt, R. B., Cooper, B. S., & Muth R. (1984). Managing for effective teaching. *Educational Leadership, 41,* 57–59.

Griffin, G. (1985). Teacher induction: Research issues. *Journal of Teacher Education, 36,* 42–46.

Grisham, D. L. (1995). Integrating the curriculum: The case of an award-winning elementary school. Paper presented at the annual meeting of the Educational Research Association, San Francisco, ERIC Document Reproduction Service, ED 385 502.

Henderson, J. G. (1992). *Reflective teaching: Becoming an inquiring educator.* Upper Saddle River, NJ: Merrill Publishers.

Hines, C. V., Cruickshank, D. R., & Kennedy, J. J. (1985). Teacher clarity and its relationship to student achievement and satisfaction. *American Educational Research Journal, 22,* 87–99.

Hirsche, E. D., Jr., (1996 Fall). Reality's revenge: Research and ideology. *American Educator, 20,* 4–6, 31–35.

Hunter, M. (1984). Knowing, teaching and supervising. In *Using what we know about teaching.* P. L. Hosford (ed.). Alexandria, VA: Association for Supervision and Curriculum Development.

Hunter, M., & Russell, D. (1981). Planning for effective instruction: Lesson design. In *Increasing your teaching effectiveness.* Palo Alto, CA: Learning Institute.

Irvin-DeVitis, L., Modlo, M., & Bromley, K. (1995 March). Science gets graphic. *Instructor, 104,* 52–56.

Joyce, B., & Weil, M. (1986). *Models of teaching.* (2nd ed.). Englewood Cliffs, NJ: Prentice-Hall.

Joyce, B., & Weil, M. (1996). *Models of teaching.* (5th ed.). Englewood Cliffs, NJ: Prentice-Hall.

Lefrançois, G. R. (1994). *Psychology for teaching.* (8th ed.). Belmont, CA: Wadsworth.

Leinhardt, G. (1992 April). What research on learning tells us about teaching. *Educational Leadership, 49,* 20–25.

Lezotte, L. (1989). School improvement based on the effective schools research. *International Journal of Educational Research, 13,* 815–825.

Mager, R. F. (1962). *Preparing instructional objectives.* Palo Alto, CA: Fearon

Manatt, R. P. (1981a). Evaluating teacher performance. Alexandria, VA: Association for Supervision and Curriculum Development. [Videotape.]

Manatt, R. P. (1981b). Manatt's exercise in selecting teacher performance evaluation criteria based on effective teaching research. Albuquerque, NM: National Symposium for Professionals in Evaluation and Research. [Mimeograph.]

Manatt, R. P. (1987). Lessons from a comprehensive performance appraisal project. *Educational Leadership, 44,* 8–14.

Medley, D. (1977). *Teacher competence and teacher effectiveness. A review of process–product research.* Washington, DC: American Association of Colleges for Teacher Education.

Mortimore, P. (1993). School effectiveness and the management of effective learning and teaching. *School Effectiveness and School Improvement, 4,* 290–310.

Oliva, P. (1993). *Supervision for today's schools.* (4th ed.). New York: Longman.

Peterson, P. (1979). Direct instruction: Effective for what and for whom? *Educational Leadership, 37,* 46–48.

Piaget, J. (1952). *The origins of intelligence.* New York: International Universities Press.

Piaget, J. (1967). *Six psychological studies.* New York: Random House.

Pinnegar, S. (1996 Fall). Sharing stories: A teacher educator accounts for narrative in her teaching. *Action in Teacher Education, 18,* 13–22.

Porter, A. C., & Brophy, J. (1988). Synthesis of research on good teaching: Insights from the work of the institute for research on teaching. *Educational Leadership, 45,* 74–85.

Prawat, R. S. (1992 April). From individual differences to learning communities: Our changing focus. *Educational Leadership, 49,* 9–13.

Purkey, S., & Smith, M. (1983). Effective schools: A review. *The Elementary School Journal, 83,* 427–452.

Raines, P., & Shadiow, L. (1995 May/June). Reflection and teaching: The challenge of thinking beyond the doing. *The Clearing House, 68,* 271–274.

Reid, E. R. (1980). *The Reader Newsletter.* Salt Lake City, UT: Exemplary Center for Reading Instruction.

Reinhartz, J., & Beach, D. M. (1997). *Teaching and learning in the elementary school: Focus on curriculum.* Upper Saddle River, NJ: Merrill Publishers.

Rosenshine, B. (1979). Content, time, and direct instruction. In *Research on teaching: Concepts, findings and implications.* P. L. Peterson & H. J. Walberg (eds.), Berkeley, CA: McCutchan Publishing Co.

Rosenshine, B. (1983). Teaching functions in instructional programs. *Elementary School Journal, 84,* 335–352.

Rosenshine, B. (1986). Synthesis of research on explicit teaching. *Educational Leadership, 43,* 60–69.

Rosenshine, B., & Furst, N. (1971). Research in teacher performance criteria. In *Research in teacher education.* B. O. Smith (ed.). Englewood Cliffs, NJ: Prentice-Hall.

Rowe, M. B. (1974). Wait-time and rewards as instructional variables, their influence on language, logic, and fate control. Part 1: Wait-time. *Journal of Research in Science Teaching, 11,* 81–94.

Rubin, L. (1985). *Artistry in teaching.* New York: Random House.

Ryan, D. G. (1960). *Characteristics of teachers.* Columbus, OH: Charles E. Merrill.

Sadowski, M. (1995). Moving beyond traditional subjects requires teachers to abandon their 'comfort zones.' *The Harvard Education Letter, 11,* 1–4.

Salomon, G. (1992). The changing role of the teacher: From information transmitter to orchestrator of learning. In *Effective and responsible teaching: The new synthesis.* F. K. Oser, A. Dick, & J. L. Patry (eds.). San Francisco: Jossey-Bass Publishers.

Sammons, P., Hillman, J., & Mortimore, P. (1995 April). Key characteristics of effective schools. ERIC Document Reproduction Service, No. ED 389 826.

Sanford, J. P., & Evertson, C. M. (1980). *Beginning the school year at a low SES junior high: Three case studies.* Austin: Research and Development Center for Teacher Education, University of Texas at Austin. ERIC Document Reproduction Service, ED 195–547.

Scheeren, J. (1992). *Effective schooling: Research, theory, and practice.* London: Cassell.

Schmoker, M. (1996). *Results: The key to continuous school improvement.* Alexandria, VA: Association for Supervision and Curriculum Development.

Schultz, F. (1996). The profession of teaching today. In *Annual editions: Education 96/97.* (23rd ed.). F. Schultz (ed.). Guilford, CT: Dushkin Publishers.

Senge, P. (1990). *The fifth discipline: The art and practice of the learning organization.* New York: Doubleday.

Sharan, S. (1980). Cooperative learning in small groups: Recent methods and effects on achievement, attitudes, and ethnic relations. *Review of Educational Research, 50,* 241–271.

Shulman, L. S. (1987). Knowledge and teaching: Foundations of the new reform. *Harvard Educational Review, 57,* 1–22.

Shulman, L. S. (1992). Research on teaching: A historical and personal perspective. In *Effective and responsible teaching: New system.* F. K. Oser, A. Dick, & J. L. Patry (eds.). San Francisco: Jossey-Bass Publishers.

Slavin, R. E. (1991 February). Synthesis of research on cooperative learning. *Educational Leadership, 48,* 71–82.

Stallings, J. A. (1978). *Teaching basic reading skills in secondary schools.* Toronto: American Educational Research Association. ERIC Document Reproduction Service, No. ED 166 634.

Stallings, J. A., & Kaskowitz, D. (1974). *Follow through classroom observation evaluation, 1972–1973.* Menlo Park, CA: Stanford Research Institute.

Vygotsky, L. S. (1978). *Mind in society.* Cambridge, MA: Harvard University Press.

Walberg, H. J., Schiller, D., & Haertel, G. D. (1979). The quiet revolution in educational research. *Phi Delta Kappan, 61,* 179–183.

Wang, M. C., Haertel, G. D., & Walberg, H. J. (1993/1994). What helps students learn? *Educational Leadership, 51,* 74–79.

Weinert, F. E., Helmke, A., & Schrader, F. W. (1992). "Research on the model teacher and the teaching model," chapter in book *Effective and responsible teaching: The new synthesis.* F. K. Oser, A. Dick, and J. L. Patry (eds.). San Francisco: Jossey-Bass Publishers.

Zeuli, J. S., & Buchmann, M. (1987 April). Implementation of teacher thinking research as curriculum deliberation. Paper presented at the annual meeting of the American Educational Research Association, Washington, DC.

10 Assessing the Complexity of Teaching

Characteristics and Components

OBJECTIVES

The objectives of this chapter are:

- Identify and describe the characteristics and components of performance assessment systems.
- Discuss various views of teaching and explain how each view relates to performance assessment.
- Describe the role of classroom observation in the assessment process.
- Discuss the use of portfolios as part of the assessment process.
- Describe the case-based method of performance assessment.
- Define and describe the purposes of formative and summative assessment.

One of the most important roles for supervisors today is assessing teacher performance as well as providing assistance to teachers in their efforts to improve instruction. Teacher performance assessment is important because it helps to validate the quality of teaching in schools and pinpoints specific areas for teacher improvement (Bronowski, Toms-Bronowski, and Bearden, 1993). It involves "collecting, synthesizing, and interpreting information" to aid teachers in improving instruction and "is always subjective to some degree" (Cruickshank, Baines, and Metcalf, 1995, p. 260). Performance assessment serves two purposes: first, promoting continuous improvement of instruction and the professional growth of teachers by providing ongoing information; second, to interpret and make judgments or decisions with regard to the level of performance or instructional efficacy.

Ralph (1995) has observed that there is "little disagreement…with the notion that the ultimate goal of good teaching (and its supervision) is to promote pupils' learning. More debate emerges, however, over the question of what, in fact, is effective teaching" and how it should be assessed (p. 42). Gage (1989) and Oberle (1991) refer to this as the paradigm war which pits a quantitative (behavioristic) process–product perspective against a more qualitative (contextual) holistic view. The assessment of teaching is impacted by the teaching as art or science debate, discussed in the previous chapter. Ralph (1995) suggests that such a bipolar reductionist view of the process does not accurately assess "teachers' practical knowledge and experience in the daily routines of actual school life" (p. 42). A more appropriate view of the assessment of teaching is "a flexible blending of several positions and methods, analogous to the creation of a mosaic" (Ralph, 1995, p. 42).

In recent years, supervisors have become an integral part of the performance assessment process as they participate in both the formative and the summative phases; they have continued in their traditional role by participating in diagnostic procedures while also making decisions concerning teacher performance. The role of the supervisor as a summative decision maker was intensified in the reform efforts of the 1980s, with one of the original reports *A Nation at Risk* (National Commission on Excellence in Education, 1983) recommending that "salary, promotion, tenure and retention decisions…be tied to an effective [assessment] system" (p. 30). However, most supervisors, unless they serve in a position of authority such as principal, have shunned making decisions about teacher performance because they view this function as counterproductive in promoting professional growth and development.

Pfeiffer and Dunlap (1982) have noted this dilemma of being both a helper and a judge when they suggest that supervisors should not be involved in "hiring, firing, or promotion, since a helping relationship is difficult to maintain with a person who makes decisions about termination" (p. 162). Teachers are reluctant to express instructional concerns to individuals who could use the information as evidence of ineffective teaching. This dilemma for supervisors continues to be one of playing a supporting and nurturing role in professional growth while becoming more directly involved in personnel decisions. As supervisors carry on professional dialogues with teachers, they come to realize that "Teachers should not be viewed as needing supervision and inspection, but as professionals who can provide their own...assessment, teaching improvement, and professional growth" (Blake et al., 1995, p. 37).

The use of a checklist of teaching behaviors to assess teacher performance reflects the kinds of assessment systems that many states and local school districts have adopted. Using paper-and-pencil instruments, which include long lists of specific teaching behaviors, has made the assessment process appear more objective and rational (Wood, 1992). It is important to recognize that assessing teaching performance is a complicated and complex task; few teachers, supervisors, or administrators are totally satisfied with the systems currently used in their school and/or district. Duke and Stiggins (1986) offer this comment regarding assessment systems: Like so many of life's ironies, they can be the most rewarding experiences, but they also have the potential for being frustrating. They summarize by saying, "Done well, [the system] can lead to improved performance, personal growth, and professional esteem. Done poorly, it can produce anxiety or ennui and drive talented teachers from the profession" (p. 9).

For us, *teacher performance assessment is an eclectic process that involves collecting information about teachers and their instructional interactions with students in the classroom using not only identified competencies (checklists and observations) but also portfolios,* reflective journals (Chapter 9), and/or case-based methods. Such a process provides a more complete view of the complexities and contexts of teaching and learning. These assessment tools can encourage teachers to continue to build and expand their professional experience based on their reflections:

> [This mosaic or eclectic view of assessment] not only promotes current educational reform goals embodied in constructivism (Cochran-Smith, 1991), collaboration (Fullan and Miles, 1992), commitment (Sergiovanni, 1992), and contextuality (Ralph, 1995), but sidesteps the contention of some educators that the assessment and "assistance" functions of the supervision process are mutually exclusive, or that the same person cannot, and should not, perform both tasks. (Ralph, 1995, p. 43)

Assessment should take into account principles of adult learning and development as well as collaboration with colleagues (Chapter 6) because teacher performance development can ultimately be viewed as human development, in which self-identity is developed (Bell and Gilbert, 1996). They continue by saying that learning means developing a sense of who teachers are as professionals.

As districts or schools construct assessment systems, one component may be emphasized more than others. As supervisors engage in performance assessment, they should first use data collected from classroom observations in a diagnostic or formative way to establish benchmarks, which serve to guide professional development activities. They can then use all the data collected from the various components of the assessment system to make a summative judgment or evaluation of a teacher's level of performance.

This chapter will provide a variety of ways for supervisors to view teacher performance assessment. The chapter begins by examining views of teaching as a basis for an assessment system. Next, characteristics and components of assessment systems are addressed; the chapter ends with a discussion of formative and summative assessment phases. The supervisor's knowledge of assessment and skill in implementing an assessment system should serve to initiate dialogue with teachers about lifelong professional improvement.

Performance Assessment and Views of Teaching

As an introduction to teacher performance assessment, this section examines the views of teaching, which were discussed in greater detail in Chapter 9. This relationship between views of teaching and the body of knowledge currently available forms the foundation of a teacher performance assessment system. This connection also provides a lens through which teaching and learning are viewed.

When teaching is viewed through the lens of process–product research, discrete teaching behaviors that have been shown to increase student achievement (Eggen and Kauchak, 1994) become the focus of the assessment system. Supervisors who view teaching from a process–product perspective engage in classroom observations that often utilize checklists of specific teacher behaviors that are to be demonstrated during the "snapshot" periods of observations. An example of a checklist used as part of an assessment system, which focuses on the presence or absence of specific teaching behaviors, is provided in Figure 10.1.

The checklist of teacher behaviors seen in Figure 10.1 requires at least one classroom observation to verify the implementation of these behaviors within the established levels of performance. These teaching behaviors, which have been correlated with student achievement, were presented and described more completely in Chapter 9.

This process–product view of teaching, and the assessment system that accompanies it, is often tied to direct instruction models and assumes that each lesson unfolds in a sequential, almost linear manner (see Chapter 9). In a direct instruction model, specific steps and teacher behaviors must occur in some sequence before other steps or behaviors are implemented. For example, the teacher begins the lesson with a focus and ends the lesson or lesson segment with closure.

The process–product research on teaching has provided educators with a core of technical teaching behaviors that have shaped the dialogue concerning the improvement of the teaching–learning process. This research has also provided pictures of what effective teachers do. As Brandt (1992) notes, process–product research laid the groundwork for the kinds of research now being done with regard to teacher performance. As teachers become more involved with studying their own teaching, they contribute to the "development of a vision that will enable us to describe with greater clarity the kind of teaching we want for every learner" (Brandt, 1994, p. 3).

The new research perspective on what constitutes effective teaching moves us beyond this process–product focus by examining the contexts that impact

FIGURE 10.1   Teacher Behavior Checklist*

Teacher's Name: _____ School: _____

Date: _____ Period/Class:_____

Teacher Behaviors	Rating Scale**				
	0 5	P 3	BE 1	U 0	
1. • Provides for focus and establishes set • Gets attention • Prepares for day's lesson • Reviews previous day's work					
2. • States instructional goals and objectives • Communicates learning expectations					
3. • Provides input and models learning tasks • Presents information • Stresses important points/content • Demonstrates aspects of learning					
4. • Demonstrates instructional clarity • Presents information in appropriate sequence • Paces lesson • Provides steps in learning					
5. • Checks for understanding and asks questions • Uses a variety of techniques to determine understanding • Asks large number of questions with high success rate at multiple levels					
6. • Provides opportunities for guided and independent practice • Provides opportunities for students to practice learning • Uses new learning strategies during class activities • Has students apply learning to examples beyond classroom					

FIGURE 10.1 *Continued*

Teacher Behaviors   Rating Scale

	0 5	P 3	BE 1	U 0	
7. • Provides feedback to students • Monitors student performance • Clarifies misunderstandings					
8. • Keeps students engaged in academic learning time • Keeps students on task • Maximizes time for learning					
9. • Demonstrates effective classroom management and organizes effectively • Specifies behavior expectations • Prevents, redirects, stops inappropriate behavior					
10. • Varies instruction • Uses different instructional strategies • Uses a variety of instructional materials					

General Comments:

Teacher Signature _____ Coach/Supervisor/Appraiser Signature _____

*Teacher behaviors identified in Chapter 9.

**Rating Scale: O = Outstanding; P = Proficient; BE = Below Expectations; U = Unsatisfactory.

teaching and learning and helps us change the way instruction is viewed (Brooks and Brooks, 1993). Searfoss and Enz (1996) call this new perspective holistic instruction. The holistic integrated instruction perspective is consistent with the constructivist philosophy, which emphasizes understanding classroom contextual issues related to the teaching–learning process.

When teaching is viewed with this new research lens, the nuances and complexities of teaching emerge as teachers reflect on not only their instructional intent but the outcomes of their efforts. The research has shown that the degree to which teachers think about their teaching experiences impacts their ability to improve instruction (Raines and Shadiow, 1995). Teacher reflection and self-assessment become important parts of an assessment system. Supervisors who have moved beyond the process–product view of teaching engage teachers in reflection, self-assessment, naturalistic inquiry (context of classroom), case-based methods, and the construction of portfolios.

Searfoss and Enz (1996) and Wood (1992) indicate that the use of a holistic orientation helps supervisors become more mindful of the multiple dimensions of the teaching–learning process, and teachers then become more of an integral part of assessment. To assess teacher performance, one must consider the instructional intent, the teaching–learning interactions, and the results of teachers' efforts. It is useful for the supervisor to engage teachers in journal writing, which causes them to reflect on their teaching ideas and the practices they have implemented or have thought about implementing (Bell and Gilbert, 1996) as well as describe in writing the goals and objectives with their perceived results. For Wood (1992), by using "this more mindful approach, they [supervisors] will accumulate more information on, more appreciation for, and better answers to the how and why of the teaching performance" (p. 58).

A sample teacher professional growth plan that requires self-assessment or reflection is provided in Figure 10.2. In a conversation with Brandt (1996), Mc-Greal talks about how, in the past, teachers have participated in individual goal-setting activities, but today these reflective activities are "referred to as professional development plans—long-term projects teachers develop and carry out" (p. 31). Listed in Figure 10.2 are questions that require the teacher to reflect on his or her instructional and professional goals and to become more of an active participant in the assessment system by describing intended outcomes and plans for accomplishing the goals. These plans address the needs of teachers who want to be involved in determining their own professional growth plans "in a collegial environment" (McGreal in Brandt, 1996).

Both the process–product perspective, which emphasizes specific teacher behaviors related to student achievement, and the holistic perspective, which recognizes the contextual nature of teaching and learning, can be useful in the development of a teacher performance assessment system. The process–product research focuses on student achievement and serves as a constant reminder that the improvement of student learning is integrally tied to improving the quality of teaching. Linking teaching with learning has been the most "important aspect of building a successful [assessment] system" (McGreal, 1983, p. 72). In light of the holistic perspective, failure to consider the contextual aspects of the classroom and engage teachers in reflection and self-assessment may result in an assessment system that is impractical and unrealistic in its attempt to have teachers become reflective professionals.

How supervisory personnel perceive teachers is also important in the implementation of an assessment system. If teachers "are considered a[s] professional …rather than [an]…object of bureaucratic scrutiny," the assessment system gains

1. Contextual Nature of Classroom: Describe the following characteristics of your classroom:

    - Characteristics of learners
    - Facilities
    - Resources/materials
    - Parental expectations/involvement
    - Learning goals

2. Statement of Targeted Personal and Professional Goal(s): What do you expect to accomplish with your students? How will you grow professionally?

3. Timeline with Tasks and Activities for Achieving Targeted Goal(s): Identify and construct a timeline. What activities are planned for you and your students to accomplish your goals?

4. Action Plan Demonstrating Evidence of Achieving Targeted Goal(s): How will you know your goals have been achieved?

5. Assessment of Results of Documented Plan: How well did you do in accomplishing your instructional and professional goals?

6. Changes to Implement: What would you do differently? What do you need to do next year?
    Next Steps:

Date of Conference:_____   Signature of Teacher: _____

FIGURE 10.2   Sample Teacher Professional Growth Plan

credibility (Wise and Darling-Hammond, 1984–1985, p. 28). On the other hand, if teachers are viewed as objects of "bureaucratic scrutiny," the task of performance assessment becomes a perfunctory duty that yields limited information and is of little assistance in promoting reflective practitioners and student achievement. How teachers are perceived also affects how the teacher performance assessment system is implemented. Performance assessment systems should be designed to provide teachers with guidance while addressing specific concerns of classroom practice (Wise and Darling-Hammond, 1984–1985). Such an assessment system is contextually based and developmentally oriented, and it is designed to foster professional growth.

Characteristics of Performance Assessment Systems

There are a variety of assessment systems that are available for schools to purchase (Harris and Hill, 1982; Iwanicki, 1981; Manatt, 1976), but if local conditions are not taken into account, the assessment system may fail. It seems evident that the implementation of any teacher performance assessment system must be based on agreed-upon components and that individuals serving in supervisory roles or positions must be trained in the system (McGreal, 1983; McGreal in Brandt, 1996). These procedural steps are crucial; before assessment systems are implemented, the characteristics of these systems should be reviewed.

McGreal (in Brandt, 1996), Nolan and Hillkirk (1991), and Nolan, Hawkes, and Francis (1993) have identified characteristics of effective assessment systems that stress continuity so that teachers have ample opportunity to construct their own knowledge regarding their professional behavior. Using the work of Shannon (1982), Hoyle, English, and Steffy (1985) developed what they call the "cardinal principles of evaluation" (p. 128). Glatthorn and Holler (1987), Good and Brophy (1987), O'Neil (1996), and Searfoss and Enz (1996) have identified similar characteristics in separate projects on effective teacher assessment systems. The following is a composite list of these eight traits:

1. The assessment system and the components used are consistent with district goals and objectives. For example, if the goal of the district is to move beyond the process–product view of teaching, the assessment system would involve multiple components for determining effective teaching.

2. There is a high level of commitment by supervisory personnel and teachers to the system as a means of improving teaching and learning. Commitment to the assessment system is critical. Without support for teacher assessment at all levels, the process will not achieve the desired goals.

3. The purpose of the assessment system is evident and clearly communicated. If the purpose is to support teachers in expanding and refining their instructional repertoire, then steps are taken and financial support provided to assist teachers in their quest to improve teaching and learning in their classrooms. Procedures, criteria, and forms are communicated to all involved, and a rebuttal response process is clearly defined and articulated.

4. Consideration is given to cost-effectiveness, legislative support, and usefulness. Essential questions that must be answered in implementing a teacher performance assessment system are:

- Is the process worth the effort and cost?
- Would another system be more effective? Why?
- Do teachers feel better about their teaching, and are they recognized and reinforced for a job well done?
- Do students achieve more as a result of the system?

5. Teacher input and involvement, which provide the basis for psychological and emotional support, are essential in the development of an assessment system. Teacher involvement in all phases—planning, implementing, and assessing—of the system encourages teachers to reflect upon their own teaching and to consider its impact on student learning.

6. Assessment is conducted on a regular, continuous basis, and multiple components are used in assessing teacher performance. These components include opportunities for both formal and informal aspects of assessment and employ components other than classroom observations.

7. The system encourages self-assessment and professional growth. Feedback from the assessment system is used for planning professional development and other teacher growth opportunities.

8. Supervisory personnel are adequately trained in the procedures of the system. All individuals responsible for the implementation of the assessment system must be trained not only in classroom observation but in portfolio development and case-based methods.

These characteristics can guide supervisors in designing and implementing more consistent, reliable, and fair teacher performance assessment systems. As one elementary teacher put it, when there is "a well-defined model, there is more trust between teacher and supervisor" (Glatthorn and Holler, 1987, p. 58). These characteristics, drawn from the sources noted, provide a conceptual framework for developing an assessment system that has many facets for "examining the efficacy of the teacher's practices, not the teacher's competence" (Nolan, Hawkes, and Francis, 1993, p. 52). Such a system attempts to assess and foster teacher growth and improvement by encouraging teachers to take the final responsibility for decisions about their own teaching behavior. In this assessment system, the supervisor serves as a catalyst who helps teachers analyze these decisions and identify an action plan (Nolan, Hawkes, and Francis, 1993). It is unfair to "press teachers to develop alternative sources of assessment and then evaluate teachers the same way we did in the 1950s" (McGreal in Brandt, 1996, p. 32).

Figure 10.3 represents our view of the components of a teacher performance assessment system that incorporates not only data from classroom observations but input from portfolios and case-based methods as well. For us, supervisors must encourage school districts to move beyond a process–product focus on assessment and the identification and documentation of lists of generic teaching behaviors to a system that includes other components. Having a variety of components within an assessment system helps to capture the complex and dynamic nature of the

FIGURE 10.3   **Suggested Components of a Teacher Performance Assessment System**

Classroom Observations	Portfolios	Case-Based Methods
• Scripting—anecdotal and verbal notes • Teacher mobility and interaction maps • Teacher–student interaction analysis	• Résumé • Reflective journals • Written instructional plans with goals, objectives, and student assessment • Student products • Classroom observations, and/or video recording	• Descriptions of classroom practices (a written record) • Dialogues about instruction • Thoughts about a specific lesson and/or strategy

classroom and the teaching–learning process. Portfolios and case-based methods should be incorporated as components; these are discussed in greater detail later in the chapter.

Components of Assessment Systems

Assessment systems utilize various components or ways of gathering meaningful data for the purpose of providing feedback to teachers regarding their performance in the teaching–learning process. Depending on the component, there is either an up-close focus, based on classroom observations, or a wide-lens focus, where portfolios and case-based methods are used.

Classroom Observation

One of the most established and commonly used components of a teacher performance assessment system is classroom observation. It involves the supervisor or peer coach/colleague in direct observation of the teaching–learning process. McGreal (1983) notes that "contemporary views of observation, based on research and experience, strongly suggest that the appropriate role for a supervisor in visiting classrooms is to be a collector of descriptive data" (p. 96). For Sergiovanni and Starratt (1993), this component is designed to answer the following questions:

- What is going on in this classroom?
- How does this work?
- Can it be explained [by the data]?
- What laws and rules govern behavior in this context?
- How can classroom events be described accurately and vividly? (p. 217)

Data collected during classroom observations help to validate teaching and learning behaviors and serve to provide pictures or snapshots of ongoing classroom events. For Hyman (1975), however, observation goes beyond seeing and includes "intentional and methodical viewing of the teacher and students" (p. 25). Observation involves careful planning and attention by the observer.

Chapter 7 provided detailed descriptions of various forms of data-collection procedures. Our purpose here is to provide a brief explanation of how classroom observations contribute to a teacher performance assessment system. Data collected during a classroom observation are normally converted to some type of assessment form. McGreal (1983) notes that supervisors can improve their classroom observations by using the following three principles to guide this component of the assessment system:

1. Supervisors need to obtain information from the teacher about the classroom and lesson prior to the observation, normally in a preobservation conference; such information is directly related to the degree to which the observational data will be valid and helpful to the teacher.

2. Supervisors should narrow the focus of their observations in order to provide an accurate description of teaching–learning events.

3. The way supervisors' observational data are collected or recorded as well as the way data are presented to teachers determines the degree to which these data impact the teachers' willingness to fully participate in instructional improvement.

As indicated in Chapter 7, a common form of data collection during classroom observations is scripting. Scripting involves taking detailed notes about what was said and/or done by the teacher and students. The data collected include anecdotal (narrative or descriptive) notes of what happened in the classroom as well as verbatim (quotations or statements of what was said by both teacher and students) notes. Later these scripted notes or script tapes can be converted to the district's formal assessment form or document. In addition to script taping, supervisors may collect data on forms that examine specific behaviors such as questioning skills, on-task and off-task behavior, teacher mobility, teacher interaction with specific students, or behavioral problems in the classroom. Mapping teacher movement in the classroom and noting teacher interactions with students using seating charts or classroom diagrams can provide valuable information about teaching–learning dynamics.

Regardless of the form of data collection, one of the difficulties supervisors often face is that their notes generally reflect the context and complexities of the classroom, while the assessment form may be based on the process–product research, which emphasizes isolated, discrete teaching behaviors. Moreover, supervisors must then take the data they have collected and make the data fit the items and structure of a checklist, which may include generic skills and competencies.

Current views of teaching, which go beyond the process–product research, deemphasize the checklist mind-set and utilize a combination of other assessment components, including portfolios and case-based methods (described in the next two sections). In these components, notes collected during classroom observations become pieces of a larger performance system; they provide opportunities for teachers to analyze what strategies they have used, the degree and quality of interactions with their students, and the ways they motivated students at the beginning of each lesson (Bell and Gilbert, 1996; Loughran, 1996).

As Oliva and Pawlas (1997) note, the information from classroom observations "features [an] analysis of the linguistic and cultural patterns of the classroom, an awareness of the metaphors in the teaching and supervisory process, and a sensitivity to the use of both verbal and nonverbal languages" (p. 417). Data collected for use with checklists serve to document the presence or absence of specific teaching–learning behaviors. Used with other assessment components, data collected from observations serve to provide a description of the many classroom dynamics of the teaching–learning process.

Portfolios

Many educators have come to view the checklists of teaching behaviors as "dinosaurs" in the teacher assessment process (Walen and DeRose, 1993). For some, lists have become outmoded because they fail to consider the contextual aspects of the classroom and "the complexities of what a teacher knows and can do" (Athanases, 1994, p. 421). A component that can be used as part of teacher performance assessment is the teaching portfolio. Darling-Hammond (1996) says that portfolios are purposeful collections of a teacher's learning, disposition, and development; portfolios represent their teaching skills and abilities. Campbell and colleagues (1997) provide the most comprehensive view of portfolios when they describe them as "an organized, goal-driven documentation of…professional growth and achieved competence in the complex act called teaching" (p. 3).

According to Wolf (1991), research has shown that portfolios are able to capture the complexities of the teaching–learning process. Portfolios serve to document personal and professional growth and are generally considered to be works in progress because they are continuous and ongoing documents. Shulman (1988) notes that portfolios serve in ways that other assessment components cannot because they reflect the complexities of teaching and learning as they occur over time, within many contexts, and in authentic settings. The use of the portfolio is more consistent with the constructivist philosophy in that it more accurately reflects the multiple dynamics of the classroom and the holistic integrated perspective (Searfoss and Enz, 1996).

Wolf (1994) notes that portfolios are "purposeful and selective collections of a person's work" and reflections about that work (p. 112). Teaching portfolios contain information about teachers and their performance or behavior in the classroom and may include such items as: (a) copies of unit and lesson plans; (b) student assignments and products; (c) teacher reflective journals or written descriptions of teaching and learning; and/or (d) audio- or videotapes of a lesson, along with more formal classroom observations by supervisors (Wolf, 1996). Wolf (1996) cautions that teachers carefully consider what they choose to include in the portfolio or else it will become a "scrapbook" or "steamer trunk." The scrapbook contains items that have emotional appeal to teachers but that may not reflect the teacher's best practice. Similarly, the "steamer trunk" becomes an unedited collection of teaching materials that the teacher has utilized along the way during the year. Rogers and Danielson (1996) remind supervisors that even though teachers have their students develop portfolios, as they prepare their own portfolios, they need guidance so that their teaching portfolios do not merely become a collection of folders.

To be effective as part of the teacher performance assessment system, portfolios should contain documents that have been carefully and thoughtfully selected and collected over an extended period of time. Langer (1996) suggests that when teachers start to create a portfolio, they begin with focusing on a classroom-based problem or issue. As teachers address the problem or issue, they engage in a process where they define or describe the situation or circumstances, develop a goal/ objective, plan, select strategies to reach their goal/objective, carry out their plan, and then (as they pull the pieces together) reflect on the outcome(s). Zubizarreta (1994) notes:

> [T]he process of putting together the narrative body of a portfolio always provides teachers with the opportunity to reflect on what, how, and why they teach. This critical process culminates in an act of writing that itself enhances the teaching of both novices and experts. (pp. 324–325)

While Langer (1996) suggests that teachers begin to establish a portfolio by focusing on a specific teaching–learning problem, Wolf (1996) observes that the heart of most portfolios involves a combination of teaching artifacts, such as lesson plans, and written reflections. He continues by saying:

> The introductory section in which the teacher broadly describes his or her teaching philosophy and goals, and the concluding section, which contains evidence of ongoing professional development and formal evaluations, provide a frame of reference for these artifacts and reflections. (p. 35)

Riggs and colleagues (1997), along with Campbell and colleagues (1997), note that the following components are appropriate for inclusion in a teacher's portfolio:

■ Introductory background information and materials in the form of résumés, teaching biographies, professional honors, leadership experience, educational philosophy, and goals as well as the philosophy of specific subject areas and/or a list of specific technology skills (computerized grade book)

■ Teaching–learning artifacts that include such items as unit and lesson plans, resources collected for teaching, video- and audiotapes of classroom instruction, specific subject-matter documents (such as laboratory reports, poems, publications, and artwork), classroom management plan (letters to parents and discipline referrals), examples of student work, and reflections about unit success and the teaching–learning process

■ Professional growth and development activities such as membership in professional organizations and associated professional involvement, letters of commendation and recommendation, and formal summative evaluations

As teachers develop the introductory portion of the portfolio, they should be careful to describe in broad, general terms the principles or beliefs that guide their professional practice. In describing their teaching experience and belief system, they provide the reader with a sense of who they are and what they hope to accomplish in the classroom. In selecting artifact components for inclusion, teachers must be careful to put them in a context with explanations as to why they are included or what they represent. A brief statement or caption can provide the necessary background information. Teachers should choose artifacts for inclusion that represent specific aspects of their teaching, illustrate their belief system, and serve to accomplish their instructional goals.

It is important that teachers include some kind of written reflection concerning the artifacts submitted (Campbell et al., 1997). Teachers may also provide a summary assessment of their work, including a statement as to why they have used certain items. Van Wagenen and Hibbard (1998) link teacher portfolios to student portfolios when they say, "A teacher's portfolio enables us to do exactly what we ask our students to do: self-assess, self-evaluate, and self-regulate" (p. 29). Figure 10.4 provides a portfolio checklist that supervisors and teachers can use when developing portfolios or assessing portfolios submitted by colleagues.

Portfolios provide teachers with the opportunity to collect examples of their teaching that they consider to be good and examine them, discuss them, modify them, and reuse them. Over the course of a year, teachers select artifacts that support their professional profile; such documented profiles are more likely to assist teachers in improving their teaching practices. What portfolios help to avoid is having "good teaching vanish…without a trace because we have no structure or tradition for preserving the best of what teachers do" (Wolf, 1996, p. 37). Campbell and colleagues (1997) say that the "portfolio is tangible evidence of a wide range of knowledge, dispositions, and skills [teachers] possess as growing professional[s]" (p. 3). Zubizarreta (1994) summarizes the importance of portfolios as a component of teacher performance assessment by noting that the teaching portfolio is a proven endeavor that fosters honest assessment of teachers' effectiveness and aids in highlighting their commitment to instructional improvement.

Case-Based Methods

The case-based method of performance assessment encourages supervisors and teachers to develop real-world scenarios of teaching episodes that can be examined and discussed as a means of reflecting on the teaching act. This method encourages teachers "to think like teachers" (Shulman, 1992; Wasserman, 1994) by

FIGURE 10.4   **Teacher Portfolio Checklist**

I. Personal introduction
   A. Description of teacher's educational background and current teaching position
   B. Statement of personal philosophy concerning student learning and role of teacher
   C. Career and teaching goals

II. Instructional component/classroom context
   A. Knowledge of subject matter revealed in lesson plans, instructional activities, and materials created (teaching–learning artifacts)
   B. Teaching–learning process—data collected from observations, journal entries, and case-based documents

III. Personal and professional growth
   A. Written reflections concerning teaching episodes
   B. Self-assessment documents—surveys, coaching and mentoring notes, and feedback from others
   C. Plan of action for personal and professional growth

IV. Student performance
   A. Student work samples
   B. Student notes or journal entries

---

focusing on real classroom incidents from which the theory underlying the best practices emerges (Merseth, 1996). Cases help teachers deal with loosely structured environments where there are few, if any, clearly right or wrong answers (Spiro, Coulson, Feltovich, and Anderson, 1988).

Ackerman, Maslin-Ostrowski, and Christensen (1996) describe a case story approach as having teachers write brief accounts of their teaching experiences, read their stories aloud, and discuss them with colleagues. It is during these conversations that the real problems of practice emerge. The case story approach "involves not just what happens…but one's responses to what happens" (Ackerman, Maslin-Ostrowski, and Christensen, 1996, p. 21).

When this component is used as part of an assessment system, the case-based method provides a common ground for discussing critical issues regarding the rationale for action, or the how and what of teaching. In the case-based method, teachers describe in detail, with prompts and questions from supervisors, exactly what happened in their classroom when they implemented a specific strategy during a lesson or series of lessons. For example, when experimenting with the concept attainment instructional strategy, the teacher plans a lesson using the supervisor as a sounding board. After the lesson, the teacher records what he or she remembers about what occurred, specifically focusing on the perceived degree of success in implementing this strategy. The teacher plans a science lesson on "eating healthy"; the teacher lists examples (green vegetable, baked potato, and fruit juice) that are healthy foods as well as nonexamples (French fries, hamburgers, and ice cream with hot chocolate sauce), foods which are not healthy. These examples and nonexamples are randomly called out, and students begin to see a pattern and inductively determine the main topic of the lesson. Together with the supervisor, this written planning document is discussed to determine if the instructional sequence is clear; if it is not, the plan is modified.

What is different in the case-based method is that the teacher is ultimately responsible for constructing the record of what will take place, then recording what did take place in the classroom. By having teachers use the case-based method as part of an assessment system, they construct their own database from which to operate; using this benchmark, they are in a better position to make changes in their performance.

The case-based method is undergirded by "research on teachers' practical knowledge,...collaborat[ion] and participat[ion]..., and emerging emphasis on teachers' voices" (Mostert, 1996, p. 2). Mostert goes on to say that "practical knowledge in the classroom is shaped by the personal history, intentions, and purposes of the teacher and by the cumulative effects of the teacher's life-history" (p. 2). For Ackerman, Maslin-Ostrowski, and Christensen (1996), when teachers share stories of predicaments and dilemmas, they gain insights and perspectives about their performance.

Lange and Burroughs-Lange (1994) view the case-based method as a means of helping teachers develop strategies for becoming comfortable with the image of who they are and as a means for resolving professional concerns and uncertainty. In addition, this method enhances professional growth by helping teachers analyze the information from their own vantage point and weave it together with the insights shared by supervisors. By combining these sources of information and integrating them according to the teachers' perceptions within classroom contexts, they can then use this information as they work to continuously improve their performance (Lampert and Clark, 1990; Lange and Burroughs-Lange, 1994). Shulman (1992) provides guidance concerning the elements of a case and recommends that it include five elements: (1) description of the contextual elements related to the classroom; (2) description of the teaching plan and instructional intentions; (3) discussion of the actual teaching episode, including unplanned events; (4) identification of decisions and/or judgments made during teaching; and (5) analysis, reflection, and new insights about the lesson taught.

For us, the case-based method is a viable component for an assessment system; it provides a means of prompting an honest conversation between the supervisor and the teacher. Getting supervisors and teachers to develop a case by talking, analyzing, observing, and then discussing a teaching episode is the first step toward establishing an assessment system in which the supervisor and teacher engage in an open dialogue. The case sheds light on the teaching–learning process, which leads to addressing critical issues that have been recorded. As a case is analyzed, issues such as responding to off-task behavior and identifying consequences or identifying appropriate types of reinforcement surface for further discussion and examination (Kauffman et al., 1993).

The case-based method can also be used in conjunction with other assessment and professional growth procedures, such as teacher journal entries, preobservation and postobservation conferences, and peer or cognitive coaching. Stahlhut and Hawkes (1997) use the term reflectivity to describe the process of going back and looking at journal entries that are a record of the teacher's professional life. An inherent part of the case-based method is to return to the entries and revisit the previous lessons and teaching behaviors employed. For Sardo Brown and Mastrilli (1997), writing, analyzing, and reflecting on case stories provides a way for teachers to recognize when change is needed and to make these changes themselves.

Formative and Summative Assessment Phases

A performance assessment system involves two different phases—formative and summative—which serve different purposes but are indirectly tied to each other. The formative phase continues and is primarily concerned with collecting data and information during classroom observations, which serve to provide an ongoing picture of the teaching–learning process. These glimpses of instructional interactions as well as teacher reflections provide guidance to the teacher and help to shape future instructional episodes. Sergiovanni and Starratt (1998) note that formative assessment emphasizes ongoing growth and development for the teacher and "is intended to increase the effectiveness of...educational programs and activit[ies]" (p. 229). It also provides feedback for redesigning lessons and modifying teaching behaviors (Oliva and Pawlas, 1997). Supervisors often participate in this phase as they work with teachers not only to identify classroom concerns and collect information about such concerns but to cooperatively develop a plan to address them (see Chapter 6).

At the end of a particular period of time (e.g., semester or school year), the summative phase is conducted and provides an opportunity to examine the data collected during the previous formative assessments and to interpret the data or make judgments about a teacher's overall performance (McCowan, Driscoll, and Roop, 1996). This second phase, then, involves making decisions about the instructional effectiveness of a teacher with regard to continuing a employment contract, dismissing or not renewing a contract, or granting merit pay/rewards. While supervisors who do not serve in administrative positions (such as principals) have not normally been directly associated with this phase, there is a growing trend to involve these supervisors in both phases, "since the two are not intrinsically distinct" and there is a substantial link between the formative and summative phases (Scriven, 1981, p. 244).

Sergiovanni and Starratt (1998) note that "In the strictest sense, formative and summative evaluation cannot be separated, for each contains aspects of the other" (p. 229). Others (Manatt, 1981; Oliva and Pawlas, 1997; Tanner and Tanner, 1987) suggest that periodic or formative assessments should ultimately become part of the summative phase. In such a system, it is important that the formative phase provide opportunities not only for the collection of classroom data but for teacher reflection as well. Reflection on the data helps to give direction for teacher instructional improvement and becomes part of the summative phase. We agree with Tanner and Tanner (1987) when they say that in order to bring about continued instructional improvement, there is a "persistent need for [both] formative and summative" phases (p. 307). As supervisors walk the assessment tightrope and balance their actions by playing the dual roles of genuinely assisting teachers while also being an assessor, they need to be aware of the various components of assessment and how to include them in the process.

Formative Assessment

As supervisors seek to provide information and resources to teachers, the performance criteria should be sufficiently differentiated to deal with individual teachers and their instructional situations and should give direction to the formative phase of teacher assessment (Glatthorn and Holler, 1987). The list of specific teacher behaviors developed from the process–product research (see Chapter 9) forms a beginning point for classroom data collection. We do not view this as an absolute list of teaching behaviors, but rather as a general core of teaching behaviors that appears frequently in the teaching effectiveness literature. These teaching behaviors can serve as part of the assessment process, especially for teachers new to the profession who may need to hone their skills. Such a list of behaviors provides a framework for collecting data and developing a written narrative based on the observation. To get the most accurate and objective information about teaching–learning behaviors, Macdonald (1979) and Reiman and Thies-Sprinthall (1998) also recommend the use of video- and/or audiotaping or the Flanders Interaction Analysis Categories System (Flanders 1967) (see Chapter 7) as a way of collecting data.

Multiple sources of data and various techniques are recommended as a means of obtaining a composite picture of teacher performance to provide feedback and hold up a mirror of what has taken place in the classroom. By including a variety of components (such as portfolios and case-based methods) as part of an assessment system along with classroom observations, the process of assessing teaching becomes more manageable and real world–based. Inherent in the assessment process is the observer, who collects, analyzes, and interprets information; who engages the teacher in dialogue; and who makes decisions about improving instruction. The coach or counselor role of the instructional supervisor during the formative phase of assessment is ongoing. The purpose of the formative phase is to help teachers improve or upgrade their teaching skills and/or add to their teaching repertoire.

Of the two phases of teacher performance assessment, we believe that the formative should take precedence. Taking the time to coach and support teachers is essential for continuous professional development. It is during the formative assessment phase that supervisors supply information (written and oral), assist in integrating these new aspects into teachers' routines of planning and teaching, respond to questions, provide guidance as teachers assimilate these new ideas into their repertoire, and focus on changes that will enhance the teachers' instructional effectiveness.

In the past, supervisors were all too often "like angels making visitations not visits" (Manatt, 1987, p. 12). As discussed in Chapter 7, supervisors need to collect information that is bias-free and valid and then present it in meaningful ways that cause teachers to reflect on the teaching–learning process. In some districts, teachers, after receiving their formative assessment, are given specific professional development activities that vary from receiving guidance in employing specific techniques to being teamed with a successful teacher. Another approach suggested by Beach and Reinhartz (1982), which can be used during formative assessment, is encouraging teachers to develop skills relative to personal instructional abilities; teachers "using inventories or self-diagnostic tools to study their own classroom teaching behavior" have a database they can use as they begin to develop an instructional profile (p. 8).

Summative Assessment

Once data have been collected and teachers have had opportunities both to reflect on their behaviors and student outcomes and to modify their instructional behavior(s) accordingly, formative assessment comes to an end; then the summative or decision-making phase begins. Summative assessment is the final phase in the assessment system. In this phase, the supervisor collects all pertinent information, reviews teacher progress, reflects on changes, discusses findings with the teacher, and makes a decision concerning the teacher's performance. Depending upon the individual assessment system a district or school campus uses, the formative phase frequently concludes at the end of a designated period such as a semester or school year. For more experienced teachers who have consistently had positive results during formative assessment, the summative phase may occur over two or three years. According to Oliva and Pawlas (1997), the summative assessment phase "culminates in a comprehensive appraisal either annually or as otherwise required"; ultimately it is "an exercise in personnel, not instructional management" (pp. 537–538). The summative phase also serves as a means of identifying areas of concern the teacher is experiencing and generates recommendations for improvement or corrections (Smith, Peterson, and Micceri, 1987).

In the summative assessment phase, the supervisor helps teachers assess progress toward predetermined goals, or what Manatt (1981) calls job improvement targets. In working with teachers in building and expanding their teaching repertoire, supervisors may choose to focus on *building blocks,* which are behaviors that teachers already exhibit but could do more often or at a more proficient level. Supervisors and teachers may also identify *targets for growth,* which involve the development of new teaching behaviors to add to their teaching repertoire. These building blocks and targets for growth may have evolved from the ongoing formative assessments, or they may arise in the summative phase of assessment when the cumulative or comprehensive picture is assembled and overall perfor-mance is discussed.

As noted earlier, the supervisor's dual role is not an easy one, since the func-tions during the formative and summative phases can conflict with each other. Glanz (1994) notes that supervisors are frequently asked to evaluate or assess teachers, yet, "On the other hand, many are responsible for promoting teacher ef-fectiveness and student learning" (p. 578). Glanz (1994) continues by saying, "Herein lies the conflict: the unresolved dilemma between the necessity to evalu-ate [assess] and the desire to genuinely assist teachers in the instructional process" (p. 578). Hazi (1994) speaks of this dilemma as entanglements with irreconcilable differences and says that "although practicing supervisors have no problem dif-ferentiating supervision from evaluation [assessment], teachers do" (p. 196). After working to develop a relationship built on trust and collegiality and establishing a climate of learning for students as well as teachers, supervisors are then asked to make judgments about teachers' performance that often undermine the trust and hinder their ability to promote the teachers' professional growth. Perhaps this is why Sergiovanni and Starratt (1993) suggest that teacher growth "should be clearly distinguished from the process of…personnel decisions [summative as-sessment and] where possible, separate personnel should perform them" (p. 247).

As supervisors are called upon more and more to participate in the summa-tive phase of teacher performance assessment, they will be required to make judg-ments based on formative assessments gathered during classroom observations, generated through portfolios and teacher reflection, and developed in case-based methods. However, Sergiovanni and Starratt (1998) offer a solution to the discom-fort that often results from having to do summative assessment:

> [I]t can be eliminated…if it is treated as a community exercise, in self-governance, as a way for the school community to maintain and strengthen its identity, commit-ted to learning, rather than as a mechanism of control exercised over segments of the [learning] community. (p. 297)

When viewed as complementary to each other, formative and summative as-sessment can lead to both improved teacher performance and continued profes-sional growth; the assessment phases need not interfere with the supportive collegiality and trust necessary for such improvement and growth to occur. Using portfolios as a component of an assessment system may help alleviate some of the burden on the supervisor. Portfolios will provide artifacts and information beyond what can be obtained during classroom observations; with this material, a more complete profile of each teacher can be compiled. The formative database for making summative decisions becomes broader and more diverse, complex, and contextual.

To achieve maximum benefit from both phases of assessment, it is essential that the teacher and supervisor work together as a team and that the rules and procedures of the assessment system be clearly articulated and understood. In order for teachers to learn these rules and to feel that the system is both fair and in their interest, they have the right, according to Hoyle, English, and Steffy (1985), to ask the following six questions:

1. What are the assessment standards?

2. Who will do the assessing?

3. What types of instruments will be used to collect the data?

4. How will the results be used in the short and long term?

5. How many times will I go through the assessment process?

6. What are the appeal procedures if I disagree with the results of the assessment?

To these questions, we would add:

7. In what ways will the system assess the complexities and content of the classroom?

8. What components other than classroom observations will be used?

9. How will this assessment system foster my continued professional growth and autonomy as a professional?

The overall teacher performance assessment system can be successful if teachers feel that the summative and formative phases are fair, equitable, and educationally sound. In the future, as Bryant and Currin (1995) envision it, new understandings on how to motivate and assess people in organizations may result in a reevaluation and elimination of practices grounded in hierarchical control.

Summary

This chapter discussed one of the most important roles for supervisors—assessing teacher performance, using the data gathered not only for improving instruction but for making decisions about teachers. Performance assessment involves collecting, analyzing, and presenting information relative to the teaching–learning process. For us, it guides teachers in their efforts to improve their teaching and to grow professionally by engaging them in reflection and dialogue and providing them with feedback on a continuous basis. Performance assessment also involves interpreting and making judgments about the level of teaching performance.

The chapter presented the dilemma that supervisors encounter as they seek both to assist teachers through interacting with them about possible actions to take with regard to classroom behavior (using classroom observations) and to make decisions or judgments about hiring, dismissal, or merit pay. Because of this dual role, teachers are often reluctant to seek assistance from supervisors, especially if their request could be interpreted as evidence of poor teaching performance. While many schools have sought to keep the roles separate, in recent years, supervisors have become more involved in personnel issues and decisions; this has created a dilemma, a dualism of assisting and assessing.

The chapter further discussed the relationship between the views of teaching and assessment. For example, if teaching is viewed through the process–product lens, the focus of the assessment system will be one of validating the presence or absence of discrete teaching–learning behaviors that have been shown to be related to academic achievement. Classroom observations and data-collection procedures seek to identify the occurrence and frequency of these generic teaching skills or behaviors. When teaching is viewed through the new research lens, the focus becomes one of examining the context of teaching and learning within the complexities of the classroom. In this contextual view of teaching, classroom observation and data collection provide opportunities for teachers to analyze and reflect on their own teaching experiences as they relate to efforts to improve their instruction. Teacher reflection and self-assessment are important parts of the assessment system as they lead to professional growth and development.

Next, the chapter presented some general characteristics of assessment systems. Procedures for conducting assessment are crucial and must be communicated to all concerned before an assessment system is implemented. Assessment systems should complement district goals and objectives, have a high level of commitment to improve from both teachers and supervisors, have support from all concerned, allow for teacher input, be conducted on a regular ongoing basis, and encourage self-assessment and reflection. The chapter also discussed components of a teacher performance assessment system. These components include not only classroom observations but portfolios and case-based methods as well.

The chapter concluded with a description of the phases of formative and summative assessment. Formative assessment allows the supervisor to play the role of diagnostician. The purpose of formative assessment is to provide a series of pictures of the teaching–learning process at various times so that, as a result of dialogue and feedback, the teacher can reshape future teaching episodes. The summative assessment phase involves the supervisor making judgments about the teacher's level of performance and instructional effectiveness.

Supervisors must walk a tightrope as they seek to balance their need to be both helper and assessor. Of the dual roles, we believe that the formative assessment phase should take priority over personnel issues or summative decisions. As supervisors are called upon to take a more active role in both the formative and summative phases of teacher performance assessment, they will have to make decisions about teachers based on formative data gathered not only during classroom observations but also through teacher reflection, portfolios, and case-based methods. The ultimate goal of an assessment system is continuous teacher growth and the development of teaching–learning behaviors that result in increased academic learning for all students.

YOUR TURN

10.1. Interview at least three teachers and three supervisors using questions related to assessment. For example, you might ask:

    a. What makes a teacher performance assessment system effective?

    b. What do you think about linking assessment results with monetary incentives or recognition?

    c. What pluses and minuses would you cite when using these incentives?

    Compile the responses of the teachers and the supervisors in a summary statement that could be helpful to you, your school, and your school district in developing and implementing a teacher performance assessment system.

10.2. Review three journal articles related to state or district teacher performance assessment systems. Then explain how the components of the teacher performance assessment system in your district or state differ from the ones you read about.

10.3. What efforts would you make to involve teachers in the development and implementation of an assessment system?

    a. How would you begin?

    b. How would you decide on the number of teachers, representative subject areas, and levels?

    c. What role would teachers play?

10.4. The superintendent has asked you to chair a committee at the district level that is charged with developing a comprehensive teacher performance assessment system.

    a. Who should be on the committee with you?

    b. What areas/topics/issues should the committee consider in assessing teacher performance?

    c. How often will teachers be assessed?

    d. By whom will they be assessed?

    e. How does the assessment system affect pay and promotion?

    f. What role should classroom observation, teacher reflection, portfolios, and case-based methods play in the assessment system?

10.5. It will be helpful to read at least one of the articles on portfolios listed in the references before beginning this task. One example is "Teaching Portfolios and the Beginning Teacher" by John Zubizarreta in the December 1994 issue of *Phi Delta Kappan* (volume 76, number 4). Or you may want to consult *How to Develop a Professional Portfolio: A Manual for Teachers* by Dorothy M. Campbell and her associates (Allyn and Bacon, 1997). This task can be done individually or in a group. You have been asked to serve on a committee to study developing one of the components of the assessment system being implemented in your district—teaching portfolios. Your role is to:

Write a rationale (a statement of purpose) and guidelines for developing a teaching portfolio.

Develop a model [of a portfolio] with appropriate artifacts to use in your sharing session with teachers in your district. It is crucial that you differentiate between a teaching portfolio and a "scrapbook/steamer trunk."

10.6. In order to understand the case-based method of performance assessment, you are to write a case story about a teaching episode—your own or one that you remember. Your case story should include the following four components:

1. A description of the context in which the teaching occurred

2. A description of your teaching plan and intentions

3. The actual experience and serendipitous events

4. The analysis, reflection, and new insights regarding the teaching–learning process

Once your case story has been developed, share it with a colleague and discuss the implications it has for focusing professional growth and development. Is the case story clear? Are there places where it can be improved? In what way(s)?

REFERENCES

Ackerman, R., Maslin-Ostrowski, R., & Christensen, C. (1996 March). Case stories: Telling tales about schools. *Educational Leadership, 53*, 21–23.

A nation at risk: The imperative for educational reform. (1983). Washington, DC.

Athanases, S. (1994). Teachers' report of the effects of preparing portfolios of literacy instruction. *The Elementary School Journal, 94*, 421–439.

Beach, D. M., & Reinhartz, J. (1982). Improving instructional effectiveness: A self-assessment procedure. *Illinois School Research and Development Journal, 19*, 5–12.

Bell, B., & Gilbert, J. (1996). *Teacher development: A model from science education.* Washington, DC: Falmer.

Blake, J., Bachman, J., Frys, M. K., Holbert, P., Ivan, T., & Sellitte, P. (1995). A portfolio-based assessment model for teachers: Encouraging professional growth. *NASSP Bulletin, 79*, 37–47.

Brandt, R. (1992). On research on teaching: A conversation with Lee Shulman. *Educational Leadership, 49*, 14–19.

Brandt, R. (1994). Overview: It's not easy. *Educational Leadership, 51*, 3.

Brandt, R. (1996). On a new direction for teacher evaluation: A conversation with Tom McGreal. *Educational Leadership, 53*, 30–33.

Bronowski, C., Toms-Bronowski, S., & Bearden, K. J. (1993). Teacher observation forms: A new look at an old technique. *NASSP Bulletin, 77*, 30–37.

Brooks, J., & Brooks, M. (1993). *In search of understanding: The case for constructivist classrooms.* Alexandria, VA: Association for Supervision and Curriculum Development.

Bryant, M., & Currin, D. (1995). Views of teacher evaluation from novice and expert evaluators. *Journal of Curriculum and Supervision, 10*, 250–261.

Campbell, D., Cignetti, P. B., Melenyzer, B. J., Nettles, D. H., & Wyman, R. M. (1997). *How to develop a professional portfolio: A manual for teachers.* Boston: Allyn & Bacon.

Cochran-Smith, M. (1991). Reinventing student teaching. *Journal of Teacher Education, 42,* 104–118.

Cruickshank, D., Baines, D., & Metcalf, K. (1995). *The act of teaching.* New York: McGraw-Hill.

Darling-Hammond, L. (1996). The quiet revolution: Rethinking teacher development. *Educational Leadership, 53,* 4–11.

Duke, D. L., & Stiggins, R. J. (1986). *Teacher evaluation: Five keys to growth.* Washington, DC: National Education Association.

Eggen, P., & Kauchak, D. (1994). *Educational psychology: Classroom connections.* (2nd ed.). Columbus, OH: Merrill.

Flanders, N. A. (1967). Teacher influence in the classroom. In *Interaction analysis: Theory, research and application.* E. J. Amidon & J. B. Hough (eds.). Reading, MA: Addison-Wesley.

Fullan, M., & Miles, M. (1992). Getting reform right: What works and what doesn't. *Phi Delta Kappan, 73,* 744–752.

Gage, N. (1989). The paradigm wars and their aftermath. *Educational Researcher, 18,* 4–10.

Glanz, J. (1994). Dilemmas of assistant principals in their supervisory role: Reflections of an assistant principal. *Journal of School Leadership, 577–593.*

Glatthorn, A., & Holler, R. L. (1987). Differentiated teacher evaluation. *Educational Leadership, 44,* 56–58.

Good, T. L., & Brophy, J. E. (1987). *Looking in classrooms.* (4th ed.). New York: Harper & Row.

Harris, B., & Hill, J. (1982). *The developmental teacher evaluation kit* (DeTEK). Austin, TX: Southwest Educational Development Laboratory.

Hazi, H. (1994). The teacher evaluation-supervision dilemma: A case of entanglements and irreconcilable differences. *Journal of Curriculum and Supervision, 9,* 1995–2161.

Hoyle, J. R., English, F. W., & Steffy, B. E. (1985). *Skills for successful school leaders.* Arlington, VA: American Association of School Administrators.

Hyman, R. (1975). *School administrator's handbook of teacher supervision and evaluation methods.* Englewood Cliffs, NJ: Prentice-Hall.

Iwanicki, E. (1981). Contract plans: A professional growth-oriented approach to evaluating teacher performance. In *Handbook of teacher evaluation.* J. Millman (ed.). Beverly Hills, CA: Sage Publications.

Kauffman, J. M., Mostert, M. P., Nuttycombe, D. G., Trent, S. C., & Hallanhan, D. P. (1993). *Managing classroom behavior: A reflective case-based approach.* New York: Allyn & Bacon.

Lampert, M., & Clark, C. M. (1990). Expert knowledge and expert thinking in teaching: A response to Floden and Klinzing. *Educational Researcher, 19,* 21–43.

Lange, J. D., & Burroughs-Lange, S. G. (1994). Professional uncertainty and professional growth: A case study of experienced teachers. *Teaching & Teacher Education, 10,* 617–631.

Langer, G. S. (1996). Teacher portfolios: Tools for improving teaching and learning. *Education Update, 38,* 1, 6.

Loughran, J. J. (1996). *Developing reflective practice: Learning about teaching and learning through modeling.* Washington, DC: Falmer.

Macdonald, J. B. (1979). Evaluation of teaching: Purpose, context, and problems. In *Planning for the evaluation of teaching.* W. R. Duckett (ed.). Bloomington, IN: Phi Delta Kappa.

Manatt, R. P. (1976). Developing a teacher performance evaluation system as mandated by Senate File 205. Des Moines: Iowa Association of School Boards.

Manatt, R. P. (1981). Evaluating teacher performance. Alexandria, VA: Association for Supervision and Curriculum Development. [Videotape.]

Manatt, R. (1987). Lessons from a comprehensive performance appraisal project. *Educational Leadership, 44,* 8–14.

McCowan, R., Driscoll, M., & Roop, P. (1996). *Educational Psychology.* (2nd ed.). Boston: Allyn & Bacon.

McGreal, T. (1983). *Successful teacher evaluation.* Alexandria, VA: Association for Supervision and Curriculum Development.

Merseth, K. K. (1996 November). Cases, case methods, and the professional development of educators. Washington, DC: ERIC Digest Clearinghouse for Teaching and Teacher Education.

Mostert, M. P. (1996 October). Cognitive aspects of case-based teaching. Paper presented at the annual meeting of the Mid-Western Educational Research Association, Chicago, IL.

National Commission on Excellence in Education.

Nolan, J. F., & Hillkirk, R. K. (1991). The effects of a reflective coaching project for veteran teachers. *Journal of Curriculum and Supervision, 7*, 62–76.

Nolan, J., Hawkes, B., & Francis, P. (1993 October). Case studies: Windows onto clinical supervision. *Educational Leadership, 51*, 52–56.

Oberle, K. (1991). Paradigm wars: Who's fighting, Who's winning? *Alberta Journal of Educational Research, 37*, 87–97.

Oliva, P. F., & Pawlas, S. (1997). *Supervision for today's schools.* (5th ed.). New York: Longman.

O'Neil, J. (1996). Teaching for performance. *Education Update, 38*, 6.

Pfeiffer, I. L., & Dunlap, J. B. (1982). *Supervision of teachers: A guide to improving instruction.* Phoenix: Oryx Press.

Raines, P., & Shadiow, L. (1995 May/June). Reflection and teaching: The challenge of thinking beyond the doing. *The Clearing House, 68*, 271–274.

Ralph, E. G. (1995). Are self-assessments accurate? Evaluating novices' teaching via triangulation. *Research in Education, 53*, 41–51.

Reiman, A. J., & Thies-Sprinthall, L. (1998). *Mentoring and supervision for teacher development.* New York: Longman.

Riggs, I. M., Sandlin, R. A., Scott, L., Childress, L., Post, P., & Edge, T. (1997 February). The use of portfolios in beginning teacher support and assessment. Paper presented at the annual meeting of the American Association of Colleges for Teacher Education, Phoenix, AZ.

Rogers, S. E., & Danielson, K. E. (1996). *Teacher portfolios: Literacy artifacts and themes.* Portsmouth, NH: Heinemann.

Sardo Brown, D., & Mastrilli, T. M. (1997 February). Secondary student teachers' cases: An analysis of dilemmas and solutions. Paper presented at the annual meeting of the Association of Teacher Educators, Washington, DC.

Scriven, M. (1981). Summative teacher evaluation. In *Handbook of teacher evaluation.* J. Millman (ed.). Beverly Hills, CA: Sage Publications.

Searfoss, L., & Enz, B. (1996). Can teacher evaluation reflect holistic instruction? *Educational Leadership, 53*, 34–37.

Sergiovanni, T. J. (1992). *Moral leadership.* San Francisco: Jossey-Bass Publishers.

Sergiovanni, T. J., & Starratt, R. (1993). *Supervision: A redefinition.* (5th ed.). New York: McGraw-Hill.

Sergiovanni, T. J., & Starratt, R. (1998). *Supervision: A redefinition.* (6th ed.). New York: McGraw-Hill.

Shannon, T. A. (1982). Teacher evaluation: Some points to ponder. *CEDR Quarterly, 15*, 18.

Shulman, J. H. (1992). *Case methods in teacher education.* New York: Teachers College Press.

Shulman, L. S. (1988). A union of insufficiencies: Strategies for teacher assessment in a period of reform. *Educational Leadership, 46*, 36–41.

Smith, B. O., Peterson, D., & Micceri, T. (1987). Evaluation and professional improvement aspects of the Florida Performance Measurement System. *Educational Leadership, 44*, 16–19.

Spiro, R., Coulson, R., Feltovich, P., & Anderson, D. (1988). Cognitive flexibility theory: Advanced knowledge acquisition in ill-structured domains. Proceedings of the tenth annual conference of the Cognitive Science Society: Hillsdale, NJ: Erlbaum.

Stahlhut, R. G., & Hawkes, R. (1997 February). Use of journals. Paper presented at the annual meeting of the Association of Teacher Educators, Washington, DC.

Tanner, D., & Tanner, L. (1987). *Supervision in education: Problems and practices.* New York: Macmillan.

Van Wagenen, L., & Hibbard, K. M. (1998 February). Building teacher portfolios. *Educational Leadership, 55*, 26–39.

Walen, E., & DeRose, M. (1993). The power of peer appraisals. *Educational Leadership, 51*, 45–48.

Wasserman, S. (1994). Using cases to study teaching. *Phi Delta Kappan, 75*, 602–611.

Wise, A., & Darling-Hammond, L. (1984–1985). Teacher evaluation and teacher professionalism. *Educational Leadership, 42*, 28–33.

Wolf, K. (1996 March). Developing an effective teaching portfolio. *Educational Leadership, 53,* 34–37.

Wolf, K. (1994). Teaching portfolios: Capturing the complexity of teaching. In *Valuing teacher's work: New directions in teacher appraisal.* L. Ingvarson & R. Chadbourne (eds.). New York: State Mutual Book & Periodical Service.

Wolf, K. (1991 October). The schoolteacher's portfolio: Issues in design, implementation, evaluation. *Phi Delta Kappan, 73,* 129–136.

Wood, C. J. (1992). Toward more effective teacher evaluation: Lessons from naturalistic inquiry. *NASSP Bulletin, 76,* 52–59.

Zubizarreta, J. (1994 December). Teaching portfolios and the beginning teacher. *Phi Delta Kappan, 76,* 323–326.

PART FOUR

Reflection, Growth, and Change

Chapter 11: Professional Growth and Development: Staff Development Opportunities for Teachers

Chapter 12: Making Decisions and Facilitating Instructional Change

Part Four serves as the capstone of the supervision process by focusing on reflection, growth, and change. In Chapter 11, professional growth and development form the centerpiece for supervisor–teacher interactions. For the supervisor, these interactions require a knowledge of the developmental characteristics of teachers and characteristics of successful professional development programs. The chapter culminates with a model for supervisors to use as they engage in their own professional growth process. Decision making and facilitating change, presented in Chapter 12, are highlighted as essential components of the supervision process. Decision making is integrally linked with the change process. These components illustrate the challenge supervisors face as they make decisions in the present while considering the possibilities of instructional changes for future school improvement.

Professional Growth and Development

Staff Development Opportunities for Teachers

OBJECTIVES

The objectives of this chapter are:

- Identify and describe various definitions and views of staff development.
- Discuss the need for staff development, including the reasons why teachers participate.
- Identify and describe the developmental characteristics of learners.
- Explain how adult developmental characteristics should be incorporated in staff development activities.
- Discuss the characteristics of successful staff development programs.

- Describe how staff development models from other organizations can be used effectively with teachers.
- Explain how supervisors can use a self-assessment model to foster their own professional growth.

Throughout this book, we have emphasized the importance of supervisors and teachers working in concert to continuously improve the teaching–learning process. Like other organizations, schools, if they are to maintain their effectiveness, must depend on the continued growth and development of their members. Darling-Hammond and Goodwin (1993) describe the importance of continued professional growth in each teacher's career by suggesting that schools, "must have effective mechanisms that help inform practitioners about their work and provide opportunity for consultation, reflection, self-assessment, and continued improvement" (p. 42). They go on to say that "competency and caring are the foundations of professional [growth and] accountability" (p. 42). This chapter describes this competency and caring relationship by examining the role of the supervisor in planning and implementing staff development opportunities for teachers. Concern for teachers' personal and professional growth becomes the focus of the staff development activities, which for us involve all teachers.

Unfortunately, such characteristics are not always found in growth opportunities for teachers. Miles (1995) has a different view and describes the current state of professional development as pedagogically naive:

> Everything that…learning…shouldn't be: radically underresourced, brief, not sustained, designed for "one size fits all," imposed rather than owned, lacking any intellectual coherence, treated as a special add-on event rather than as part of a natural process and trapped in…a bureaucratic system. (p. vii)

To counteract this negative image, Hargreaves (1995) says that "what we want for our children, we should also want for their teachers—that schools be places of learning for both of them and that such learning be suffused with excitement, engagement, passion, challenge, creativity, and joy" (pp. 27–28).

The role of supervisors is critical to promoting passion, creativity, and joy in teaching and enhancing the professional growth and development of teachers by facilitating instructional effectiveness and strengthening commitment. Joyce and Showers (1988) link the degree of success in promoting professional development with school improvement. Helping teachers grow and develop their expertise becomes a part of the larger system of overall improvement for individual classrooms, campuses, and the entire school district. Fullan (1995) supports this position when he says that professional development is "integral to accomplishing a moral purpose,…central to continuous improvements in professional work cultures, and…embedded in the continuum of initial and career long teacher education" (pp. 264–265). The task of the supervisor is to achieve a workable combination of meeting individual and organizational needs within the context of a complex environment such as a school (Fullan, 1995; Guskey, 1995). Kyle (1995) suggests that professional development involves all educational professionals in the process of change and renewal and summarizes the situation when he says that "Professional development ought to be a process whereby education professionals regularly enhance their academic knowledge and pedagogical understandings, as well as question the purposes and parameters of what they do" (p. 679).

This chapter begins by discussing various definitions and views of staff development and provides reasons why teachers participate in staff development. It also examines developmental characteristics of teachers and presents implications for staff development. Next, the chapter describes successful staff development programs and outlines steps for initiating and implementing such programs. The chapter also includes a discussion of models for professional development gleaned from other organizations. The chapter concludes with a model for linking supervisor development to self-assessment.

Definitions and Views of Staff Development

Professional development is not unique to the teaching profession and is widely recognized by other organizations as an important means of maintaining and upgrading the quality of personnel. For teachers, supervisors, and other instructional leaders, staff development provides an opportunity to continually expand their repertoire of teaching, supervisory, and/or administrative skills. However, Hammond and Foster (1987) note that "designers of staff development often forget that adults learn when they perceive there is a need to learn" (p. 42). It is important, then, to focus on the professional needs of teachers when examining the issues that are currently being raised about the nature of professional development programs.

With an understanding of the purpose of professional development, supervisors are in a better position to identify the specific objectives to be accomplished. Over two decades ago, Edefelt and Johnson (1975) saw staff development as any "development activity that a teacher undertakes singly or with other teachers after receiving his or her initial teaching certificate and after beginning professional practice" (p. 5). Such a definition provides a foundation for understanding the purposes of professional development. For us, the terms professional development, staff development, in-service, and continuing education are terms that have been and continue to be used interchangeably.

Edefelt (1979) later suggested that a definition of staff development should be expanded to include all personnel in a school if the total program development and professional performance are to improve. He notes that the teaching staff as well as administrators influence the quality and climate of schools. Professional development activities are also designed to include other professionals, such as members of college faculties, state department personnel, and staff of teacher organizations, who often play important roles in the professional development process.

McCleary and colleagues (1993) view staff development through a wide-angle lens and include such activities as:

- Working with faculty and staff to identify professional needs
- Planning, organizing, and facilitating programs that improve faculty and staff effectiveness and that are consistent with institutional goals and needs

- Supervising individuals and groups
- Providing feedback on performance
- Arranging for remedial assistance
- Engaging faculty and others to plan and participate in recruitment and development activities, and to initiate self-development

For other authorities in the field of staff development, the ultimate goal is to improve instruction (Landon and Shirir, 1986; Sheerlin, 1991). According to work done and reported by Joyce, Murphy, Showers, and Murphy (1989), Pink (1989), and Stallings (1989), gains in student achievement can be linked to ongoing staff development programs that are well designed, with clearly established implementation plans, and that have adequate resources (McCleary et al., 1993).

Other researchers have characterized staff development programs in different ways. Dillon-Peterson (1980) has suggested that such activities should: (a) accommodate a variety of situations, (b) meet human needs, (c) be implemented to meet local needs, and (d) utilize free and inexpensive resources available to school districts. Orlich (1984) recommends that programs address identified needs and be "planned and designed for a specific groups of individuals in school districts"; he goes on to say that professional development activities should be built around a specific set of objectives that "are designed to extend, add, or improve job-oriented skills or knowledge" (p. 34).

Yet another perspective is offered by Reinhartz, Hadaway, and Trask (1992), who examined the critical variables for restructuring staff development efforts, based on the work of Corrigan (1990), Griffin (1983), Little (1981), and Wideen (1987). Reinhartz, Hadaway, and Trask (1992) identified the following eight critical variables related to effective staff development:

1. The teacher is central to the process of staff development, serving as a partner or prime mover in implementing change.

2. There is a comprehensive and collaborative focus, which emphasizes the participation of all stakeholders.

3. The focus is on each school or campus as building sites form centers of inquiry for students and teachers.

4. Staff development is context-sensitive to meet local needs.

5. Programs utilize cumulative knowledge on effective teaching and staff development.

6. Staff development is continuous and ongoing, providing a thread of continuity.

7. The staff development process is developmental, allowing for passage through personal and professional stages.

8. Staff development encourages teachers to be reflective about planning and teaching.

For us, professional growth and development can be defined as all the learning experiences, both formal and informal, that teachers encounter that support their continued instructional effectiveness as they adjust to the dynamic nature of the school environment. Such development includes activities that: (a) are intended for all teachers regardless of professional and/or developmental level; (b) are systematic, long term, individualized, and oriented toward improved student achievement; (c) encourage the exploration of new knowledge, skills, and attitudes to remain intellectually alert; (d) foster the pursuit of personal and professional goals to achieve excellence; and (e) help teachers stay current with new developments in curriculum. In the final analysis, professional development occurs with groups of teachers who continue to grow professionally as they work together to ensure that their school functions effectively and that their students learn.

Little (1990) notes that the main reason teachers are motivated to work together and support each other is found in their work of teaching: "To the extent that teachers find themselves truly dependent on one another to manage the tasks and reap the rewards of teaching, joint participation will be worth the investment of time and other resources" (p. 509). Ultimately, the success of professional development depends on the ability and willingness of supervisors and teachers to work together to transform the total school culture.

Reasons Why Teachers Participate in Staff Development

To be successful in planning professional development programs, supervisors need to move away from the notion that teachers are ineffective or that they are lacking in skills and knowledge (Darling-Hammond, 1994; Kyle, 1995; Smylie and Conyers, 1991). Such a deficit model of professional development perceives teachers as implementors rather than developers and creators, and it contradicts the current view that teaching is a professional endeavor, not just a job. According to Sergiovanni and Starratt (1993), it is helpful if supervisors think of professional development as renewal in which "Teacher growth is less a function of polishing existing skills or keeping up with the latest development and more a function of solving problems and changing as individuals" (p. 267). They continue by suggesting that professional growth occurs "when teachers see themselves, the school, the curriculum, and the students…in a new light" (p. 267).

Growth and development sessions should therefore take place in forums where teachers can exchange ideas and examine their own performance (Goodwin, 1987). The literature supports professional development that is grounded in a sound conceptual base. Most recently, Hatano (1993) and Howe and Stubbs (1996) have proposed a professional development model based on constructivist theory and sociocultural perspectives. In such a model, teachers are empowered as they look to themselves to construct their own response to a question or problem and as they involve their colleagues in a collaborative problem-solving process. Teachers take charge of their own professional growth and development and become less dependent on others in their quest for professional renewal. The literature continues to substantiate Howey's (1977) original six factors that helped explain why teachers participate in staff development activities:

1. *Handling the transition from a preservice role as student to an in-service role as teacher.* Today, the terms induction and mentoring are used and promoted to ease this transition into teaching. Teaching seems to be one of the very few, if not the only, profession that requires new employees to be proficient on their first day of work (Reinhartz, 1989). Bey (1992) and Odell (1992) point out that if new teachers are to feel successful, they need support from their experienced colleagues in their building; without such support, they are likely to drop out of the profession within the first few years. Guy (1993) states:

> As new teachers enter…schools, they are strongly influenced by existing norms they encounter among those already teaching…[and].... [to] make significant changes to the schools…attention must be paid [to the] continuing professional development of the whole staff. (p. 3)

Nearly two decades ago, Schlechy and Vance (1983) estimated that 30 percent of new teachers left the profession within the first or second year of teaching, and 50 percent by the end of the fourth year; those figures remained constant. More recently, data suggest that new teachers are leaving the profession even earlier: 19 percent leave during the first year, 12 percent leave during the second year, and 50 percent leave by the fifth year (*Mentoring Texas: Texas Teacher Preparation Study,* 1995). The need for continued support through staff development is critical during these early years, and new approaches to staff development (Howe and Stubbs, 1996) offer supervisors a conceptual framework for working with new teachers.

2. *Meeting specific classroom needs.* The effort to reform and restructure schools "ultimately turns on teachers' success in accomplishing the…tasks of learning the skills and perspectives assumed by new visions of practice and unlearning the practices and beliefs…that have dominated their professional lives to date" (Darling-Hammond and McLaughlin, 1995, p. 597). For example, teachers in the last decades have needed assistance in understanding the implementation of programs such as quality schools advocated by Glasser (1990); total quality management as suggested by Bronstingl (1992) and Deming (1981); alternative assessment strategies recommended by Wiggins (1994); and cooperative learning as proposed by Johnson, Johnson, and Holubec (1994a, 1994b). Marczely (1996) emphasizes the need for staff development to personalize programs to reach individual teachers. Enhancing the professional lives of teachers by providing programs that help them as they function daily in the classroom is an essential function of staff development (McCleary et al., 1993). In response to the need to improve test scores or address what some have called results-driven education (Sparks and Hirsh, 1997), teachers are being required to "acquire new instructional knowledge and skills" (p. 4). Successful staff development depends on "locally constructed responses to specific teacher and learner needs" (Darling-Hammond and McLaughlin, 1995, p. 603).

3. *Meeting mandates set forth by local school districts and/or states.* According to Herman and Herman (1992), managing schools at the campus level is becoming increasingly commonplace and is at the forefront of the current national restructuring movement. To be effective, campus-level management must focus on teamwork, cooperation, and student needs (Reinhartz, 1993). Several studies have been conducted to investigate the topics of site-based decision making; faculty, staff, parents, and even students work toward a vision that transcends any one group. Such a vision guides decisions regarding learning and teaching goals, staffing, resources, assessment, staff development, and allocations (Glickman, Gordon, and Ross-Gordon, 1995). For David (1995/1996), "site-based management is basically an attempt to transform schools into communities where the appropriate people participate constructively in major decisions that affect them" (p. 4). This idea complements the new model of professional development.

4. *Remaining current.* Caldwell (1988), Duke (1990), and Joyce (1990) also support the notion that professional development activities serve to introduce teachers to innovations and new ideas currently being developed and implemented. As in any field, conditions in teaching change; teachers need continuous updating and assistance in using a variety of new instructional approaches, technology, materials, textbooks, equipment, and programs. To assist teachers in remaining current, supervisors seek to provide opportunities for receiving new information, discussing the issues, practicing the skills with colleagues, and implementing the skills in their classrooms. Such a framework engenders confidence in learning and uses information about constructivism, systems thinking, educational technology, and alternative assessment, to name a few.

5. *Progressing in career-related matters.* As career teachers complete several years of teaching, many are looking for additional ways to be more effective not only with their students but in their school and community. They are interested in helping their school be the best it can be. This mirrors the components of a "teacher career cycle," which identifies various stages as teachers move from career entry to career disengagement (Huberman, 1995). In the past, teachers were passive recipients of staff development, but today job-embedded staff development "links learning to the immediate and real-life problems faced by teachers and administrators" and becomes an endeavor that all participate in (Sparks and Hirsh, 1997, p. 52).

6. *Meeting personal needs.* Beyond the desire to help others, teachers are interested in growing personally as well, particularly as they enter middle adulthood. There is a need to be physically fit, have a positive frame of mind, look at all children as having the ability to succeed, and have a desire to want to come to school each day. Personal development goes hand-in-hand with professional development; one without the other is futile. Professional development helps teachers engage in meaningful intellectual, social, and emotional experiences with new ideas, materials, equipment, and other individuals (Little, 1993).

An inventory of professional development sessions reveals the typical kinds of options presented to teachers: Some sessions primarily offer inspiring speeches; others are make-and-take workshops; and still others feature presentations on specific skills and/or particular curricular strategies or programs. Although these efforts can provide a way of bringing about professional growth and development, which leads to instructional improvement, the results have been only marginal (Dillon-Peterson, 1981; Showers, Joyce, and Bennett, 1987; Sparks and Hirsh, 1997; Yarger, Howey, and Joyce, 1980). In examining these older models of staff development that feature the presentation and transfer of information, Darling-Hammond and Goodwin (1993) say they are no longer viable for they fail to foster collaboration and collegiality as the basis for teacher growth.

As instructional leaders, supervisors should promote staff development activities that include all members of the educational community. The greatest possibility for teacher change exists when the relationship between supervisor and teacher is based on cooperation and mutual respect as they work toward common professional and personal goals.

The kinds of professional development activities presented in the literature over the last 20 years suggest that change is needed to energize the professional development process. Such a change will require a shift in the current model—a different way of thinking on the part of supervisors as they work cooperatively in planning, organizing, implementing, and rethinking teacher development. Such a vision must include "teacher networks, enriched professional roles, and collegial work," which foster a more positive feeling about remaining in the profession (Darling-Hammond, 1996, p. 71).

Teachers as Learners: Developmental Characteristics

Nearly two decades ago, Andrews (1981) identified the problems associated with professional development programs, and staff development programs in particular:

> [They] are not designed for adults. While many of the principles of learning are the same for adults and children, differences do exist, and only by careful attention to those differences will consistently successful learning programs for adults be offered. (pp. 11–12)

Showers (1990) points out that "good" staff development is centered around who determines the content of the session, the attitudes of teachers toward the training, and the teaching of adult learners. It is only in the last few years that staff developers and other school personnel have come to recognize that teaching adults requires different strategies. According to Southerland and Hardin (1992), "The field of adult education has pointed to…differences between the way children and adults learn" (p. 270). Coupled with this idea of being sensitive to the developmental characteristics of the audience is the realization that teachers should teach each other rather than bring in "outsiders" who present "dog and pony shows." Professional development must be more than having teachers just enduring it or what Sparks and Hirsh (1997) call "sit and get." Joyce (1990) concurs when he says that the success of schools "will be fashioned largely by how staff development systems evolve. How good schools will be as educational institutions will be functions of the energy and quality of the investment in their personnel" (p. xv).

Professional development must also incorporate research in the fields of learning styles (Tennant, 1988), constructivism (Sparks and Hirsh, 1997), and hemisphericity (Sonnier, 1990) to help refute the notion that teachers lack "the maturity, experience, a readiness to learn, and a motivation to learn" (Southerland and Hardin, 1992, p. 270). Professional development activities can be more productive if the research in these areas is used in the planning stages.

To be effective in planning and implementing staff development activities, supervisors need to consider the different stages and the variety of ranges in teachers' development. When viewing teachers as learners, supervisors should keep in mind some general principles of development: As adult learners, teachers have unique identifiable stages or periods of development with common characteristics; movement from one stage or period to another is sequential; and the rate of development and movement from one period or stage to the next is unique for each teacher.

When considering professional development activities, it is important to address the psychological makeup of the adult learner. Until recently, little research had been done concerning how adults learn; in fact, adult development has been a neglected area of inquiry for scholars (Knowles, 1978). Christensen (1985), however, notes that as long "as changes in life styles, technology, career patterns and life span continue, there will be an ever increasing emphasis on adult education" (p. 158). In this section, a brief overview will be provided regarding adult growth and development and the career patterns of teachers. Secondly, implications will be discussed as to how this information can be useful when planning professional development sessions.

Recognizing that adult learning is different from that of children is the key to understanding adult growth and development. Lindeman (1926) addressed this topic when he wrote *The Meaning of Adult Education,* which provides the foundation for adult learning and education today. He identified adults who needed to be learners, those who required freedom, and those who were creative. More recently, Knowles (1980, 1984) proposed a theory of adult learning called *andragogy* that is guided by the following five assumptions. First, adults have a fundamental need to be self-directing; they take the initiative for learning. Second, adults have a wealth of experience that should be part of their learning process. Third, adults are more receptive to learning when it addresses real-life problems or is related to adult developmental tasks. Fourth, adults are performance-oriented and seek immediate application of their learning. Finally, adults are generally self-motivated learners who seek opportunities to learn in a variety of settings. Knowing that adults are different and have different needs and styles of learning has implications for staff developers. Butler (1989) conducted a review of adult learning and staff development. Apps (1981), building on the work of Lindeman, identified the following nine principles that are helpful for those who work with teachers:

1. Get to know the teachers you work with.

2. Use their prior knowledge as a way to introduce new information.

3. Relate theory to practice.

4. Provide a supportive, nonthreatening environment.

5. Present material in a variety of ways (e.g., cooperative learning, expert groups).

6. Present the information in a variety of formats.

7. Provide feedback within an appropriate time frame.

8. Assist teachers in locating resources and materials.

9. Meet with teachers outside of sessions to follow up.

It was Fuller (1969) and the response of teachers to her Teacher Concerns Questionnaire that opened the way for research on the career development stages of teachers. As reported by Fuller and Brown (1975), teachers had concerns about making the transition from college student to teacher, surviving the first month and then the year, teaching students what they needed to know, and then worrying about their students. The teachers progressed from a concern about self to a concern for the task of teaching to a concern for their students and how to make an impact on their lives.

Teachers, like students, move through developmental stages that have distinct characteristics and involve various tasks (Glickman, Gordon, and Ross-Gordon, 1995). Levine (1987, 1989) suggests that an understanding of life cycles can be an important resource for school leaders because seldom, if ever, will all the teachers a supervisor works with be at the same stage of development. The work of Erikson (1978, 1980, 1982), Gould (1978, 1980), Levinson (1978, 1980, 1990), Havighurst (1972, 1980), and Loevinger (1976) suggests three distinctive periods of adult development with corresponding developmental characteristics. These periods and their corresponding characteristics are summarized in Figure 11.1.

Just as developmental characteristics help young people construct knowledge based on their experiences in the world, likewise adults construct their knowledge based on their understanding of the world (Clinchy, 1995). By combining the basic principles of development with an understanding of teacher devel-

FIGURE 11.1 Stages of Adult Development

Period of Development	Age	Task/Characteristics
Early adulthood	20 to 30/40	Seeks intimacy through collegial relationships at work rather than isolation; optimistic and idealistic; motivated by work and family; forms a life dream or vision and establishes mentor relationships; may be self-protective
Middle adulthood	30/40 to 55/60	Seeks generativity and renewal of career while developing self rather than stagnating; serves as mentor to others in their career goals; demonstrates conformist behavior and seeks to belong; desires continuity and stability; modifies dream or vision of life
Later adulthood	55/60 to death	Seeks integrity rather than despair by directing energy toward advanced status, building a legacy, or celebrating success; copes with physical and physiological changes and limitations; reflective and conscientious

opment, the following implications for supervisors emerge. According to Smylie (1995), teachers need:

■ Opportunities to work collaboratively with others by engaging in ongoing activities that foster shared goals and responsibilities; agendas are flexible

■ Participation in shared decision making in areas including curriculum and instruction, staff development, and general school operations

■ An environment characterized by egalitarianism among colleagues, with working and learning relationships based on individual talents and expertise

■ Clear goals that guide individual and group activities and give meaning and direction to work, learning, and innovation

■ Opportunities for the integration of work and learning

■ Access to a variety of sources of information and feedback concerning performance and accomplishments

Because of the number of teachers who participate in professional development sessions and the differences in their ages, the number of years of teaching experience, and the grade levels and subjects taught, many (if not most) function at different developmental levels. Supervisors should recognize these differences in conceptual development (Glickman, 1985; Glickman, Gordon, and Ross-Gordon, 1998; Harvey, Hunt, and Schroder, 1961; Santmire, 1979). Likewise, there needs to be a recognition that teachers, like students, are individuals with varying cognitive abilities, and that they have different levels of professional commitment to personal growth and change.

Differences in cognitive functioning influence the degree to which teachers will process the information presented and the degree to which they will implement the information in their classrooms. Some teachers can, with little assistance, absorb information from staff development sessions and use it the next day in their classrooms because they have the background, experience, and ability to think at a high conceptual level (Glickman, 1981; Glickman, Gordon, and Ross-Gordon, 1998; Wilsey and Killion, 1982). The challenge for supervisors is to initiate staff development activities that provide the conditions under which the change process can occur. According to Bents and Howey (1981), for behavioral or developmental change to occur, the teacher's schemata must be affected. Teachers should be viewed as individuals who have different instructional needs, interests, and cognitive abilities. The composite profiles of Cheryl Moore, Ann Marie Rayfield, and Cal Green in Figure 11.2 illustrate developmental diversity found among teachers in schools today.

In planning for staff development, it would be helpful to identify those teachers who can assimilate the new information because they have prior knowledge and experience related to what is presented. Also, it is important to identify those who may have more difficulty in accommodating this new information because they have had very little, if any, experience with the concept or strategy that is presented. Supervisors need to keep these two groups in mind as they plan and implement professional development activities and programs. Without a comprehensive approach that accommodates these cognitive differences among teachers, those with little familiarity with the session topic will not likely adopt any new ideas or implement any new strategies in their classrooms. If change, in the form of improved instruction, does not occur, the entire process is often seen as useless and meaningless.

Within the school organization, the need for professional growth models has historically been heightened by two factors: the relative stability of the teaching profession and a young group of beginning teachers. Sergiovanni and Starratt (1983) sum up the situation this way: "When teachers land a decent job they are likely to stay. Combine this phenomenon with a relatively young teaching force and many districts are faced with large numbers of teachers who are likely to stay employed in the same school and system for...decades" (p. 326). Professional development for teachers becomes critical in promoting instructional competency and enhancing the commitment of teachers to their work. As Duke (1993) notes, "Adults learn all the time, but growth, particularly professional growth is rarer....

FIGURE 11.2

Teacher Profile: Cheryl Moore

Miss Moore is in her mid-twenties and has been teaching for three years. Prior to coming to this school, she had limited experience in working with children. She is anticipating marriage within the year and is looking forward to starting her own family. Initially, she attempted to try and implement what she learned in her teacher preparation program, and the veteran teachers often viewed her as naive and idealistic as she sought to fulfill her vision of what teaching should be like. She has been teaming with another veteran teacher at her grade level and has built on what she learned in the university; as a result, she has modified some of her expectations about teaching. Mostly, she has learned skills and strategies with the help of her mentor that have helped her survive as a teacher. She knows she will be successful as a teacher and has begun to focus more on her students and less on her own survival. She is even thinking about going back to school and getting her master's degree but will wait and see what demands marriage and family place on her.

During her first couple of years at this campus, Miss Moore felt that her first principal was easygoing and that the school was run by the parents. This teacher's inexperience and lack of direction from the principal caused some tentative moments in the first two years, and she questioned her decision to become a teacher. With the help of her mentor and the arrival of a new principal at the school last year, this young teacher is now convinced that teaching is for her. Parents, teachers, and students have come together and created a really exciting learning environment. Miss Moore is looking forward to next year and the possibilities for professional growth as well as her own personal growth.

Teacher Profile: Ann Marie Rayfield

Mrs. Rayfield has been teaching for 15 years and is nearing the midpoint of her career. She was married for 9 years, 7 of which were during the first years of her teaching career. Following a difficult divorce from another teacher in the district, she relocated to her present school and position. She remained single until last year when she married a counselor at her school. Presently, her personal and professional interests center on her school, but she is looking forward to having a family and became pregnant during the past school year. The baby is due over the summer, and she looks forward to spending some time with the new baby and then returning to school. She served as a mentor teacher this past school year.

In the last couple of years, Mrs. Rayfield has achieved her vision of her teaching self and feels confident about her ability as a teacher and educator. Her principal has consulted her on numerous issues this year; with this professional acknowledgment, she feels empowered. She likes working as a mentor teacher and is considering other positions within the school district that will draw upon her experience and expertise. She is regularly complimented by her principal and other teachers on her insights and her ability to suggest new programs that produce learning results. The expertise she has gained in her teaching duties is also evident in her work in the larger community where she has served on several committees. She has been approached by a sales representative from a book company and asked to work for them and is faced with the dilemma of deciding

(continued)

FIGURE 11.2

what she wants to do with the rest of her professional career while also experiencing motherhood for the first time. One of her concerns is that the teacher salary schedule works against her. In her district and the state in general, veteran teachers top out within 20 years; unless things change, her potential income will be limited. She has such mixed feelings because she truly enjoys what she does, but she is afraid that if she remains in the classroom, she may become bitter over her stagnant salary and her potential to grow professionally.

Teacher Profile: Cal Green

Mr. Green has been teaching for 25 years and filters information based on this experience. He has a strong perception that educational issues and innovations recycle. He has often said, "There is nothing new in education; we just rename the old." He has a strong dislike of change, not only at school but in his personal life as well. When he came to this community from an urban teaching assignment, he wanted the largest and most urban-like school setting because that was what he was used to. One of the factors that frustrates Mr. Green is that he has more years of experience in education than his principal does; in those years, he has seen six principals come and go. As Mr. Green says, "Some were good; most were mediocre or bad." For him to grow professionally, Mr. Green has to see the activity as meaningful. He has a strong sense of self but still seeks recognition for his performance as a teacher.

Mr. Green uses his own standards to judge his performance and has little value for the checklist mentality of the current teacher assessment system the district uses. "Frankly," he says, "the current system is an insult to most experienced teachers. It might serve a purpose to help beginning teachers in their first year or two, but beyond that it is worthless and demeaning." There have been times when Mr. Green regrets not having taken advantages of opportunities to move on to other positions in the district or even in the community. Sometimes, because of his maximum salary and the years of experience, he feels trapped. This is when he becomes the most discouraged and has to work hard to "psych himself up." Mr. Green seldom seeks connections through collegial relationships. He spends most of his free time with his family. He has parents nearby whom he must tend to, and he has adult children and teenage children who also occupy much of his out-of-school time.

New knowledge is…filtered through well-informed cognitive structures, with the result that dissonant information is often excluded or discredited" (p. 703).

In spite of the importance of continued professional development, on the average, teachers in the United States participate in approximately three to five staff development activities each year; only rarely are these sessions scheduled for more than one day at a time (Joyce and Showers, 1983; Showers, Joyce, and Bennett, 1987; Shroyer, 1990). Duke (1993) reports that schools need to examine practices that create barriers to professional growth and points out "that teachers, like other human beings, vary in their motivation and capacity to grow…depending on life circumstances, personal health, and work-related commitments. Policies that mandate that all teachers must grow according to a fixed schedule and in similar ways are mindless" (p. 711).

Successful Staff Development Programs: What Research Says

It is a difficult if not impossible task to keep up with the growing body of research on staff development. Within this vast array of information, studies often tend to present conflicting views, leaving readers without a clear picture of what to do. With new views and models being implemented, a quiet revolution has been taking place that promises to transform teacher professional development into an era of reform (Darling-Hammond, 1996; Darling-Hammond and McLaughlin, 1995). These changes in professional development involve new forms of teacher preparation, new institutional arrangements, new structures and opportunities for growth outside schools (including extra-school learning communities), and policies that support growth within schools. These new structures are "networks [that] engage people in collective work on authentic problems [which] brings them face to face with other people and possibilities" (Darling-Hammond and McLaughlin, 1995, p. 599). As teachers become part of professional development schools, accelerated schools, and other new structures, they find themselves in an environment and a climate of personal and professional growth.

Joyce and Showers (1980) have made significant contributions to the knowledge base of staff development; early on, they identified three messages from research that continue to guide and improve staff development programs. These messages are:

1. Teachers are good learners.
2. Certain conditions are needed in order for teachers to learn.
3. Research continues to reveal what these conditions are.

The first message for organizers of staff development programs is a hopeful one, but it is essential that the conditions are conducive for learning. Conditions that seem to maximize teacher learning include the involvement of teachers in planning the program and basing the program on the interests, background, developmental level, and degree of preparation of teachers. Other conditions related to the effectiveness of staff development come from the research literature.

Over a decade ago, McCleary (1984) stated that staff development activities should take place at individual school campuses. In 1993, she and her team repeated these reasons for campus-specific staff development programs. Sparks and Hirsh (1997), in their book *A New Vision for Staff Development*, cite specific campus- and district-based models and programs that have proved successful. These case-based examples serve to reinforce the notion that staff development should help meet the diverse needs of specific school campuses. School-based programs will be more meaningful and useful to the faculty and staff when the case-based strategies are practiced and implemented at the classroom and school levels.

Borrowing from staff development research in mathematics and science, the following principles have been shown to be successful. These seven principles suggest that effective staff development programs:

1. Are driven by a clear understanding of practices that promote effective teaching and learning

2. Give teachers the chance to expand their knowledge and skills, which broaden their teaching repertoire

3. Use instructional strategies that are consistent with adult learning and, when possible, mirror the methods to be learned by students

4. Enhance the idea of the school as a community of learners that fosters collegiality and collaborative endeavors between and among teachers

5. Foster the development of teacher leaders beyond their classrooms

6. Link activities to other components of the educational community by combining them with other school initiatives, aligning them with the curriculum and assessment standards, and supporting them not only within the school but in the district and community as well

7. Conduct continuous assessment to ascertain the degree of satisfaction and commitment, the impact on teacher–student achievement, and the overall school community (Loucks-Horsley, Stiles, and Hewson, 1996)

As supervisors, teachers, and staff members plan staff development programs, these principles can serve to guide these activities. In the View from the Field section that follows, a description of a staff development process that incorporates many of these principles, which has been used in the Anchorage Schools, is presented.

A View from the Field
The Staff Development Process
Bobbette M. Morgan

As I worked with teachers in the Anchorage, Alaska, schools, bringing in "experts" for the transmission of skills and knowledge to teachers was a comfortable model but largely ineffective. When viewed by teachers, the "expert" would blow in, blow off, and blow out. Some people would listen; some didn't. I have also been that "expert" on many occasions, and no matter how positive the evaluations were at the end of the day or week, I found the role to be very unsatisfactory. I have never had any follow-up or feedback about the implementation of the ideas presented. In many cases, the supervisors or administrators in the district did not even attend the session(s). I have always wondered, "How can they support teachers in implementing instructional improvement if they are not a part of the process themselves?"

In reflecting on my own experience and becoming more aware of what research says, it seems that an effective staff development program should provide opportunities to learn for all employees within the school district, not just teachers. Anyone and everyone who comes in contact with students is part of creating the school climate. The program should also be designed to address the district's goals, mission statement, and/or motto or slogan. Such statements as "Helping every child achieve," "All children can learn," and "Achieving success one student at a time" provide a focus for action. Staff development should be positive and rewarding; it should help people move toward self-improvement while building on the talents of all employees of the school. Staff development in the district should have a clearly defined long-term plan, which recognizes that change does not occur quickly. Unfortunately, all too often development efforts are fragmented or piecemeal and intended to be a quick fix to an immediate problem. The idea that staff development is to "fix" a teacher having problems puts the entire program in a negative light.

For staff development to effect long-term change, teachers have to be actively involved in planning the activities and in learning about instructional strategies and processes. Every school faculty has dedicated, enthusiastic staff members who welcome the opportunity to attend a workshop and bring back new information. Support for these people is crucial, and sending them in pairs or in groups of three or four provides for the creation of a district training team. The ideas they gain form the basis for staff development and will be shared with their faculty at a later date. The instructional team is less threatening to individuals and creates a stronger model for working with their peers. Staff development should not only provide time for teachers to plan and organize an event but also provide them with skills and techniques on how to work with adult learners.

School-focused, school-defined, and teacher-designed plans for staff development that are based on needs assessments of the faculty are much more likely to produce training topics of interest and concern to teachers than those identified and conducted by those in the central office. In Anchorage, we found that teachers know what they need and want and should be given a say in staff development activities.

We also developed needs assessments that were designed to identify training topics tied to campus improvement efforts, focusing on students' needs and student learning. The training opportunities we developed centered on meeting the needs of teachers as they attempted to meet the learning needs of students. Needs assessment was to be done very informally through suggestions from various campus groups as well as more formal structures, such as districtwide questionnaires. Here are two examples of needs assessment instruments that can be used to solicit input from teachers concerning staff development:

Staff Needs Assessment for Planning Staff Development

Example 1: Open-Ended Response

In terms of staff development, please complete the following:

1. What do we do well as a faculty? a school?
2. What do we do at our school or in our grade levels/subject areas that is satisfactory but that needs improvement?
3. What are we doing now as a faculty or school that really ought to stop?
4. What are we not doing that we really should do?
5. What specific topics would you like to see addressed during next year's staff development sessions that would help us achieve our goals?

Planning Staff Development Sessions

Example 2: Forced Response

Next year, we will have the opportunity to plan five staff development days. Topics must relate to campus and department needs. This survey is designed to obtain your input on how to best use those days. Your input is important to the decision-making process as we plan for staff development sessions.

The following traits represent seven broad characteristics research has found to be present in effective schools. Circle the number that best describes your view as to the degree the characteristic is present in our school today.

	Obviously Present		To Some Degree		Not Present
1. *Commonly Held Academic Expectations:* There are high teacher expectations, staff agreements regarding achievement standards, homework expectations, and a system for monitoring each individual's progress.	1	2	3	4	5
2. *Commonly Accepted Student Discipline Standards:* Student behavior expectations are consistent schoolwide; students understand the reasons for the existing rules.	1	2	3	4	5
3. *Commonly Understood Sense of Purpose, Direction, and Community:* Parents, staff, and students have a sense of pride or spirit and an understanding of the purpose of schooling in the building; peer pressure is present for adherence to agreed-upon values and norms; there is high parent involvement and cooperation; teachers feel a sense of efficacy (I can do it!).	1	2	3	4	5

	Obviously Present		To Some Degree		Not Present
4. *Cooperative and Productive Classroom Climate:* The climate is businesslike but caring, with high academic engaged time and appropriate pacing; teachers use a variety of instructional methods.	1	2	3	4	5
5. *School Climate Fostering Student Involvement, Recognition, and Caring:* There is a consistent and daily high ratio of praise to punishment in the classrooms, public display of student work, student perception that teachers care about them personally, and opportunities for students to accept responsibility.	1	2	3	4	5
6. *Teacher Interaction, Involvement, and Sense of Community:* Teachers plan cooperatively, exchange ideas and successful strategies, and seek understanding of common expectations in items 1, 2, and 3.	1	2	3	4	5
7. *Effective, Strong, Involved Administrative Leadership:* Administration fosters the conditions that will bring about the previous six characteristics, provides direction, builds commitment, and is involved (and involves staff) in decisions.	1	2	3	4	5

Training schedules are no longer confined to just staff development. We found in Anchorage that there were many options for teachers; for example, university classes can be scheduled at the school. The schedule can be arranged so that part of the time comes from the end of the workday after students leave and part of the time comes from teachers staying longer (their contribution). We also used another strategy, which was to bring in a small group of substitute teachers at the same time. The substitutes went into classes for an hour and a half; then the teachers could do joint planning for thematic units, observe other teachers using new strategies, attend a staff development session, or work together to design an upcoming staff development session. The teachers then returned to their classes, and the substitutes were used to free up another set of teachers.

Topics for staff development were also the focus of instructional team meetings. These could occur daily for 15 minutes as reports were made concerning progress or problems. Such activities need to be monitored and be part of the minutes kept to demonstrate progress by the team. Staff development such as this was job-embedded, not just training either away from the job or on days when students have the day off.

Professional Growth: Using Models from Other Organizations

While not necessarily presented as a staff development model per se, some of the most widely recognized approaches for people development have been influenced by Deming (1981) and proposed by Blanchard and Johnson (1982) and Blanchard (1989). These models not only provide a framework for fostering development but also suggest the need to work collaboratively in seeking ways of enhancing performance. Blanchard and Johnson (1982) note that professional growth and development begins with cooperative goal setting. Blanchard (1989) recommends a collaborative, coaching approach; Deming (1981) and Bronstingl (1992) affirm that cooperation rather than competition is at the heart of the staff development process.

The One Minute Manager Approach. In the early 1980s, Blanchard and Johnson (1982) suggested in their book, *The One Minute Manager,* a model of staff development that they call a way of training "winners." They state that if organizations don't want to invest in people through staff development activities, then they have only two other choices: one is to hire only "winners," which is expensive and sometimes impossible; the other is to pray. Neither option seems viable, so it is therefore incumbent on organizations, including schools, to put forth the time and effort necessary to provide staff development opportunities that can help people not only be more successful but feel more committed to and responsible for their efforts. Such a model, then, may prove helpful to supervisors as they work with teachers.

The One Minute Manager approach places an emphasis on principles of people development and is designed to get quality results from the people in any organization. Perhaps this emphasis on people is best summarized when Blanchard and Johnson (1982) note that the One Minute Manager's symbol is "a one minute readout from…a digital watch [that] is intended to remind…us to take a minute out of our day to look into the faces of the people we…[supervise and] realize that they are our most important resources" (p. 5).

In applying this view to schools, instructional supervisors must realize that teachers are the schools' greatest resource and, as such, must nurture and support them. The following steps describe how this approach can be used with teachers. The first step in the model is goal setting. In this step, the supervisor and teachers: (a) develop and agree on instructional and professional goals; (b) look at examples that demonstrate or illustrate the desired goals; (c) write out their own personal and professional goals, using less than 250 words; and (d) read and reflect on the goals regularly (weekly).

The second step, designed to encourage people to develop their full potential, is especially important during professional and development activities. This step involves praising people. In implementing this step, the supervisor: (a) communicates with teachers about their successes; (b) gives praise immediately and is specific about what was accomplished; (c) affirms teachers by telling them how good he or she feels about their performance; (d) encourages teachers to continue to do more of the same and communicates support for their success.

In the One Minute Manager approach, the key to developing people is to support teachers as they are successful and then recognizing them for it. Finding the strengths rather than the faults serves to motivate individuals to continue to work toward personal and professional goals.

The One Minute Manager provides an approach that can be a tool for supervisors to use when assisting teachers in developing personal and professional goals that will help them strengthen their classroom performance. Three principles from this model further serve to guide supervisors and instructional leaders in staff development. First, according to Blanchard and Johnson (1982), "everyone is a potential winner. Some people are disguised as losers; don't let their appearances fool you" (p. 71). Second, they say, "people who feel good about themselves produce good results" (p. 19). Finally, the approach emphasizes that the best minute that supervisors can spend is the one they invest in people with whom they work.

The Managing the Journey Approach.   Blanchard (1989) has also developed a program called Managing the Journey, which is collaborative in its orientation. The supervisor coaches and supports teachers as learners along the path toward professional development and improvement. The Managing the Journey program focuses on changing behaviors within a model that provides various types and kinds of information about the implementation of a new technique or program and lends support throughout the entire process. Blanchard (1989) contrasts his program with ones that use the telling and "zap" approaches.

Blanchard (1989) suggests ways to manage new skills, techniques, materials, and equipment. These four approaches are (1) directive, (2) coaching, (3) supporting, and (4) delegating. During the phase when the directive approach is used, the teacher gains new information and knowledge about the topic under study as the supervisor models what is expected and sets the tone and climate for the change to take place. It is a time of "barrel filling" as the supervisor provides input so the teacher can become more familiar with the new concept or procedure. This is followed by a coaching phase in which teachers experience what has been demonstrated or explained; they try the technique with a supervisor, coach, or mentor at their side. As the teacher becomes more comfortable with the technique and has opportunities to talk with colleagues and to ask questions, the supervisor provides support so the teacher does not feel alone. The supervisor is there in case questions come up or if modifications are needed for individual situations. The fourth phase is delegating. It is the time in the learning cycle when teachers, on their own, feel confident about what they are doing and why they are doing it;

they implement or use the strategy independently. Using this approach as a framework for professional development programming helps teachers maintain their focus as they work with supervisors to gain proficiency with the new skill or concept.

The Total Quality Management (TQM) Approach.   The final example, the Total Quality Management approach, illustrates how business has influenced educational practice in the decades of the 1980s and early 1990s. Many school districts have used Total Quality Management (TQM) to revitalize teaching and learning practices. The guiding principles of TQM are found in the work of W. E. Deming (1981). As Brandt (1992) points out, Deming's ideas are not new to instructional leaders because of the emphasis on "cooperation rather than competition, intrinsic rather than extrinsic rewards, and supervision as helping people instead of evaluating them" (p. 3). However, with all the policies and procedures that educators have to adhere to, the Total Quality Movement model presents interesting challenges and opportunities. Achieving quality depends on how well leaders internalize the basic values of TQM (Brandt, 1992).

The TQM movement is based on Deming's work, which, according to Bronstingl (1992), can be understood within four fundamental tenets when applied to schools:

1. Organizations must focus on their consumers.

2. Everyone must be committed to continuous development (personally and collectively) in a mutual agreement.

3. Organizations are systems, and teaching–learning activities within the system are seen as an ongoing process.

4. Success of the TQM model is the responsibility of those involved and who are committed to ensuring that the principles and practices are part of the school culture.

As supervisors and teachers use the TQM model when planning and implementing professional development sessions, they work toward the goal of creating quality schools. Embodied in the TQM movement is the belief that learning is ongoing and requires a commitment to quality first in all endeavors. Supervisors work to model and support these characteristics for teachers during the initial stages of implementation in order to avoid pitfalls. School leaders must pledge continual support to teachers as teachers pledge support to each other. Such a pledge helps all move toward the goal of quality and therefore school improvement (Bronstingl, 1992).

The approaches presented represent a few examples of how leaders in business and education have come together in order to improve the teaching and learning practices in schools across the United States. As each approach has found its way into schools, the principles and tenets serve to inspire the types of sessions that will become part of professional development offerings.

Self-Assessment for Supervisors: Linkages to Professional Growth

Throughout this book, Your Turn activities have been included as a way of providing opportunities for application, involvement, and self-assessment. We have tried to identify personal and professional characteristics as well as leadership practices and procedures that are associated with effective supervisors. Prospective supervisors should now be able to reflect on the kinds of behavior they would like to exhibit. To become truly effective, supervisors need to be in control of their own learning, capitalize on their abilities, and have a keen sense of their own strengths as well as their liabilities and deficiencies. By coupling knowledge of the characteristics of the teachers with whom they work with an understanding of their own strengths and weaknesses, supervisors can be more effective in selecting and conducting staff development activities.

In order for supervisors to be their best, a self-analysis is encouraged. According to Eble (1978), the instructional leader's ability to develop "his or her own self lies in bringing out and using wisely those qualities of personality and character essential to the complex task of bringing out the best in others" (p. 81). With the theoretical foundations and the models and mechanics of practice presented in earlier chapters, introspection now becomes the key to the supervisor's professional development and ultimate effectiveness. Before supervisors confront realistic situations in school settings, introspection provides a way for them to assess their supervisory style, leadership skills, attitudes about the teaching–learning process, and ability to work with a diverse faculty and staff population in schools. As Fullan and Hargreaves (1991) suggest, supervisors need professional development opportunities that expand their understanding of the school culture, increase their valuing of teachers with whom they work, encourage greater cooperation and collegiality, and promote connectedness with the wider community.

As individuals involved in a professional field of human resources management, instructional leaders should have an understanding of their strengths and weaknesses as well as their roles. One way supervisors can gain a greater understanding of their personal and professional traits is through the use of a modified Johari Window, developed by Joseph Luft and Henry Ingram (1955). Their framework serves as a way for supervisors to identify their known traits or characteristics while acknowledging their hidden traits or behaviors. Using this conceptual framework, we have shown in Figure 11.3 the components of the relationship between a supervisor and teachers expressed in known and unknown supervisor behavior traits.

According to Figure 11.3, there are some personal characteristics and professional traits of the supervisor that are known to both the supervisor and the teachers. This part of the window is called the "public or open self." Some traits of a supervisor, however, are known only to the supervisor. This area of the window is call the "hidden or private self" and consists of knowledge of personal assessments the supervisor makes about how he or she relates to others. There are some traits that are known to the teachers but are unknown to the supervisor. This area

	What the teacher knows about the supervisor	What the teacher does not know about the supervisor
What the supervisor knows about himself or herself	Public or open self	Hidden or private self
What the supervisor does not know about himself or herself	Blind self	Undiscovered or unknown self

FIGURE 11.3   **Components of Known and Unknown Supervisor Traits**

of the window is called the "blind self" because the supervisor is not aware of these behaviors and does not receive or understand the feedback from others. Finally, there are traits that are unknown to both the supervisor and teachers. This area of the window is called the "undiscovered or unknown self" because this is the part of the supervisor's personality or behavior that remains unknown. Supervisors can modify the shapes of the different "window panes" by disclosing or withholding information or guarding information. The Johari Window provides a useful mechanism for self-recognition when supervisors reflect on the insights about their behavior, seek out new information, and try to see themselves as others see them. For instance, at a staff development session, a supervisor may overlook useful feedback in the form of questions from teachers about his or her handling of the program. Instead of becoming defensive, a supervisor with an awareness of the Johari Window's "blind" windowpane might be more attuned to information from others so that he or she could assess behaviors and improve professional competence.

One way for supervisors to assess their ability to work with different types of teachers who may be from diverse cultural and ethnic backgrounds is to participate in programs related to gender and ethnicity. One such program, Gender/Ethnic Expectations and Student Achievement (GESA) developed by Grayson and Miller (1993), has as its objective an increase in "the use of non-stereotypical interactions, materials and activities" (mimeographed). The GESA program was developed over 10 years ago in an attempt to help participants deal with students and colleagues in way that reduces the disparity in people-to-people interactions. The program focuses on five areas of disparity: instructional contact, grouping in the organization, classroom management/discipline, enhancing of self-esteem, and evaluation of performance. Each of these areas has a corresponding interaction and curriculum component. The areas of disparity are generic and, according to Grayson and Miller (1993), can be applied to concerns related to: "gender, race, national origin, developmental or physical disability, socioeconomic class, perceived ability, or any of the labels which tend to deal people out or permit them to deal themselves in or out of the educational system" (mimeographed). For supervisors to ensure quality and excellence in their performance and interactions with students, teachers, and parents, they need to examine their beliefs and values regarding the issues of gender, race, and ethnic biases. Once supervisors confront these issues honestly and directly, they will be better at making changes in their actions with others.

Reinhartz and Beach (1993) have developed a Self-Assessment Model for Supervisors (SAMS) similar to the self-assessment model for teachers, which can be used by supervisors and instructional leaders to assess and reflect on their performance, using input and assistance from teachers and other school personnel. This self-assessment system is designed to address the professional development of supervisors. The Self-Assessment Model for Supervisors is shown in Figure 11.4 and illustrates a cyclical nature. As stated in the first chapter, professional growth for supervisors, like teachers, is a life-long reciprocal process. As teachers and supervisors interact in a variety of contexts they engage in two-way growth and development.

According to SAMS, one of the first things that supervisors do to gain insights about themselves is solicit information through diagnostic inventories and feedback from others. These data become the basis for the development of a professional profile, using a portfolio approach. The portfolio becomes the receptacle for various types of data, which include information from colleagues, responses recorded on inventories/instruments over time, and personal journal entries.

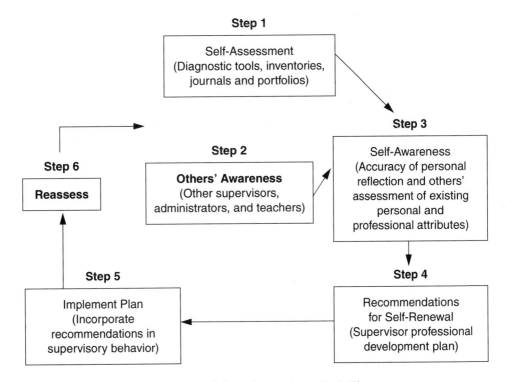

FIGURE 11.4   Self-Assessment Model for Supervisors (SAMS)

Using the data collected, the SAMS approach provides a framework that supervisors use in addressing specific areas of their performance or aspects they may want to target. Journal writing is especially helpful to get supervisors to reflect on specific situations, interactions, and behaviors they experience over time as they perform their job. These entries both provide a record of events and document feelings of the supervisor about specific situations. Such a record is valuable in providing insights.

After the supervisor has had an opportunity to analyze, evaluate, and reflect on what has been collected, he or she begins to sort out and clarify what was done and why and brings these data to a level of consciousness. As supervisors get to know more about themselves using SAMS, they become connoisseurs and self-critics; and they learn to look at their behavior more objectively as they balance the need for individuality with that of diversity. In step 3 of the model, they have to make a professional decision about the accuracy of the information they have received.

Introspection, coupled with the information about specific supervisory roles, responsibilities, and skills, gives direction to supervisors in their quest for excellence. Bruner (1966) has suggested that, in obtaining knowledge, "unless the learner [supervisor] also masters himself [or herself], disciplines his [or her] taste, deepens his [or her] view of the world, the 'something' learned…is hardly worth the effort" (p. 73). In step 4, the supervisor is ready to develop a plan of action based on the feedback and reflection. Professional growth should be viewed from a learning perspective. For supervisors to develop professionally, they need the freedom to determine their own direction and growth, to interact with other supervisors in a cooperative manner, and to discuss new ideas and break the feeling of isolation. In step 5, supervisors begin to implement a plan and, where appropriate, to modify their behavior. They also need time to plan and initiate SAMS so they can consider new ways to grow professionally and personally as they continually reassess (step 6) their progress.

Knowing yourself as a supervisor takes time and effort. According to Daresh (1986), there is a need for supervisors to grow personally and professionally if they are to be successful in their assignments. Professional development for supervisors, as well as teachers, is a lifelong process; supervisors should take a proactive approach as they seek to improve their own performance and behaviors. We believe that self-assessment means that supervisors look at who they are, what they are doing, and why they are doing it in order to be more effective in assisting teachers to improve instruction and to bring about change in the overall quality of schools.

Summary

Professional development, the focus of Chapter 11, serves to enhance the skills and abilities of both supervisors and teachers. It is important to note that continued development is for all, both supervisors and teachers, because of the need for personal and professional growth. Such goals as improved skills and professional commitment are possible to accomplish if supervisors attend to what the research literature says not only about professional development but about adult development and teachers as learners.

The chapter began with a discussion of various definitions and views of staff development. Development activities should (a) include all teachers; (b) be systematic, long term, and oriented toward improving the teaching–learning process; (c) encourage the development of new knowledge and skills that foster continued success; (d) foster the pursuit of personal and professional goals; and (e) help teachers remain current.

The supervisor should consider the six factors that motivate teachers to attend staff development activities: (1) making transitions from preservice to inservice, (2) meeting classroom needs, (3) addressing mandates from the district or state, (4) remaining current, (5) progressing in personal and professional career goals, and (6) meeting personal needs. It is essential to explain and state the purposes of staff development activities so that teachers experience programs that are truly meaningful and that help them realize their potential.

To be considered a success, sessions should be designed with adult learners (teachers) in mind and recognize the developmental characteristics of teachers. Supervisors also plan staff development activities that are research-based so that teachers can cognitively process the information, have opportunities for active involvement, and have follow-up sessions with feedback. Examples of professional development from organizations in the corporate community were described. Various aspects of these models are being adopted and used in schools. These approaches include: the One Minute Manager, Managing the Journey, and Total Quality Management (TQM). Each approach was described, along with its applicability to education. The supervisor builds cooperative structures between and among teachers and colleagues as well as establishes collaborative settings in which staff development can be developed. Finally each supervisor needs to take a look at who he or she is and what his or her role is in helping teachers to grow professionally. The Self-Assessment for Supervisors (SAMS) model provides a strategy for helping supervisors self-analyze as a way of developing their full potential.

YOUR TURN

11.1. As a part of the introspection phase of knowing yourself, keep a journal and record interactions with other teachers and administrators. After a week or two, review your entries:

   a. What do you think is your dominant leadership style?

   b. What did you learn about yourself that you did not know before?

   c. What changes, if any, will you make in your supervisory behavior?

   Refer to in the self-assessment model journal writing in Chapter 6 as a way to start.

11.2. There is a video of Blanchard's Managing the Journey model. If possible, try to obtain a copy and listen to what he has to say about assisting people in making changes in their professional lives. In your journal, record your feelings as Blanchard describes the four-step approach he advocates. Compare his approach with that in *The One Minute Manager*. What are the similarities and the differences? How can you use them when planning and implementing professional development programs?

11.3. After reviewing Deming's 14 points of Total Quality Management below, develop a professional development action plan for yourself (or your district).

1. Create a constancy of purpose based on customer need.
2. Adopt the new philosophy.
3. Cease dependence on mass inspection.
4. Cease bottom-line management.
5. Improve constantly and forever the system and its processes.
6. Institute training.
7. Institute leadership.
8. Drive out fear.
9. Break down barriers.
10. Eliminate slang and exhortations.
11. Eliminate quotas and standards for the purpose of measuring people.
12. Remove barriers to pride of workmanship.
13. Institute a program of education and self-improvement.
14. Have everyone work together to accomplish the transformation.

11.4. Reflect on the following question that focuses on how you, as a supervisor/coach/mentor, will contribute to the growth of teachers in the two scenarios given: What steps would you take if a teacher came to you with the following situations?

a. A teacher meets you in the hall and appears upset. She tells you that one of her classes is so frustrating. The students in this particular class have such a wide range of abilities. What do you say? Where does the teacher go from here?

b. A teacher barges into your room. The teacher informs you that his kids are a bunch of unruly students who do not have any regard or respect for authority. The class is a zoo, and he says he is not going to put up with it anymore. He is interested in your ideas of what can be done in the short and long term. Where does the discussion begin?

11.5. You have been asked by the superintendent to prepare a white-paper report on the status and needs of staff development in your district. As you plan for your assignment, especially identify how you would obtain input from elementary and secondary teachers, those at the central office staff, and members of professional organizations regarding the perceptions among these various individuals and groups of the status and needs of staff development in the district. Draft a needs assignment and share with colleagues to get input.

REFERENCES

Andrews, T. E. (1981). Improving adult learning programs. In *Adult learners: A research study.* T. E. Andrews, W. R. Houston, & B. L. Bryany (eds.). Washington, DC: Association of Teacher Educators.

Apps, J. W. (1981). *The adult learner on campus.* Chicago: Follett.

Bey, T. M., (1992). Mentoring in teacher education: Diversifying support for teachers. In *Mentoring: Contemporary principles and issues.* T. M. Bey & C. T. Holmes (eds.). Reston, VA: Association of Teacher Educators.

Bents, R. H., & Howey, K. R. (1981). Staff development = change in individual. In *Staff development/organization development.* B. Dillon-Peterson (ed.). Alexandria, VA: Association for Supervision and Curriculum Development.

Blanchard, K. (1989). *Managing the journey.* Escondido, CA: Blanchard Training and Development.

Blanchard, K., & Johnson, S. (1982). *The one minute manager.* New York: William Morrow.

Brandt, R. (1992). Overview. Are we committed to quality. *Educational Leadership, 50,* 3.

Bronstingl, J. J. (1992). The quality revolution in education. *Educational Leadership, 50,* 4–9.

Bruner, J. (1966). *Toward a theory of instruction.* New York: Norton.

Butler, J. (1989). A review of adult learning theory and staff development research. Washington, DC: Office of Education Research and Improvement, ED 308 334.

Caldwell, S. D. (1988). School-based improvement. *Educational Leadership, 46,* 50–53.

Christensen, J. C. (1985). Adult learning and teacher career stage development. In *Career long teacher education.* P. J. Burke & R. G. Heideman (eds.). Springfield, IL: C. C. Thomas.

Clinchy, B. M. (1995). Goals 200: The student as object. *Phi Delta Kappan, 76,* 389–392.

Corrigan, D. (1990 March). Collaborative development of integrated services for children and families. Resource paper presented to the National Symposium on Integrated Services for Children and Families, Alexandria, VA.

Daresh, J. C. (1986 October). Principals' perceptions of the quality of alternative administrative inservice models. Paper presented at the annual meeting of the Mid-Western Educational Research Association. Chicago, IL. [Mimeograph.]

Darling-Hammond, L. (1994 February). Standards for teachers. Thirty-fourth Charles W. Hunt Memorial Lecture presented at the meeting of the American Association for Colleges of Teacher Education, Chicago, IL.

Darling-Hammond, L. (1996). The quiet revolution: Rethinking teacher development. *Educational Leadership, 53,* 70–76.

Darling-Hammond, L., & Goodwin, A. L. (1993). Progress toward professionalism in teaching. In *Challenges and achievements of American education.* G. Cawelti (ed.). Alexandria, VA: Association for Supervision and Curriculum Development.

Darling-Hammond, L., & McLaughlin, M. W. (1995). Policies that support professional development in an era of reform. *Phi Delta Kappan, 76,* 597–604.

David, J. L. (1995/1996). The who, what, and why of site-based management. *Educational Leadership, 53,* 4–9.

Deming, W. E. (1981). *Out of crisis.* Boston: MIT Press.

Dillon-Peterson, B. (1980). Conducting a workshop program/staff improvement. In *Staff development and educational change.* W. R. Houston & R. Pankratz (eds.). Reston, VA: Association of Teacher Educators.

Dillon-Peterson, B. (ed.). (1981). *Staff development/organization development.* Alexandria, VA: Association for Supervision and Curriculum Development.

Duke, D. L., (1990). Setting goals for professional development. *Educational Leadership, 47,* 71–75.

Duke, D. L. (1993). Removing barriers to professional growth. *Phi Delta Kappan, 74,* 702–712.

Eble, K. (1978). *The art of administration.* San Francisco: Jossey-Bass Publishers.

Edefelt, R. A. (1979). Inservice teacher education: A concept, an overview. In *Inservice.* Syracuse, NY: National Council of States on Inservice Education.

Edefelt, R. A., & Johnson, M. (eds.). (1975). *Rethinking in-service education*. Washington, DC: National Education Association.

Erikson, E. H. (ed.). (1978). *Adulthood*. New York: Norton.

Erikson, E. H. (1980). *Identity and the life cycle*. New York: Norton.

Erikson, E. H. (1982). *The life cycle completed: A review*. New York: Norton.

Fullan, M. G. (1995). The limits and the potential of professional development. In *Professional development in education: New paradigms and practices*. T. R. Guskey & M. Huberman (eds.). New York: Teachers College Press.

Fullan, M. G., & Hargreaves, A. (1991). *What's worth fighting for in your school*. Toronto: Ontario Public School Teachers Federation.

Fuller, F. F. (1969). Concerns of teachers: A developmental conceptualization. *American Educational Research Journal, 6*, 207–226.

Fuller, F. F., & Brown, O. H. (1975). Becoming a teacher. In *Teacher Education*. Seventy-fourth yearbook of the National Society for the Study of Education. Part 2. Chicago: University of Chicago Press.

Glasser, W. (1990). *The quality school: Managing students without coercion*. New York: Harper & Row.

Glickman, C. (1981). *Developmental supervision: Alternative practices for helping teachers improve instruction*. Alexandria, VA: Association for Supervision and Curriculum Development.

Glickman, C. (1985). *Supervision of instruction: A developmental approach*. Boston: Allyn & Bacon.

Glickman, C., Gordon, S., & Ross-Gordon, J. (1995). *Supervision of instruction: A developmental approach*. (3rd ed.). Boston: Allyn & Bacon.

Glickman, C., Gordon, S., & Ross-Gordon, J. (1998). *Supervision of instruction: A developmental approach*. (4th ed.). Boston: Allyn & Bacon.

Goodwin, A. L. (1987). Vocational choices and the realities of teaching. In *Teacher renewal*. F. S. Bolin & J. M. Falk (eds.). New York: Teachers College Press.

Gould, R. L. (1978). *Transformations: Growth and change in adult life*. New York: Simon & Schuster.

Gould, R. L. (1980). Transformations during early and middle years. In *Themes of work and love in adulthood*. N. Smelser & E. H. Erikson (eds.). Cambridge, MA: Harvard University Press.

Grayson, D. A., & Miller, P. (1993). Gender/ethnic expectations and student achievement. Presentation at the annual Eisenhower Conference. Austin, TX. [Mimeograph.].

Griffin, G. A. (1983). *Staff development*. 83rd yearbook of the National Society for the Study of Education. Chicago: University of Chicago Press.

Griffin, G. A. (1987). The school in society and social organization of the school: Implications for staff development. In *Staff development for school improvement*. M. F. Wideen & I. Andrews (eds.). New York: Falmer.

Guskey, T. R. (1995). Professional development in education: In search of the optimal mix. In *Professional development in education*. T. R. Guskey & M. Huberman (eds.). New York: Teachers College Press.

Guy, M. (1993 January 28). Will teacher preparation play a major role in the reauthorization of elementary/secondary programs? In *Teacher Education Reports, 15*, 1–3.

Hammond, J., & Foster, K. (1987). Creating a professional learning partnership. *Educational Leadership, 44*, 42–44.

Hargreaves, A. (1995). Development and desire: A postmodern perspective. In *Professional development in education*. T. R. Guskey & M. Huberman (eds.). New York: Teachers College Press.

Harvey, O., Hunt, D., & Schroder, H. M. (1961). *Conceptual systems and personality organization*. New York: Wiley.

Hatano, G. (1993). Time to merge Vygotskian and constructivist conceptions of knowledge acquisition. In *Contexts for learning*. E. Forman, N. Minick, & C. Stone (eds.). New York: Oxford University Press.

Havighurst, R. J. (1972). *Developmental tasks and education*. (3rd ed.). New York: McKay.

Havighurst, R. J. (1980). More thoughts on developmental tasks. *Personnel and Guidance Journal, 58*, 330–335.

Herman, J. J., & Herman, J. L. (1992). Business officials and school-based management. *School Business Affairs, 57,* 34–37.

Howe, A. C., & Stubbs, H. S. (1996). Empowering science teachers: A model for professional development. *Journal of Science Teacher Education, 8,* 167–182.

Howey, K. R. (1977). Organization for inservice teacher education. In *Inservice.* Syracuse, NY: National Council of States on Inservice Education.

Huberman, M. (1995). Professional careers and professional development: Some intersections. In *Professional development in education.* T. R. Guskey & M. Huberman, (eds.). New York: Teachers College Press.

Johnson, D. W., Johnson, R. T., & Holubec, E. J. (1994a). *Cooperative learning in the classroom.* Alexandria, VA: Association for Supervision and Curriculum Development.

Johnson, D. W., Johnson, R. T., & Holubec, E. J. (1994b). *The new circles of learning: Cooperation in the school.* Alexandria, VA: Association for Supervision and Curriculum Development.

Joyce, B. (1990). *Changing school culture through staff development.* Reston, VA: Association for Supervision and Curriculum Development.

Joyce, B., & Showers, B. (1980). Improving inservice training. The message from research. *Educational Leadership, 37,* 379–385.

Joyce, B., & Showers, B. (1983). *Power in staff development through research on training.* Alexandria, VA: Association for Supervision and Curriculum Development.

Joyce, B., & Showers, B. (1988). *Student achievement through staff development.* New York: Longman.

Joyce, B., Murphy, C., Showers, B., & Murphy, B. (1989). Restructuring the workplace: School renewal as cultural change. Paper presented at the annual meeting of the American Educational Research Association, San Francisco, CA.

Knowles, M. (1978). *The adult learner: A neglected species.* (2nd ed.). Houston: Gulf.

Knowles, M. (1980). *The modern practice of adult education: From pedagogy to andragogy.* (2nd ed.). Chicago: Association/Follett.

Knowles, M. (1984). *Andragogy in action: Applying modern principles of adult learning.* San Francisco: Jossey-Bass Publishers.

Kyle, W. C., Jr. (1995 September). Professional development: The growth and learning of teachers as professionals over time. *Journal of Research in Science Teaching, 32,* 679–681.

Landon, G. L., & Shirir, W. (1986). A practical approach to school improvement. *Educational Leadership, 44,* 73–75.

Levine, S. L. (1987). Understanding life cycle issues: A resource for school leaders. *Journal of Education, 169,* 7–19.

Levine, S. L. (1989). *Promoting adult growth in schools: The promise of professional development.* Boston: Allyn & Bacon.

Levinson, D. (1978). *The seasons of a man's life.* New York: Ballantine.

Levinson, D. (1980). Conceptions of the adult life course. In *Themes of work and love in adulthood.* N. Smelser & E. H. Erikson (eds.). Cambridge, MA: Harvard University Press.

Levinson, D. (1990). A theory of life structure in adulthood. In *Higher stages of human development: Perspectives on adult growth.* C. N. Alexander and E. J. Langer (eds.). New York: Oxford University Press.

Lindeman, E. C. (1926). *The meaning of adult education.* New York: New Republic.

Little, J. W. (1981). *School success and staff development: The role of staff development in urban desegregated schools.* Boulder, CO: Center for Action Research.

Little, J. W. (1990). The persistence of privacy: Autonomy and initiative in teachers' professional relations. *Teacher College Record, 91,* 509–536.

Little, J. W. (1993 Summer). Teachers' professional development in a climate of educational reform. *Educational Evaluation and Policy Analysis, 15,* 129–151.

Loevinger, J. (1976). *Ego development: Conceptions and theories.* San Francisco: Jossey Bass Publishers.

Loucks-Horsley, S., Stiles, K., & Hewson, P. (1996 May). Principles of effective professional development for mathematics and science education: A synthesis of standards. *NISE Brief, 1,* 1–7.

Luft, J., & Ingram, H. (1955). The Johari window: A graphic model of interpersonal awareness. Proceedings of the Western Training Laboratory in Group Development. University of California, Los Angeles Extension Office.

Marczely, B. (1996). *Personalizing professional growth: Staff development that works.* Thousand Oaks, CA: Corwin Press.

McCleary, L. E. (1984). Staffing and staff development. In *Educational administration today.* D. Orlosky (ed.). Columbus, OH: Merrill Publishers.

McCleary, L. E., Baker, D. R., Martin, M., & McDonald, M. (1993). Staff development. In *Principals for our changing schools.* Scott D. Thomson (ed.). Fairfax, VA: National Policy Board for Educational Administration.

Mentoring Texas: Texas Teacher Preparation Study. (1995 May). Interim report. Austin, TX: Policy Research—Teacher Retention, Mobility and Attrition.

Miles, M. B. (1995). Foreword. In *Professional development in education: New paradigms and practices.* T. R. Guskey & M. Huberman (eds.). New York: Teachers College Press.

Odell, S. J. (1992). Evaluating mentoring programs. In *Mentoring: Contemporary principles and issues.* T. M. Bey & C. T. Holmes (eds.). Reston, VA: Association of Teacher Educators.

Orlich, D. C. (1984). Inservice education: A problem or a solution? *Science and Children, 21,* 33–35.

Pink, W. (1989). Effective development of rural school improvement. Paper presented at the annual meeting of the American Educational Research Association, San Francisco, CA.

Reinhartz, J. (1989). The teacher induction process: Preserving the old and welcoming the new. *Teacher induction.* Washington, DC: National Education Association.

Reinhartz, J. (1993). Site-based decision-making: Deregulation school style. In *Integration or a fragmentation of site-based decision-making.* L. Avila (ed.). 1993 yearbook. The Texas Association for Supervision and Curriculum Development. Austin: Texas Association for Supervision and Curriculum Development.

Reinhartz, J., & Beach, D. M. (1993 Fall/Winter). A self-assessment model for supervisors: Increasing supervisor effectiveness. *Record in Educational Administration and Supervision 14,* 35–40.

Reinhartz, J., Hadaway, N., & Trask, J. A. (1992). Teacher preparation programs and educational change. *Contemporary Education, 63,* 294–297.

Santmire, T. E. (1979). Developmental differences in adult learners: Implications for staff development. Lincoln: University of Nebraska. [Mineograph.]

Schlechy, P., & Vance, V. (1983). Recruitment, selection, and retention: The shape of the teaching force. *Elementary School Journal, 83,* 469–487.

Sergiovanni, T. J., & Starratt, R. J. (1983). *Supervision: Human perspectives.* (3rd ed.). New York: McGraw-Hill.

Sergiovanni, T. J., & Starratt, R. J. (1993). *Supervision: A redefinition.* (5th ed.). New York: McGraw-Hill.

Sheerlin, J. (1991). How instructional leaders view staff development. *NASSP Bulletin, 75,* 8–14.

Showers, B. (1990 May/June). Aiming for superior classroom instruction for all children: A comprehensive staff development model. *RASE (Remedial and Special Education), 11,* 35–39.

Showers, B., Joyce, B., & Bennett, B. (1987). Synthesis of research on staff development: A framework for future study and a state-of-the-art analysis. *Educational Leadership, 45,* 77–87.

Shroyer, G. M. (1990). Effective staff development for effective organization development. *Journal of Staff Development, 11,* 2–6.

Smylie, M. A. (1995). Teacher learning in the workplace: Implications for school reform. In *Professional development in education: New paradigms & practices.* T. R. Guskey & M. Huberman (eds.). New York: Teachers College Press.

Smylie, M. A., & Conyers, G. (1991). Changing conceptions of teaching influence the future of staff development. *Journal of Staff Development, 12,* 12–16.

Sonnier, I. (1990). *Affective education: Methods and techniques.* Englewood Cliffs, NJ: Educational Technology Publications.

Southerland, A. R., & Hardin, D. T. (1992 Summer). Wanted: A new level of precision for staff development in education. *Contemporary Education, 63,* 270–273.

Sparks, G. M. (1983). Synthesis of research on staff development for effective teaching. *Educational Leadership, 41,* 3, 65–72.

Sparks, D., & Hirsh, S. (1997). *A new vision for staff development.* Alexandria, VA: Association for Supervision and Curriculum Development.

Stallings, J. (1989). Effective use of time: In-service workshops to help middle school teachers. The National Dissemination Study Group. *Educational programs that work.* (15th ed.). Longmont, CO: Sopris West Inc.

Tennant, M. (1988). *Psychology and adult learning.* London: Routledge.

Wideen, M. F. (1987). Perspectives on staff development. In *Staff development for school improvement.* M. F. Wideen & I. Andrews (eds.). New York: Falmer Press.

Wiggins, G. (1994 July). None of the above. *The Executive Educator, 16,* 14–18.

Wilsey, C., & Killion, J. (1982). Making staff development programs work. *Educational Leadership, 40,* 36–43.

Yarger, S. J., Howey, K. R., & Joyce, B. R. (1980). *Inservice teacher education.* Palo Alto, CA: Booksend Library.

12 Making Decisions and Facilitating Instructional Change

OBJECTIVES

The objectives of this chapter are:

- Describe the decision-making process.
- Identify the steps in decision making.
- Apply the principles that guide effective decision making.
- Describe the kinds of and reasons for resistance to change.
- Identify and describe the stages in the planned change model.
- Discuss the relationship of change to school culture.
- Describe ways to facilitate change in schools.
- Apply the principles that facilitate the change process.

The ability to make decisions and the capacity to foster change are essential components of the supervision process. As school leaders, supervisors are involved in making decisions on a daily basis, and their ability to make rational, logical choices not only impacts areas of the school program but is essential to the operation of schools (Alfonso, Firth, and Neville, 1981). Likewise, supervisors are charged with initiating and facilitating change while at the same time helping others deal with change. This involves functioning in the present while simultaneously considering courses of action for the future. To achieve balance in approaching change, Osguthorpe and Patterson (1998) suggest that schools "foster a culture of inquiry, receive questions as gifts, experience edification, and blend the champion and critic roles" (p. 63).

As indicated throughout this book, supervision exists for the primary purpose of promoting effective instruction, which results in improved student achievement (learning). The relationship between improved teaching–learning and change was noted by Lovell and Wiles (1983) nearly two decades ago when they stated that "instructional improvement implies change, [and] it is our assumption that the coordination and facilitation of instructional and curricular change are fundamental [to]…supervision" (p. 114).

Decision making is integrally linked with the change process. Without sound decisions, changes that are not productive or in the best interests of the process of school improvement may be initiated. Fullan and Stiegelbauer (1991) observe:

> One of the most fundamental problems in education today is that people do not have a clear, coherent sense of…what educational change is…, and how it proceeds. Thus there is much faddish superficiality, confusion, failure of…programs, unwarranted and misdirected resistance, and misunderstood reform. What is needed is a more coherent picture that people who are involved in or affected by educational change can use to make sense of what they and others are doing. (p. 4)

Supervisors must therefore provide meaning for the changes that are to be implemented in schools, and they must keep student learning as the primary focus. However, the path of change is littered with potholes (Guskey and Peterson, 1995–1996). Rather than relying on "sound bites, simplistic explanation, and exposés," educators and society as well must become more intelligent so that we can reconceive the issues and problems as well as possible solutions (Caine and Caine, 1997, p. 3). We must also reexamine the change process as well.

This chapter will focus first on the decision-making process, the steps involved in making good decisions, and some general principles that can guide decision making. The chapter includes an examination of the change process and accompanying barriers to change as well as stages in a planned change model. The chapter concludes by discussing change and school culture, the facilitation of change, and some principles that guide the change process.

The Decision-Making Process

Many decisions are made directly or indirectly every day in schools about curriculum issues, teaching and learning, and programmatic concerns…"that fundamentally shape the character and direction of…policy" (Huddleston (1996) p. 296). It has been suggested that principals may make as many as 400 decisions in one day (Calebrese and Zepeda, 1997). With so many decisions to make, the process may become routine or haphazard when it should involve careful analysis. Research into the decision-making process of the past reveals that when supervisors muddle through, the results of their decision may not be relevant to the original context that required a decision (Gorton, 1987, p. 4).

This muddling-through type of decision making found in education has been called the garbage can model (Cohen, March, and Olson, 1972; Gorton, 1987). Such a process suggests that unless supervisors are constantly monitoring their decision making, they are candidates for being "dumped on" and are then left with the task of sorting through the "garbage."

To help supervisors avoid the garbage can approach, two models of decision making may prove helpful. The first model, *normative,* sees decision making as a way to logically address issues by following a series of steps, which solves a problem and produces a resolution (Draft, 1986; Schultz and Schultz, 1998). Thus in the normative model, decisions are made according to sound principles of analysis performed in a series of rational steps. The second model, *descriptive,* sees decision making as the product of organizational factors that help to shape what actually occurs; decisions are made in response to circumstances and situations (Gorton, 1987). The second model can often be likened to the garbage can approach and reflects what is done when organizational protocol, instead of analysis and logic, forms the basis for a response. The descriptive model tends to maintain the status quo, and decisions that can lead to change seldom take place. A vision rarely materializes when a descriptive model is used because the focus is on the here and now, not on the future and its possibilities.

Current perspectives on decision making generally favor the normative model over the descriptive model, and definitions tend to emphasize the rational, data-driven, problem-solving dimension of good decision making. However, in the pressure of daily routines and operating procedures, people often take the descriptive approach as they respond to the immediate need to achieve results. It should be noted that supervisors must constantly and consciously follow procedures that help to identify relevant questions, generate pertinent data, and determine which data are relevant to the decision (Crowther and Grashel, 1997). *Decision making,* then, can be defined as a process in which an individual or group considers information within the context of a value system when proposing various solutions to a problem, a concern, or a need. Ideally, choices are made from several alternatives and then implemented (Greenberg and Baron, 1997). For example, when supervisors and teachers are considering an evaluation system for their school district, they would obtain information from the literature and from personal visits to other schools in order to establish parameters for a potential system. Once the information has been analyzed and local needs have been addressed, components of the evaluation system that are compatible with the district and campus goals are selected. As seen in this example, decision making does not occur in a vacuum. It should also be noted that "no decision making techniques, no matter how carefully drawn, can guarantee success" (Huddleston, 1996, p. 297).

Osguthorpe and Patterson (1998) encourage educators to go beyond the traditional view of decision making in order for change and collaborative renewal to occur. They suggest a process called *shared discernment* which involves constantly searching for the right decision which eventually emerges. This approach makes decision making a continuous problem-solving process.

Steps in Decision Making

As supervisors work individually or with groups of teachers to make decisions, they can use an analytic model to improve the quality of the decision-making process. Huddleston (1996) has identified 4 steps that are essential to rational decision making. These include: (1) clarifying and ranking goals, (2) considering all alternatives, (3) weighing the possible outcomes of each alternative, and (4) selecting the alternative that is the best match for the goal. Calebrese and Zepeda (1997), Greenberg and Baron (1997), and Wedley and Field (1984) have expanded this mode of decision making to include 10 steps. It should be noted that not all decisions will necessarily conform to these 10 steps because, in individual situations, steps may be combined or eliminated.

The first step in the model is *identification of the problem*. Proper problem identification is essential if effective decisions are to be made. This is not always easy because people often distort, ignore, or omit information that might have a bearing on problem identification (Cowan, 1986). To correct an identified problem, supervisors must acknowledge the symptoms, causes, and sources. Symptoms frequently involve visible signs such as discord, poor results, and/or chronic behaviors. Causes are the underlying reasons for the problem. For example, in working with teachers who are interested in improving the reading scores of students in the fourth grade, the supervisor will note poor reading scores as the symptom, but an inconsistent reading program may be the cause of the problem. The source becomes the underlying substrata for the cause and symptoms. The source of the poor scores may be the reading program and materials, which will need to be addressed. If shared discernment is applied, the group members find solutions together which is a "compromise or tactics for wooing reluctant members to a particular position" (Osguthorpe and Patterson, 1998, p. 58).

The second step is the *collection of data* that are relevant to the problem. The supervisor must determine what information to gather and when there is enough information to make a decision. The use of computer-generated reports and analyses may prove helpful in this step. For example, in examining the issue of the reading scores, the task for supervisors and teachers is to disaggregate the data to examine subscores, such as comprehension or vocabulary by gender, socioeconomic status, and ethnicity, to determine particular areas of need. The data can suggest possible courses of action for reteaching and opportunities for differentiating instruction by offering all students options to grow as much as possible (Tomlinson, 1999).

The third step involves the *establishment of solution criteria*. These criteria define the parameters of the problem and ways to resolve it. The supervisor and teachers determine the characteristics that would be evident in a viable solution. Supervisor and teachers establish benchmarks or criteria for reading improvement; these benchmarks guide the teachers' behavior and indicate how and when the problem will be resolved.

The fourth step centers on the *generation of possible alternatives,* all of which are considered valid. The supervisor and teachers engage in creative brainstorming to generate a list of possibilities for consideration (Greenberg and Baron, 1997). Relying solely on previously used approaches or ready-made answers is something supervisors should avoid in the brainstorming phase. By generating a great number of solutions, there is a higher probability that participants will make an appropriate decision (Calebrese and Zepeda, 1997). As the supervisor and teachers consider ways to address current reading scores, options may range from making individual adjustments to completely revamping the reading program using both the basal and literature-based approaches. Having variety may help reach more children with different learning styles. As the supervisor and teachers work collaboratively to seek solutions to a problem, it is choosing from a range of possibilities that makes a solution possible. To investigate the effectiveness of different educational reading programs, teachers can conduct action research in their classrooms and generate data which contributes to their knowledge base. Such professional knowledge produced by classroom research provides rich insightful descriptions which guide teachers toward systems of thinking regarding programs under consideration (Kennedy, 1997).

The fifth step that the supervisor and teachers use is *weighing the alternatives against the established criteria* to determine the feasibility of a course of action. Aspects to consider might include financial as well as legal and ethical parameters. It would be impractical to recommend a new reading curriculum K–6 if the school budget would not accommodate such a recommendation. It is equally important to consider the philosophical beliefs of teachers, parents, and administrators when making decisions that go counter to the existing school culture. Having personal beliefs for or against a program and/or approach can pose an ethical dilemma for those making key decisions. As Strike, Haller, and Soltis (1998) note, to act morally and ethically is making a decision requires that supervisors use emotion as well as reason to emphasize and demonstrate caring for others.

The sixth step involves the *selection of the best alternatives* from among the range of choices. The supervisor and teachers sort through the alternatives and eliminate various options if they do not fit the previously established criteria or benchmarks. The goal of this step is to determine which solution is best and why (Greenberg and Baron, 1997). For example, in addressing individual as well as class reading scores, the supervisor and teachers must follow school or state policy and pick those alternatives that have the greatest potential for solving the problem. The seventh step incorporates *consideration of the consequences* with the action or strategies selected. Here the supervisor becomes part of the fourth-grade team to monitor and assess the potential shortcomings and benefits of the action selected. For example, if they decide on a procedure that tracks and segregates the students into separate reading groups and/or programs, then the risk of a potential lawsuit would impact the final decision.

In the eighth step, as the supervisor and teachers arrive at the moment of decision, a *plan of action is selected and implemented.* The supervisor and teachers review the highest-rated alternatives, based on action research data generated, reflect on the context, and then select a course of action that best meets the needs of all students. In this step, as a solution is implemented, planning, involvement, and coordination are important to the process. Huddleston (1996) notes that "Implementation is about follow-through. It involves recognizing that [decisions] unfold in complex and uncertain environments" (p. 319). As the supervisor and teachers work collaboratively, chances for success are increased if the reasons for the decision, along with the expectations for changes, are communicated to parents and students.

The ninth step, the *evaluation of the decisions or solution,* and the tenth step, *modification of the implemented solution,* provide a way to monitor the decision-making process on the basis of outcomes. Consideration should be given to pilot the program to glean any issues that had not been considered. When decisions produce poor results, the consequences should be recorded. If criteria or benchmarks are violated during implementation, the supervisor and teachers may need to rethink the course of action and modify the proposed solution. As Calebrese and Zepeda (1997) note, supervisors and teachers must guard against traps…that are formed because of biases, hidden decision-making styles, and information filters" (p. 103).

As illustrated in this model, decision making is a complex process that (as steps are followed) takes a great deal of time and thought. The foundation of decision making is problem solving, which provides a pathway for achieving greater results. Quality decision-making experiences require problem solving.

Principles to Guide Decision Making

Some general principles guide the decision-making process. These 10 principles, based on the work of Alfonso, Firth, and Neville (1981), Calebrese and Zepeda (1997), and Gorton (1987), are summarized below:

1. Effective decision making requires that judgments be made on the basis of data collected about the school organization and its goals and members; the nature and causes of constraints (time, resources, and data available) should be analyzed and efforts should be made to decrease their impact on the decision-making process.

2. Effective decision making requires risk taking because the outcome of a decision cannot be determined with total accuracy.

3. Decision making requires the thoughtful, careful analysis of issues and the identification of actions to be taken; choices should be made from a range of alternatives, with opportunities for growth and refinement as part of the process.

4. Decision making is more effective when it is encouraged by the organization, when it increases the commitment of individuals to the goals and objectives of the school organization, and when past decisions have produced positive results that were rewarded or reinforced by the organization.

5. An effective supervisor recognizes the political nature of the decision-making process as it relates to the power structure, control, and resources of the school organization.

 6. Group members will be more supportive of decision making when they recognize that decisions are not perfect solutions but merely the best choices from among possible options.

7. Decision making is influenced by the social, political, and historical contexts in which the decision is being made and by the psychological makeup of the individual making the decision.

8. Effective decision making requires limiting personal bias, filters, and prior experience from the situation and establishing an open and objective mind-set; decision makers should not assume more authority than exists.

9. Decision making is enhanced when the school organization encourages and provides an atmosphere of collaboration and problem solving.

10. Decision making will be more effective when there is a continuous process for evaluating decisions that have been made and the procedures for making them.

Gorton (1987) has also observed several personal variables that can influence the actions of the decision maker. The five types of personal attitudes or values that affect the decision maker's choices are: (1) risk orientation, (2) attitude toward people, (3) educational philosophy, (4) concern for status, and (5) concern for authority and control. The kinds of personal thoughts involved in the decision-making process and the values or attitudes that are evident in the thought process can be seen in the following examples. In a risk orientation, the supervisor is willing to take chances in pursuing possible solutions. The supervisor's attitude toward people is reflected in the belief that if a certain individual recommends a course of action, it must be a good decision. The educational philosophy helps to set parameters about practices that are appropriate or inappropriate for the teachers or students. Concern about status requires that the decision allows people to save face or to follow protocol. If the supervisor is concerned with authority and control, then the focus of the process is on who is in charge or who calls the shots.

As these variables suggest, there are personal as well as organizational dimensions to the decision-making process. By utilizing the suggested steps and the 10 principles and guidelines, supervisors can implement the decision-making process in a more rational and organized manner. In addition, systematic inquiry and collaboration with others will increase the likelihood of finding solutions that are more long lasting. This will be beneficial to all who are affected by changes to instructional problems by making good decisions.

The Change Process

Change is part of life for both individuals and organizations. Philosophers have observed that the only thing permanent is change. According to Greenberg and Baron (1997), "Nothing is sacred when it comes to organizational change [even] traditions are not immune" (p. 545). For Alfonso, Firth, and Neville (1981), there is a sense of urgency associated with change; there seems to be "a belief that our survival as a civilized society depends on our willingness to initiate and accept change" (p. 244). On an individual level, Fritz (1996) notes that people seek change rather than simply tolerate it. Wheatley (1993) reinforces the importance of change which results in more adaptive and healthier organizations that have the ability to self-organize as they constantly grow and respond.

Bolman and Deal (1991) have identified environmental pressures that can prompt change: globalization, information technology, deregulation, and demographic shifts. As supervisors team with teachers and others in schools to promote changes that can transform the organization, the multinational and multiethnic nature of students, the use of all forms of technology, the competition for resources through deregulation, and shifts in the populations of school communities are important to keep in mind. Belasco (1990) creates a helpful mental image of the difficulties associated with the change process in the title of his book, *Teaching the Elephant to Dance: Empowering Change in Your Organization.* One can imagine the effort it takes to teach elephants to dance. Supervisors may have to exert effort as they seek to foster change in school cultures.

If change is often difficult to achieve and often resisted, why is there a need for it? What does the change process accomplish? Gorton (1987) provides a description of a rationale for change based on the following four premises:

> (1) Although the status quo is not necessarily bad, there is usually room for improvement; (2) while all change does not necessarily lead to improvement, improvement is not likely to occur without change; (3) unless we attempt change, we are not likely to know whether a proposed innovation is better than the status quo; and (4) participation in the change process can result in greater understanding and appreciation of the desirable features of the status quo and…a better understanding and appreciation of, and skill in, the change process itself. (p. 136)

Whether change is planned, or occurs spontaneously, due to natural circumstances, there are cumulative consequences for the organization. Hanson (1996) has described three types of change. One is planned change, which "is a conscious and deliberate attempt to manage events so that the outcome is redirected by design to some predetermined end" (p. 284). A second is spontaneous change, an alteration that is "the result of natural circumstances and random occurrences" (p. 284). Third, evolutionary change "refers to the long-range, cumulative consequences of major and minor alterations in the organization" (p. 284).

Schools are not immune to these types of changes. The intense changes occurring in most organizations today, including schools, "may be remembered as a historic event, the Western equivalent of the collapse of communism" (Sherman, 1993, p. 123). Knezevich (1984) notes that "the professional behaviors of teachers. …methods of instruction, design of facilities…are very different now from what they were a generation ago, much less a century ago" (p. 102). Beginning as early as the 1800s and continuing into the present, changes—or innovations, as they have sometimes been called—have increasingly found their way into the schools and ultimately into individual classrooms. However, changes often take the form of new subject matter, revised materials, and instructional strategies; organization of pupils by criteria such as age, grade, or ability; and building designs that are functional and practical as well as accommodating to all learners.

In order to understand the change process and its impact on the teaching–learning process, Hanson (1996) has defined change as "the process of altering the behavior, structures, procedures, purposes, or outputs…within an organization" (p. 283). One example of the impact of change on the teaching–learning process is technology, particularly the use of computers in schools. Many schools are creating their own Web pages on the Internet (Monahan and Tomko, 1996), while others use the Internet to connect with scientists, who serve as mentors to high school students and (through E-mail) provide feedback to both students and teachers (O'Neill, Wagner, and Gomez, 1996). As computers become more common in individual classrooms, teachers take advantage of the word processing capabilities and an evaluation system for recording and calculating grades.

The trend of integrating innovations into schools and classrooms will continue, and if the past is any indication, it will be at a much faster rate. Supervisors and teachers have a wide variety of strategies and models to choose from to implement changes to promote instructional excellence (Guskey, 1990). There are many innovations that have attracted the attention of all educators: they include: (a) cooperative learning (Johnson and Johnson, 1987; Johnson, Johnson, and Holubec, 1994a, 1994b; Slavin, 1983, 1991, 1994); (b) effective and high-performance schools model (Brookover et al., 1987; Mohrman, Wohlstetter, and associates, 1994); (c) learning styles, including learning modalities (de Bono, 1983; Carbo, Dunn, and Dunn, 1986; Dunn and Dunn, 1993, 1996; Thomson and Mascazine, 1997); (d) standards-based curriculum (National Center for History in the Schools, 1994; National Council of Teachers of Mathematics, 1995; National Research Council, 1994; National Council of Teachers of English, 1996). Individuals who function in their capacity as instructional supervisor will be called upon to help manage or facilitate the implementation of the changes or innovations.

Resistance to Change

Whenever change is mentioned, a frequent and natural response is one of resistance. As Osguthorpe and Patterson (1998) note, "Whenever people perceive the need for change in something that is important to them, tension will occur"

(p. 106). Supervisors, teachers, and students can become so conditioned to the routine of school that they come to love the security of the status quo; the lack of tension or conflict that such conditions produce makes change a difficult task. The statements below are typical of the kinds of reactions that supervisors may receive when they mention change:

- "Everything is going all right, so why change?"
- "People aren't ready for change."
- "We've never done it that way before in this school."
- "That's too radical for us."
- "It's too complicated; it won't work with our students."

Perhaps as a supervisor, you will not encounter too many negative reactions, but the mention of change often brings them out in force, and statements like those listed above will have to be acknowledged in order for change to be truly effective. In anticipating reactions to change, the following factors have been identified as the primary reasons to resist change (Basom and Crandall, 1991; Bolman and Deal, 1991; Gorton, 1987):

- *Habit.* People tend to behave the same way they have always behaved, so a change represents a challenge to their accustomed behavior. For example, teachers often develop routines or curriculum units for their classrooms; they do things out of habit. To suggest that they modify their routine or change their curriculum plans may create tension and be met with resistance. As Osguthorpe and Patterson (1998) observed, as a teacher investigates "new literacy methods and makes comments...other teachers [become] defensive about the methods they have used for many years" (pp. 106–107).

- *Bureaucratic structure of schools and top-down approaches.* As a bureaucracy, the school emphasizes order, rationality, and stability. The decision-making process engenders authority in prompting change. For example, teachers may lack the initiative to bring about program changes because the approval process is tedious and involves authorities not only at the campus level but at the district level as well.

- *Lack of incentive and preparation.* If a change seems threatening and frustrating, it is difficult to motivate others to consider the innovation unless some form of incentive is offered. Change is more difficult to initiate when teachers have not been properly prepared to deal with the called-for complexities. A commonly cited example is the introduction of technology into the classroom. If teachers are to use the Internet as an integral component of instruction, they must be given support and training in the use of computers and have knowledge of the Internet's potential to support teaching and learning.

- *Nature of the proposed change and resource allocations.* Some innovations are more difficult to implement because of their complexity, cost, or other factors. For example, the introduction of a new reading series and literacy program may require the purchase of materials in grades K through 12; if the approach is significantly different from before, it may require ongoing support and training.

- *Alteration of relationships as well as school and community norms.* Change alters the clarity and stability of relationships, which creates confusion and ambiguity. Group norms also act as effective barriers to change because individuals are reluctant to go against their peers or community expectations. For example, elementary schools in one district changed the grade-level combinations. The school system moved from having neighborhood K–5 elementary school campuses to separate campuses for grades K through 2, 3 through 6, and 6 through 8. This change involved moving students as well as faculty and staff from building to building. It took several months to get everyone settled.

- *Lack of understanding and loss of meaning and purpose.* Many people resist change simply because they do not understand all the aspects, implications, or benefits of the proposed change or have a misunderstanding of the proposed innovation. For example, teachers may reject an instructional strategy (e.g., cooperative learning) because they fail to understand the potential of this approach for improving student achievement. They may also feel that it is a fad and, as such, lacks purpose or meaning for their school or classroom.

- *Differences of opinion and competing visions.* Some changes may be resisted simply because there is an honest difference of opinion; some people may not feel that the proposed innovation is the proper course of action to take because there are competing views of what should happen in schools. For example, some teachers may favor a subject-centered approach to curriculum while others prefer a thematic, integrated approach to curriculum design. These enduring differences will continue and make change difficult, if not impossible.

- *Lack of skill.* People often resist change because they do not possess the necessary skills to implement the change, and they are reluctant to learn new skills. For example, elementary teachers frequently indicate that they take time away from science to teach something else or to provide time for guest speakers or special programs because they do not feel prepared to teach science using the recommended hands-on approach.

- *Fear and feelings of incompetency and loss of power.* Fear is a strong reason for resistance to change because people fear the unknown, they fear for their jobs, and they fear for their position. Change could disrupt any and all of these areas, which can result in feelings of incompetence and powerlessness. For example, teachers may be reluctant to adopt a new assessment process because they are concerned that they do not have the skills and/or knowledge to effectively implement performance-based assessment, portfolios, or other alternative measures. As a result, they will not be as prepared to explain the reasons for the grade on an assignment, group task, or project.

Resistance to change is a complex phenomenon with many causes that vary from individual to individual and from context to context. The supervisor should work closely with teachers and try to anticipate those individuals who might resist change and then diagnose a possible reason for the resistance. It is important to work to bring about successful changes because change efforts can create an attitude of cynicism that makes the change process difficult in the future (Reichers, Wanous, and Austin, 1997).

Stages in the Planned Change Model

For Guskey (1991), change is a highly personal and individual endeavor. But too often, change is implemented by those who are concerned with organizational policies because they expedite the change process. The differing concerns of "street-level bureaucrats" (macro-level) and those responsible for actual implementation of the change (micro-level) make facilitating change even more complicated (McLaughlin, 1990; Weatherley and Lipsky, 1997). Even if change is viewed as personal and empowering, it can be threatening unless a supportive environment is provided (Guskey, 1991).

While many factors determine whether personnel will accept and implement change and their chances of success in doing so, supervisors are critical to the success of the process. The seven stages to planned change, originally proposed by Lippit, Watson, and Westley (1958), have been expanded and modified by others (Frohman and Sashin, 1970; Gorton, 1987; Schein, 1972; Smither, 1998). These seven stages are helpful in introducing and initiating change; they involve: (1) conducting a needs assessment, (2) orienting the target group to the change, (3) deciding if a change is needed, (4) developing a plan of action, (5) implementing the change, (6) evaluating the change, and (7) refining and institutionalizing the practices embedded in the change.

In *stage 1*, the supervisor conducts a needs assessment to determine the readiness for change. The process involves developing a new approach or evaluating and selecting a model that will replace the current system(s). Questions that help to focus the discussion are: (a) What are the purposes of the proposed change, and what is the change supposed to accomplish? (b) Are the objectives relevant to the needs of the campus or district? (c) Are the people ready for a change?

In *stage 2*, the supervisor orients the target group to the proposed change by creating an awareness or interest in the proposed new model or change. The supervisor and teachers examine the barriers that would prevent the group from reaching the proposed innovation; they identify the strengths and weaknesses of the group as well. Next, pilot tests help to refine the goals prior to full implementation of the change. With the help of members of the target group, the necessary commitments, such as resources, training, or building modifications, are identified.

For *stage 3*, the supervisor, working individually or with teachers, determines whether to introduce and implement the change (based on results in the previous step) and identifies the individuals who should participate in this decision. Here the supervisor, in collaboration with the target group, decides whether or not to proceed with the implementation of change and answers the questions: Why? Why not? The strengths and weaknesses or advantages and disadvantages of the change should also be identified.

Stage 4 involves the development of an action plan, which charts the implementation process. Working collaboratively with members of the target group, the supervisor and a team of teachers conduct staff development programs for all individuals involved who are affected by the proposed change. In addition, written information that further explains the changes is provided. The supervisor must supply the necessary support and resources to the degree possible to implement the change and, working with the teachers, anticipate and try to resolve in advance any operational problems that may be encountered.

In *stage 5*, the proposed change is implemented. Following the established guidelines and procedures, the supervisor, in collaboration with teachers and other stakeholders, implements the proposed change. During the implementation process, the supervisor should ensure that a chronicle of events is recorded and shared periodically with target groups.

Stage 6 involves in-process or formative assessment. Using open-ended or structured feedback procedures, data are collected from teachers and other members of the target group to determine the degree to which the proposed change is accomplishing the objectives or meeting the goals as drafted. By analyzing aspects of the innovation that need improvement, the supervisor and teachers can propose modifications and additional support as needed. Guiding questions for stage 6 are: What evidence will be provided that the innovation is accomplishing the objectives? How will we know if the innovation is being successful?

Finally, in *stage 7*, the change is refined and institutionalized. Based on the results of the formative assessment, the innovation is refined, modified, or redesigned. Gaining acceptance for the innovation as a regular and ordinary part of the educational program is the goal of the change process.

To successfully navigate through the seven stages of planned change requires that supervisors use their skills as leaders, planners, organizers, and communicators as they collaboratively work with teachers. As supervisors become partners in the change process, it is essential to keep in mind the vision of the organization and the reality of the changes being implemented without lessening the aspirations and the rapidly moving actions that implement the change (Fritz, 1996). The following questions can help to guide the implementation of change:

- What is the purpose of the proposed change? What is the change supposed to accomplish? What are the objectives of the proposed change?

- Is the change relevant to the needs of the school or district?

- What evidence will be used to determine if the change has accomplished the objectives?

- How difficult is the proposed innovation to understand and implement?

■ What prerequisite skills do teachers as well as students need in order to implement change? If these skills are lacking, how will they be developed?

■ What are the financial obligations involved, and what other resources will be needed?

■ What are the strengths and weaknesses or advantages and disadvantages of the proposed change?

■ How will the success of the change be measured?

It should be clear from these questions and the previously cited stages of planned change that the supervisor works in concert with others in the school in planning, organizing, training, diagnosing, and assessing the effectiveness of change.

Once the change or innovation has been agreed on, the supervisor must shepherd it through until it is implemented. It is risky to make changes, but risk is involved in any alternative to current practice because disequilibrium is created. In addition, there is no guarantee that the change will be an improvement over what currently exists because the outcomes of change are difficult to predict with certainty. "It is possible to regress...change for the worse rather than better" (Knezevich, 1984, p. 103). That is why the initial step—needs assessment and determination of the appropriate change—is so critical to the overall effectiveness of the change process.

Finally, if the innovation is acceptable to teachers and others in the target group in the preliminary stages, the wholesale adoption process is the next critical step. It must be stressed that change is a complex process that is initiated and carried out by individuals. Because change involves developmental growth, it also requires time for members of the target group to process all the information and to test the innovation in their classrooms with children (Hord et al., 1987). Taking a metacognitive approach to the change process can be valuable as supervisors assist teachers individually or in cohort groups to initiate and adopt new strategies, procedures, or materials that will improve classroom instruction.

These insights into the change process can be valuable to supervisors as they work with teachers individually or in groups to initiate and adopt new strategies, procedures, or materials that will improve classroom instruction. By focusing on the previously identified stages and the above points, supervisors may be able to overcome some of the initial resistance and negative feelings that are often associated with educational change.

Change and School Culture

Any attempt to initiate change is more effective if it builds on a school's culture—a culture that includes traditions, ceremonies, heroes and heroines, and a sense of the past and future. It is the culture of a school that becomes the "tool for processing new data and generating new knowledge and understandings" (Pajak, 1993,

p. 177). Schein (1985) says that the culture, as a learning function, helps organizations through times of change and uncertainty. Hargreaves (1995) calls change renewal a time of continuous paradox; to help supervisors promote change, he suggests six action items that can guide school renewal. First, schools should have continuously evolving missions as teachers and supervisors review and revise their goals over time. Second, schools should develop procedures that allow policies to be developed by communities of people at the level where they can be realized. Third, the school must engage in reculturing so that collaboration and dialogue can occur between and among teachers and others in the school community. Fourth, schools must examine the focus that shapes relationships and restructure so that teachers can be more effective working within the structure rather than against it. Fifth, schools must also become learning organizations, not only for the students but for the faculty and staff who work there, so teachers then become problem solvers and expand their ability to accomplish their goals. Finally, schools must engage in positive politics in order to secure the necessary support and resources to accomplish their mission, reclaim the focus of the educational program, and in so doing empower others.

Any attempted change not only includes the supervisor but all members of the organization who share the same culture. Change requires everyone to do their part; no one person has the solution. There needs to be a common collective ethos that motivates all to work together. As Dewey (1902) suggested decades ago, if schools are not good places for children, they will not be good places for teachers either.

The supervisor is at the heart of the change process model because he or she must work with teachers and others to give meaning to this process. It is the supervisor who helps to interpret the big picture and who should be able to answer the question, Is this change good for students? Torbert (1990) suggests that Dewey's cooperative approach accommodates diverse perspectives and seems to hold the most promise for achieving successful change. For Krupp (1989), incentives to change come from within; unless change is internalized, the innovation will not be fully and successfully implemented. She agrees with Covey (1989), who recognizes that change takes place at the personal level, not just at the organizational level. It is the individual who has to accommodate the change before it is institutionalized in any meaningful way.

Change is a complex process through which instructional supervisors must navigate. In the implementation of change, supervisors build bridges and passages that assist teachers in understanding and appreciating the purpose of the change and how it works within their school culture. Such a system of building bridges encourages teachers to connect to the change, which provides opportunities for them to become involved and interested. As changes are implemented, teachers move from a state of uncertainty to one of certainty; as they move through this process, the supervisor serves as coach and supporter.

When supervisors acknowledge the role of school culture in change, they recognize the importance of establishing collegial relationships between and among supervisors and teachers. The positive interactions that occur between teachers and supervisors and among teachers themselves as crucial to the success of any change effort. All too often, the change process has required heroic efforts among participants, but as Corbett and D'Amico (1986) state:

> Educational improvements should not have to rely on heroic efforts. We must begin to think about how to support innovation.... At least four organizational conditions can facilitate improvement [change]: (1) available time, (2) cushions against interference, (3) opportunities for encouragement, and (4) recognition of the need for incorporation. (p. 71)

Facilitating Change

It seems that change surrounds the school environment more today than ever before and has become a concern for teachers as well as instructional supervisors. Supervisors, as they work with teachers, play various roles as they initiate plan, and provide direction for changes that result in instructional improvement. According to Pajak (1993), "The image of the supervisor as 'organizational change agent' [was] developed during the 1960s and 1970s" (p. 162). It was during this time when many changes—such as Operation Head Start, new mathematics, teaching teams, open classrooms, and bilingual education programs—were implemented. As early as 1963, Cunningham recommended that supervisors consider themselves as agents of change, individuals designated by the school to foster and implement change. So facilitating change is not a new role; it is one with a long history.

In thinking through the steps involved in initiating and adopting change, it is helpful to examine what others have learned about change and innovation. According to Hord and colleagues (1987), it is important to remember as they initiate or facilitate change that change:

- Is a process, not an event
- Is accomplished by individuals
- Is highly personal
- Involves developmental growth
- Is best understood in operational terms
- Focus[es]…on individuals, innovations, and context (pp. 5–6)

Change in the schools, when not planned and orderly, may seem chaotic, and supervisors may become caught up in all the negative aspects associated with the change process. Bolman and Deal (1991) note that "investments in change must be matched with collateral investments in training" (p. 376). For Ackerman and colleagues (1996), change can be best facilitated if supervisors have "practitioners write brief stories of their own experiences, then read them aloud and discuss them…It is during these discussions that real-life, close-to-the bone problems of practice come to life" (p. 21). After writing and discussing stories, teachers begin to think in different ways, which lead to thinking more deeply.

Dealing with change, then, is part of the supervision process; supervisors help provide direction and meaning to the changes that occur in schools through the shared stories. They need to empower themselves and others using a collaborative effort to ensure that the innovation is successful. When all the stakeholders work together as the result of a commitment to and belief in their collective action, change becomes a bottom-up process, not the reverse.

As noted earlier, reluctance to change is a reality that supervisors will need to address. As testimony to this reluctance, many schools are littered with the failed innovations of the past, such as the "new math," tracking systems, and merit pay. In the foreword to the book *Taking Charge of Change* (Hord et al., 1987), Knoll notes the problems encountered when facilitating educational changes when she states:

> One only has to search obscure storage closets or bookrooms in schools or talk with those who have been involved with education and its improvement over a period of time to understand the frustration involved in changing the status quo. Innovations involved with instructional strategies and curriculum have usually failed.

Supervisors need to take the necessary precautions to overcome the possible negativism and resistance they may encounter. Supervisors can be encouraged by the research suggesting that change is not always resisted by a target group (Gorton, 1987; Parish and Arends, 1983; Herriott and Gross, 1979). The role of facilitator, then, is crucial to the ultimate success of any innovation.

It is clear that innovators come in all shapes and sizes—young, mature, high social status, unusual, unorthodox, and committed (Rogers, 1965). Instructional supervisors often find themselves in a bind: On the one hand, they are entrusted with routine maintenance activities of the school (such as writing reports, conducting meetings, and ordering textbooks and supplies); yet they also are expected to be innovators who not only inspire change but can manage change through to the successful implementation stage. There is no easy solution to this dilemma. However, supervisors should seize every opportunity to utilize their creative and innovative abilities to foster and facilitate change in others. A well-conceived plan is necessary for facilitating the adoption of change or innovation.

Principles of Change

For supervisors to function as effective change agents, they should be knowledgeable about the general principles of change as reflected in the literature. These eight guiding principles that provide direction for the implementation of change within organizations are a condensation of various sources (Alfonso, Firth, and Neville, 1981; Fullan and Stiegelbauer, 1991; Krupp, 1989):

1. Change is more effective when it addresses organizational goals and objectives or problems, is planned for, and influences or impacts some outcome.

2. Change will be more effective when it is noncompetitive and when the people who will be affected are involved in the planning and feel they have some control over their own fate.

3. Change is more effective when the change efforts shift from "selling" to "diffusion."

4. Changes that are primarily technological will be more effective if they are supported by direct experience and support in implementation.

5. Change is more effective if it is not perceived as causing a loss in prestige or esteem, if it does not require a significant shift in values, if it is not perceived as giving advantage to groups or individuals, and if it does not threaten the vested interests of powerful groups and individuals.

6. Change efforts will be more effective when the restraining factors that inhibit an individual's normal desire for change are recognized and dealt with and when the personality fluctuations that occur with age are acknowledged.

7. Change will be more effective when group norms are recognized and when change produces a new force field or cohesiveness within a group while clarifying roles, fostering understanding, and enhancing affiliative relationships.

8. Change will be more effective when continuously evaluated and when supported by the organization.

Summary

This chapter examined the aspects of decision making and change as related to the supervision process. Both decision making and change are critical aspects of the work of a supervisor. Decision making helps individuals and organizations improve by seeking rational, logical solutions to problems. Both serve to enhance what happens instructionally in schools.

The chapter began by describing the nature of the decision-making process and listing several steps that are involved in making good decisions. These 10 steps include: (1) identification of the problem; (2) collection of data; (3) establishment of solution criteria; (4) generation of possible alternatives; (5) weighing of alternatives against criteria; (6) selection of best alternatives; (7) consideration of consequences; (8) selection and implementation of a plan of action; (9) evaluation of decisions or solutions; and (10) modification of the implemented solution. The chapter advocated a proactive process, which involves developing and selecting from among alternative choices, rather than a reactive approach, which responds to problems after they have developed. This section closed with a list of 10 principles to guide instructional supervisors in the decision-making process.

The chapter then described the change process, noting that change is a part of life in organizations. Next, the chapter presented various kinds of resistance to change that supervisors may encounter. Stages were outlined for promoting planned change. These seven stages involve: (1) conducting a needs assessment; (2) orienting the target group; (3) determining to implement change; (4) developing an action plan; (5) implementing the proposed change; (6) conducting formative assessment; and (7) refining and institutionalizing the change. Then a discussion of the role of school culture and change was presented, along with ways to facilitate change. Finally, the chapter ended with a list of eight principles that can guide supervisors as they serve as change agents.

YOUR TURN

12.1. You have been asked to make a decision about year-round schools. Your school district is experiencing financial difficulties, and top administrators are looking for ways to save money. One alternative might be year-round schooling. Your superintendent wants your feelings and reasons to support your decision. Research the topic and find six pros and six cons for year-round schooling. Then decide whether you favor the proposal or not. Prepare the most convincing case you can, based on the decision you made.

12.2. You are working with a teacher who is experiencing a personal problem (it could be substance abuse). In your opinion, the problem is affecting the teacher's productivity and effectiveness in the classroom. As a result, the students are receiving less than adequate instruction. You must decide if the situation is serious enough to call it to the attention of the proper authorities. Your chief concern is that you have been this teacher's friend and much of what you know was told to you in confidence. What do you do? Do you let things go, or do you bring the situation to someone's attention? You have to make a decision. Outline several alternative courses of action you might take.

12.3. Part of decision making is to establish priorities. Obtain a copy of a campus school budget. It will tell you how resources are being allocated, which will provide insight into some of the decisions that have been made regarding support for the instructional program.

Using this budget, identify those areas that you would modify funding for and provide a rationale for your decisions.

12.4. You have attended several conferences on a new reading program. You are excited about the prospect of implementing such a program in your district. You have briefly introduced the key components of the new program to the teachers, but you are aware that there is some resistance to adopting and implementing it. Moreover, some teachers (as well as other supervisors and administrators) have been frank with you and have said, "Why us? We'll change the reading program in five years anyway." Under these circumstances, what steps will you take to facilitate change and implement the new reading program? Review the suggestions offered in the chapter; then describe the strategies you will use to shepherd the change process.

12.5. It has been said that teachers as well as students love routine; in fact, "they love the bonds that enslave them." What does this statement mean to supervisors? How could you go about fostering or promoting change in your classroom, school, and/or school district in light of probable resistance from both teachers and students? What techniques would you use for overcoming resistance?

REFERENCES

Ackerman, R., Maslin-Ostrowski, P., & Christensen, C. (1996 March). Case stories: Telling tales about school. *Educational Leadership, 53*, 21–23.

Alfonso, R. J., Firth, G. R., & Neville, R. F. (1981). *Instructional supervision: A behavior system.* (2nd ed.). Boston: Allyn & Bacon.

Basom, R. E., & Crandall, D. P. (1991). Implementing a redesign strategy: Lessons from educational change. *Educational Horizons, 69*, 73–77.

Belasco, J. A. (1990). *Teaching the elephant to dance: Empowering change in your organization.* New York: Crown.

Bolman, L. G., & Deal, T. E. (1991). *Reframing organizations: Artistry, choice, and leadership.* San Francisco: Jossey-Bass Publishers.

Brookover, W. L., Beamer, L., Efthim, H., Hathaway, D., Lezotte, L., Miller., Passalacqua, J., & Tornatzky, L. (1987). *Creating effective schools.* Holmes Beach, FL: Learning Publications.

Caine, R. N., & Caine, G. (1997). *Education on the edge of possibility.* Alexandria, VA: Association for Supervision and Curriculum Development.

Calebrese, R. L., & Zepeda, S. J. (1997). *The reflective supervisor: A practical guide for educators.* New York: Eye on Education.

Carbo, M. R., Dunn, R., & Dunn, K. (1986). *Teaching students to read through their individual learning styles.* Reston, VA: Prentice-Hall.

Cohen, M. D., March, J. G., & Olson, J. A. (1972 March). A garbage can model of organizational choice. *Administrative Science Quarterly, 44*, 70–72.

Corbett, H. D., & D'Amico, J. J. (1986). No more heroes: Creating systems to support change. *Educational Leadership, 44*, 70–72.

Covey, S. (1989). *The 7 habits of highly effective people.* New York: Simon & Schuster.

Cowan, D. A. (1986). Developing a process model of problem recognition. *Academy of Management Review, 11*, 763–776.

Crowther, S., & Grashel, J. (1997 November 17). Ongoing professional development institute. Paper presented at the U.S. Department of Education's Regional Conference on Improving America's Schools, Dallas, TX.

Cunningham, L. L. (1963). Effecting change through leadership. *Educational Leadership, 21*, 75–79.

de Bono, E. (1983). The cognitive research trust (CoRT) thinking program. In *Thinking: An expanding frontier.* W. Maxwell, (ed.). Philadelphia: Franklin Institute Press.

Dewey, J. (1902). *The child and the curriculum.* Chicago: University of Chicago Press.

Draft, R. (1986). *Organizational theory and design.* San Francisco: West.

Dunn, R., & Dunn, K. (1993). *Teaching secondary students through their individual learning styles: Practical approaches for grades 7–12.* Needham Heights, MA: Allyn & Bacon.

Dunn, R., & Dunn, K. (1996). *How to implement and supervise a learning style program.* Alexandria, VA: Association for Supervision and Curriculum Development.

Fritz, R. (1996). *Corporate tides: The inescapable laws of organizational structure.* San Francisco: Berrett-Koehler Publishers.

Frohman, M. A., & Sashkin, M. (1970 October). The practice of organizational development: A selection review. Ann Arbor: University of Michigan, Institute for Social Research. [Technical report.]

Fullan, M. G., & Stiegelbauer, S. (1991). *The new meaning of educational change.* New York: Teachers College Press.

Gorton, R. A. (1987). *School leadership and administration.* Dubuque, IA: Wm. C. Brown.

Greenberg, J., & Baron, R. A. (1997). Behavior in organizations: Understanding and managing the human side of work. (6th ed.). Upper Saddle River, NJ: Prentice-Hall.

Guskey, T. R. (1990 February). Integrating innovations. *Educational Leadership, 47,* 11–15.

Guskey, T. R. (1991). Enhancing the effectiveness of professional development programs. *Journal of Educational and Psychological Consultation, 2,* 239–247.

Guskey, T. R., & Peterson, K. D. (1995–1996). The road to classroom change. *Educational Leadership, 53,* 10–14.

Hanson, E. M. (1996). *Educational administration and organizational behavior.* (4th ed.). Boston: Allyn & Bacon.

Hargreaves, D. (1995). Renewal in the age of paradox. *Educational Leadership, 52,* 14–19.

Herriott, R. E., & Gross, N. (eds.). (1979). *The dynamics of planned educational change.* Berkeley, CA: McCutchan Publishing Co.

Hord, S. M., et al. (1987). *Taking charge of change.* Alexandria, VA: Association for Supervision and Curriculum Development.

Huddleston, M. W. (1996). *The public administration workbook.* (3rd ed.). White Plains, NY: Longman.

Johnson, D. W., & Johnson, R. T. (1987). *Learning together and alone.* (2nd ed.). Englewood Cliffs, NJ: Prentice-Hall.

Johnson, D. W., Johnson, R. T., & Holubec, E. J. (1994a). *Cooperative learning in the classroom.* Alexandria, VA: Association for Supervision and Curriculum Development.

Johnson, D. W., Johnson, R. T., & Holubec, E. J. (1994b). *The new circles of learning: Cooperation in the school.* Alexandria, VA: Association for Supervision and Curriculum Development.

Kennedy, M. M. (1997). The connection between research and practice. *Educational Researcher, 26,* 4–12.

Knezevich, S. J. (1984). *Administration and public education.* (4th ed.). New York: Harper & Row.

Krupp, J. (1989). *The change process.* Alexandria, VA: Association for Supervision and Curriculum Development. [Audiotape.]

Lippit, R., Watson, J., & Westley, B. (1958). *The dynamics of planned change.* New York: Harcourt, Brace & World.

Lovell, J. T., & Wiles, K. (1983). *Supervision for better schools.* (5th ed.). Englewood Cliffs, NJ: Prentice-Hall.

McLaughlin, M. W. (1990). The Rand change agent study revisited: Macro perspectives and micro realities. *Educational Researcher, 19,* 11–16.

Mohrman, S. A., Wohlstetter, P. (1994). *School-based management: Organizing for high performance.* San Francisco: Jossey-Bass Publishers.

Monohan, B., & Tomko, S. (1996 November). How schools can create their own web pages. *Educational Leadership, 54,* 37–38.

National Center for History in the Schools. (1994). *National standards for history: Expanding children's world in time and space.* Los Angeles: National Center for History in the Schools, National Council of Teachers of English, Urbana, IL.

National Council of Teachers of English. (1996). *Standards for the English language arts.* Urbana, IL: National Council of Teachers of English.

National Council of Teachers of Mathematics. (1995). *Curriculum and evaluation standards for school mathematics.* Reston, VA: National Council of Teachers of Mathematics.

National Research Council. (1994). *National science education standards.* Washington, DC: National Research Council.

O'Neill, D. K., Wagner, R., & Gomez, L. M. (1996 November). Online mentors: Experimenting in science class. *Educational Leadership, 54,* 39–42.

Osguthorpe, R. T., & Patterson, R. S. (1998). *Balancing the tensions of change: Eight keys to collaborative educational renewal.* Thousand Oaks, CA: Corwin Press.

Pajak, E. (1993). Concepts of supervision and leadership: Change and continuity. In *Challenges and achievements of American education, 1993 Yearbook.* G. Cawelti (ed.). Alexandria, VA: Association for Supervision and Curriculum Development.

Parish, R., & Arends, R. (1983). Why innovative programs are discontinued. *Educational Leadership, 40,* 62–65.

Reichers, A. E., Wanous, J. P., & Austin, J. T. (1997). Understanding and managing cynicism about organizational change. *Academy of Management Executive, 11,* 48–59.

Rogers, E. M. (1965). What are innovators like? In *Change process in the public schools.* R. O. Carlson, et al. (eds.). Eugene, OR: Center for the Advanced Study of Educational Administration.

Schein, E. H. (1972). *Professional education: Some new directions.* New York: McGraw-Hill.

Schein, E. H. (1985). *Organizational culture and leadership.* San Francisco: Jossey-Bass Publishers.

Schultz, D. P., & Schultz, S. E. (1998). *Psychology and work today.* (7th ed.). Upper Saddle River, NJ: Prentice-Hall.

Sherman, S. (1993 December 13). How will we live with the tumult? *Fortune, 128,* 123–125

Slavin, R. E. (1983). *Cooperative learning.* White Plains, NY: Longman.

Slavin, R. E. (1991 February). Synthesis of research on cooperative learning. *Educational Leadership, 48,* 71–82.

Slavin, R. E. (1994). *Using student team learning.* (4th ed.). Baltimore, MD: The Johns Hopkins University Center for Research on Elementary and Middle Schools.

Smither, R. D. (1998). *The psychology of work and human performance.* (3rd ed.). New York: Longman.

Strike, K., Haller, E., & Soltis, J. (1998). *The ethics of school administration.* (2nd ed.). NY: Teachers College Press.

Thomson, B. S., & Mascazine, J. R. (1997 June). Attending to learning styles in mathematics and science classrooms. *ERIC Clearinghouse for Science, Mathematics, and Environmental Education DIGEST.*

Tomlinson, C. A. (1998) *The differentiated classroom: Responding to the needs of all learners.* Alexandria, VA: Association for Supervision and Curriculum Development.

Torbert, W. R. (1990). Reform from the center. In *Educational leadership and changing contexts of families, communities, and schools.* B. Mitchell & L. L. Cummingham (eds.). Eighty-ninth Yearbook of the National Society for the Study of Education. Chicago: University of Chicago Press.

Weatherley, R., & Lipsky, M. (1997). Street-level bureaucrats and institutional innovation: Implementation of special education reform. *Harvard Educational Review, 47,* 171–197.

Wedley, W. C., & Field, R. H. G. (1984). A predecision support system. *Academy of Management Review, 9,* 696–703.

Wheatley, M. J. (1993). *Leaders' guide to leadership and the new science.* Carlsbad, CA: CRM Films.

AUTHOR INDEX

Acheson, A. A., 137, 153, 162, 164, 168, 181
Ackerman, R. H., 76, 98, 247, 248, 256, 311, 315
Alexander, L. T., 212, 228
Alexander, W. M., 202, 208
Alfonso, R. J., 8, 14, 22, 31, 33, 34, 43, 50, 62, 68, 88, 90, 98, 118, 122, 297, 301, 303, 312, 315
Anderson, D., 247, 258
Anderson, E. M., 144, 153
Anderson, L. M., 216, 227
Anderson, R. H., 5, 8, 10, 12, 14, 22, 57, 69, 76, 88, 99, 114, 122, 130, 131, 132, 153, 160, 171, 172
Andrews, P. H., 178, 181
Andrews, R., 72, 98
Andrews, T. E., 270, 291
Aoki, T. T., 211, 227
Apps, J. W., 272, 291
Arends, R., 312, 317
Argyris, C., 55, 68
Armstrong, T., 222, 227
Arrendondo, D. E., 77, 98, 141, 153
Association for Supervision and Curriculum Development, 34, 43, 75, 77, 88, 98, 121, 122
Athanases, S., 244, 256
Austin, J. T., 307, 317
Ausubel, D. P., 218, 227
Avolio, B. J., 74, 86, 98

Bachman, J., 256
Baines, 233, 257
Baker, D. R., 294
Barell, J., 216, 227
Barnard, C. I., 50, 68
Barnes, S., 216, 227
Baron, R. A., 49, 59, 69, 73, 74, 75, 76, 90, 91, 99, 298, 299, 300, 303, 316
Barr, A. S., 34, 43
Barr, D., 103, 108, 110, 112, 114, 122
Basom, R. E., 305, 315
Bass, B. M., 74, 86, 98
Baudhuin, S. E., 123
Beach, D. M., 5, 10, 12, 13, 16, 22, 23, 30, 32, 38, 39, 41, 45, 132, 145, 153, 155, 186, 187, 188, 195, 200, 201, 207, 210, 213, 215, 224, 227, 230, 251, 256, 287, 294
Beamer, L., 315
Beane, J. A., 199, 207
Bearden, K. J., 233, 256
Belasco, J. A., 303, 315

Bell, B., 234, 238, 244, 256
Bennett, B., 270, 276, 294
Bennis, W., 73, 75, 76, 77, 88, 90, 98
Bents, R. H., 129, 153, 274, 291
Berelson, B., 118, 122
Berliner, D., 188, 207, 215, 228, 229
Berlo, D. K., 106, 122
Berrien, F. K., 49, 68
Bessent, W., 8, 22
Bey, T., 145, 153, 268, 291
Biddle, B. J., 170, 181
Bigge, M. L., 193, 194, 207
Blake, J., 234, 256
Blake, R. R., 83, 87, 99
Blanchard, K. H., 38, 44, 47, 55, 68, 85, 100, 282, 283, 291
Blase, J. L., 59, 68, 79, 90, 99, 100
Block, A. W., 65, 68
Bloom, B. S., 193, 195, 207
Blumberg, A., 136, 153
Bobbitt, F., 187, 207
Bolin, F., 33, 36, 44
Bolman, L. G., 5, 9, 22, 61, 68, 72, 99, 303, 305, 311, 315
Bondi, J., 8, 24, 33, 59, 60, 70, 72, 73, 101, 187, 208
Boswell, M., 216, 228
Bower, M, 61, 68
Bowlby, J., 80, 99
Boyan, N. J., 10, 22, 72, 99, 110, 112, 122, 134, 153
Bradsher, M., 27, 44
Brandt, R., 215, 221, 223, 228, 235, 238, 256, 284, 291
Brewer, W. K., 13, 22
Bridges, E. M., 80, 99
Brody, J. E., 77, 98, 141, 153
Bromley, K., 218, 229
Bronowski, C., 233, 256
Bronstingl, J. J., 268, 282, 284, 291
Brookover, L. G., 304, 315
Brooks, J. G., 222, 228, 237, 256
Brooks, M. G., 222, 228, 237, 256
Brophy, J. E., 5, 22, 159, 160, 182, 215, 216, 218, 219, 222, 223, 227, 228, 229, 230, 240, 257
Brown, O. H., 272, 292
Bruckner, L. J., 29, 34, 43, 44
Bruner, J., 36, 44, 197, 207, 288, 291
Bryant, M., 253, 256
Bryk, A. S., 65, 68
Buchmann, M., 211, 231
Buckley, R. B., 27, 44
Burlingame, M., 70

Burmeister, L. E., 117, 122
Burroughs-Lange, S. G., 248, 257
Burton, W. H., 29, 34, 43, 44
Butler, J., 272, 291

Caine, G., 297, 315
Caine, R. N., 297, 315
Calabrese, R. L., 4, 15, 22, 77, 99, 158, 159, 181, 298, 299, 300, 301, 315
Calderhead, J., 144, 154
Caldwell, J. H., 216, 228
Caldwell, S. D., 269, 291
Campbell, D., 244, 245, 246, 255, 257
Campbell, R. F., 59, 68
Capie, W., 216, 228
Carbo, M., 304, 315
Carr, A. A., 16, 22, 77, 87, 88, 99
Champy, J. A., 108, 122
Chang, Y. S., 79, 99
Charan, R., 49, 68
Chatman, J. A., 61, 68
Childress, L., 258
Chinn, C. A., 13, 22
Christensen, J. C., 129, 153, 247, 248, 256, 271, 291
Cignetti, P. B., 257
Clark, C. M., 248, 257
Clements, B., 172, 181
Clinchy, B. M., 272, 291
Cline, D., 136, 155
Coates, T., 160, 181
Cochran-Smith, M., 234, 257
Cogan, M. L., 129, 136, 154
Cohen, M. D., 298, 315
Coker, H., 216, 228
Coker, J., 216, 228
Coleman, J. S., 35, 44
Coleman, P., 87, 100
Colton, A, B., 140, 156
Combs, F. S., 70
Comer, J., 66, 68
Commission on the Role and Preparation of Mentor Teachers, 144, 154
Conley, D. T., 77, 99
Conoley, C. W., 177, 181
Conoley, J. C., 177, 181
Conrad, M., 29, 44
Conyers, G., 267, 294
Coons, A. E., 73, 100
Cooper, B. S., 215, 229
Cooper, J. M., 41, 45
Copeland, W. D., 10, 22, 110, 112, 122, 134, 153

Corbett, H. D., 311, 315
Corrigan, D., 266, 291
Costa, A., 5, 18, 22, 39, 44, 76, 78, 99, 107, 109, 122, 142, 143, 149, 154
Coulson, R. , 247, 258
Covey, S. K., 39, 44, 75, 78, 82, 83, 92, 93, 99, 107, 112, 122, 310, 315
Cowan, D. A., 299, 315
Coyle, S., 65, 68
Crandall, D. P., 305, 315
Creemer, B. P. M., 221, 228
Cresso, D. W., 61, 62, 66, 68
Crowson, R. L., 73, 100, 123
Crowther, S., 298, 315
Cruickshank, D., 216, 229, 233, 257
Cunningham, L. L., 36, 44, 68, 311, 315
Cunningham, W. E., 61, 62, 66, 68, 212, 228
Currin, D., 253, 256

D'Amico, J. J., 311, 315
da Costa, J. L., 160, 181
Daloz, L. A., 144, 145, 154
Daniel, L. G., 7, 12, 24
Danielson, C., 224, 228
Danielson, K. E., 245, 258
Daresh, J. C., 7, 17, 22, 72, 84, 99, 288, 291
Darling-Hammond, L., 239, 240, 244, 257, 259, 264, 267, 268, 269, 270, 277, 291
David, J. L., 269, 291
Davis, R. H., 212, 228
Dawe, H. A., 211, 228
de Bono, E., 304, 315
De Rose, M., 244, 258
Deal, T. E., 5, 9, 22, 60, 61, 62, 64, 68, 72, 99, 303, 305, 311, 315
Delorme Mapping, 201, 207
Deming, W. E., 268, 282, 284, 291
Devine, T. E., 59, 69
Dewey, J., 34, 44, 190, 207, 310, 315
Dickson, W., 55, 70
Dillon-Peterson, B., 266, 270, 291
Dinkmeyer, D., 17, 22
Dishaw, M. M., 216, 228
Doll, R. C., 8, 22
Donaldson, G. A., 76, 98
Donnellon, A., 57, 69
Downer, D. F., 65, 68
Doyle, W., 159, 181, 216, 228
Draft, R., 298, 315
Driscoll, M., 249, 257
Drory, A., 59, 68
Drucker, P., 49, 58, 68
Drummond, H. D., 31, 45
Dubois, D. J., 176, 177, 181
Duke, D. L., 234, 257, 269, 274, 276, 291

Dunkin, M. J., 170, 181
Dunlap, J. B., 8, 13, 23, 50, 53, 70, 103, 116, 117, 123, 233, 258
Dunn, K., 304, 315
Dunn, R., 304, 315

Eaker, R. E., 132, 154
Eble, K., 285, 291
Eby, J. W., 27, 44, 211, 228
Eccles, R. G., 49, 69
Eckstein, D., 17, 22
Edefelt, R. A., 145, 155, 265, 291
Edge, T., 258
Edmonds, R., 64, 68
Efthim, H., 315
Eggebrecht, J., 199, 207
Eisner, E. W., 136, 154, 210, 211, 228
Eggen, P., 199, 207, 215, 228, 235, 257
Ellett, C. D., 216, 228
Elliott, R., 144, 154
Elmes, R., 103, 108, 110, 112, 114, 122
Emmer, E. T., 216, 228
English, F. W., 187, 207, 240, 253, 257
Enz, B., 237, 238, 240, 244, 258
Erikson, E. H., 272, 292
Etchison, C., 27, 44
Etzioni, A., 47, 50, 67, 68, 90, 99
Evans, T. J., 87, 99
Evertson, C., 172, 181, 216, 227, 228, 230

Falbe, C. M., 93, 101
Fayol, H., 53, 69
Feltovich, P., 247, 258
Field, R. H. G., 299, 317
Fielder, F. E., 72, 99
Fifer, F., 168, 181
Filby, N., 216, 228
Firth, G. R., 4, 8, 14, 22, 31, 33, 34, 43, 50, 62, 68, 88, 90, 98, 118, 122, 297, 301, 303, 312, 315
Fisher, C., 216, 228
Flanders, N. A., 170, 181, 250, 257
Fleishman, E. A., 74, 99
Flesch, R., 117, 122
Floyd, K., 103, 104, 122
Foster, G. E., 65, 69
Foster, K., 265, 292
Francis, P., 134, 155, 240, 241, 258
Francke, D., 117, 123
Franseth, J., 34, 44
Frazee, B., 27, 44, 186, 197, 198, 207
Fredericks, A. D., 27, 44
Freiberg, H. J., 165, 182
French, J. R., 91, 99
Fritz, R., 77, 99, 303, 308, 315
Frohman, M. A., 307, 315
Frys, M. K., 256
Fullan, M. G., 41, 44, 80, 99, 234, 257, 264, 285, 292, 297, 312, 315

Fuller, F. F., 272, 292
Furst, N., 215, 216, 217, 230

Gage, N. L., 215, 229, 233, 257
Gall, M. D., 137, 153, 162, 164, 168, 181
Gardner, H., 222, 229
Gardner, J., 85, 99
Garman, N. B., 133, 154, 158
Garmston, R., 5, 18, 22, 39, 44, 76, 78, 99, 107, 109, 122, 142, 143, 149, 154
Gaus, J. M., 50, 69
Gendler, T., 65, 69
Getzels, J. W., 12, 22, 58, 69
Giaconia, R., 215, 229
Giammatteo, M. C., 87, 99
Gilbert, J., 234, 238, 244, 256
Gillman, J. N., 145, 154
Glanz, J., 7, 22, 77, 99, 252, 257
Glasser, W., 27, 44, 75, 99, 268, 292
Glatthorn, A. A., 8, 22, 57, 69, 132, 154, 187, 207, 240, 241, 250, 257
Glenn, S. A., 131, 154
Glickman, C. D., 5, 8, 22, 39, 44, 87, 99, 128, 129, 134, 137, 139, 146, 154, 160, 164, 186, 207, 269, 272, 274, 292
Goldhammer, R., 5, 8, 10, 11, 14, 22, 57, 69, 76, 88, 99, 114, 122, 129, 130, 131, 132, 136, 146, 154, 160, 171, 172
Goldsberry, L. F., 128, 136, 154
Gomez, L. M., 304, 316
Gomez, M. L., 223, 229
Good, T. L., 5, 22, 159, 160, 182, 215, 216, 229, 240, 257
Goodlad, J., 31, 45, 219, 229
Goodwin, A. L., 264, 267, 270, 291, 292
Gordon, B. G., 132, 133, 154
Gordon, S. P., 5, 8, 22, 39, 44, 128, 137, 138, 139, 154, 160, 186, 207, 269, 272, 274, 292
Gorton, R. A., 85, 93, 99, 103, 115, 117, 122, 298, 301, 302, 303, 305, 307, 312, 315
Gould, R. L., 272, 292
Gould, S., 57, 69
Graeber, A. O., 216, 228
Grashel, J., 298, 315
Grayson, D. A., 286, 292
Greenberg, J., 49, 59, 69, 73, 74, 75, 76, 90, 91, 99, 298, 299, 300, 303, 316
Greenblatt, R. B., 215, 229
Greenleaf, R. K., 76, 79, 100
Gresso, D. W., 212, 228
Griffin, F., 174, 182
Griffin, G., 220, 221, 229
Griffin, G. A., 266, 292
Gifffiths, D., 72, 100
Grisham, D. L., 222, 229
Gross, B. M., 48, 69

Gross, N., 312, 316
Grouws, D. A., 216, 229
Guba, E. G., 58, 69
Guskey, T. R., 27, 44, 264, 292, 297, 304, 307, 316
Guy, M., 268, 292

Hadaway, N., 266, 294
Haertel, G. D., 215, 216, 231
Hallanhan, D. P., 257
Haller, E., 300, 317
Halpin, A. W., 74, 100
Hamilton, C., 103, 109, 122
Hammond, J., 265, 292
Hanaka, M., 109, 123
Hanson, E. M., 303, 304, 316
Hardin, D. T., 271, 294
Hargreaves, A., 80, 99
Hargreaves, D., 264, 285, 292, 310, 316
Harper, S. C, 54, 69
Harris, B., 8, 22, 240, 257
Harris, E. F., 74, 99
Harrow, A. J., 196, 207
Harvey, K. R., 129, 153
Harvey, O., 274, 292
Hatano, G., 267, 292
Hathaway, D., 315
Havinghurst, R. J., 272, 292
Hawkes, B., 240, 241, 258
Hawkes, R., 249, 258
Hawkins, B., 109, 123, 134, 155
Hazi, H., 252, 257
Head, F. A., 144, 154
Healy, C. C., 144, 154
Helmke, A., 215, 231
Helms, D. B., 12, 23
Hemphill, J. K., 73, 100
Henderson, J. C., 27, 44
Henderson, J. G., 215, 229
Herriott, R. E., 312, 316
Herman, J. J., 269, 293
Herman, J. L., 269, 293
Herschel, R. T., 178, 181
Hershey, P., 47, 69, 85, 100
Herzberg, F., 57, 69
Hewson, P., 278, 293
Hibbard, K. M., 246, 258
Hill, J., 240, 257
Hill, P. T., 65, 69
Hillkirk, R. K., 240, 258
Hillman, J., 230
Hilty, E. B., 158, 182
Hines, C. V., 216, 229
Hinkin, T. R., 93, 101
Hirsche, E. D., 215, 229
Hirsh, S., 268, 269, 270, 271, 277, 295
Hitt, W. D., 73, 100
Hohn, R. L., 193, 194, 207
Holbert, P., 256
Holifield, M., 136, 155
Holler, R. L., 240, 241, 250, 257

Holubec, E. J., 268, 293, 304, 316
Hong, L., 77, 100
Hopkins, D., 129, 155
Hord, S. M., 309, 311, 312, 316
Howe, A. C., 267, 268, 293
Howey, K. R., 268, 270, 274, 291, 293, 295
Hoy, W. K., 119, 123
Hoyle, J. R., 240, 253, 257
Huberman, M., 27, 44, 269, 293
Huddleston, M. W., 298, 299, 301, 316
Huitt, W. G., 216, 228
Hunkins, F. P., 12, 23, 198, 199, 207
Hunt, D., 274, 292
Hunter, M., 134, 137, 155, 163, 211, 216, 225, 229
Hurwitz, E., 123
Hyman, R., 243, 257

Iannaccone, L., 55, 69
Ingram, H., 285, 294
Irvin-DeVitis, L., 218, 229
Ivan, T., 256
Iwanicki, E., 240, 257

Jacobs, R. M., 103, 104, 105, 122, 123
Jaworski, J., 82, 83, 100
Jehn, K. A., 61, 68
Jewell, L. N., 60, 69, 73, 100, 103, 104, 123
Johnson, C. E., 216, 228
Johnson, D. W., 268, 292, 304, 316
Johnson, M., 265, 292
Johnson, R. T., 268, 293, 304, 316
Johnson, S., 38, 44, 55, 68, 282, 283, 291
Johnson, S. M., 50, 69
Joyce, B., 5, 23, 27, 39, 45, 137, 141, 142, 148, 149, 155, 156, 213, 217, 229, 264, 266, 269, 270, 271, 276, 277, 293, 294, 295

Kahn, R., 47, 69
Kanter, R. M., 61, 69
Kaskowitz, D., 216, 231
Katz, D., 47, 69
Kauchak, D., 199, 207, 215, 228, 235, 257
Kauffman, J. M., 248, 257
Keating, D. E., 57, 69
Kelly, E. C., 104, 123
Kennedy, A., 61, 68
Kennedy, J. J., 216, 229
Kennedy, M. M., 16, 23, 300, 316
Kerr, B. J., 133, 155
Killon, J., 129, 156, 274, 295
King, F. L., 109, 123
King, M., 62, 70
Kirby, P. C., 79, 99, 141, 142, 155
Knezevich, S. J., 74, 80, 100, 104, 123, 304, 309, 316
Knight, G. R., 188, 207

Knowles, M., 271, 293
Koestenbaum, P., 40, 44
Komoski, P. K., 199, 207
Kondrasuk, J. N., 59, 69
Kosmoski, G. J., 14, 16, 23, 130, 155
Kotter, J. P., 75, 100
Kowalski, T. J., 49, 69
Krajewski, R. J., 5, 7, 8, 10, 14, 22, 57, 69, 76, 88, 99, 114, 122, 130, 131, 132, 133, 155, 160, 171, 172
Krathwohl, D. R., 196, 207
Kreps, G., 111, 123
Krupp, J., 310, 312, 316
Kujawa, E., 27, 44, 211, 228
Kuralt, R. C., 163, 182
Kyle, W. C., 264, 267, 293

Labovitz, G., 79, 99
Lafrancois, G. R., 211, 229
Lambert, L., 73, 100
Lampert, M., 248, 257
Landon, G. L., 266, 293
Lange, J. D., 248, 257
Langer, G. S., 245, 257
Larocque, L., 86, 100
Lashway, L., 77, 100
Lee, V. E., 65, 68
Leinhardt, G., 221, 222, 229
Leithwood, K., 87, 100
Letven, E., 57, 69
Levering, R., 55, 69, 103, 123
Levin, H., 66, 69
Levine, D. U., 188, 207
Levine, S. L., 272, 293
Levinson, D., 272, 293
Levinson, H., 79, 100
Lewin, K., 55, 69
Lezotte, L., 219, 220, 229, 315
Lindeman, E. C., 271, 293
Lipham, J. M., 117, 123
Lipitt, R., 307, 316
Lipsky, M., 307, 317
Little, J. W., 79, 100, 145, 155, 266, 267, 270, 293
Liu, C., 72, 100
Loevinger, J., 272, 293
Lorentz, C. W., 216, 228
Lorenz, K., 80, 100
Loucks-Horsley, S., 278, 293
Loughran, J. J., 244, 257
Lovell, J., 8, 14, 22, 24, 62, 69, 88, 100, 118, 123, 297
Lucasse-Shannon, A., 144, 153
Lucio, W. H., 34, 44
Luft, J., 285, 294
Lysaught, J. P., 103, 123

Maccoby, M., 83, 84, 100
Macdonald, J. B., 250, 257
Machell, J., 72, 80, 101
Machiavelli, N., 80, 100

MacNaughten, R., 4, 23, 103, 108, 123, 176
Mager, R. F., 195, 207, 212, 229
Makibbin, S. S., 18, 23
Manatt, R. P., 131, 155, 161, 163, 215, 216, 229, 230, 240, 249, 251, 257
Manz, C. C., 57, 69
March, J. G., 298, 315
Marczely, B., 268, 294
Marliave, R., 216, 228
Martin, M., 294
Mascazine, J. R., 304, 317
Maslin-Ostrowski, R., 247, 248, 256, 315
Mastrilli, T. M., 249, 258
Mathews, D., 77, 100
Mayo, E., 55, 69
McAdams, R. P., 16, 18, 23
McCanse, A. A., 83, 87, 99
McCleary, L. E., 265, 266, 268, 277, 294
McCowan, R., 249, 257
McDevitt, M. A., 158, 182
McDonald, M., 294
McGreal, T., 17, 23, 238, 240, 241, 242, 243, 257
McGregor, D., 81, 100
McLaughlin, M. W., 268, 269, 277, 291, 307, 316
McNeely, S. L., 163, 182
McNeil, J. D., 34, 44
McPherson, R. B., 73, 100
Medley, D., 216, 230
Meinbach, A. M., 27, 44
Melenyzer, B. J., 257
Mentoring Texas, 268, 294
Merseth, K. K., 247, 257
Metcalf, K., 233, 257
Meza, J., 141, 142, 155
Micceri, T., 251, 258
Midas, M. T., 59, 69
Miles, M., 234, 257
Miles, M. B., 264, 294
Miller, P., 286, 292
Minor, M., 110, 111, 123
Miskel, C. G., 119, 123
Modlo, M., 218, 229
Moffett, C. A., 77, 98, 141, 153
Mohrman, S. A., 304, 316
Monahan, B., 304, 316
Morgan, B. M., 278
Morris, V., 119, 123
Morrison, G. S., 197, 207
Mortensen, C. D., 104, 123
Mortimore, P., 72, 100, 221, 230
Mosher, R. L., 136, 155
Mostert, M. P., 248, 257, 258
Mouton, J. S., 83, 87, 99
Murphy, B., 266, 293
Murphy, C., 266, 293
Muth, R., 215, 229

Naisbitt, J., 84, 100
Nanus, B., 73, 75, 76, 77, 88, 90, 98
National Center for History in the Schools, 304, 316
National Council of Teachers of English, 304, 316
National Council of Teachers of Mathematics, 304, 316
National Education Association, 7, 23, 199, 207
National Research Council, 304, 316
Neill, A. S., 191, 207
Nelton, S., 94, 100
Nettles, D. H., 257
Neuhauser, P. C., 61, 69
Neville, R. F., 7, 8, 14, 22, 31, 33, 34, 43, 50, 62, 68, 88, 90, 98, 118, 122, 297, 301, 303, 312, 315
Newman, F. M., 27, 44
Nohria, N., 49, 69
Nolan, J. F., 134, 155, 240, 241, 258
Nuttycombe, D. G., 257
Nystrand, R. O., 68

O'Hare, M., 90, 100
O'Neil, J., 240, 258
O'Neill, D. K., 304, 316
Oberle, K., 233, 258
Odell, S. J., 145, 155, 268, 294
Oja, S. N., 137, 155
Oliva, P. F>, 8, 14, 18, 23, 103, 123, 158, 182, 219, 230, 244, 249, 251, 258
Olson, J. A., 298, 315
Olson, L. C., 39, 43, 44
Orlich, D. C., 266, 294
Ornstein, A., 12, 23, 188, 198, 199, 207
Osborn, M., 109, 114, 117, 118, 123
Osborn, S., 109, 114, 117, 118, 123
Osguthorpe, R. T., 297, 299, 304, 305, 316
Ott, J. S., 61, 69
Owens, R. G., 52, 55, 56, 58, 60, 64, 69

Pajak, E., 12, 23, 34, 36, 37, 40, 45, 136, 142, 143, 155, 172, 182, 309, 311, 316
Parish, R., 312, 317
Parker, C., 103, 109, 122
Parsons, T., 49, 70
Pasch, M., 188, 190, 201, 202, 207
Passalacqua, J., 315
Patterson, R. S., 297, 299, 304, 305, 316
Pawlas, G. E., 8, 14. 18, 23, 103, 123, 158, 182, 244, 249, 251, 258
Pediwell, J. A., 205, 207
Pellicer, L. O., 134, 155
Peters, T. J., 38, 45, 55, 70
Peterson, D., 251, 258
Peterson, K. D., 60, 62, 64, 68, 297, 316
Peterson, P., 216, 230
Pfeiffer, I. L., 8, 13, 23. 50, 53, 70, 103, 116, 117, 123, 233, 258

Piaget, J., 222, 230
Pierce, P. R., 30, 31, 45
Pink, W., 266, 294
Pinnegar, S., 223, 230
Pitner, N. J., 73, 100
Place, N., 27, 45
Playko, M. A., 7, 17, 22, 72, 84, 99
Poole, W. L., 40, 45
Porter, A. C., 218, 219, 223, 230
Porter-Gehrie, C., 123
Post, P., 258
Prawat, R. S., 221, 230
Purkey, S. C., 62, 64, 65, 70, 216, 230
Purpel, D. E., 136, 155

Raines, P., 212, 230, 238, 258
Raiola, E., 103, 107, 110, 118, 123
Ralph, E. G., 233, 234, 258
Rasey, M. I., 104, 123
Raven, R., 91, 99
Ravitich, D., 41, 45
Reavis, C. A., 129, 133, 155
Reichers, A. E., 307, 317
Reid, E. R., 216, 230
Reiman, A. J., 5, 23, 128, 131, 142, 144, 145, 148, 154, 155, 250, 258
Reinhartz, J., 5, 10, 12, 13, 16, 22, 23, 30, 32, 38, 39, 41, 45, 109, 123, 132, 145, 153, 155, 186, 187, 188, 195, 200, 201, 207, 210, 213, 215, 224, 227, 230, 251, 256, 266, 268, 269, 287, 294
Reisner, E. H., 30, 45
Reitzug, U. C., 49, 69
Rickert, S. R., 145, 154
Riggs, I. M., 245, 258
Riordan, G., 160, 181
Roethlisberger, F., 55, 70
Rogers, C., 56, 70
Rogers, E. M., 312, 317
Rogers, S. E., 245, 258
Romm, T., 59, 68
Roop, P., 249, 257
Rosansky, V., 79, 99
Rosen, B., 190, 207
Rosenshine, B, 215, 216, 217, 230
Ross-Gordon, J. M., 5, 8, 22, 39, 44, 128, 137, 138, 139, 154, 160, 186, 207, 269, 272, 274, 292
Rothlein, L., 27, 44
Rowe, M. B., 216, 230
Rubin, L., 211, 230
Rudnitski, R. A., 27, 44, 74, 100, 186, 197, 198, 207
Russell, D., 216, 229
Ryan, D. G., 215, 230
Ryan, K., 41, 45

Sadowski, M., 222, 224, 230
Sahakian, P., 160, 162, 182
Salomon, G., 212, 230

Sammons, P., 72, 100, 221, 230
Sandlin, R. A., 258
Sanford, J. P., 216, 230
Santmire, T. E., 274, 294
Saphier, J., 62, 70
Sardo-Brown, 201, 207, 249, 258
Sashkin, M., 307, 315
Saylor, J. G., 202, 208
Scheeren, J., 221, 230
Schein, E. H., 61, 70, 73, 100, 307, 310, 317
Schiller, D., 215, 216, 231
Schlechy, P., 268, 294
Schomoker, M., 72, 79, 101, 222, 230
Schrader, F. W., 215, 231
Schriesheim, C. A., 93, 101
Schroder, H. M., 274, 292
Schubert, W. H., 187, 208
Schuelke, D. L., 123
Schultz, D. P., 53, 54, 55, 70, 298, 317
Schultz, F., 212, 230
Schultz, S. E., 53, 54, 55, 70, 298, 317
Scriven, M., 249, 258
Seager, G. B., 129, 132, 155
Searfoss, L., 237, 238, 240, 244, 258
Seiler, W. J., 106, 123
Sellitte, P., 256
Senge, P. M., 40, 45, 80, 101, 221, 231
Sergiovanni, T., 7, 8, 23, 48, 54, 57, 62, 70, 72, 77, 85, 101, 234, 242, 249, 252, 258, 267, 274, 294
Shadiow, L., 212, 230, 238, 258
Shanker, A., 149, 156
Shannon, T. A., 240, 258
Sharan, S., 216, 231
Sheerlin, J., 266, 294
Sheppard, B., 4, 23, 72, 86, 101
Sherman, S., 304, 317
Shinn, J. L., 133, 156
Shirir, W., 266, 293
Showers, B., 5, 23, 27, 39, 45, 137, 141, 142, 148, 149, 155, 156, 264, 266, 270, 276, 277, 293, 294
Shroyer, G. M., 276, 294
Shulman, J. H., 246, 248, 258
Shulman, L. S., 210, 211, 231, 244, 258
Shuma, K. Y., 133, 156
Sizer, T., 66, 70
Slavin, R. E., 216, 231, 304, 317
Small, W. H,, 29, 45
Smith, B. O., 251, 258
Smith, J. B., 65, 68
Smith, J. M., 7, 23
Smith, M. D., 197, 208
Smith, M. S., 62, 64, 65, 70, 216, 230
Smither, R. D., 307, 317
Smyer, R., 63, 66, 70
Smylie, M. A., 57, 70, 267, 273, 294
Smyth, J., 146, 156
Snyder, K., 134, 156

Soltis, J., 300, 317
Sonnier, I., 271, 294
Sorenson, D., 80, 101
Southerland, A. R., 271, 294
Spain, C., 31, 45
Sparks, D., 268, 269, 270, 271, 277, 295
Sparks-Langer, G. M., 140, 156
Spencer, H., 80, 101
Spiro, R., 247, 258
Sprague, M. M., 18, 23
Spring, J., 29, 45
Sprinthall, N. A., 137, 156
Stacey, R. D., 47, 49, 61, 70
Stahlhut, R. G., 249, 258
Stallings, J., 165, 182, 216, 231, 266, 295
Starratt, R. J., 7, 8, 23, 242, 249, 252, 258, 267, 274, 294
Steffy, B. E., 240, 253, 257
Steiner, G. A., 118, 122
Stiegelbauer, S., 297, 312, 315
Stiggins, R. J., 27, 45, 234, 257
Stiles, K., 278, 293
Stockard, J. W., 198, 208
Stockton, J., 160, 162, 182
Strike, K., 300, 317
Stubbs, H. S., 267, 268, 293

Tanner, D., 26, 29, 31, 45, 134, 156, 186, 187, 191, 208, 249, 250, 258
Tanner, L., 26, 29, 31, 45, 134, 156, 186, 187, 191, 208, 249, 250, 258
Taylor, F. W., 52, 70
Teacher Education Reports, 10, 23
Tennant, M., 271, 295
Terry, R. W., 73, 92, 101
Texas Education Agency, 174, 176, 177, 182
Thies-Sprinthall, L., 5, 23, 128, 131, 137, 142, 144, 145, 148, 154, 155, 156, 250, 258
Thompson, B. S., 7, 23, 304, 317
Thoresen, C., 160, 181
Thurston, P. W., 70
Tobin, K. G., 216, 228
Tomko, S., 304, 316
Tomlinson, C. A., 300, 317
Toms-Bronowski, S., 233, 256
Torbert, W. R., 310, 317
Tornatsky, L., 315
Townsend, R., 54, 70
Tracey, J. B., 93, 101
Tracey, S. J., 4, 23, 103, 108, 123, 176
Trask, J. A., 266, 294
Trent, S. C., 257
Turner, J. S., 12, 23
Turner, M., 144, 156
Tye, K. A., 90, 101
Tye, B. B., 90, 101
Tyler, R., 187, 192, 208

Usdan, M. D., 68

Valencia, S., 27, 45
Van der Bogert, R., 76, 98
Van Wagenen, L., 246, 258
Vance, V., 268, 294
Vygotsky, L. S., 222, 231

Wagner, R., 304, 316
Waite, D., 17, 23
Walberg, H. J., 215, 216, 231
Waldman, D. A., 86, 98
Walen, E., 244, 258
Walker, B., 103, 108, 110, 112, 114, 122
Wang, M. C., 215, 231
Wanous, J. P., 307, 317
Wasserman, S., 246, 258
Waterman, R. H., 38, 45, 55, 70
Watson, J., 307, 316
Weatherly, R., 307, 317
Weber, M., 52, 70
Wedley, W. C., 299, 317
Wehlage, G., 27, 44
Weil, M., 213, 217, 229
Weinert, F. E., 215, 231
Welchert, A. J., 144, 154
Westley, B., 307, 316
Wheatley, M., 4, 5, 7, 24, 72, 80, 101, 303, 317
Wheeler, P., 160, 182
White, B. L., 7, 12, 24
Wideen, M. F., 266, 295
Wiggins, G., 27, 45, 268, 295
Wiles, J., 8, 24, 33, 59, 60, 70, 72, 73, 101, 187, 208
Wiles, K., 8, 14, 23, 24, 62, 69, 88, 100, 118, 123
Wilsey, C., 129, 156, 274, 295
Wise, A., 239, 240, 259
Witcher, A., 65, 68
Wohlstetter, P., 63, 66, 70
Wolf, K., 244, 245, 246, 259
Wolfinger, D. M., 198, 208
Wood, C. J., 234, 238, 259
Wood, J. R., 29, 45
Wyman, R. M., 257

Yammarino, F. J., 86, 98
Yarger, S. J., 270, 295
Yelon, S. L., 212, 228
Youn, J. Y., 93, 101
Yukl, G. A., 73, 74, 85, 93, 101

Zangwill, I., 32, 45
Zepeda, S. J., 4, 5, 22, 77, 99, 158, 159, 181, 298, 299, 300, 301, 315
Zeuli, J. S., 211, 231
Zigarelli, M. A., 63, 65, 70
Zimmerman, D. P., 77, 98, 141, 153
Zubizarreta, J., 245, 246, 255, 259

SUBJECT INDEX

Abstract thinking. *See* Developmental supervision
Adult development, 270–276
  characteristics, 270
  needs, 273
  principles, 272
  profiles, 275–276
  See also Staff development
Assessing teaching. *See* Performance assessment
Assessing teaching and learning, 202
  alternative procedures, 202
  See also Curriculum development.
Assessment systems, 242–249
  case-based methods, 246–249
  observations, 242–243
  portfolios, 244–246
  See also Performance assessment
Authority, 90–93
  See also Power and authority

Behavioral language
  See descriptive, nonjudgmental communication
Behavioral organizational process, 58–59

Change process, 303–313
  facilitating, 311
  premises of, 303
  principles of, 312–313
  resistance to, 305–306
  school culture, 309
  stages in process, 307–308
Classroom Observation, 159–172
  data analysis, 171–172
  data collection procedures, 162–170
  feedback: interacting and conversing with teachers, 174–176
  general guidelines for conducting, 160–162
  preparing to observe, 159
  See also Procedures for collecting data and Conferencing with teachers
Clinical supervision, 129–141
  compared with developmental supervision, 139–141
  five step process, 130–132
  guidelines for use, 132
Cognitive coaching, 142
  See also Collegial and collaborative supervision

Collegial and Collaborative supervision, 141
Communication, 103–119
  barriers to, 112–113
  characteristics of, 103–104
  components of, 105–106
  definitions of, 103
  effective supervisor responses, 109–112
  model, 106
  principles of, 118–119
  other forms (written, nonverbal, nonjudgmental, and descriptive), 109–117
Communication map, 104–105
  cause and effect, 104
  interactive, 105
  pragmatic, 105
  psychological, 104
  semiotic, 105
Conferencing with teachers, 174–177
  components of successful conference, 176–177
  See also Interacting and conversing with teachers
Culture. *See* Organizational culture
Curriculum, 187–191
  definitions and views, 187
  philosophies in developing (essentialist, pragmatist, existentialist), 188–191
  See also Curriculum model and Curriculum designs
Curriculum designs, 197–198
  broad fields, 198
  integrated or thematic, 198
  problem solving, 198
  student or learner centered, 197
  subject-centered or field-based, 197
Curriculum development, 192–197, 199, 202
  goals, 192
  model, 192–197
  operationalizing, 199
  resources, 202
  screens, 192–193
  sources of, 192

Data analysis, 171–172
  See also Classroom observation
Data collection procedures, 162–170
  on-task and off-task checklists, 164
  teacher mobility and management, 168

timelines, 162
  topical data capture, 163
  transitions and pacing, 166
  verbal interaction coding, 170
Decision-making, 298–302
  principles to guide process, 301–302
  steps in the process, 299–301
Developmental supervision, 137–141
  compared with clinical, 139–141
Domains of learning, 195–197
  affective, 196
  cognitive, 195
  psychomotor, 196–197
  See also Instructional objectives

Educational change. *See* Change
Effective leaders. *See* Leadership
Effective teaching behaviors, 215–220
  identifying and labeling, 218–220
  See also Teaching
Evaluation. *See* Performance assessment

Flanders Interaction Analysis categories. *See* Data collection procedures
Formative assessment/evaluation, 249–250
  See also Performance assessment

Goals and objectives. *See* Curriculum development

Instructional leaders. *See* Leadership
Instructional objectives, 194–197
  taxonomies of, 195–197
Instructional problems. *See* Teaching
Instructional supervision. *See* supervision
Instructional Supervision Training program, 134–136
  See also Clinical supervision.
Interacting and conversing with teachers, 174
  See also Conferencing with teachers and Classroom observation

Leaders and managers, 75–76
Leadership, 73–78
  building and bonding, 86
  definitions of, 73–74
  models and theories of, 80–87
  principles of, 88–90

Leadership *(continued)*
  qualities of, 76–80
  styles, 82–86
  supervisory, 87–88
  traits, 80
  views of, 73–75
Lesson planning and implementation.
  See Curriculum development
Lesson transitions and pacing. *See* data
  collection procedures

Management. *See* Leaders and
  managers
Mentoring, 144
  See also Collegial and collaborative
    supervision
Models of curriculum development.
  See Curriculum development
Models of supervision, 129–147

Observation. *See* Classroom
  observation
On-task and off-task behavior. *See*
  Data collection procedures
Organizations, 38–39, 48–52
  characteristics of, 48–50
  common themes in, 50
  descriptions and definitions, 50
  effective characteristics, 38–39
  formal, 52
  historical views of, 51
Organizational culture, 60–62
Organizational effectiveness,
  62–66
  principles of, 62–63
  school characteristics, 63–66
  schools and organizations, 64
  variables, 65
Organizational environment of
  schools, 48
  See also Organizational structures
    and Organizational culture

Organizational functions and
  relationships, 54–57
  determinants of, 56
  dissonance, 55
  group dynamics and field theory, 55
  job enrichment and motivation
    hygiene, 57
Organizational influence, 59–60
Organizational processes, 58–69
Organizational structure, 52–54
  bureaucratic, 52
  formal, 53

Peer coaching, 141–142
  See also Collegial and collaborative
    supervision
Performance assessment, 235–238,
  240–252
  characteristics of systems, 240–241
  components of assessment systems,
    242–249
  formative assessment, 249–250
  summative assessment, 252–252
  views of, 235–238
Planning for teaching and learning,
  199
  See also Curriculum development
    and Curriculum designs
Power and authority, 90–93
  coercive, 90
  identitive, 91
  other finds of, 91–92
  utilitarian, 90
Professional growth, 282–284
  managing the journey, 283
  one minute manager approach, 282
  total quality approach, 284
Professional growth plan, 239
  See also Performance assessment

School effectiveness, 63–66
Self-assessment supervision, 145–147

Self-assessment for supervisors,
  285–287
Staff development, 265–277
  definitions and views, 265–266
  principles of, 278
  reason to participate in, 267–269
  successful programs, 277
  teachers as learners, 270–276
  variables related to, 266
  See also Adult development and
    Professional growth
Summative assessment/evaluation,
  250–252
  See also Performance assessment
Supervision, 5–15, 28
  assumptions related to, 9–11
  changes in practice, 28
  definitions, 8, 14–15
  instructional, 8, 12
  principles of, 5–6
  theoretical framework, 12
  views and perspectives, 7–9
Supervisor, 16–18, 31, 41
  duties of, 31
  guiding principles for, 41
  roles of, 16–18

Teaching, 211–223
  concerns related to, 212–213
  definitions and views, 211
  effective behaviors, 215–220
  role of supervisor in, 223
  selection of strategies, 213–214
Teaching behaviors, 215–220
Teaching research, 215,
  221–222
  beyond process-product,
    221–222
  process-product focus, 215

Verbal interactions, 170
  See also Data collection procedures